# MCSA

# Windows Server® 2016

## Study Guide

# MCSA

# Windows Server® 2016

## Study Guide

## Exam 70-740: Installation, Storage, and Compute with Windows Server 2016

Will Panek

Senior Acquisitions Editor: Kenyon Brown
Development Editor: Kim Wimpsett
Technical Editors: Rodney R. Fournier, Chris Crayton
Production Editor: Rebecca Anderson
Copy Editor: Judy Flynn
Editorial Manager: Mary Beth Wakefield
Production Manager: Kathleen Wisor
Executive Editor: Jim Minatel
Book Designers: Judy Fung and Bill Gibson
Proofreader: Nancy Carrasco
Indexer: J & J Indexing
Project Coordinator, Cover: Brent Savage
Cover Designer: Wiley
Cover Image: ©Getty Images Inc./Jeremy Woodhouse



Published simultaneously in Canada

ISBN: 978-1-119-35934-0
ISBN: 978-1-119-35949-4 (ebk.)
ISBN: 978-1-119-35947-0 (ebk.)

Manufactured in the United States of America



For general information on our other products and services or to obtain technical support, please contact our Customer Care Department within the U.S. at (877) 762-2974, outside the U.S. at (317) 572-3993 or fax (317) 572-4002.

Wiley publishes in a variety of print and electronic formats and by print-on-demand. Some material included with standard print versions of this book may not be included in e-books or in print-on-demand. If this book refers to media such as a CD or DVD that is not included in the version you purchased, you may download this material at http://booksupport.wiley.com. For more information about Wiley products, visit www.wiley.com.

**Library of Congress Control Number:** 2017939769



10 9 8 7 6 5 4 3 2

*This book is dedicated to the three ladies of my life: Crystal, Alexandria, and Paige.*

# Acknowledgments

I would like to thank my wife and best friend, Crystal. She is always the light at the end of my tunnel. I want to thank my two daughters, Alexandria and Paige, for all of their love and support during the writing of all my books. The three of them are my support system and I couldn't do any of this without them.

I want to thank all of my family and friends who always help me when I'm writing my books. I want to thank my brothers Rick, Gary, and Rob. I want to thank my great friends Shaun, Jeremy, and Gene.

I would like to thank all of my friends and co-workers at StormWind Studios. I want to especially thank the team who I work with on a daily basis, and that includes Tom W, Dan Y, Corey F, Ronda, Dan J, Jessica, Dave, Tiffany, Tara, Ashley, Brittany, Doug, Mike, Vince, Desiree, Ryan, Ralph, Dan G, Tyler, Jeff B, Shayne, Patrick, Noemi, Michelle, Zachary, Colin, and the man who makes it all possible, Tom Graunke. Thanks to all of you for everything that you do. I would not have been able to complete this book without all of your help and support.

I want to thank everyone on my Sybex team, especially my development editor Kim Wimpsett, who helped me make this the best book possible, and Rodney R. Fournier, who is the technical editor of many of my books. It's always good to have the very best technical guy backing you up. I want to thank Rebecca Anderson, who was my production editor, and Judy Flynn for being the copy editor.

I want to also thank Chris Crayton and Nancy Carrasco for being my proofreaders. Special thanks to my acquisitions editor, Kenyon Brown, who was the lead for the entire book. Finally, I want to thank everyone else behind the scenes that helped make this book possible. It's truly an amazing thing to have so many people work on my books to help make them the very best. I can't thank you all enough for your hard work.

# Acknowledgments

# About the Author

**William Panek** holds the following certifications: MCP, MCP+I, MCSA, MCSA+ Security and Messaging, MCSE-NT (3.51 & 4.0), MCSE 2000, 2003, 2012/2012 R2, MCSE+Security and Messaging, MCDBA, MCT, MCTS, MCITP, CCNA, CCDA, and CHFI. Will is also a four time and current Microsoft MVP winner.

After many successful years in the computer industry, Will decided that he could better use his talents and his personality as an instructor. He began teaching for schools such as Boston University and the University of Maryland, just to name a few. He has done consulting and training for some of the biggest government and corporate companies in the world including the United States Secret Service, Cisco, the United States Air Force, and the US Army.

In 2015, Will became a Sr. Microsoft Instructor for StormWind Studios (`www.stormwindstudios.com`). He currently lives in New Hampshire with his wife and two daughters. Will was also a Representative in the New Hampshire House of Representatives from 2010 to 2012. In his spare time, he likes to do blacksmithing, shooting (trap and skeet), snowmobiling, playing racquetball, and riding his Harley. Will is also a commercially rated helicopter pilot.

# Contents at a Glance

# Contents

# Table of Exercises

# Introduction

This book is drawn from more than 20 years of IT experience. I have taken that experience and translated it into a Windows Server 2016 book that will help you not only prepare for the MCSA: Windows Server 2016 exams but also develop a clear understanding of how to install and configure Windows Server 2016 while avoiding all of the possible configuration pitfalls.

Many Microsoft books just explain the Windows operating system, but with *MCSA: Windows Server 2016 Complete Study Guide*, I go a step further by providing many in-depth, step-by-step procedures to support my explanations of how the operating system performs at its best.

Microsoft Windows Server 2016 is the newest version of Microsoft's server operating system software. Microsoft has taken the best of Windows Server 2003, Windows Server 2008, and Windows Server 2012 and combined them into the latest creation, Windows Server 2016.

Windows Server 2016 eliminates many of the problems that plagued the previous versions of Windows Server, and it includes a much faster boot time and shutdown. It is also easier to install and configure, and it barely stops to ask the user any questions during installation. In this book, I will show you what features are installed during the automated installation and where you can make changes if you need to be more in charge of your operating system and its features.

This book takes you through all the ins and outs of Windows Server 2016, including installation, configuration, Group Policy Objects, auditing, backups, and so much more.

Windows Server 2016 has improved on Microsoft's desktop environment, made networking easier, enhanced searching capability, and improved performance—and that's only scratching the surface.

When all is said and done, this is a technical book for IT professionals who want to take Windows Server 2016 to the next step and get certified. With this book, you will not only learn Windows Server 2016 and ideally pass the exams, but you will also become a Windows Server 2016 expert.

# The Microsoft Certification Program

Since the inception of its certification program, Microsoft has certified more than 2 million people. As the computer network industry continues to increase in both size and complexity, this number is sure to grow—and the need for proven ability will also increase. Certifications can help companies verify the skills of prospective employees and contractors.

The Microsoft certification tracks for Windows Server 2016 include the following:

**MCSA: Windows Server 2016** The MCSA is now the lowest-level certification you can achieve with Microsoft in relation to Windows Server 2016. It requires passing three exams: 70-740, 70-741, and 70-742.

**MCSE: Cloud Platform and Infrastructure** The MCSE certifications, in relation to Windows Server 2016, require that you become an MCSA first and then pass two additional exams. The additional exams will vary depending on which of the two MCSE tracks you choose. For more information, visit Microsoft's website at `www.microsoft.com/learning`.

## How Do You Become Certified on Windows Server 2016?

Attaining Microsoft certification has always been a challenge. In the past, students have been able to acquire detailed exam information—even most of the exam questions—from online "brain dumps" and third-party "cram" books or software products. For the new generation of exams, this is simply not the case.

Microsoft has taken strong steps to protect the security and integrity of its new certification tracks. Now prospective candidates must complete a course of study that develops detailed knowledge about a wide range of topics. It supplies them with the true skills needed, derived from working with the technology being tested.

The new generations of Microsoft certification programs are heavily weighted toward hands-on skills and experience. It is recommended that candidates have troubleshooting skills acquired through hands-on experience and working knowledge.

Fortunately, if you are willing to dedicate the time and effort to learn Windows Server 2016, you can prepare yourself well for the exam by using the proper tools. By working through this book, you can successfully meet the requirements to pass the Windows Server 2016 exams.

## MCSA Exam Requirements

Candidates for MCSA certification on Windows Server 2016 must pass at least the following three Windows Server 2016 exams:

- 70-740: Installation, Storage, and computer with Windows Server 2016
- 70-741: Networking with Windows Server 2016
- 70-742: Identity with Windows Server 2016

For those who have a qualifying certification, they can take the Upgrading exam "Upgrading Your Skills to MCSA: Windows Server 2016" (Exam 70-743). The objectives for this exam span the three individual exams. This book covers all of the objectives for the Upgrading exam. For details about the exam, visit Microsoft's website at `www.microsoft.com/learning`.

Microsoft provides exam objectives to give you a general overview of possible areas of coverage on the Microsoft exams. Keep in mind, however, that exam objectives are subject to change at any time without prior notice and at Microsoft's sole discretion. Visit the

Microsoft Learning website (www.microsoft.com/learning) for the most current listing of exam objectives. The published objectives and how they map to this book are listed later in this introduction.

For a more detailed description of the Microsoft certification programs, including a list of all the exams, visit the Microsoft Learning website at www.microsoft.com/learning.

## Tips for Taking the Windows Server 2016 Exams

Here are some general tips for achieving success on your certification exam:

- Arrive early at the exam center so that you can relax and review your study materials. During this final review, you can look over tables and lists of exam-related information.
- Read the questions carefully. Do not be tempted to jump to an early conclusion. Make sure you know *exactly* what the question is asking.
- Answer all questions. If you are unsure about a question, mark it for review and come back to it at a later time.
- On simulations, do not change settings that are not directly related to the question. Also, assume the default settings if the question does not specify or imply which settings are used.
- For questions about which you're unsure, use a process of elimination to get rid of the obviously incorrect answers first. This improves your odds of selecting the correct answer when you need to make an educated guess.

### Exam Registration

At the time this book was released, Microsoft exams are given using more than 1,000 Authorized VUE Testing Centers around the world. For the location of a testing center near you, go to VUE's website at www.vue.com. If you are outside of the United States and Canada, contact your local VUE registration center.

Find out the number of the exam that you want to take and then register with the VUE registration center nearest to you. At this point, you will be asked for advance payment for the exam. The exams are $165 each, and you must take them within one year of payment. You can schedule exams up to six weeks in advance or as late as one working day prior to the date of the exam. You can cancel or reschedule your exam if you contact the center at least two working days prior to the exam. Same-day registration is available in some locations, subject to space availability. Where same-day registration is available, you must register a minimum of two hours before test time.

When you schedule the exam, you will be provided with instructions regarding appointment and cancellation procedures, ID requirements, and information about the testing center location. In addition, you will receive a registration and payment confirmation letter from VUE.

Microsoft requires certification candidates to accept the terms of a nondisclosure agreement before taking certification exams.

# Who Should Read This Book?

This book is intended for individuals who want to earn their MCSA: Windows Server 2016 certification.

This book will not only help anyone who is looking to pass the Microsoft exams, it will also help anyone who wants to learn the real ins and outs of the Windows Server 2016 operating system.

# What's Inside?

Here is a glance at what's in each chapter:

**Chapter 1: Installing Windows Server 2016** In the first chapter, I explain the requirements and steps required to install and configure Windows Server 2016.

**Chapter 2: Installing in the Enterprise** This chapter shows you how to install Windows Server 2016 in an enterprise environment.

**Chapter 3: Configuring Storage and Replication** I take you through the advantages and benefits of Windows Server 2016 storage and replication configurations.

**Chapter 4: Understanding Hyper-V** This chapter will show you how to implement and configure Windows Server Hyper-V and virtual machines. You will learn about virtual networking, virtual hard disks, migration types, and Integration Services.

**Chapter 5: Configuring High Availability** This chapter takes you through the different ways to create and manage Network Load Balancing (NLB) and high availability.

**Chapter 6: Understanding Clustering** You will see the different ways that you can setup and configure clustering. I will explain how to setup clustering for applications or Hyper-V servers.

**Chapter 7: Configuring Windows Containers** In this chapter I will explain the advantages of using Microsoft Containers. I will also explain how containers and images are created and managed using Docker.

**Chapter 8: Maintaining Windows Server** This chapter shows you how to maintain your Windows Server 2016 system.

**Chapter 9: Understanding Monitoring** This chapter will show you how to implement and configure monitoring. Monitoring allows you to look at the different resources on a system and fine-tune those resources for best performance.

# What's Included with the Book

This book includes many helpful items intended to prepare you for the MCSA: Windows Server 2016 certification.

**Assessment Test** There is an assessment test at the conclusion of the introduction that can be used to evaluate quickly where you are with Windows Server 2016. This test should be taken prior to beginning your work in this book, and it should help you identify areas in which you are either strong or weak. Note that these questions are purposely more simple than the types of questions you may see on the exams.

**Objective Map and Opening List of Objectives** Later in this introduction, I include a detailed exam objective map showing you where each of the exam objectives is covered. Each chapter also includes a list of the exam objectives that are covered.

**Helpful Exercises** Throughout the book, I have included step-by-step exercises of some of the more important tasks that you should be able to perform. Some of these exercises have corresponding videos that can be downloaded from the book's website. Also, in the following section I have a recommended home lab setup that will be helpful in completing these tasks.

**Exam Essentials** The end of each chapter also includes a listing of exam essentials. These are essentially repeats of the objectives, but remember that any objective on the exam blueprint could show up on the exam.

**Chapter Review Questions** Each chapter includes review questions. These are used to assess your understanding of the chapter and are taken directly from the chapter. These questions are based on the exam objectives, and they are similar in difficulty to items you might actually receive on the MCSA: Windows Server 2016 exams.

The Sybex Test Engine can be obtained at `www.wiley.com/go/sybextestprep`.

**Sybex Test Engine** Readers can access the Sybex Test Engine, which includes the assessment test and chapter review questions from the book in electronic format. In addition, it includes the following:

**Practice Exams** There are a total of three practice exams included with the Sybex test engine: one each for Exams 70-740, 70-741, and 70-742.

**Electronic Flashcards** Flashcards are included for quick reference. They are a great tool for learning important facts quickly. You may even consider these as additional simple practice questions, which is essentially what they are.

**PDF of Glossary of Terms** There is a glossary included that covers the key terms used in this book.

# Recommended Home Lab Setup

To get the most out of this book, you will want to make sure you complete the exercises throughout the chapters. To complete the exercises, you will need one of two setups. First, you can set up a machine with Windows Server 2016 and complete the labs using a regular Windows Server 2016 machine.

The second way to set up Windows Server 2016 (the way I set up Server 2016) is by using virtualization. I set up Windows Server 2016 as a virtual hard disk (VHD), and I did all the labs this way. The advantages of using virtualization are that you can always just wipe out the system and start over without losing a real server. Plus, you can set up multiple virtual servers and create a full lab environment on one machine.

I created a video for this book showing you how to set up a virtual machine and how to install Windows Server 2016 onto that virtual machine.

# How to Contact Sybex/Author

Sybex strives to keep you supplied with the latest tools and information you need for your work. Please check the `Sybex.com` website at `www.sybex.com/go/mcsawin2016`, where I'll post additional content and updates that supplement this book should the need arise.

You can contact me by going to my website at `www.willpanek.com`. You can also watch free videos on Microsoft networking at `www.youtube.com/c/williampanek`. If you would like to follow information about Windows Server 2016 from Will Panek, please visit Twitter `@AuthorWillPanek`.

# Certification Objectives Maps

Table I.1 provides the objective mappings for the 70-740 exam. In addition to the book chapters, you will find coverage of exam objectives in the flashcards, practice exams, and videos on the book's companion website:

```
http://www.wiley.com/WileyCDA/WileyTitle/
productCd-1119359341,miniSiteCd-SYBEX.html
```

**TABLE I.1** 70-740 exam objectives

| Objective | Chapter |
|---|---|
| **Install Windows Servers in host and compute environments (10–15%)** | |
| Install, upgrade, and migrate servers and workloads | 1 |
| Determine Windows Server 2016 installation requirements; determine appropriate Windows Server 2016 editions per workloads; install Windows Server 2016; install Windows Server 2016 features and roles; install and configure Windows Server Core; manage Windows Server Core installations using Windows PowerShell, command line, and remote management capabilities; implement Windows PowerShell Desired State Configuration (DSC) to install and maintain integrity of installed environments; perform upgrades and migrations of servers and core workloads from Windows Server 2008 and Windows Server 2012 to Windows Server 2016; determine the appropriate activation model for server installation, such as Automatic Virtual Machine Activation (AVMA), Key Management Service (KMS), and Active Directory-based Activation | 1 |
| Install and configure Nano Server | 1 |
| Determine appropriate usage scenarios and requirements for Nano Server, install Nano Server, implement Roles and Features on Nano Server, manage and configure Nano Server, manage Nano Server remotely using Windows PowerShell | 1 |
| Create, manage, and maintain images for deployment | 2 |
| Plan for Windows Server virtualization; plan for Linux and FreeBSD deployments; assess virtualization workloads using the Microsoft Assessment and Planning (MAP) Toolkit; determine considerations for deploying workloads into virtualized environments; update images with patches, hotfixes, and drivers; install roles and features in offline images; manage and maintain Windows Server Core, Nano Server images, and VHDs using Windows PowerShell | 2 |
| **Implement storage solutions (10–15%)** | |
| Configure disks and volumes | 3 |
| Configure sector sizes appropriate for various workloads, configure GUID partition table (GPT) disks, create VHD and VHDX files using Server Manager or Windows PowerShell, mount virtual hard disks, determine when to use NTFS and ReFS file systems, configure NFS and SMB shares using Server Manager, configure SMB share and session settings using Windows PowerShell, configure SMB server and SMB client configuration settings using Windows PowerShell, configure file and folder permissions | 3 |

**TABLE I.1** 70-740 exam objectives *(continued)*

| Objective | Chapter |
|---|---|
| Implement server storage | 3 |
| Configure storage pools; implement simple, mirror, and parity storage layout options for disks or enclosures; expand storage pools; configure Tiered Storage; configure iSCSI target and initiator; configure iSNS; configure Datacenter Bridging (DCB); configure Multi-Path IO (MPIO); determine usage scenarios for Storage Replica; implement Storage Replica for server-to-server, cluster-to-cluster, and stretch cluster scenarios | 3 |
| Implement data deduplication | 3 |
| Implement and configure deduplication, determine appropriate usage scenarios for deduplication, monitor deduplication, implement a backup and restore solution with deduplication | 3 |
| **Implement Hyper-V (20–25%)** | |
| Install and configure Hyper-V | 4 |
| Determine hardware and compatibility requirements for installing Hyper-V, install Hyper-V, install management tools, upgrade from existing versions of Hyper-V, delegate virtual machine management, perform remote management of Hyper-V hosts, configure virtual machines using Windows PowerShell Direct, implement nested virtualization | 4 |
| Configure virtual machine (VM) settings | 4 |
| Add or remove memory in running a VM, configure dynamic memory, configure Non-Uniform Memory Access (NUMA) support, configure smart paging, configure Resource Metering, manage Integration Services, create and configure Generation 1 and 2 VMs and determine appropriate usage scenarios, implement enhanced session mode, create Linux and FreeBSD VMs, install and configure Linux Integration Services (LIS), install and configure FreeBSD Integration Services (BIS), implement Secure Boot for Windows and Linux environments, move and convert VMs from previous versions of Hyper-V to Windows Server 2016 Hyper-V, export and import VMs, implement Discrete Device Assignment (DDA) | 4 |
| Configure Hyper-V storage | 4 |
| Create VHDs and VHDX files using Hyper-V Manager, create shared VHDX files, configure differencing disks, modify virtual hard disks, configure pass-through disks, resize a virtual hard disk, manage checkpoints, implement production checkpoints, implement a virtual Fibre Channel adapter, configure storage Quality of Service (QoS) | 4 |

| Objective | Chapter |
|---|---|
| Configure Hyper-V networking | 4 |
| Add and remove virtual network interface cards (vNICs), configure Hyper-V virtual switches, optimize network performance, configure MAC addresses, configure network isolation, configure synthetic and legacy virtual network adapters, configure NIC teaming in VMs, configure virtual machine queue (VMQ), enable Remote Direct Memory Access (RDMA) on network adapters bound to a Hyper-V virtual switch using Switch Embedded Teaming (SET), configure Bandwidth Management | 4 |
| **Implement Windows containers (5–10%)** | |
| Deploy Windows containers | 7 |
| Determine installation requirements and appropriate scenarios for Windows containers, install and configure Windows Server container host in physical or virtualized environments, install and configure Windows Server container host to Windows Server Core or Nano Server in a physical or virtualized environment, install Docker on Windows Server and Nano Server, configure Docker daemon start-up options, configure Windows PowerShell for use with containers, install a base operating system, tag an image, uninstall an operating system image, create Windows Server containers, create Hyper-V containers | 7 |
| Manage Windows containers | 7 |
| Manage Windows or Linux containers using the Docker daemon, manage Windows or Linux containers using Windows PowerShell, manage container networking, manage container data volumes, manage Resource Control, create new container images using Dockerfile, manage container images using DockerHub repository for public and private scenarios, manage container images using Microsoft Azure | 7 |
| **Implement high availability (30–35%)** | |
| Implement high availability and disaster recovery options in Hyper-V | 5 |
| Implement Hyper-V Replica, implement Live Migration, implement Shared Nothing Live Migration, configure CredSSP or Kerberos authentication protocol for Live Migration, implement storage migration | 5 |
| Implement failover clustering | 6 |

**TABLE I.1** 70-740 exam objectives *(continued)*

| Objective | Chapter |
|---|---|
| Implement Workgroup, Single, and Multi Domain clusters; configure quorum; configure cluster networking; restore single node or cluster configuration; configure cluster storage; implement Cluster-Aware Updating; implement Cluster Operating System Rolling Upgrade; configure and optimize clustered shared volumes (CSVs); configure clusters without network names; implement Scale-Out File Server (SoFS); determine different scenarios for the use of SoFS versus clustered File Server; determine usage scenarios for implementing guest clustering; implement a Clustered Storage Spaces solution using Shared SAS storage enclosures; implement Storage Replica; implement Cloud Witness; implement VM resiliency; implement shared VHDX as a storage solution for guest clusters | 6 |
| Implement Storage Spaces Direct | 6 |
| Determine scenario requirements for implementing Storage Spaces Direct, enable Storage Spaces direct using Windows PowerShell, implement a disaggregated Storage Spaces Direct scenario in a cluster, implement a hyper-converged Storage Spaces Direct scenario in a cluster | 6 |
| Manage failover clustering | 6 |
| Configure role-specific settings, including continuously available shares; configure VM monitoring; configure failover and preference settings; implement stretch and site-aware failover clusters; enable and configure node fairness | 6 |
| Manage VM movement in clustered nodes | 5 |
| Perform a live migration; perform a quick migration; perform a storage migration; import, export, and copy VMs; configure VM network health protection; configure drain on shutdown | 5 |
| Implement Network Load Balancing (NLB) | 5 |
| Install NLB nodes, configure NLB prerequisites, configure affinity, configure port rules, configure cluster operation mode, upgrade an NLB cluster | 5 |
| **Maintain and monitor server environments (10–15%)** | |
| Maintain server installations | 8 |

| Objective | Chapter |
|---|---|
| Implement Windows Server Update Services (WSUS) solutions; configure WSUS groups; manage patch management in mixed environments; implement an antimalware solution with Windows Defender; integrate Windows Defender with WSUS and Windows Update; perform backup and restore operations using Windows Server Backup; determine backup strategies for different Windows Server roles and workloads, including Hyper-V Host, Hyper-V Guests, Active Directory, File Servers, and Web Servers using Windows Server 2016 native tools and solutions | 8 |
| Monitor server installations | 9 |
| Monitor workloads using Performance Monitor; configure Data Collector Sets; determine appropriate CPU, memory, disk, and networking counters for storage and compute workloads; configure alerts; monitor workloads using Resource Monitor | 9 |

Exam objectives are subject to change at any time without prior notice and at Microsoft's sole discretion. Please visit Microsoft's website (`www.microsoft.com/learning`) for the most current listing of exam objectives.

# Assessment Test

1. Which of the following is a valid role for a Windows Server 2016 computer?
   - **A.** Stand-alone server
   - **B.** Member server
   - **C.** Domain controller
   - **D.** All of the above

2. You need to add a new Windows Server 2016 image to your WDS server. You want to use a command-line command to complete this task. What command would you use?
   - **A.** `WDSUTIL /Add`
   - **B.** `WDSUTIL /image`
   - **C.** `WDSUTIL /prepareimage`
   - **D.** `WDSUTIL /addimage`

3. You have been hired to help a small company set up its first Windows network. It has had the same 13 users for the entire two years it has been open, and the company has no plans to expand. What version of Windows Server 2016 would you recommend?
   - **A.** Windows Server 2016 Datacenter (Desktop Experience)
   - **B.** Windows Server 2016 Standard (Desktop Experience)
   - **C.** Windows Server 2016 Datacenter
   - **D.** Windows Server 2016 Essentials

4. You are using WDS to deploy Windows Server 2016 images across your organization, and you are using the WDSUTIL command-line utility to perform this task. You want to copy a previously created image from the image store using this utility. Which option of WDSUTIL should you use?
   - **A.** `/move`
   - **B.** `/copy-image`
   - **C.** `/get`
   - **D.** `/enable`

5. You want to install a group of 25 computers using disk images created in conjunction with the System Preparation Tool. Your plan is to create an image from a reference computer and then copy the image to all the machines. You do not want to create an SID on the destination computer when you use the image. Which `Sysprep.exe` command-line option should you use to set this up?
   - **A.** `/specialize`
   - **B.** `/generalize`
   - **C.** `/oobe`
   - **D.** `/quiet`

6. You have a Hyper-V host that runs Windows Server 2016. The host contains a virtual machine named Virtual1. Virtual1 has resource metering enabled. You need to use resource metering to track the amount of network traffic that Virtual1 sends to the 10.10.16.0/20 network. Which command would you run?

   A. `Add-VMNetworkAdapteiAd`

   B. `Set-VMNetworkAdapter`

   C. `New-VMResourcePool`

   D. `Set-VMNetworkAdapterRoutingDomamMapping`

7. You need to ensure that the companies two Virtual Machines, VM1 and VM2, can communicate with each other only. The solution must prevent VM1 and VM2 from communicating with Server1. Which cmdlet should you use?

   A. `Set-NetNeighbor`

   B. `Remove-VMSwitchTeamMember`

   C. `Set-VMSwitch`

   D. `Enable-VMSwitchExtension`

8. You want to make sure the hard disk space for your virtual machines is occupied only when needed. What type of virtual hard disk would you recommend?

   A. Dynamically expanding disk

   B. Fixed-size disk

   C. Differencing disk

   D. Physical or pass-through disk

9. What is the command to install Hyper-V on a Windows Server 2016 machine that was installed in Server Core?

   A. `start /w ocsetup Hyper-V`

   B. `start /w ocsetup microsoft-hyper-v`

   C. `start /w ocsetup Microsoft-Hyper-V`

   D. `start /w ocsetup hyper-v`

10. You are a network administrator for a small company that uses Hyper-V. You need to reboot your virtual machine. What PowerShell command can you use?

    A. `Restart-VM`

    B. `Reboot-VM`

    C. `Shutdown-VM`

    D. `ShutStateOff`

11. You are the administrator for a mid-size organization. You have been asked by the owner to set up a NLB cluster. You want to use PowerShell to set up the cluster. What command would you use?
   A. `New-NlbCluster`
   B. `Create-NlbCluster`
   C. `Setup-NlbCluster`
   D. `Set-NlbCluster`
12. Which of the following actions should be performed against a NLB cluster node if maintenance needs to be performed while not terminating current connections?
   A. Evict
   B. Drainstop
   C. Pause
   D. Stop
13. If you have a running cluster and need to run the Validate a Configuration Wizard again, which of the following tests may require cluster resources to be taken offline?
   A. Network tests
   B. Storage tests
   C. System configuration tests
   D. Inventory tests
14. What PowerShell command would you use to run a validation test on a cluster?
   A. `Test-Cluster`
   B. `Validate-Cluster`
   C. `Set-Cluster`
   D. `Add-Cluster`
15. You download the wrong image from docker. What command allows you to delete an image?
   A. `docker del`
   B. `docker rm`
   C. `docker kill`
   D. `docker dl`
16. You have built a bunch of containers. What PowerShell command allows you to view the containers?
   A. `docker view`
   B. `docker see`
   C. `View-Container`
   D. `Get-Container`

17. What command allows you to see your container images?

    A. `docker images`

    B. `docker info`

    C. `docker view`

    D. `docker see`

18. You need to use an Active Directory application data partition. Which command can you use to create and manage application data partitions?

    A. `DCPromo.exe`

    B. `NTDSUtil.exe`

    C. `ADUtil.exe`

    D. `ADSI.exe`

19. What command-line command would you type in to start Performance Monitor?

    A. `Netmon.exe`

    B. `Perfmon.exe`

    C. `Performon.exe`

    D. `Resmon.exe`

20. What command-line command would you type in to start Resource Monitor?

    A. `Netmon.exe`

    B. `Perfmon.exe`

    C. `Performon.exe`

    D. `Resmon.exe`

# Answers to Assessment Test

1. D. Based on the business needs of an organization, a Windows 2016 Server computer can be configured in any of the roles listed. See Chapter 1 for more information.

2. A. The `WDSUTIL /Add` command allows an administrator to add an image to a WDS server. See Chapter 1 for more information.

3. D. Windows Server 2016 Essentials is ideal for small businesses that have as many as 25 users and 50 devices. Windows Server 2016 Essentials has a simpler interface and preconfigured connectivity to cloud-based services but no virtualization rights. See Chapter 1 for more information.

4. B. You should use the `/copy-image` option of the WDSUTIL utility to copy an image from the image store. See Chapter 2 for more information.

5. B. The `/generalize` option prevents system-specific information from being included in the image. The `Sysprep.exe` command can be used with a variety of options. You can see a complete list by typing **`sysprep/?`** at a command-line prompt. See Chapter 2 for more information.

6. B. The `Set-VMNetworkAdapter` command allows an administrator to configure features of the virtual network adapter in a virtual machine or the management operating system. See Chapter 3 for more information.

7. C. The `Set-VMSwitch` cmdlet allows an administrator to configure a virtual switch. See Chapter 3 for more information.

8. A. The only virtual hard disk that increases in size is the dynamically expanding disk. See Chapter 4 for more information.

9. C. This question relates to the setup command used to install the Hyper-V server role on a Windows Server 2016 Server Core machine. It's important to remember that these commands are case sensitive and that the correct command is `start /wocsetup Microsoft-Hyper-V`. See Chapter 4 for more information.

10. A. The PowerShell command `Restart-VM` restarts a virtual machine. See Chapter 4 for more information.

11. A. To create a new NLB cluster, you would use the PowerShell command `New-NlbCluster`. See Chapter 5 for more information.

12. B. If an administrator decides to use the drainstop command, the cluster stops after answering all of the current NLB connections. So the current NLB connections are finished but no new connections to that node are accepted. See Chapter 5 for more information.

13. B. The storage tests require the clustered disk resource to be offline. If you need to run the storage tests, the Validate a Configuration Wizard will prompt you to make sure you want to take the resources offline. See Chapter 6 for more information.

14. A. Administrators would use `Test-Cluster` to complete validation tests for a cluster. See Chapter 6 for more information.

15. B. The `docker rm` command is the command that is used to delete an image. You should run `docker images` first and get the ID number or name of the image that you want to delete. See Chapter 7 for more information.

16. D. The `Get-Container` PowerShell command allows an administrator to view information about containers. See Chapter 7 for more information.

17. A. The `docker images` command gives you the ability to see your images. The `docker info` command allows you to see how many images you have on a host, but it does not give you details about the images. See Chapter 7 for more information.

18. B. The primary method by which system administrators create and manage application data partitions is through the `ntdsutil` tool. See Chapter 8 for more information on TTL.

19. B. `Perfmon.exe` is the command-line command to start Performance Monitor. See Chapter 9 for more information on DDNS.

20. D. `Resmon.exe` is the command-line command to start Resource Monitor. See Chapter 9 for more information.

# MCSA

# Windows Server® 2016

## Study Guide

# Installing Windows Server 2016

## THE FOLLOWING 70-740 EXAM OBJECTIVES ARE COVERED IN THIS CHAPTER:

✓ **Install, upgrade, and migrate servers and workloads**

- This objective may include but is not limited to: Determine Windows Server 2016 installation requirements; determine appropriate Windows Server 2016 editions per workloads; install Windows Server 2016; install Windows Server 2016 features and roles; install and configure Windows Server Core; manage Windows Server Core installations using Windows PowerShell, command line, and remote management capabilities; implement Windows PowerShell Desired State Configuration (DSC) to install and maintain integrity of installed environments; perform upgrades and migrations of servers and core workloads from Windows Server 2008 and Windows Server 2012 to Windows Server 2016; determine the appropriate activation model for server installation, such as Automatic Virtual Machine Activation (AVMA), Key Management Service (KMS), and Active Directory-based Activation.

✓ **Install and configure Nano Server**

- This objective may include but is not limited to: Determine appropriate usage scenarios and requirements for Nano Server; install Nano Server; implement Roles and Features on Nano Server.

So, you have decided to start down the track of Windows Server 2016. The first question you must ask yourself is what's the first step? Well, the first step is to learn about what Windows Server 2016 features and benefits are available and how these features can help improve your organization's network.

So that's where I am going to start. I will talk about the different Windows Server 2016 versions and what version may be best for you. After I show you some of the new and improved Windows Server 2016 features, I will then show you how to install these different versions onto your network.

I will also show you how to use some PowerShell commands in the Windows Server 2016 installation. Let's dive right into the server by talking about some of the new features and advantages of Windows Server 2016.

The Windows Server 2016 installations will all be done on a virtual server. You can use any virtual software as long as its supports Windows Server 2016 and 64-bit processors.

# Features and Advantages of Windows Server 2016

Before I show how to install and configure Windows Server 2016, let's take a look at some of the new features and the advantages it offers. Microsoft has stated that Windows Server 2016 is "the cloud-ready operating system." This means that many of the features of Windows Server 2016 are built and evolve around cloud based software and networking.

Since many of you will be upgrading from previous versions of Windows Server, these are the new and/or improved features introduced by Microsoft since then. I will specifically identify any new features or advantages that are new to Windows Server 2016 only.

I will talk about all of these features in greater detail throughout this book. What follows are merely brief descriptions.

**Built-in Security** Microsoft has always tried to make sure that their operating systems are as secure as possible, but with Windows Server 2016, Microsoft has included built-in breach resistance. This feature helps stop attackers on your system and allows a company to meet any compliance requirements.

**Active Directory Certificate Services** *Active Directory Certificate Services (AD CS)* provides a customizable set of services that allow you to issue and manage *public key infrastructure (PKI) certificates*. These certificates can be used in software security systems that employ public key technologies.

**Active Directory Domain Services** *Active Directory Domain Services (AD DS)* includes new features that make deploying domain controllers simpler and that let you implement them faster. AD DS also makes the domain controllers more flexible, both to audit and to authorize for access to files. Moreover, AD DS has been designed to make performing administrative tasks easier through consistent graphical and scripted management experiences.

**Active Directory Rights Management Services** *Active Directory Rights Management Services (AD RMS)* provides management and development tools that let you work with industry security technologies, including encryption, certificates, and authentication. Using these technologies allows organizations to create reliable information protection solutions.

**BitLocker** *BitLocker* is a tool that allows you to encrypt the hard drives of your computer. By encrypting the hard drives, you can provide enhanced protection against data theft or unauthorized exposure of your computers or removable drives that are lost or stolen.

**BranchCache** *BranchCache* allows data from files and web servers on a wide area network (WAN) to be cached on computers at a local branch office. By using BranchCache, you can improve application response times while also reducing WAN traffic. Cached data can be either distributed across peer client computers (distributed cache mode) or centrally hosted on a server (hosted cache mode). BranchCache is included with Windows Server 2016 and Windows 10.

**Containers** Windows Server 2016 has started focusing on an isolated operating system environment called Dockers. Dockers allow applications to run in isolated environments called Containers. Containers are a separate location where applications can operate without affecting other applications or other operating system resources. To understand Dockers and Containers, think of virtualization.

Virtual machines are operating systems that run in their own space on top of another operating system. Well Dockers and Containers allow an application to run in its own space and because of this, it doesn't affect other applications. There are two different types of containers to focus on.

> **Windows Server Containers** Windows Server 2016 allows for an isolated application to run by using a technology called process and namespace isolation. Windows Server 2016 containers allow applications to share the system's kernel with their container and all other containers running on the same host.
>
> **Hyper-V Containers** Windows Server 2016 Hyper-V Containers add another virtual layer by isolating applications in their own optimized virtual machine. Hyper-V Containers work differently than Windows Server Containers in the fact that the Hyper-V Containers do not share the system's kernel with other Hyper-V Containers.

**Credential Guard** Credential Guard helps protect a system's credentials and this helps avoid pass the hash attacks. Credential Guard offers better protection against advanced persistent threats by protecting credentials on the system from being stolen by a compromised administrator or malware.

Credential Guard can also be enabled on Remote Desktop Services servers and Virtual Desktop Infrastructure so that the credentials for users connecting to their sessions are protected.

**DHCP** *Dynamic Host Configuration Protocol (DHCP)* is an Internet standard that allows organizations to reduce the administrative overhead of configuring hosts on a TCP/IP-based network. Some of the features are DHCP failover, policy-based assignment, and the ability to use Windows PowerShell for DHCP Server.

**DNS** *Domain Name System (DNS)* services are used in TCP/IP networks. DNS will convert a computer name or fully qualified domain name (FQDN) to an IP address. DNS also has the ability to do a reverse lookup and convert an IP address to a computer name. DNS allows you to locate computers and services through user-friendly names.

**Failover Clustering** *Failover Clustering* gives an organization the ability to provide high availability and scalability to networked servers. Failover clusters can include file share storage for server applications, such as Hyper-V and Microsoft SQL Server, and those that run on physical servers or virtual machines.

**File Server Resource Manager** *File Server Resource Manager* is a set of tools that allows administrators to manage and control the amount and type of data stored on the organization's servers. By using File Server Resource Manager, administrators have the ability to set up file management tasks, use quota management, get detailed reports, set up a file classification infrastructure, and configure file-screening management.

**Group Policy Objects** *Group Policy Objects* are a set of rules and management configuration options that you can control through the Group Policy settings. These policy settings can be placed on users' computers throughout the organization.

**Hyper-V** *Hyper-V* is one of the most changed features in Windows Server 2016. Hyper-V allows an organization to consolidate servers by creating and managing a virtualized computing environment. It does this by using virtualization technology that is built into Windows Server 2016.

Hyper-V allows you to run multiple operating systems simultaneously on one physical computer. Each virtual operating system runs in its own virtual machine environment.

Windows Server 2016 Hyper-V now allows an administrator to protect their corporate virtual machines using the new feature called Shielded Virtual Machine. Shielded Virtual Machines are encrypted using BitLocker and the VMs can only run on approved Hyper-V host systems.

Hyper-V also now includes a new feature called containers. Containers add a new unique additional layer of isolation for a containerized applications.

**IPAM** *IP Address Management (IPAM)* is one of the features introduced with Windows Server 2012. IPAM allows an administrator to customize and monitor the IP address infrastructure on a corporate network.

**Kerberos Authentication** Windows Server 2016 uses the *Kerberos authentication* (version 5) protocol and extensions for password-based and public key authentication. The Kerberos client is installed as a *security support provider (SSP)*, and it can be accessed through the *Security Support Provider Interface (SSPI)*.

**Managed Service Accounts (gMSAs)** Stand-alone *group managed service accounts*, originally created for Windows Server 2008 R2 and Windows 7, are configured domain accounts that allow automatic password management and *service principal names (SPNs)* management, including the ability to delegate management to other administrators. Service accounts are accounts that an administrator creates so that the account can be used to start a service. Managed service accounts are accounts that are created using PowerShell, and then Active Directory manages the account. This includes changing the password on a regular frequency.

**Nano Server** Windows Server 2016 has introduced a brand-new type of server installation called Nano Server. Nano Server allows an administrator to remotely administer the server operating system. It was primarily designed and optimized for private clouds and datacenters. Nano Server is very similar to Server Core, but the Nano Server operating system uses significantly less hard drive space, has no local logon capability, and only supports 64-bit applications and tools.

**Nested Virtualization** Windows Server 2016 introduces a new Hyper-V feature called Nested Virtualization. Nested Virtualization allows administrators to create virtual machines within virtual machines. As an instructor, I think this is an awesome new feature. Now I can build a Windows Server 2016 Hyper-V server with a training virtual machine. Then when I get to the part when I need to teach Hyper-V, I can just do that right in the classroom virtual machine. There are numerous possibilities and we will talk more about them throughout this book.

**Networking** There are many networking technologies and features in Windows Server 2016, including BranchCache, Data Center Bridging (DCB), NIC Teaming, and many more.

**PowerShell Direct** Windows Server 2016 includes a new simple way to manage Hyper-V virtual machines called PowerShell Direct. PowerShell Direct is a new powerful set of parameters for the PSSession cmdlet called VMName. This will be discussed in greater detail in the Hyper-V chapters.

**Remote Desktop Services** Before Windows Server 2008, we used to refer to this as Terminal Services. *Remote Desktop Services* allows users to connect to virtual desktops, RemoteApp programs, and session-based desktops. Using Remote Desktop Services allows users to access remote connections from within a corporate network or from the Internet.

**Security Auditing** *Security auditing* gives an organization the ability to help maintain the security of an enterprise. By using security audits, you can verify authorized or unauthorized access to machines, resources, applications, and services. One of the best advantages of security audits is to verify regulatory compliance.

**Smart Cards** Using *smart cards* (referred to as *two-factor authentication*) and their associated *personal identification numbers (PINs)* is a popular, reliable, and cost-effective way to provide authentication. When using smart cards, the user not only must have the physical card but also must know the PIN to be able to gain access to network resources. This is effective because even if the smart card is stolen, thieves can't access the network unless they know the PIN.

**TLS/SSL (Schannel SSP)** *Schannel* is a security support provider (SSP) that uses the *Secure Sockets Layer (SSL)* and *Transport Layer Security (TLS)* Internet standard authentication protocols together. The Security Support Provider Interface is an API used by Windows systems to allow security-related functionality, including authentication.

**Windows Deployment Services** *Windows Deployment Services* allows an administrator to install Windows operating systems remotely. Administrators can use Windows Deployment Services to set up new computers by using a network-based installation.

**Windows PowerShell Desired State Configuration** Windows Server 2016 created a new PowerShell management platform called Windows PowerShell Desired State Configuration (DSC). DSC enables the deploying and managing of configuration data for software services and it also helps manage the environment in which these services run.

DSC allows administrators to use Windows PowerShell language extensions along with new Windows PowerShell cmdlets, and resources. DSC allows you to declaratively specify how a corporation wants their software environment to be configured and maintained.

DSC allows you to automate tasks like enabling or disabling server roles and features, manage Registry settings, manage files and directories, manage groups and users, deploy software, and run PowerShell scripts to just name a few.

**Windows Server Backup Feature** The *Windows Server Backup* feature gives an organization a way to back up and restore Windows servers. You can use Windows Server Backup to back up the entire server (all volumes), selected volumes, the system state, or specific files or folders.

# Planning the Windows Server 2016 Installation

Before you install Windows Server 2016, you must first ask yourself these important questions: What type of server do I need? Will the server be a domain controller? What roles do I need to install on this server?

Once you have figured out what you need the server to do, you can make a game plan for the installation. So, let's start by looking at some of the server roles and technologies that can be installed on a Windows Server 2016 computer.

## Server Roles in Windows Server 2016

When you install Windows Server 2016, you have to decide which roles and features are going to be installed onto that server. This is an important decision in the computer world. Many administrators not only overuse a server but also underutilize servers in their organization.

For example, many administrators refuse to put any other roles or features on a domain controller. This may not be a good use of a server. Domain controllers help authenticate users onto the network, but after that the domain controllers are really not very busy all day long. Domain controllers have tasks that they must perform all day, but the server on which they reside is not heavily used when compared to a SQL Server machine or an Exchange mail server. This is where monitoring your server can be useful.

If your domain controller is a virtual machine or if you have more than enough servers, then having a domain controller with no other applications on it (except DNS) may be fine. But if servers are limited, then think about putting other services or applications on your server if the server can handle them. Just remember, some applications work better on member servers than on domain controllers. So before just adding any application to a domain controller, make sure you research the application and find out best practices.

Now let's take a look at some of the roles and features you can install onto a Windows Server 2016 machine. Knowing the different roles and features you can install will help you to design, deploy, manage, and troubleshoot technologies in Windows Server 2016. Figure 1.1 shows the Add Roles and Features Wizard in Server Manager. It shows you just some of the roles that can be installed on a Windows Server 2016 machine.

**FIGURE 1.1** Available roles in Windows Server 2016

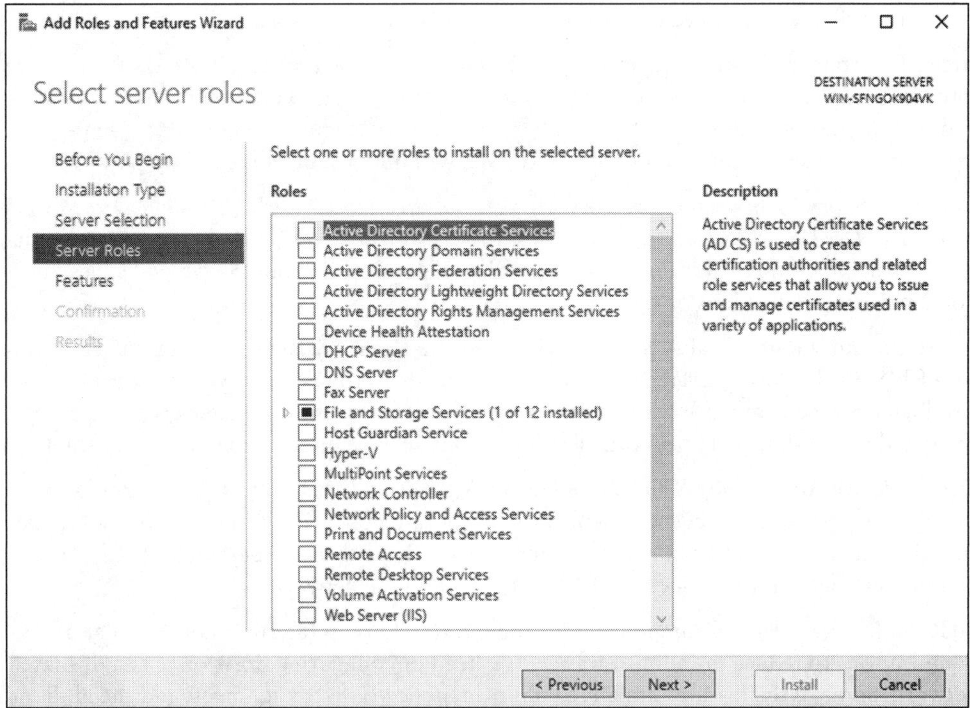

**Roles and Features**

Many of these roles were discussed in the section "Features and Advantages of Windows Server 2016." I include them here again because they are also *roles* that can also be installed on Windows Server 2016.

The following roles are available in Windows Server 2016:

**Active Directory Certificate Services** The AD CS server role in Windows Server 2016 allows you to build a PKI and provide public key cryptography, digital certificates, and digital signature capabilities for your organization.

**Feature** AD CS provides a customizable set of services that allows you to issue and manage PKI certificates. These certificates can be used in software security systems that employ public key technologies.

**Role** AD CS in Windows Server 2016 is the server role that allows you to build a PKI and provide public key cryptography, digital certificates, and digital signature capabilities for your organization.

**Active Directory Domain Services** The AD DS server role allows you to create a scalable, secure, and manageable infrastructure for user and resource management and to provide support for directory-enabled applications, such as Microsoft Exchange Server.

**Active Directory Federation Services** *Active Directory Federation Services (AD FS)* provides Internet-based clients with a secure identity access solution that works on both Windows and non-Windows operating systems. AD FS gives users the ability to do a *single sign-on (SSO)* and access applications on other networks without needing a secondary password.

**Active Directory Lightweight Directory Services** *Active Directory Lightweight Directory Services (AD LDS)* is a *Lightweight Directory Access Protocol (LDAP)* directory service that provides flexible support for directory-enabled applications, without the dependencies and domain-related restrictions of AD DS.

**Active Directory Rights Management Services** Active Directory Rights Management Services (AD RMS) in Windows Server 2016 is the server role that provides you with management and development tools that work with industry security technologies including encryption, certificates, and authentication to help organizations create reliable information protection solutions.

**Device Health Attestation** The Device Health Attestation helps protect your corporate network by verifying that client systems meet corporate policy. For example, you can make sure that all computers that connect to your network have their proper updates, antivirus, and proper configuration policies before connecting to the network.

**DHCP** *Dynamic Host Configuration Protocol (DHCP)* is an Internet standard that allows organizations to reduce the administrative overhead of configuring hosts on a TCP/IP-based network. Some of the features are DHCP failover, policy-based assignment, and the ability to use Windows PowerShell for DHCP Server.

**DNS** *Domain Name System (DNS)* services are used in TCP/IP networks. DNS will convert a computer name or fully qualified domain name (FQDN) to an IP address. DNS also has the ability to do a reverse lookup and convert an IP address to a computer name. DNS allows you to locate computers and services through user-friendly names.

**Fax Server** The fax server allows you to send and receive faxes, and it also allows you to manage fax resources such as jobs, settings, reports, and fax devices on a specific computer or on the network.

**File and Storage Services** *File and Storage Services* allows an administrator to set up and manage one or more file servers. These servers can provide a central location on your network where you can store files and then share those files with network users. If users require access to the same files and applications or if centralized backup and file management are important issues for your organization, administrators should set up network servers as a file server.

**Host Guardian Service** The Host Guardian Service (HGS) allows you to have a more secure environment for your network's virtual machines. The HGS role provides the Attestation & Key Protection services that enable Guarded Hosts to run Shielded virtual machines.

**Hyper-V** The Hyper-V role allows administrators to create and manage a virtualized environment by taking advantage of the technology built into the Windows Server 2016 operating system. When an administrator installs the Hyper-V role, all required virtualization components are installed.

Some of the required components include the Windows hypervisor, Virtual Machine Management Service, the virtualization WMI provider, the virtual machine bus (VMbus), the virtualization service provider (VSP), and the virtual infrastructure driver (VID).

**MultiPoint Services** MultiPoint Services allows multiple users, each with their own independent and familiar Windows experience, to simultaneously share one computer.

**Network Controller** The Network Controller provides the point of automation needed for continual configuration, monitoring, and diagnostics of virtual networks, physical networks, network services, network topology, address management, and so on within a datacenter.

**Network Policy and Access Services** Use the *Network Policy and Access Services* server role to install and configure *Network Policy Server (NPS)*, which helps safeguard the security of your network.

**Print and Document Services** *Print and Document Services* allows an administrator to centralize print server and network printer tasks. This role also allows you to receive scanned documents from network scanners and route the documents to a shared network resource, Windows SharePoint Services site, or email addresses. Print and Document Services also provides fax servers with the ability to send and receive faxes while also giving the administrator the ability to manage fax resources such as jobs, settings, reports, and fax devices on the fax server.

**Remote Access** Remote Access provides connectivity through DirectAccess, VPN, and Web Application Proxies. DirectAccess provides an Always On and Always Managed experience. Remote Access provides VPN access including site-to-site connectivity. Web Application

Proxies enable web-based applications from your corporate network to client devices outside of the corporate network. Remote Access also includes routing capabilities, including Network Address Translation (NAT).

**Remote Desktop Services** Remote Desktop Services allows for faster desktop and application deployments to any device, improving remote user effectiveness while helping to keep critical data secure. Remote Desktop Services allows for both a *virtual desktop infrastructure (VDI)* and session-based desktops, allowing users to connect from anywhere.

**Volume Activation Services** Windows Server 2016 *Volume Activation Services* will help your organization benefit from using this service to deploy and manage volume licenses for a medium to large number of computers.

**Web Server (IIS)** The *Web Server (IIS)* role in Windows Server 2016 allows an administrator to set up a secure, easy-to-manage, modular, and extensible platform for reliably hosting websites, services, and applications.

**Windows Deployment Services** Windows Deployment Services allows an administrator to install a Windows operating system over the network. Administrators do not have to install each operating system directly from a CD or DVD.

**Windows Server Essentials Experience** Windows Server Essentials Experience allows an administrator to set up the IT infrastructure, and it also provides powerful functions such as PC backups to help protect your corporate data and Remote Web Access that allows access to business information from anywhere in the world. Windows Server Essentials Experience also allows you to easily connect to cloud-based applications and services.

**Windows Server Update Services** *Windows Server Update Services (WSUS)* allows administrators to deploy application and operating system updates. By deploying WSUS, administrators have the ability to manage updates that are released through Microsoft Update to computers in their network. This feature is integrated with the operating system as a server role on a Windows Server 2016 system.

## Migrating Roles and Features to Windows Server 2016

Once you decide on which roles and features you are going to install onto your Windows Server 2016 system, then you either have to install those roles and features from scratch or migrate them from a previous version of Windows server.

Windows Server 2016 includes a set of migration tools that administrators can use to help ease the process of migrating server roles, features, operating system settings, and data. Administrators can migrate this data from an existing server that are running Windows Server 2008 R2, Windows Server 2012, Windows Server 2012 R2, or Windows Server 2016 to a computer that is running Windows Server 2016.

Using Windows Server Migration Tools to migrate roles, role services, and features can simplify the deployment of new servers. You can migrate roles and features on any server, including Server Core, installation option of Windows Server 2016, and virtual servers. By using Windows Server Migration Tools, an administrator can reduce migration downtime, increase the accuracy of the migration process, and help eliminate conflicts that could otherwise occur during the migration process.

One advantage of using the migration tools is that most of them support cross-architecture migrations (x86-based to x64-based computing platforms), migrations between physical and virtual environments, and migrations between both the full and Server Core installation options of the Windows Server operating system. In Windows Server 2016, Windows Server Migration Tools also supports cross-subnet migrations.

To use Windows Server Migration Tools, the feature must be installed on both the source and destination computers. Windows Server Migration Tools installation and preparation can be divided into the following stages:

1. Installing Windows Server Migration Tools on destination servers that run Windows Server 2016
2. Creating deployment folders on destination servers that run Windows Server 2016 for copying to source servers
3. Copying deployment folders from destination servers to source servers
4. Registering Windows Server Migration Tools on source servers

If you plan to use Windows Server Migration Tools, you must be a member of the Administrators group on both the source and destination servers to install, remove, or set up the tools.

Administrators can install Windows Server Migration Tools 2016 by using either the Add Roles Or Features Wizard in Server Manager or Windows PowerShell deployment cmdlets for Server Manager.

To install Windows Server Migration Tools on a Server Core installation of Windows Server 2016, you would complete the following steps:

1. Open a Windows PowerShell session by typing **`powershell.exe`** in the current command prompt session and then pressing Enter.
2. In the Windows PowerShell session, install Windows Server Migration Tools by using the Windows PowerShell `Install-WindowsFeature` cmdlet for Server Manager. In the Windows PowerShell session, type the following, and then press Enter. (Omit the `ComputerName` parameter if you are installing the Windows Server Migration Tools on the local server.)

   ```
   Install-WindowsFeature Migration -ComputerName computer_name
   ```

## Deciding Which Windows Server 2016 Versions to Use

You may be wondering which version of Windows Server 2016 is best for your organization. After all, Microsoft offers the following six versions of Windows Server 2016.

At the time this book was written, there were six versions of Windows Server 2016. But Microsoft is always improving and creating new versions of their products. Be sure to check out Microsoft's website for any other versions or changes.

**Windows Server 2016 Datacenter** This version is designed for organizations that are looking to migrate to a highly virtualized, private cloud environment. Windows Server 2016 Datacenter has full Windows Server functionality with unlimited virtual instances.

**Windows Server 2016 Standard** This version is designed for organizations with physical or minimally virtualized environments. Windows Server 2016 Standard has full Windows Server functionality with two virtual instances.

**Windows Server 2016 Essentials** This version is ideal for small businesses that have as many as 25 users and 50 devices. Windows Server 2016 Essentials has a simpler interface and preconfigured connectivity to cloud-based services but no virtualization rights.

**Windows Hyper-V Server 2016** Microsoft Hyper-V Server 2016 has the exact same Hyper-V role components as Windows Server 2016. Hyper-V 2016 Server is a stand-alone version that has the Windows hypervisor, the Windows Server driver model, and the other virtualization components only. Windows Hyper-V Server 2016 allows you to have a simple virtualization solution which allows you to reduce costs.

**Windows Storage Server 2016** Windows Storage Server 2016 is not openly available for sale to the general public. Windows Storage Server 2016 is only available as an integrated hardware offering or as an available field upgrade from your hardware manufacturer. Windows Storage Server 2016 fully supports upgrades from previous versions.

**Windows MultiPoint Premium 2016 Server** Windows MultiPoint Premium Server 2016 is a Stand-Alone Windows product designed for environments that have multiple users simultaneously sharing one computer. Windows MultiPoint Premium 2016 Server is the same as a Windows Server 2016 with Multipoint Services Installed. MultiPoint Services allows multiple users, each with their own independent and familiar Windows experience to simultaneously share one computer.

Once you choose what roles are going on your server, you must then decide how you're going to install Windows Server 2016. There are two ways to install Windows Server 2016. You can upgrade a Windows Server 2012 or Windows Server 2012 R2 machine to Windows Server 2016, or you can do a clean install of Windows Server 2016. If you decide that you are going to upgrade, there are specific upgrade paths you must follow.

Your choice of Windows Server 2016 version is dictated by how your current network is designed. If you are building a network from scratch, then it's pretty straightforward. Just choose the Windows Server 2016 version based on your server's tasks. However, if you already have a version of Windows Server 2012 installed, you should follow the recommendations in Table 1.1, which briefly summarize the supported upgrade paths to Windows Server 2016.

**TABLE 1.1** Supported Windows Server 2016 upgrade path recommendations

| Current System | Upgraded System |
|---|---|
| Windows Server 2012 Standard | Windows Server 2016 Standard or Datacenter |
| Windows Server 2012 Datacenter | Windows Server 2016 Datacenter |

| Current System | Upgraded System |
|---|---|
| Windows Server 2012 R2 Standard | Windows Server 2016 Standard or Datacenter |
| Windows Server 2012 R2 Datacenter | Windows Server 2016 Datacenter |
| Windows Server 2012 R2 Essentials | Windows Server 2016 Essentials |
| Hyper-V Server 2012 R2 | Hyper-V Server 2016 |
| Windows Storage Server 2012 Standard | Windows Storage Server 2016 Standard |
| Windows Storage Server 2012 Workgroup | Windows Storage Server 2016 Workgroup |
| Windows Storage Server 2012 R2 Workgroup | Windows Storage Server 2016 Workgroup |

If your version of Microsoft Windows Server is not 64-bit, you can't upgrade to Windows Server 2016.

## Deciding on the Type of Installation

One of the final choices you must make before installing Windows Server 2016 is what type of installation you want. There are three ways to install Windows Server 2016.

**Windows Server 2016 (Desktop Experience)** This is the version with which most administrators are familiar. This is the version that uses *Microsoft Management Console (MMC)* windows, and it is the version that allows the use of a mouse to navigate through the installation.

**Windows Server 2016 Server Core** This is a bare-bones installation of Windows Server 2016. You can think of it this way: If Windows Server 2016 (Desktop Experience) is a top-of-the-line luxury car, then Windows Server 2016 Server Core is the stripped-down model with no air-conditioning, manual windows, and cloth seats. It might not be pretty to look at, but it gets the job done.

**Windows Server 2016 Nano Server** Windows Server 2016 has introduced a brand new type of server installation called Nano Server. Nano Server allows an administrator to remotely administer the server operating system. It was primarily designed and optimized for private clouds and datacenters. Nano Server is very similar to Server Core, but the Nano Server operating system uses significantly smaller hard drive space, has no local logon capability, and only supports 64-bit applications and tools.

## Real World Scenario

### Server Core

Here is an explanation of Server Core that I have used ever since it was introduced in Windows Server 2008.

I am a *huge* sports fan. I love watching sports on TV, and I enjoy going to games. If you have ever been to a hockey game, you know what a hockey goal looks like. Between hockey periods, the stadium workers often bring out a huge piece of Plexiglas onto the ice. There is a tiny square cut out of the bottom of the glass. The square is just a bit bigger than a hockey puck itself.

Now they pick some lucky fan out of the stands, give them a puck at center ice, and then ask them to shoot the puck into the net with the Plexiglas in front of it. If they get it through that tiny little square at the bottom of the Plexiglas, they win a car or some such great prize.

Well, Windows Server 2016 (Desktop Experience) is like regular hockey with a net, and Windows Server 2016 Server Core is the Plexiglas version.

Server Core supports a limited number of roles:

- Active Directory Certificate Services (AD CS)
- Active Directory Domain Services (AD DS)
- Active Directory Federation Services (AD FS)
- Active Directory Lightweight Directory Services (AD LDS)
- Active Directory Rights Management Services (AD RMS)
- DHCP Server
- DNS Server
- Fax Server
- File and Storage Services
- BITS Server
- BranchCache
- Hyper-V
- Network Policy and Access Services
- Print and Document Services
- Remote Access

- Remote Desktop Services
- Volume Activation Services
- Web Server (IIS)
- Windows Deployment Services
- Windows Server Update Services
- .NET Framework 3.5 Features
- .NET Framework 4.6 Features
- Streaming Media Services
- Failover Clustering
- iSCSI
- Network Load Balancing
- MPIO
- qWave
- Telnet Server/Client
- Windows Server Migration Tools
- Windows PowerShell 4.0

Server Core does not have the normal Windows interface or GUI. Almost everything has to be configured via the command line or, in some cases, using the Remote Server Administration Tools from a full version of Windows Server 2016. While this might scare off some administrators, it has the following benefits:

**Reduced Management** Because Server Core has a minimum number of applications installed, it reduces management effort.

**Minimal Maintenance** Only basic systems can be installed on Server Core, so it reduces the upkeep you would need to perform in a normal server installation.

**Smaller Footprint** Server Core requires only 1GB of disk space to install and 2GB of free space for operations.

**Tighter Security** With only a few applications running on a server, it is less vulnerable to attacks.

The prerequisites for Server Core are basic. It requires the Windows Server 2016 installation media, a product key, and the hardware on which to install it.

After you install the base operating system, you use PowerShell or the remote administrative tools to configure the network settings, add the machine to the domain, create and format disks, and install roles and features. It takes only a few minutes to install Server Core, depending on the hardware.

**Real World Scenario**

**Better Security**

When I started in this industry more than 20 years ago, I was a programmer. I used to program computer hospital systems. When I switched to the networking world, I continued to work under contract with hospitals and with doctors' offices.

One problem I ran into is that many doctors are affiliated with hospitals, but they don't actually have offices within the hospital. Generally, they have offices either near the hospital or, in some cases, right across the street.

Here is the issue: Do we put servers in the doctors' offices, or do we make the doctor log into the hospital network through a remote connection? Doctors' offices normally don't have computer rooms, and we don't want to place a domain controller or server on someone's desk. It's just unsafe!

This is where Windows Server 2016 Server Core can come into play. Since it is a slimmed-down version of Windows and there is no GUI, it makes it harder for anyone in the office to hack into the system. Also, Microsoft has a domain controller in Windows Server 2016 called a *read-only domain controller (RODC)*. As its name suggests, it is a read-only version of a domain controller.

With Server Core and an RODC, you can feel safer placing a server on someone's desk or in any office. Server Core systems allow you to place servers in areas that you would never have placed them before. This can be a great advantage to businesses that have small, remote locations without full server rooms.

## NIC Teaming

*NIC Teaming*, also known as *load balancing and failover (LBFO)*, gives an administrator the ability to allow multiple network adapters on a system to be placed into a team. Independent hardware vendors (IHVs) have required NIC Teaming, but until Windows Server 2012, NIC Teaming was *not* part of the Windows Server Operating System.

To be able to use NIC Teaming, the computer system must have at least one Ethernet adapter. If you want to provide fault protection, an administrator must have a minimum of two Ethernet adapters. One advantage of Windows Server 2016 is that an administrator can setup 32 network adapters in a NIC Team.

NIC Teaming is a very common practice when setting up virtualization. It is one way that you can have load balancing with Hyper-V.

NIC Teaming gives an administrator the ability to allow a virtual machine to use virtual network adapters in Hyper-V. The advantage of using NIC Teaming in Hyper-V is that the administrator can use it to connect to more than one Hyper-V switch. This allows Hyper-V to maintain connectivity even if the network adapter under the Hyper-V switch gets disconnected.

An administrator can configure NIC Teaming in either Server Manager or PowerShell.

## Installing Windows Server 2016

In the following sections, I am going to walk you through two different types of installs. I will show you how to do a full install of Windows Server 2016 Datacenter (Desktop Experience), and then I will show you how to install the Server Core version of the same software and Nano Server.

For these labs, I am using the full release of Windows Server 2016 Datacenter, but you can use Windows Server 2016 Standard.

### Installing with the Desktop Experience

In Exercise 1.1, I will show you how to install Windows Server 2016 Datacenter (Desktop Experience). This installation will have a Graphical User Interface (GUI) and this means that an administrator will be able to control the applications on the Desktop and the operating system functions with a mouse.

**Windows Installation**

At the time of this writing, I used the first full release of Windows Server 2016 Datacenter. For this reason, there may be screens that have changed somewhat since this book was published.

**EXERCISE 1.1**

**Installing Windows Server 2016 Datacenter (Desktop Experience)**

1. Insert the Windows Server 2016 installation DVD, and restart the machine from the installation media.
2. At the first screen, Windows Server 2016 (see Figure 1.2) will ask you to configure your language, time and currency, and keyboard. Make your selections, and click Next.
3. At the next screen, click Install Now.
4. Depending on what version of Windows Server 2016 you have (MSDN, TechNet, and so on), you may be asked to enter a product key. If this screen appears, enter your product key, and click Next. If this screen does not appear, just go to step 5.

**EXERCISE 1.1 *(continued)***

**FIGURE 1.2** Windows Server 2016 Setup

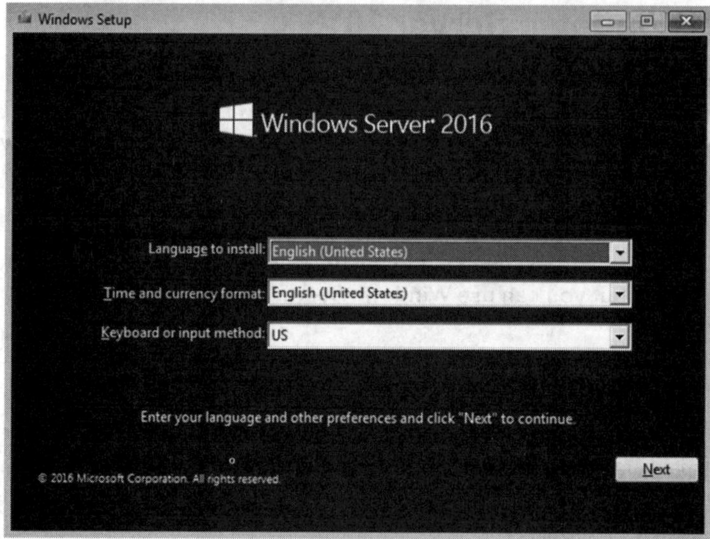


5. The Select The Operating System That You Want To Install screen then appears. Choose the Windows Server 2016 Datacenter (Desktop Experience) selection (see Figure 1.3) and click Next.

**FIGURE 1.3** Windows Server Edition

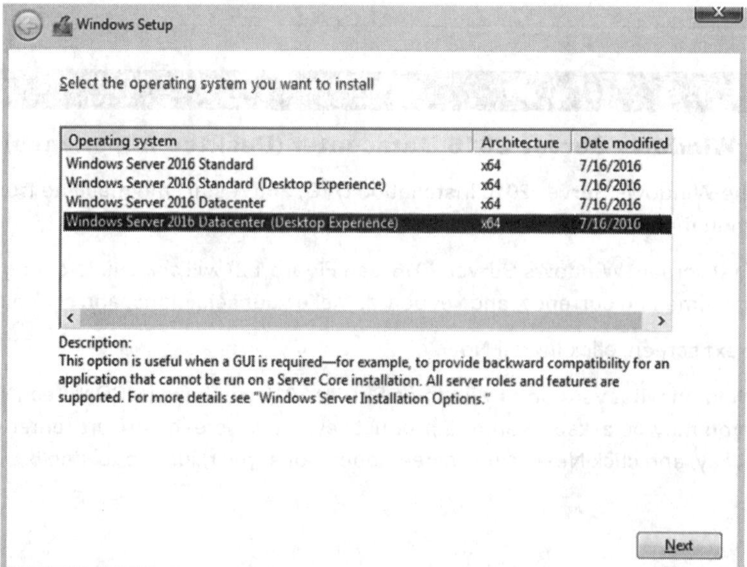

6. The license terms screen appears. After reading the Windows Server 2016 license agreement, check the I Accept The License Terms check box, and click Next.

7. On the Which type of installation do you want? Screen (see Figure 1.4), choose Custom: Install Windows Only (Advanced).

**FIGURE 1.4** Windows Server Installation

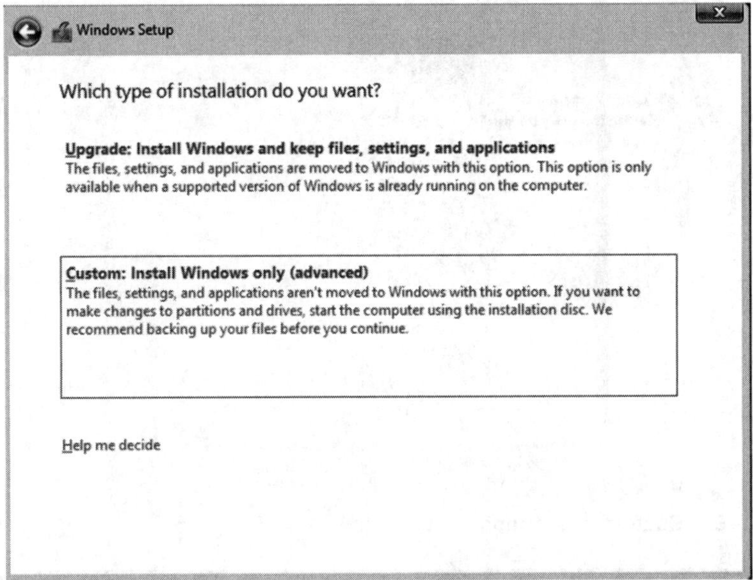


8. The next screen will ask you where you want to install Windows. If your hard disk is already formatted as NTFS, click the drive, and then click Next. If the hard disk is not yet set up or formatted, choose the New link, and create a partition. After creating the partition, click the Format link. Once the format is done, make sure you choose the new partition, and click Next.

9. The Installing Windows screen will appear next. This is where the files from your media will be installed onto the system (see Figure 1.5). The machine will reboot during this installation.

10. After the machine is finished rebooting, a screen requesting the administrator password will appear (see Figure 1.6). Type in your password. (P@ssword is used in this exercise.) Your password must meet the password complexity requirements. (Three of the following four are needed for complexity: one capitalized letter, one lowercase letter, one number, and/or one special character.) Click Finish.

**EXERCISE 1.1 *(continued)***

**FIGURE 1.5** Installing Windows screen

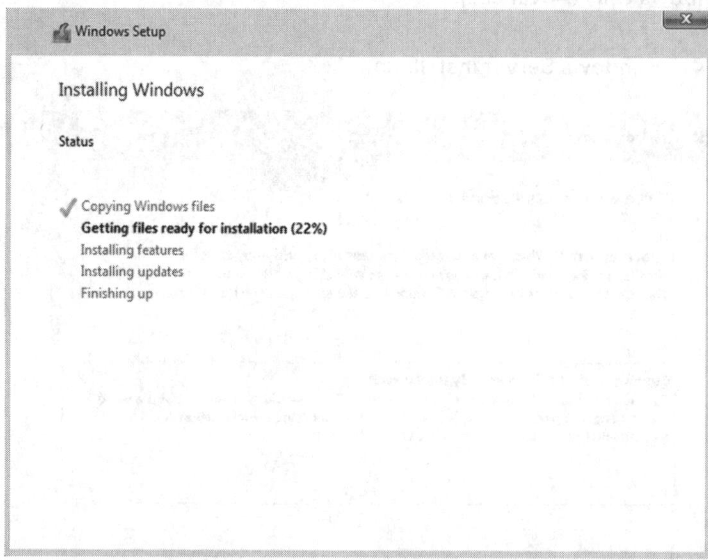


**FIGURE 1.6** Customize settings

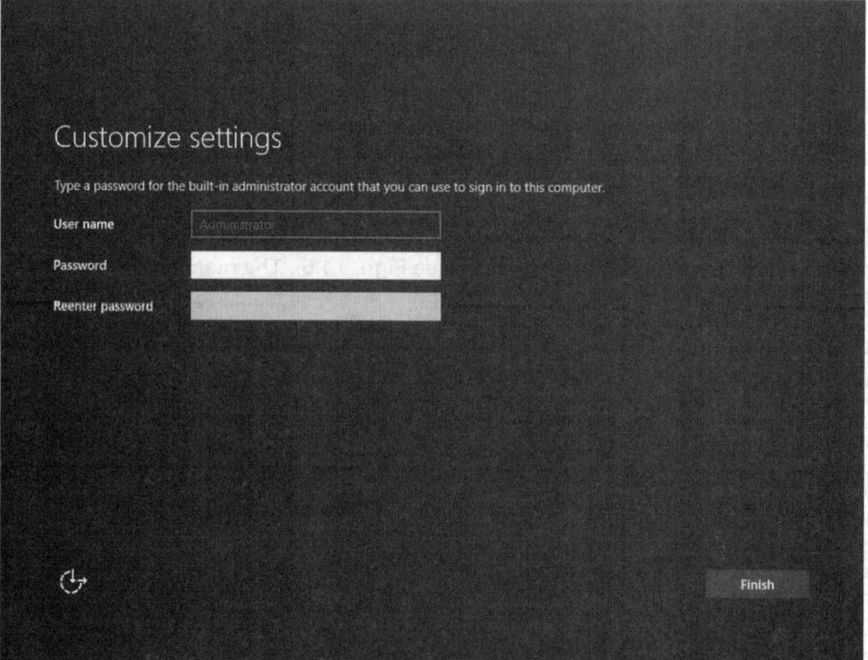

11. Next, log into the system. Press Ctrl+Alt+Del, and type in the administrator password. The machine will set up the properties of the administrator account.
12. Notice that the Server Manager dashboard automatically appears. Your Windows Server 2016 installation is now complete.
13. Close Server Manager.

After you have logged into the Windows Server 2016 Datacenter system, you will notice some features right away. The first is that there is a Start button in the lower-left corner of the screen.

Administrators can also access the Start button by pressing the Windows key on a standard keyboard.

## Installing Windows Server 2016 Server Core

In Exercise 1.2, you will learn how to install Windows Server 2016 Server Core. You'll notice that the steps are similar to the ones in Exercise 1.1, with a couple of exceptions. As mentioned earlier, Server Core is a command line configuration of Windows Server 2016.

**EXERCISE 1.2**

### Installing Windows Server 2016 Using Server Core

1. Insert the Windows Server 2016 installation DVD, and restart the machine from the installation media.
2. At the first screen, Windows Server 2016 will prompt you to configure your language, time and currency, and keyboard. Make your selections, and click Next.
3. At the next screen, click Install Now.
4. Depending on what version of Windows Server 2016 you have (MSDN, TechNet, and so on), you may be asked to enter a product key. If this screen appears, enter your product key, and click Next. If this screen does not appear, just go to step 5.
5. The Select The Operating System That You Want To Install screen then appears. Choose the Windows Server 2016 Datacenter selection (see Figure 1.7) and click Next.
6. The license terms screen appears. After reading the Windows Server 2016 license agreement, check the I Accept The License Terms check box and click Next.
7. At the Which Type Of Installation Do You Want? screen, choose Custom: Install Windows Only (Advanced).

**EXERCISE 1.2 *(continued)***

**FIGURE 1.7** Windows Server Edition

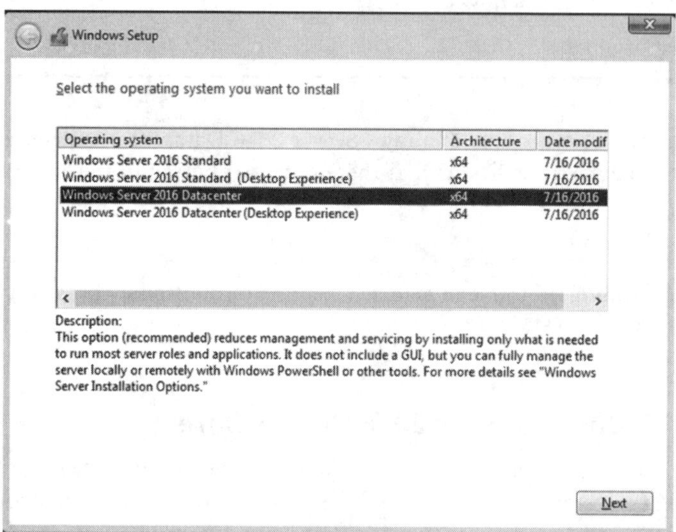


8. The next screen will ask you where you want to install Windows. If your hard disk is already formatted as NTFS, click the drive and then click Next. If the hard disk is not set up or formatted, choose the New link and create a partition. After creating the partition, click the Format link. Once the format is done, make sure you choose the new partition and click Next.

9. The Installing Windows screen will appear next. This is where the files from your media will be installed onto the system. The machine will reboot during this installation.

10. After the machine is finished rebooting, a screen requesting the administrator password will appear. Click OK (see Figure 1.8) and then type in your password. (P@ssword is used in this exercise.) Your password must meet the password complexity requirements (one capitalized letter, one number, and/or one special character).

**FIGURE 1.8** Change Password Screen

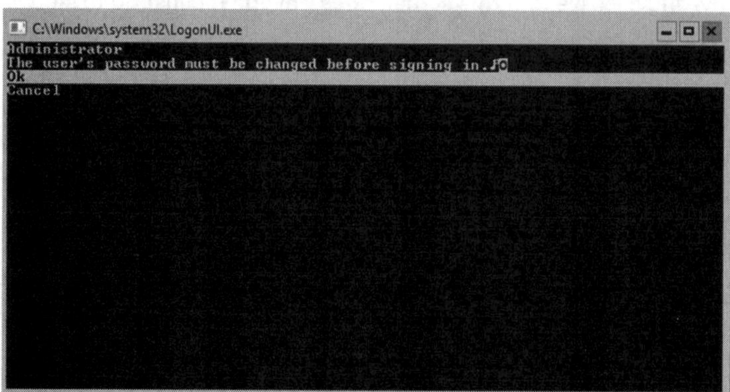

11. After the password is changed, a screen will appear telling you that the password has changed (see Figure 1.9). Hit the Enter key.

**FIGURE 1.9** Password Changed Screen

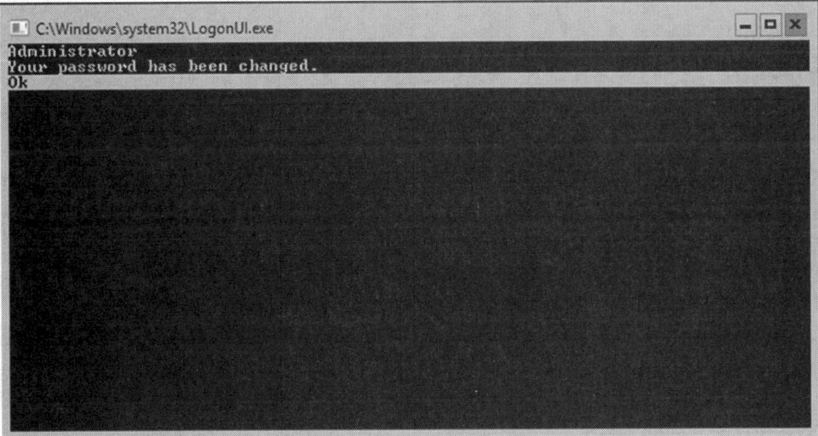


12. You will automatically get logged in. You will notice that the command prompt will automatically appear (see Figure 1.10). Your Windows Server 2016 Server Core installation is now complete. To turn off the machine, type **Shutdown /s /t 0**.

**FIGURE 1.10** Server Core Command Prompt

We will be showing many PowerShell commands throughout this book. The new Windows Server 2016 exams will be PowerShell intensive. I will show you the PowerShell commands needed to configure and maintain Windows Server 2016 Server Core throughout this entire book.

## Installing Windows Server 2016 Nano Server

With the release of Windows Server 2016, Microsoft has released a brand new installation option called Nano Server. Nano Server is a version of Windows Server 2016 that is controlled remotely and it was specifically designed to optimize the Windows Server for private cloud and Datacenter installations.

Windows Server 2016 Nano Server is a lot like Server Core but the advantage is that it is even a smaller installation of the operating system. Nano Server has *NO* local logon or GUI capabilities and it will allow only 64-bit applications and utilities.

Since Nano Server takes much less hard drive space and does not have many of the normal server components, its allows Nano Server to be much faster when it comes to setups, reboots, and even updates. Nano Server is available for both Standard and Datacenter editions of Windows Server 2016.

When Microsoft created Nano Server, they had some very specific ideas of how companies would use this version. For example, Nano Server is a good option for a DNS server, an IIS server, an application server for cloud based applications, or even a storage machine for file servers.

Now that you have seen some of the options on how to use Nano Server, let take a look at some of the disadvantages of Nano Servers. The first downside to using a Nano Server is that it cannot act as Domain Controller (this is a server with a copy of Active Directory installed onto the system). Also, Group Policy Objects (rules that you can put on machines or users) are also not supported on Nano Servers. Finally, Nano Servers can't be configured to use System Center Configuration Manager, System Center Data Protection Manager, NIC Teaming, or as proxy servers. Nano Servers also use a version of Windows PowerShell which has many differences as a server with regular PowerShell.

At the time this book was written, Nano Server only supports the Current Branch for Business (CBB) licensing model. But be sure to check the Microsoft website before taking any of the Microsoft Windows Server 2016 exams to make sure that this has not changed.

When it comes to installing Nano Servers, there are a few different options. There is no downloadable version of just Windows Server 2016 Nano Server. Nano Server is included on the Windows Server 2016 Standard or Datacenter physical media. Both server versions have a folder called NanoServer. The NanoServer folders contain a .wim image and a subfolder called Packages. The Packages subfolder is needed when you want to add server roles and features to the image.

But if you want a real easy way to create a Nano Server virtual hard drive (VHD), you can just download the Nano Server Image Builder. This software will help you easily create a Nano Server VHD that you can then use to boot up a server with or use in Microsoft's Hyper-V server.

In Exercise 1.3, you will learn how to install the Nano Server Image Builder and build a Nano Server VHD. For this exercise, you must have a copy of Windows Server 2016 downloaded.

**EXERCISE 1.3**

### Creating a Nano Server VHD

1. Download the Nano Server Image Builder (see Figure 1.11) at Microsoft's website (`https://www.microsoft.com/en-us/download/details.aspx?id=54065`) by clicking the Download button. I saved the downloaded file under my Windows Server 2016 Downloads folder.

**FIGURE 1.11** Nano Server Image Builder

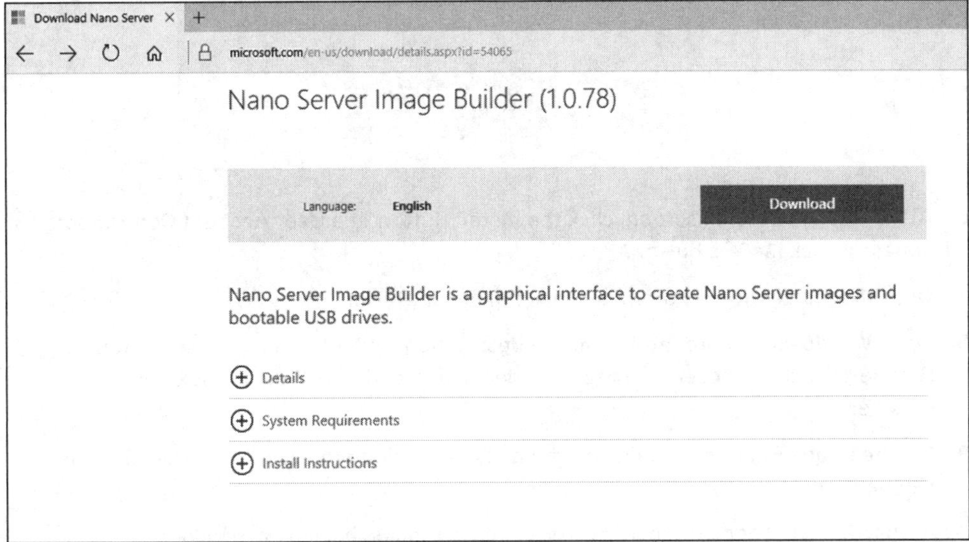


2. A file named `NanoServerImageBuilder.msi` will be created. Double-click on the file. If an Open File Security Warning Dialog box appears, click the Run button.
3. The Nano Server Image Builder Setup wizard will begin. Click Next at the intro screen.
4. At the Licensing screen, click the I accept the terms checkbox and click Next.
5. At the Destination Folder screen, choose the directory where you want to install the Nano Server Image Builder files (see Figure 1.12). Click Next.

**EXERCISE 1.3 *(continued)***

**FIGURE 1.12** Nano Server Image Builder Destination

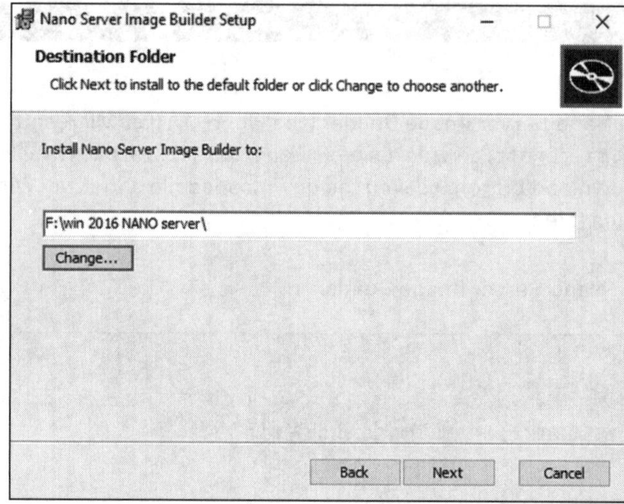


6. At the Ready to Install screen, click the Install Button. If a User Account Control box appears, click the Yes button.
7. Once the Installation is complete, click the Finish Button.
8. Open Windows Explorer and go to the destination folder that you chose in step 5. Double-click the `NanoServerImageBuilder.exe` file. If a UAC dialog box appears, click Yes.
9. For the Image Builder to work, you must also download the Windows ADK kit. This can be done at

   `https://developer.microsoft.com/en-us/windows/hardware/windows-assessment-deployment-kit`

   Click the get Windows ADK Download button.
10. It will ask you if you want to run or save the file. I saved the file to the same destination folder as the Nano Server Image Builder. Once it's downloaded, double-click the `adksetup.exe` file. If a dialog box appears, click Run.
11. Specify the destination of where you want the Windows ADK files to install and click Next.
12. At the Windows Kit Privacy screen, you can choose either option. By choosing Yes, you will participate in Microsoft's feedback program. For this exercise, I chose No. Click Next.
13. At the License Agreement screen, click Accept.

14. At the Features screen, accept the defaults and click Install. If a UAC screen appears, click Yes.
15. After the installation is complete, click the Close button.
16. Double-click on the `NanoServerImageBuilder.exe` file. When the UAC screen appears, click Yes.
17. So we now have the ability to create a Nano Server image or a bootable USB. We are going to create an Image. So click on the top choice "Create a new Nano Server image" (see Figure 1.13).

**FIGURE 1.13** Nano Server Image Choice

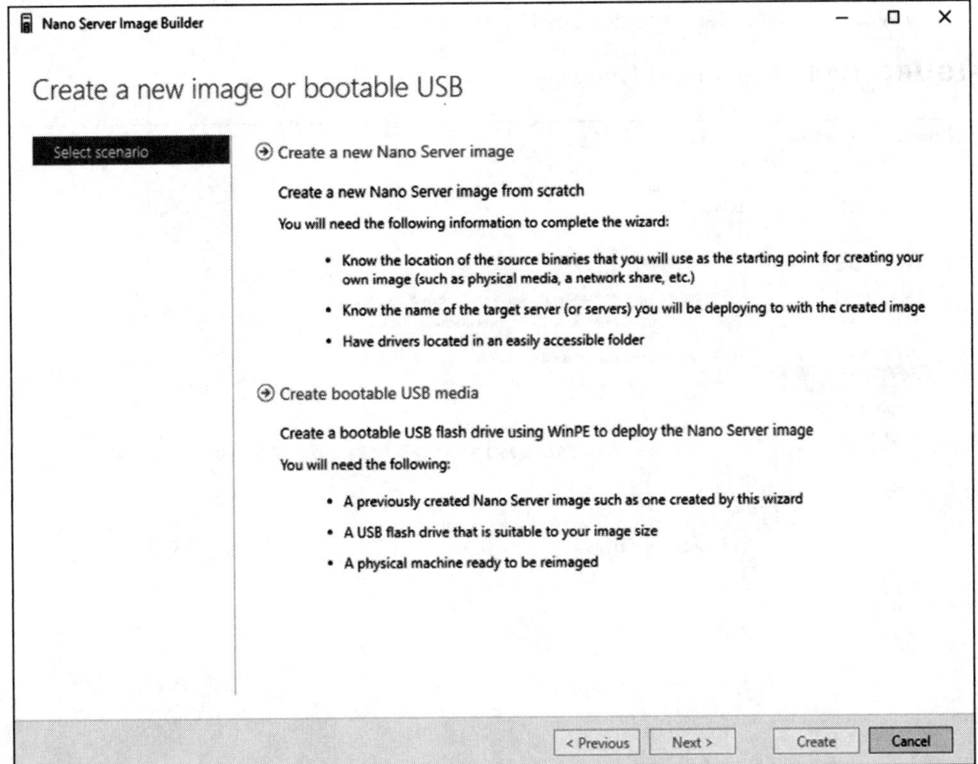


18. At the Before you begin screen, click Next.
19. At the Select Installation Media screen, point the folder to your Windows Server 2016 installation files where the NanoServer Folder resides. Click Next.

**EXERCISE 1.3 *(continued)***

If you only have a Windows Server 2016 .ISO image, right click on the ISO image and choose Open With ➤ Windows Explorer. Then copy the NanoServer folder to another location. Then in step 20, just point to the location of the NanoServer folder.

20. At the License agreement screen, click the box that states I have read and agree to the terms. Then click Next.
21. At the Deployment type screen. I am going to choose to create a Virtual machine image named Pluto.vhd. I am keeping the default of 8 GB and I am placing the VHD in my Win 2016 Nano Server folder (see Figure 1.14). Click Next.

**FIGURE 1.14** Deployment Type

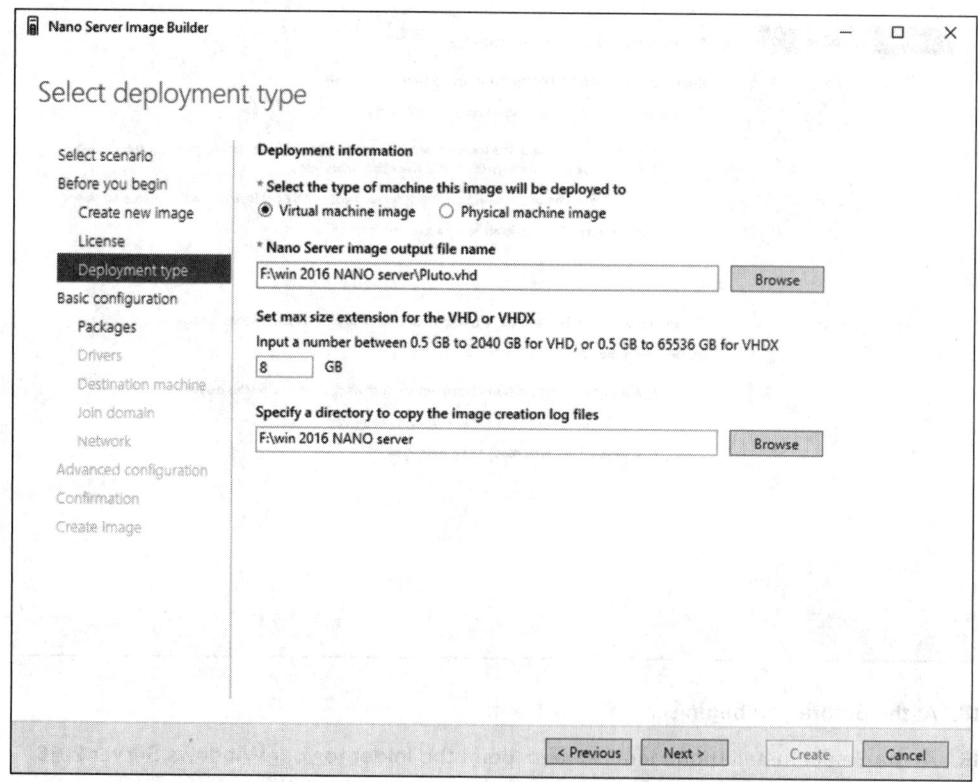


22. At the Basic Installation screen, click Next.
23. At the Select Optional Packages screen, you can choose any other options you want to install like DNS, IIS, etc. I am just going to click Next.

24. At the Drivers screen, add any drivers that may be needed for your installation and click Next.

25. Next the Destination screen will appear. Here is where you will enter the name of the computer and the Administrator's password. I am using Pluto as the computer name and P@ssw0rd as the password. Make sure your Time Zone is correct and click Next.

26. At this time, I am not going to join a domain. So I am just going to click Next.

27. I will leave the default network settings and click Next.

28. At the Advanced Configuration Screen, I am going to choose the top option "Create a Basic Nano Server Image" (see Figure 1.15).

**FIGURE 1.15** Advanced Configuration Screen

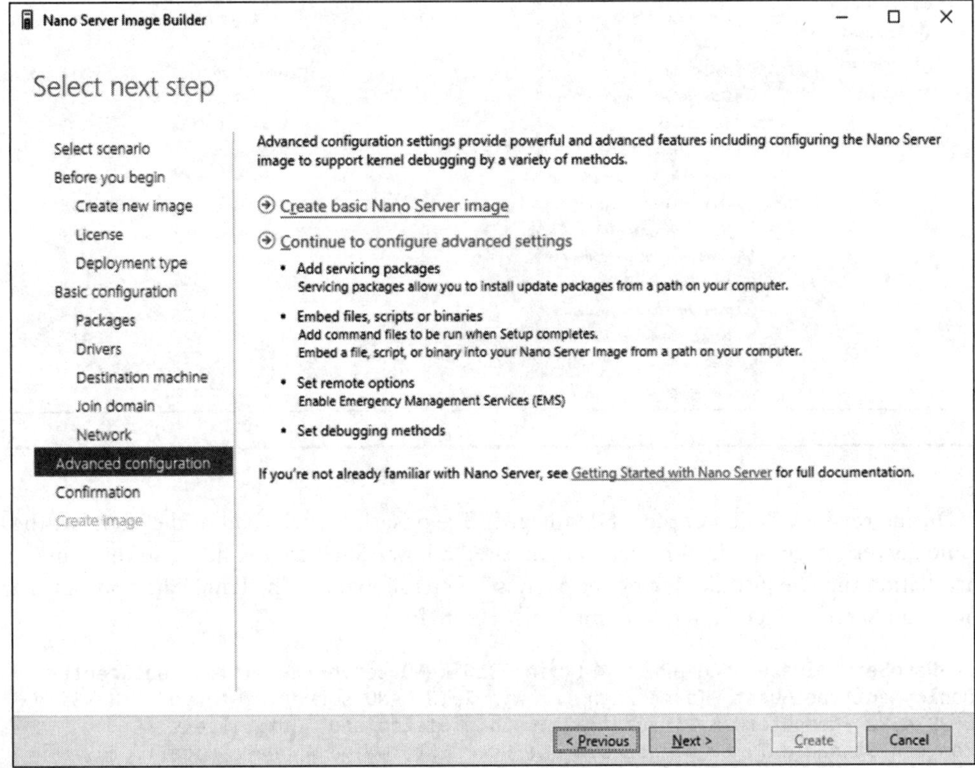


29. After you click the link, it will automatically take you to a Confirmation screen. Just click the Create button.

30. Once the image is complete, click the Close button.

**EXERCISE 1.3** ***(continued)***

31. Open Windows Explorer and go to the folder where you created the VHD (see Figure 1.16). Make sure the VHD (My VHD is named Pluto.vhd) has been created. You can now run this VHD in Microsoft Hyper-V.

**FIGURE 1.16** Verifying the Created VHD

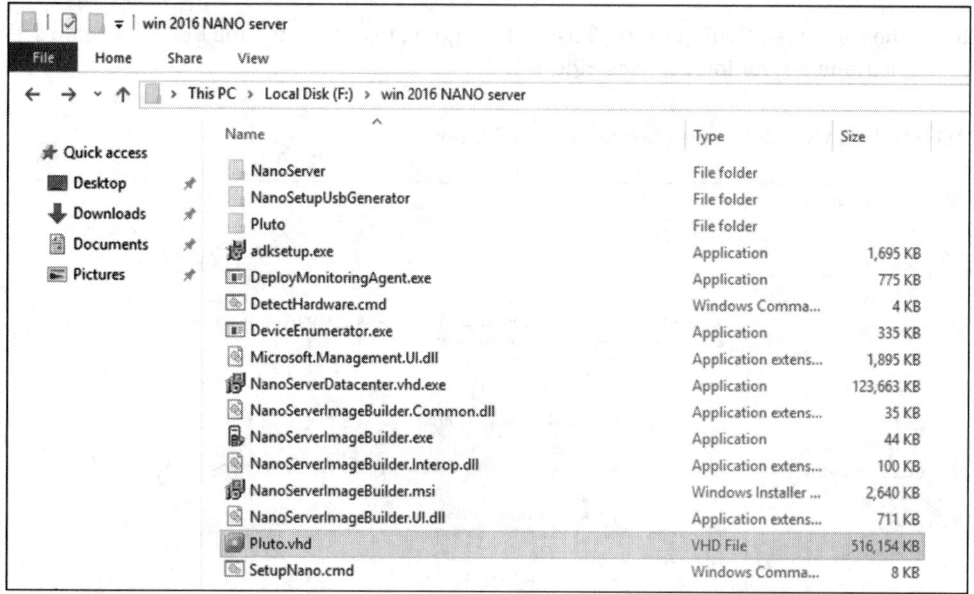


During the installation of the VHD image in Exercise 1.3, at the end of the exercise, the Nano Server Image Builder automatically created a PowerShell command to do the same installation that we just did during the exercise. The following is the PowerShell output that the Nano Server Image Builder automatically created:

```
New-NanoServerImage -MediaPath 'F:\win 2016 NANO server' -Edition 'Datacenter'
-DeploymentType Guest -TargetPath 'F:\win 2016 NANO server\Pluto.vhd' -MaxSize
8589934592 -ComputerName 'Pluto' -SetupCompleteCommand ('tzutil.exe /s
"Eastern Standard Time"') -LogPath 'C:\Users\StormWind\AppData\Local\Temp\
NanoServerImageBuilder\Logs\2016-11-13 17-48'
```

At the time this book was written, Nano Server PowerShell did not allow the following features (this list was taken directly from Microsoft's website);

- ADSI, ADO, and WMI type adapters
- Enable-PSRemoting, Disable-PSRemoting (PowerShell remoting is enabled by default.)
- Scheduled jobs and PSScheduledJob module

- Computer cmdlets for joining a domain { Add | Remove }
- Reset-ComputerMachinePassword, Test-ComputerSecureChannel
- Profiles (You can add a startup script for incoming remote connections with Set-PSSessionConfiguration.)
- Clipboard cmdlets
- EventLog cmdlets { Clear | Get | Limit | New | Remove | Show | Write } (Use the New-WinEvent and Get-WinEvent cmdlets instead.)
- Get-PfxCertificate cmdlet
- TraceSource cmdlets { Get | Set }
- Counter cmdlets { Get | Export | Import }
- Some web-related cmdlets { New-WebServiceProxy, Send-MailMessage, ConvertTo-Html }
- Logging and tracing using PSDiagnostics module
- Get-HotFix
- Implicit remoting cmdlets { Export-PSSession | Import-PSSession }
- New-PSTransportOption
- PowerShell transactions and Transaction cmdlets { Complete | Get | Start | Undo | Use }
- PowerShell Workflow infrastructure, modules, and cmdlets
- Out-Printer
- Update-List
- WMI v1 cmdlets: Get-WmiObject, Invoke-WmiMethod, Register-WmiEvent, Remove-WmiObject, Set-WmiInstance (Use CimCmdlets module instead.)

After Windows Server 2016 server is installed, you need to look at how to activate the server. In the next section, you will learn about the different ways you can activate a Windows Server 2016 system.

# Activating and Servicing Windows

After you complete the installation of Windows Server 2016, the next step is activating the operating system. Windows Server 2016 gives you a few different options when it comes to activation.

In the past, many administrators would use the Volume Activation Management Tool (VMAT) to activate both Microsoft operating systems and Microsoft products like Office. Administrators can still use VMAT to activate Microsoft products like Office but with the release of Windows Server 2016, there are some new ways to help administrators activate the operating systems.

So let's take a look at some of the different activation options that you have with the Windows Server 2016 operating system.

## Key Management Service

Windows Server 2016 Key Management Service (KMS) gives your Windows computers an easy and automated way to get activated. KMS allows your computers to get activated right on your local network without the need of contacting Microsoft. For this to happen, you must setup a KMS client-server network. KMS clients are able to contact KMS servers as long as your network uses either a static TCP/IP configuration or you have a Domain Name System (DNS) server setup.

To configure KMS hosts systems, you must configure and retrieve Volume Activation information. This is done by using a Software License Manager (referred to as SL Manager) script (Slmgr.vbs). This script can be run on a local system or a remote system but it needs to be run from a user's account that uses an elevated command prompt. KMS host systems can be any Windows client operating system running Windows Vista or higher and any Server above Windows Server 2003.

To create or modify the slmgr.vbs script, an administrator can use either the `Wscript.exe` or `Cscript.exe` application. `Slmgr.vbs` uses the `Wscript.exe` scripting engine by default. After an administrator makes any changes to the `Slmgr.vbs` script, the Software Licensing Service must be restarted. This can be done by using the Services Microsoft Management Console (MMC) or by running the `net stop` and `net start` commands at an elevated command prompt (`net stop sppsvc` and `net start sppsvc`).

The `Slmgr.vbs` script has different command line switches that you can use. Table 1.2 shows you some of the different switches that you can use with the `Slmgr.vbs` script.

**TABLE 1.2** `Slmgr.vbs` switches

| Parameter | Description |
|---|---|
| `/ato` | This switch is used for retail and volume systems editions with a KMS host key or a Multiple Activation Key (MAK) installed. The `/ato` command prompts Windows to try to do an online activation. For any systems that are using a Generic Volume License Key (GVLK), this will make the system attempt to do a KMS activation. |
| `/cdns` | This switch allows an administrator to disable KMS host automatic DNS publishing. |
| `/cpri` | Administrators can use this switch to lower the priority of KMS host processes. |
| `/dli` | Administrators can use this switch on the KMS host to view the current KMS activation count. |
| `/dlv` | When an administrator uses this switch, the license information for the installed operating system is displayed. |

| Parameter | Description |
|---|---|
| `/ipk` | This command will try to install a 5x5 product key. |
| `/sai activationInterval` | This switch allows an administrator to change how often a KMS client attempts to activate itself when it cannot find a KMS host. The default setting is 120 minutes, but you can change the interval by replacing `ActivationInterval` with the number of minutes you want to set. |
| `/sdns` | This switch allows an administrator to enable KMS host automatic DNS publishing. |
| `/spri` | This allows an administrator to set the CPU priority of the KMS host processes to Normal. |
| `/sprt PortNumber` | Using this switch allows an administrator to change the default TCP communications port on a KMS host from 1688 to whichever port the admin wants to use. To change the default port number, replace the `PortNumber` switch with the TCP port number to use. |
| `/sri RenewalInterval` | This switch allows an administrator to change how often a KMS client attempts to renew its activation by contacting a KMS host. If you need to change the default of 10080 (7 days), just replace `RenewalInterval` with a number of minutes you want to use. |

To run `Slmgr.vbs` remotely, administrators must supply additional parameters. They must include the computer name of the target computer as well as a username and password of a user account that has local administrator rights on the target computer. If run remotely without a specified username and password, the script uses the credentials of the user running the script.

```
slmgr.vbs TargetComputerName [username] [password] /parameter [options]
```

## Automatic Virtual Machine Activation

Another Windows Server 2016 activation method is called Automatic Virtual Machine Activation (AVMA). The main advantage of AVMA is that is works the same way a proof-of-purchase works. Once that there is proof that the Windows Server 2016 operating system is used in accordance with Microsoft Software License terms, AVMA allows you to install virtual machines on that Windows Server operating system without the need of using or managing product keys for each virtual machine.

AVMA attaches the virtual machine activation to the properly activated Hyper-V machine during the startup process. One of the nice advantages to using AVMA is that AVMA will provide administrators with real time reporting data. When your virtual servers are properly activated using volume or OEM licensing, AVMA gives an organization many benefits, like activating virtual machines in remote areas and also activating virtual machines even if no Internet connection is present.

One advantage to AVMA activations is that virtual machines are activated as long as the Hyper-V server is legally licensed. This helps consulting companies in the fact that they do not need to access client virtual machines to activate the machines as long as the Hyper-V server is properly licensed. Also, hosting companies can use the server logs to help keep the virtual machines running properly.

AVMA requires Windows Server 2016 with the Hyper-V role installed. AVMA can also run on Windows Server 2012 and Windows Server 2012 R2 if needed. Table 1.3 shows the Windows Server 2016 AVMA (5x5) Keys that are available from Microsoft's website.

**TABLE 1.3** Windows Server 2016 AVMA Keys

| Edition | AVMA Key |
|---|---|
| Datacenter | TMJ3Y-NTRTM-FJYXT-T22BY-CWG3J |
| Standard | C3RCX-M6NRP-6CXC9-TW2F2-4RHYD |
| Essentials | B4YNW-62DX9-W8V6M-82649-MHBKQ |

## Active Directory–Based Activation

One of the best advantages of using Windows Servers is the ability to install Active Directory onto your corporate network. Active Directory is just a centralized database of objects for a corporation called a domain.

For companies running Active Directory, administrators can use this towards their advantage when it comes to activation. Active Directory-Based Activation (ADBA) allows administrators to activate computers right through the domain connection.

Many organizations have remote locations and at these locations there is company owned software that needs to be registered. Normally administrators would use a retail key or a Multiple Activation Key (MAK) to get these products activated. The nice thing about ADBA is that as long as the computers are connected to the domain, the software and products can be activated through the domain.

When an Administrator joins a Windows computer to the domain, the ADBA will automatically activate the computers version of Windows either online with Microsoft or through the use of an activation proxy.

## Servicing Windows Server 2016

Now that we looked at some of the ways to activate your Windows Server 2016 systems, let's take a look at how you can service your Windows Server systems. Table 1.4 will show the different versions for Windows Server 2016 and which servicing model each version uses.

**TABLE 1.4** Servicing Models for Windows Server 2016

| Installation Option | LTSB Servicing | CBB Servicing |
|---|---|---|
| Desktop Experience | Yes | No |
| Server Core | Yes | No |
| Nano Server | No | Yes |

### Long Term Servicing Branch

Before the release of Windows Server 2016, Windows operating systems used the "5+5" servicing models. What this meant was there were 5 years of mainstream support and 5 years of extended support for the different versions of the Windows operating systems. This model will continue to be used in Windows Server 2016 (Desktop Support and Server Core) but it will be known as Long Term Servicing Branch (LTSB).

### Current Branch for Business

Administrators who decide to install Windows sever 2016 Nano Server will be choosing to use the Current Branch for Business (CBB) servicing model. This version of servicing is a more aggressive version and it was specifically designed with the cloud in mind. As the cloud continues to quickly evolve, the CBB servicing model is meant for that lifecycle. The CBB servicing model will continue to provide new features and functions to Windows Server allowing the server to evolve and grow with the rapidly changing industry. Microsoft's goal is to release updates multiple times per year for Nano Server thus keeping it changing with the industry.

## Using Windows Deployment Services

Another way that many IT departments deploy operating systems has been through the use of Windows Deployment Services (WDS). WDS allows an IT administrator to install a Windows operating system without using an installation disc. Using WDS allows you to deploy the operating system through a network installation. WDS can deploy Windows XP, Windows Server 2003, Windows Vista, Windows 7, Windows 8, Windows 10, Windows Server 2008/2008 R2, Windows Server 2012, Windows Server 2012 R2, and Microsoft Windows Server 2016.

The following are some of the advantages of using WDS for automated installation:

- You can remotely install Windows 7/8/10.
- The procedure simplifies management of the server image by allowing you to access Windows 7/8/10 distribution files from a distribution server.
- You can quickly recover the operating system in the event of a computer failure.

Here are the basic steps of the WDS process from a PXE-enabled WDS client:

1. The WDS client initiates a special boot process through the PXE network adapter (and the computer's BIOS configured for a network boot). On a PXE client, the user presses F12 to start the PXE boot process and to indicate that they want to perform a WDS installation.
2. A list of available Windows PE boot images is displayed. The user should select the appropriate Windows PE boot image from the boot menu.
3. The Windows Welcome screen is displayed. The user should click the Next button.
4. The WDS user is prompted to enter credentials for accessing and installing images from the WDS server.
5. A list of available operating system images is displayed. The user should select the appropriate image file to install.
6. The WDS user is prompted to enter the product key for the selected image.
7. The Partition And Configure The Disk screen is displayed. This screen provides the ability to install a mass storage device driver, if needed, by pressing F6.
8. The image copy process is initiated, and the selected image is copied to the WDS client computer.

The following sections describe how to set up the WDS server and the WDS clients and how to install Windows 7/8/10 through WDS.

## Preparing the WDS Server

With the WDS server, you can manage and distribute Windows 7/8/10 operating system images to WDS client computers. The WDS server contains any files necessary for PXE booting, Windows PE boot images, and the Windows 7/8/10 images to be deployed.

The following steps for preparing the WDS server are discussed in the upcoming sections:

1. Make sure that the server meets the requirements for running WDS.
2. Install WDS.
3. Configure and start WDS.
4. Configure the WDS server to respond to client computers (if this was not configured when WDS was installed).

For WDS to work, the server on which you will install WDS must meet the requirements for WDS and be able to access the required network services.

## WDS Server Requirements

The WDS server must meet these requirements:

- The computer must be a domain controller or a member of an Active Directory domain.
- At least one partition on the server must be formatted as NTFS.

- WDS must be installed on the server.
- The operating system must be Windows Server 2003, Windows Server 2008/2008 R2, Windows Server 2012 / 2012 R2, or Windows Server 2016.
- A network adapter must be installed.

## Network Services

The following network services must be running on the WDS server or be accessible to the WDS server from another network server:

- TCP/IP installed and configured
- A DHCP server, which is used to assign DHCP addresses to WDS clients (Ensure that your DHCP scope has enough addresses to accommodate all of the WDS clients that will need IP addresses.)
- A DNS server, which is used to locate the Active Directory controller
- Active Directory, which is used to locate WDS servers and WDS clients as well as authorize WDS clients and manage WDS configuration settings and client installation options

## Installing the WDS Server Components

You can configure WDS on a Windows Server 2003/2008/2008 R2, Windows Server 2012 / 2012 R2, or Windows Server 2016 computer by using the Windows Deployment Services Configuration Wizard or by using the WDSUTIL command line utility. Table 1.5 describes the `WDSUTIL` command line options.

**TABLE 1.5** `WDSUTIL` command line options

| WDSUTIL Option | Description |
|---|---|
| `/initialize-server` | Initializes the configuration of the WDS server |
| `/uninitialized-server` | Undoes any changes made during the initialization of the WDS server |
| `/add` | Adds images and devices to the WDS server |
| `/convert-ripimage` | Converts Remote Installation Preparation (RIPrep) images to WIM images |
| `/remove` | Removes images from the server |
| `/set` | Sets information in images, image groups, WDS servers, and WDS devices |

**TABLE 1.5** WDSUTIL command line options *(continued)*

| WDSUTIL Option | Description |
|---|---|
| /get | Gets information from images, image groups, WDS servers, and WDS devices |
| /new | Creates new capture images or discover images |
| /copy-image | Copies images from the image store |
| /export-image | Exports to WIM files images contained within the image store |
| /start | Starts WDS services |
| /stop | Stops WDS services |
| /disable | Disables WDS services |
| /enable | Enables WDS services |
| /approve-autoadddevices | Approves Auto-Add devices |
| /reject-autoadddevices | Rejects Auto-Add devices |
| /delete-autoadddevices | Deletes records from the Auto-Add database |
| /update | Uses a known good resource to update a server resource |

The first step in setting up WDS to deploy operating systems to the clients is to install the WDS role. You do this by using Server Manager.

One of the advantages of using the Windows deployment server is that WDS can work with Windows image (`.wim`) files. Windows image files can be created through the use of the Windows Sysprep utility.

One component to which you need to pay attention when using the Windows deployment server is *Preboot Execution Environment (PXE)* network devices. PXE boot devices are network interface cards (NICs) that can talk to a network without the need for an operating system. PXE boot NIC adapters are network adapters that have a set of preboot commands within the boot firmware.

This is important when using WDS because PXE boot adapters connect to a WDS server and request the data needed to load the operating system remotely. Remember, most of the machines for which you are using WDS do not have an operating system on the computer. You need NIC adapters that can connect to a network without the need for an operating system for WDS to work properly.

For the same reason, you must set up DHCP to accept PXE machines. Those machines need a valid TCP/IP address so that they can connect to the WDS server.

## Preparing the WDS Client

The WDS client is the computer on which Windows 7/8/10 will be installed. WDS clients rely on a technology called PXE, which allows the client computer to boot remotely and connect to a WDS server.

To act as a WDS client, the computer must meet all of the hardware requirements for Windows 7/8/10 and have a PXE-capable network adapter installed, and a WDS server must be present on the network. Additionally, the user account used to install the image must be a member of the Domain Users group in Active Directory.

After the WDS server has been installed and configured, you can install Windows 7/8/10 on a WDS client that uses a PXE-compliant network card.

To install Windows 7/8/10 on the WDS client, follow these steps:

1. Start the computer. When prompted, press F12 for a network service boot. The Windows PE appears.
2. The Windows Welcome screen appears. Click the Next button to start the installation process.
3. Enter the username and password of an account that has permission to access and install images from the WDS server.
4. A list of available operating system images stored on the WDS server appears. Select the image to install and click Next.
5. Enter the product key for the selected Windows 7/8/10 image and click Next.
6. The Partition And Configure The Disk screen appears. Select the desired disk-partitioning options, or click OK to use the default options.
7. Click Next to initiate the image-copying process. The Windows Setup process will begin after the image is copied to the WDS client computer.

# Understanding Features On Demand

One of the problems in previous versions of Windows Server was how roles and features were stored on the hard disk. Before the introduction of Windows Server 2012, even if a server role or feature was disabled on a server, the binary files for that role or feature were still present on the disk. The problem with this approach is that, even if you disable the role, it still consumes space on your hard drive.

Features On Demand in Windows Server 2012 solves this issue because not only can administrators disable a role or feature, they can also completely remove the role or feature's files. Windows Server 2016 has continued with Features on Demand and administrators can choose what Roles and Features they want to use, when they want to use them.

Once this is done, a state of Removed is shown in Server Manager, or the state of Disabled With Payload Removed is shown in the Deployment Image Servicing and Management (`Dism.exe`) utility. To reinstall a role or feature that has been completely removed, you must have access to the installation files.

The Deployment Image Servicing and Management (`Dism.exe`) utility is talked about throughout this entire book. DISM will be discussed in great detail when we discuss Windows imaging.

If you want to remove a role or feature completely from the system, use `-Remove` with the `Uninstall-WindowsFeature` cmdlet of Windows PowerShell.

If you want to reinstall a role or feature that has been removed completely, use the Windows PowerShell `-Source` option of the `Install-WindowsFeature Server Manager` cmdlet. Using the `-Source` option states the path where the WIM image files and the index number of the image will be located. If an administrator decides not to use the `-Source` option, Windows will use Windows Update by default.

When you're using the Features On Demand configuration, if feature files are not available on the server computer and the installation requires those feature files, Windows Server 2016 can be directed to get those files from a side-by-side feature store, which is a shared folder that contains feature files. It is available to the server on the network, from Windows Update, or from installation media. This can be overwritten using the `-Source` option in the Windows PowerShell utility.

**Source Files for Roles or Features**

Offline virtual hard disks (VHDs) cannot be used as a source for installing roles or features that have been completely removed. Only sources for the same version of Windows Server 2016 are supported.

To install a removed role or feature using a WIM image, follow these steps:

1. Run the following command:

   ```
   Get-windowsimage -imagepath \install.wim
   ```

   In step 1, *`imagepath`* is the path where the WIM files are located.

2. Run the following command:

   ```
   Install-WindowsFeature featurename -Source wim: path:index
   ```

   In step 2, *`featurename`* is the name of the role or feature from `Get-WindowsFeature`. *`path`* is the path to the WIM mount point, and *`index`* is the index of the server image from step 1.

To add or remove a role or feature, you must have administrative rights to the Windows Server 2016 machine.

# Summary

In this chapter, you studied the latest advantages of using Windows Server 2016. You also learned about the different roles and features you can install on a Windows Server 2016 machine. You also explored how to migrate those roles and features from a Windows Server 2008, 2008 R2, and Windows Server 2012 machine to a Windows Server 2016 machine.

I discussed the different upgrade paths that are available and which upgrades are best for your current network setup. You learned that another important issue to decide when installing Windows Server 2016 is whether to use Server Core or the GUI installation.

You learned how to install Windows Server 2016 Datacenter (Desktop Experience), and you installed the Windows Server 2016 Server Core. Remember, Server Core is a slimmed-down version of Windows Server. With no GUI desktop available, it's a safer alternative to a normal Windows install.

I discussed a feature called Features On Demand. This feature allows you to remove roles and features from the operating system and remove the associated files completely from the hard drive, thus saving disk space.

# Video Resources

There are videos available for the following exercises:

1.1

1.2

You can access the videos at `http://sybextestbanks.wiley.com` on the Other Study Tools tab.

# Exam Essentials

**Understand the upgrade paths.** It's important to make sure you understand the different upgrade paths from Windows Server 2012 and Windows Server 2012 R2 to Windows Server 2016.

**Understand Windows Server 2016 server roles.** Understand what the Windows Server 2016 server roles do for an organization and its users.

**Understand Features On Demand.** Understand the feature called Features On Demand. Microsoft loves to ask exam questions about its new features, and this will be no exception. Understand how features and roles stay on the system until you physically remove them from the hard drive.

**Understand Windows Deployment Services.** Know how to install and configure a Windows Deployment Services (WDS) server. Know the WDS network requirements and components.

# Review Questions

1. You are the administrator for the ABC Company. You are looking to install Windows Server 2016, and you need to decide which version to install. You need to install a version of Windows that is just for logon authentication and nothing else. You want the most secure option and cost is not an issue. What should you install?
   - **A.** Windows Server 2016 Datacenter (Desktop Experience)
   - **B.** Windows Server 2016 Datacenter Server Core
   - **C.** Windows Server 2016 Standard (Desktop Experience)
   - **D.** Windows Server 2016 Web Server Core
2. You are the IT manager for a large organization. One of your co-workers installed a new Windows Server 2016 Datacenter Server Core machine, but now the IT team has decided that it should be a Windows Server 2016 Datacenter (Desktop Experience). What should you do?
   - **A.** Reinstall Windows Server 2016 Datacenter Server Core on the same machine.
   - **B.** Install a new machine with Windows Server 2016 Datacenter Server Core.
   - **C.** Convert the current Windows Server 2016 Datacenter Server Core to the Windows Server 2016 Datacenter (Desktop Experience) version.
   - **D.** Dual-boot the machine with both Windows Server 2016 Datacenter Server Core and Windows Server 2016 Datacenter (Desktop Experience).
3. You are the administrator for your company, and you are looking at upgrading your Windows Server 2012 Standard with GUI to Windows Server 2016. Which version of Windows Server 2016 does Microsoft recommend you use to keep the GUI interface?
   - **A.** Windows Server 2016 Datacenter (Desktop Experience)
   - **B.** Windows Server 2016 Standard (Desktop Experience)
   - **C.** Windows Server 2016 Datacenter
   - **D.** Windows Server 2016 Standard
4. You are looking at upgrading your Windows Server 2012 R2 Datacenter with GUI machine to Windows Server 2016. Your organization is considering virtualizing its entire server room, which has 25 servers. To which version of Windows Server 2016 would you upgrade while keeping the GUI interface?
   - **A.** Windows Server 2016 Datacenter (Desktop Experience)
   - **B.** Windows Server 2016 Standard (Desktop Experience)
   - **C.** Windows Server 2016 Datacenter
   - **D.** Windows Server 2016 Standard
5. You have been hired to help a small company set up its first Windows network. It has had the same 13 users for the entire two years it has been open, and the company has no plans to expand. What version of Windows Server 2016 would you recommend?
   - **A.** Windows Server 2016 Datacenter (Desktop Experience)
   - **B.** Windows Server 2016 Standard (Desktop Experience)

C. Windows Server 2016 Datacenter

D. Windows Server 2016 Essentials

6. You have been hired to help a small company set up its Windows network. It has 20 users, and it has no plans to expand. What version of Windows Server 2016 would you recommend?

   A. Windows Server 2016 Datacenter

   B. Windows Server 2016 Standard

   C. Windows Server 2016 Essentials

   D. Windows Server 2016 Datacenter (Desktop Experience)

7. Which of the following are benefits of using Windows Server 2016 Server Core? (Choose all that apply.)

   A. Reduced management

   B. Minimal maintenance

   C. Smaller footprint

   D. Tighter security

8. You are a server administrator, and you are trying to save hard drive space on your Windows Server 2016 Datacenter machine. Which feature can help you save hard disk space?

   A. `HDSaver.exe`

   B. Features On Demand

   C. ADDS

   D. WinRM

9. You are the IT Director for your company. Your company needs to install a version of Windows Server 2016 that uses the Current Branch for Business servicing model. What version would you install?

   A. Windows Server 2016 Datacenter

   B. Windows Server 2016 Standard

   C. Windows Server 2016 Essentials

   D. Windows Server 2016 Nano Server

10. What type of domain controller would you install into an area where physical security is a concern?

    A. Primary domain controller

    B. Backup domain controller

    C. Read-only domain controller

    D. Locked-down domain controller

Chapter 2

# Installing in the Enterprise

## THE FOLLOWING 70-740 EXAM OBJECTIVES ARE COVERED IN THIS CHAPTER:

✓ **Create, manage, and maintain images for deployment.**

- This objective may include but is not limited to the following subobjectives: Plan for Windows Server virtualization; plan for Linux and FreeBSD deployments; assess virtualization workloads using the Microsoft Assessment and Planning (MAP) Toolkit; determine considerations for deploying workloads into virtualized environments; update images with patches, hotfixes, and drivers; install roles and features in offline images; manage and maintain Windows Server Core, Nano Server images, and VHDs using Windows PowerShell

Installing Windows Server 2016 is quick and easy, but as an IT manager or IT professional, you may have to install dozens of copies of Windows Server 2016. It is not a good practice to install them one at a time. It's important to understand how to automate a Windows Server 2016 deployment for the Windows Server 2016 (70-740) exam, but you'll also use automated deployments in a corporate environment. Many companies use third-party tools to create and deploy Windows Server 2016 machines, but there are other ways.

You can automate the installation of Windows Server 2016 in several ways. You can install Windows Server 2016 by using an unattended installation, by using Windows Deployment Services (WDS) to remotely deploy unattended installations, by using Hyper-V, or by using the System Preparation Tool for disk imaging. To help customize these options for automating remote installations, you can also use answer files to provide answers to the questions that are normally asked during the installation process. After you've installed Windows Server 2016, you can also automate the installation of applications by using Windows Installer packages.

This chapter includes an overview of the automated deployment options available with Windows Server 2016. Also included in this chapter is information on how to access the deployment tools available for Windows Server 2016 and the use of unattended installation, how the System Preparation Tool (along with Deployment Image Servicing and Management DISM utility) is used to create disk images for automated installation, and how to use Windows System Image Manager (SIM) to create unattended answer files.

# Understanding Automated Deployment Options

If you need to install Windows Server 2016 on multiple computers, you could manually install the operating system on each computer, as described in Chapter 1, "Installing Windows Server 2016." However, automating the deployment process will make your job easier, more efficient, and more cost effective if you have a large number of client computers on which to install Windows Server 2016.

Windows Server 2016 comes with several utilities that can be used for deploying and automating the Windows Server 2016 installation. With access to multiple utilities with different functionality, administrators have increased flexibility in determining how to best deploy Windows Server 2016 within a large corporate environment.

The following sections contain overviews of the automated deployment options, which will help you choose which solution is best for your requirements and environment. The options for automated deployment of Windows Server 2016 are as follows:

- Microsoft Deployment Toolkit (MDT) 2013 Update 2
- Unattended installation, or unattended setup, which uses `Setup.exe`
- Microsoft Assessment and Planning (MAP) Toolkit
- Windows Automated Installation Kit (Windows AIK)
- Windows Assessment and Deployment Kit for Windows Server 2016
- WDS (covered in Chapter 1 "Installing Windows Server 2016")
- System Preparation Tool (`Sysprep.exe`), which is used to set up a machine to be imaged or cloned
- Deployment Image Servicing and Management (DISM)

Another option that you have to deploy Windows Server 2016 is through System Center Configuration Manager (SCCM). Since SCCM is its own application with an additional cost, it is beyond the scope of this book. You can learn more about SCCM on the Microsoft website at `https://technet.microsoft.com/en-us/system-center-docs/system-center`.

## An Overview of the Microsoft Deployment Toolkit 2013 Update 2

Microsoft released a deployment assistance toolset called the *Microsoft Deployment Toolkit (MDT) 2013 Update 2*. It is used to automate desktop and server deployment. The MDT provides an administrator with the following benefits:

- Administrative tools that allow for the deployment of desktops and servers through the use of a common console (see Figure 2.1)
- Quicker deployments and the capabilities of having standardized desktop and server images and security
- Zero-touch deployments of Windows Server 2016, Windows Server 2012/2012 R2, Windows Server 2008/2008 R2, Windows 10/8/7

To install the MDT 2013 package onto your computer (regardless of the operating system being deployed), you must first meet the minimum requirements of MDT. These components need to be installed only on the computer where MDT 2013 is being installed:

- Windows Server 2016, Windows Server 2012/2012 R2, Windows Server 2008/2008 R2, Windows 10, Windows 8.1, Windows 8, or Windows 7.
- The Windows Assessment and Deployment Kit (ADK) for Windows Server 2016 is required for all deployment scenarios.

- System Center 2016 Configuration Manager Service Pack 1 with the Windows ADK for Windows Server 2016 is required for zero-touch installation (ZTI) and user-driven installation (UDI) scenarios.
- If you are using ZTI and/or UDI, you are allowed to add the MDT SQL database to any version of System Center Configuration Manager with SQL Technology; if you are using LTI, you must use a separately licensed SQL Server product to host your MDT SQL database.

**FIGURE 2.1** Microsoft Deployment Toolkit console

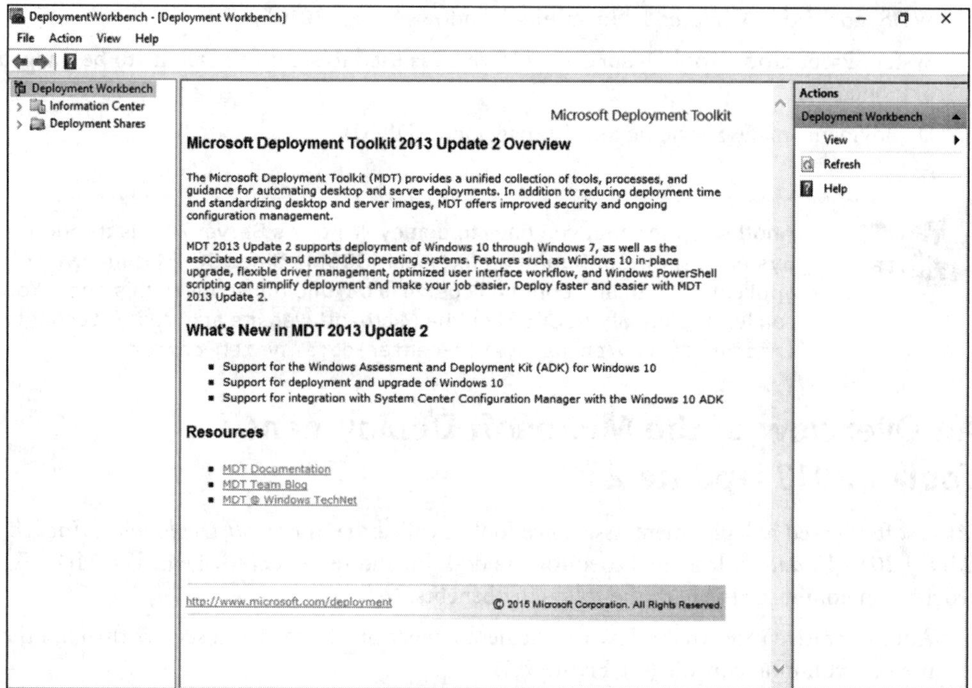

You can install MDT 2013 without installing Windows (ADK) first, but you will not be able to use the package fully until Windows (ADK) is installed. I will explain all of the benefits of Windows (ADK) in the section called "Overview of the Windows Assessment and Deployment Kit" later in this chapter. I recommend you install Windows ADK first at `https://developer.microsoft.com/en-us/windows/hardware/windows-assessment-deployment-kit`.

In Exercise 2.1, you will download and install MDT 2013. You can install MDT 2013 on the Windows Server 2016 operating system machine that you installed in Chapter 1. If you decide to install the MDT 2013 onto a server or production machine, I recommend that you perform a full backup before completing Exercise 2.1. Installing MDT 2013 will replace any previous version of MDT that the machine may currently be using.

**EXERCISE 2.1**

### Downloading and Installing MDT 2013

To download and install MDT 2013, follow these steps:

1. Download the MDT 2013 Update 1 utility from Microsoft's website (`https://www.microsoft.com/en-us/download/details.aspx?id=48595`).
2. Click the Download button (see Figure 2.2).

**FIGURE 2.2** Microsoft Deployment Toolkit Download

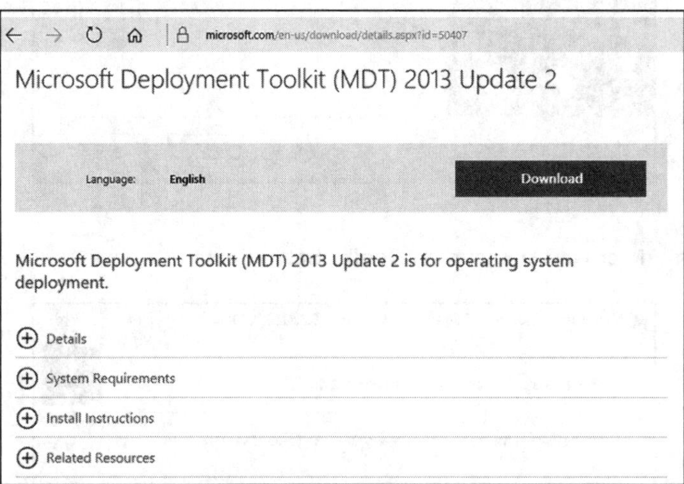


3. You get a screen asking "Choose the download you want". Choose the x64 or x86 version (I chose the x64 version). Click Next.
4. A message box may appear asking if you want to run or save the MDT. I clicked the down arrow next to Save As and saved the files into the downloads directory.
5. Double-click `MicrosoftDeploymentToolkit_xxx.exe` you choose to start the installation.
6. At the Welcome screen, click Next as shown in Figure 2.3.
7. At the License screen, click the I Accept The Terms In The License Agreement radio button and click Next.
8. At the Custom Setup screen, click the down arrow next to Microsoft Deployment Toolkit and choose Entire Feature Will Be Installed On Local Hard Drive. Click Next as shown on Figure 2.4.

**EXERCISE 2.1 *(continued)***

**FIGURE 2.3** Microsoft Deployment Toolkit Setup Screen

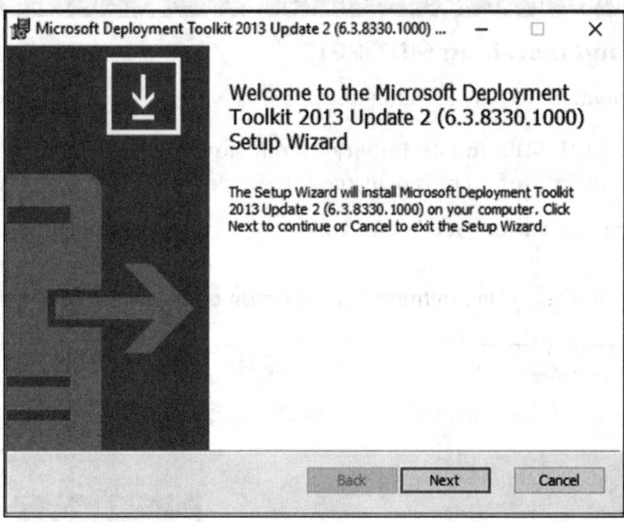


**FIGURE 2.4** Microsoft Deployment Toolkit Setup Screen

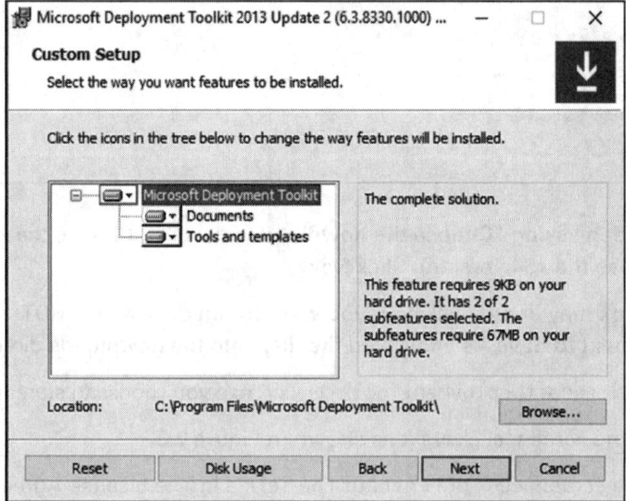


9. At the Customer Experience Improvement Program screen, choose if you want to participate or not and choose Next.
10. At the Ready To Install screen, click the Install button (shown in Figure 2.5).

**FIGURE 2.5** Ready to Install Screen

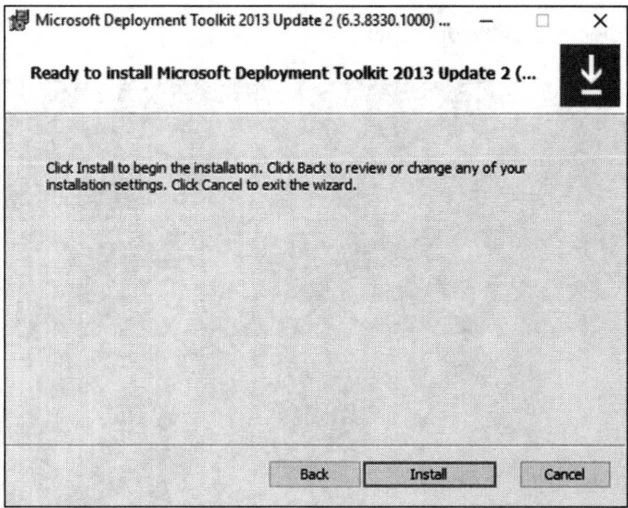


11. If a User Account Control dialog box appears, click the Yes button.
12. When the installation completes, click the Finish button.

---

Now that you have installed MDT 2013, you are going to configure the package. In Exercise 2.2, you will configure MDT 2013 and set up a distribution share and database. I am creating the MDT 2013 on a Windows Server 2016 so that we can distribute Windows Server 2016. Make sure the Windows Assessment and Deployment Kit (ADK) for Windows Server 2016 is installed because it is required for all deployment scenarios.

**EXERCISE 2.2**

### Configuring MDT 2013

To configure MDT 2013, follow these steps:

1. Create a shared folder on your network called `Distribution`, and give the Everyone group full control to the folder for this exercise.
2. Open the MDT workbench by choosing Start ➢ Microsoft Development Toolkit ➢ Deployment Workbench (see Figure 2.6).
3. In the left-hand pane, click Deployment Shares, and then right-click the deployment shares and choose New Deployment Share.
4. The New Deployment Share Wizard begins (As shown in Figure 2.7). At the first screen, you will choose the directory where the deployments will be stored. Click the Browse button and choose the Distribution share that you created in step 1. Then click Next.

**EXERCISE 2.2 (continued)**

**FIGURE 2.6** Deployment Workbench

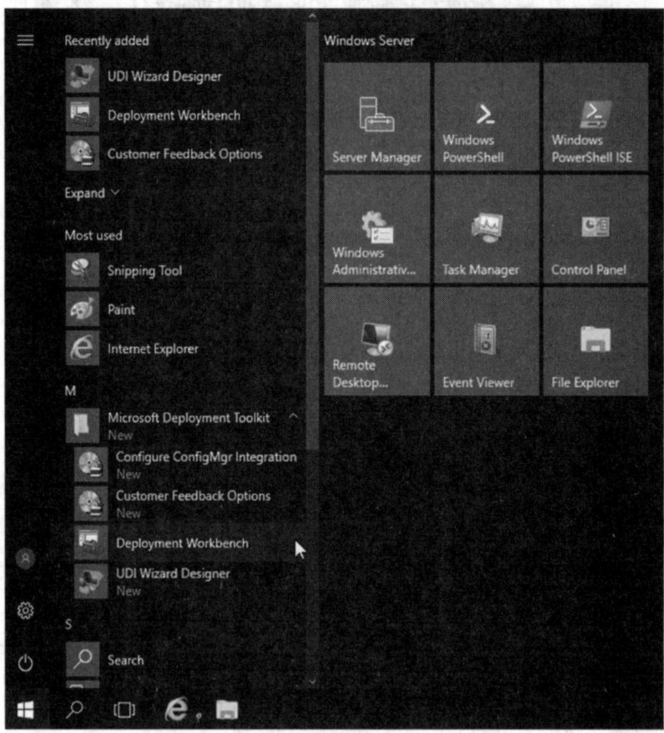


**FIGURE 2.7** Microsoft Deployment Toolkit Setup Screen

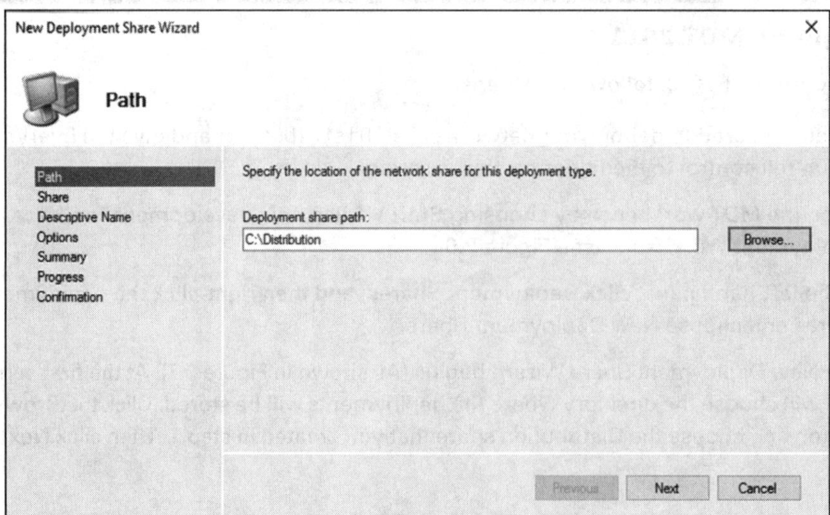

5. At the Share Name screen, accept the default, Distribution. Click Next.
6. At the Descriptive Name screen, accept the default description name (as shown in Figure 2.8) and click Next.

**FIGURE 2.8** Descriptive Name Screen

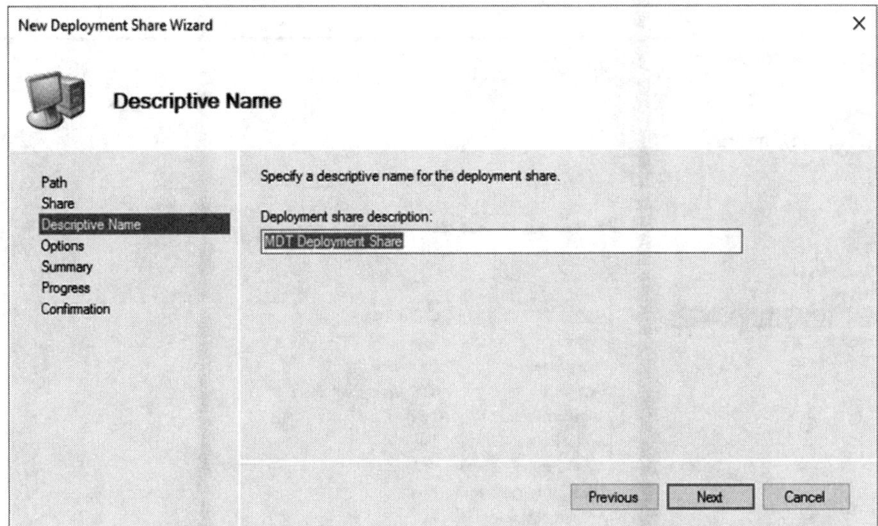


7. At the Options Screen, Make sure all check boxes are checked as shown in Figure 2.9.

**FIGURE 2.9** Options Screen

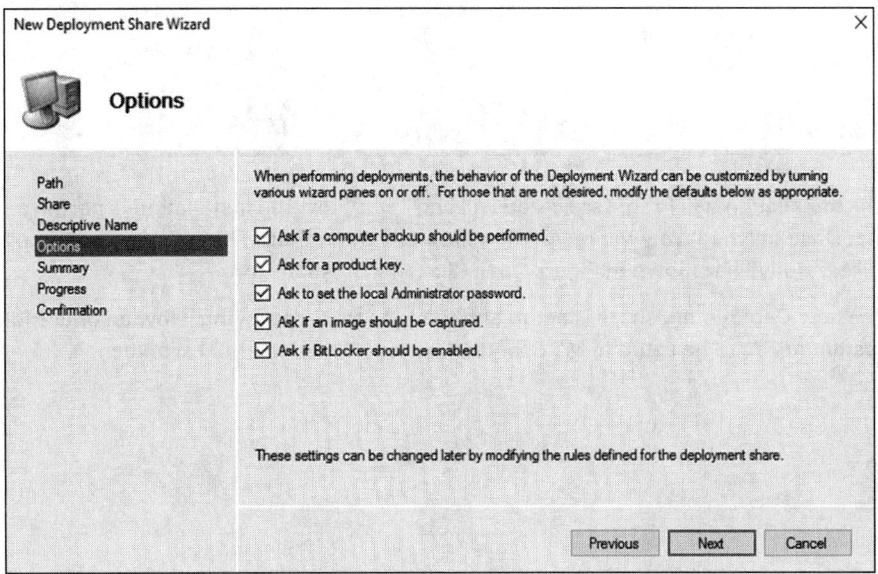

**EXERCISE 2.2 *(continued)***

8. At the Summary screen, look over the options and choose the Next button (shown in Figure 2.10).

**FIGURE 2.10** Summary Screen

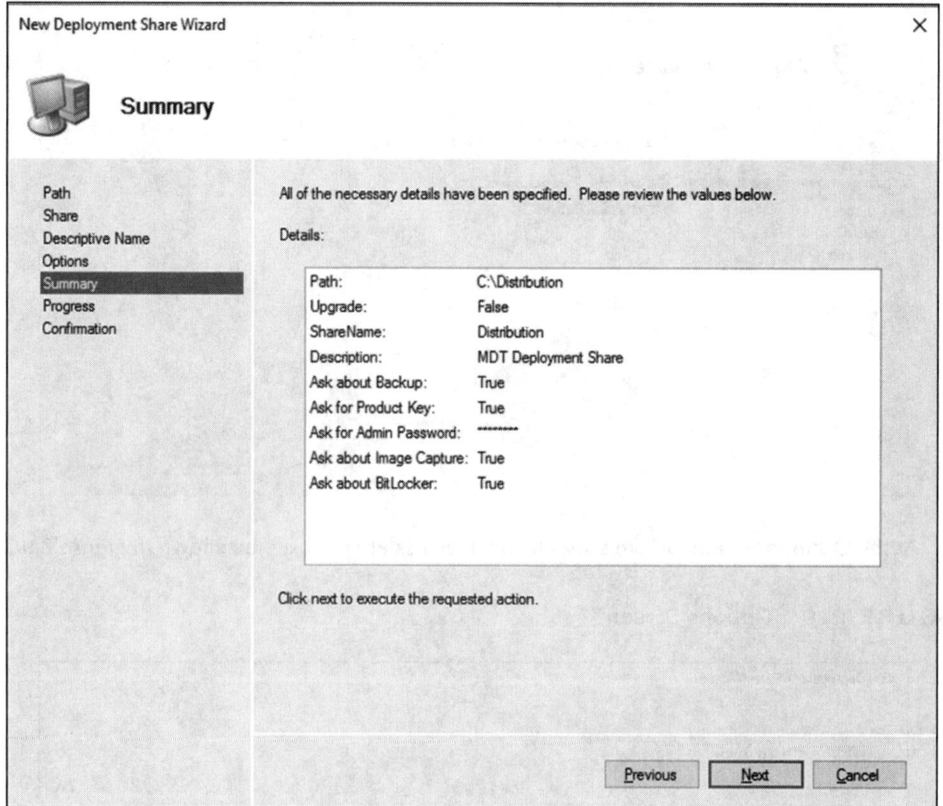


9. The installation will Progress screen will show you how the installation is performing. Once finished, you will receive a message stating that "The process completed successfully" (as shown in Figure 2.11). Click the Finish button.

10. The new Deployment share is setup and ready to start deploying. Now an operating system needs to be setup in MDT for deployment. Close the MDT workbench.

**FIGURE 2.11** Confirmation Screen

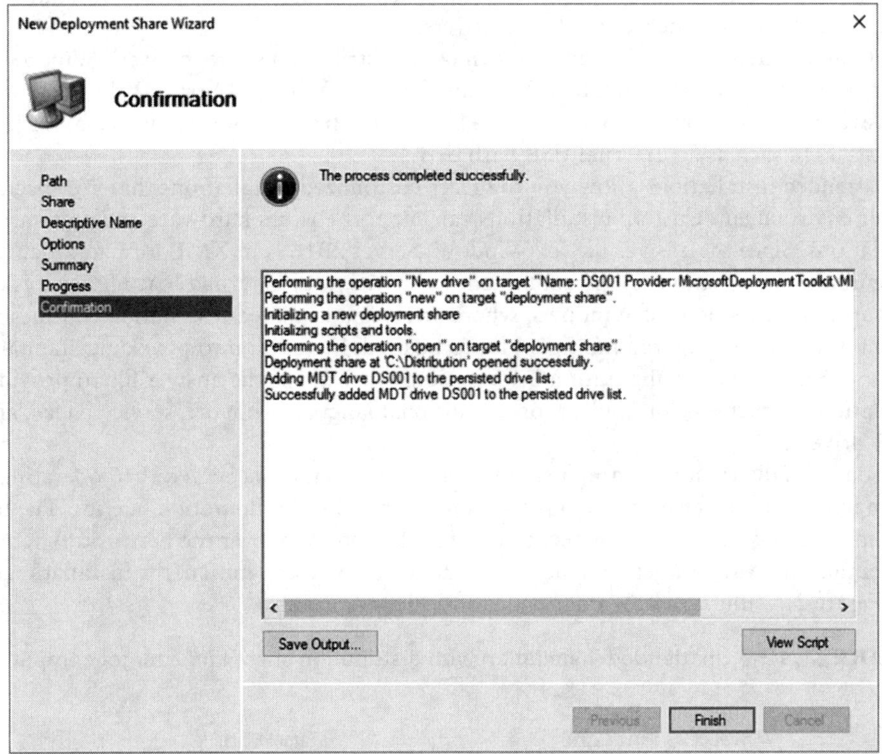


Now that you have seen how to install the MDT 2013 utility, let's take a look at some other ways to automatically install Windows Server 2016.

## An Overview of Unattended Installation

Unattended installation is a practical method of automating deployments when you have a large number of clients to install and the computers require different hardware and software configurations. Unattended installations allow you to create customized installations that are specific to your environment. Custom installations can support custom hardware and software installations.

Unattended installations utilize an answer file called `Autounattend.xml` to provide configuration information during the installation process. Think about the Windows Server 2016 installation from the previous chapter. You are asked for your locale, type of installation, and so on. The answer file allows these questions to be answered without user interaction. In addition to providing standard Windows Server 2016 configuration information, the answer file can provide installation instructions for applications, additional language support, service packs, and device drivers.

With an unattended installation, you can use a distribution share to install Windows Server 2016 on the target computers. You can also use a Windows Server 2016 DVD with an answer file located on the root of the DVD, on a floppy disk, or on a universal flash device (UFD), such as an external USB flash drive.

Unattended installations allow you to create customized installations that are specific to your environment. Custom installations can support custom hardware and software installations. Since the answer file for Windows Server 2016 is in XML format, all custom configuration information can be contained within the `Autounattend.xml` file. This is different from past versions of Windows, where creating automated installation routines for custom installations required multiple files to be used. In addition to providing standard Windows Server 2016 configuration information, you can use the answer file to provide installation instructions for applications, additional language support, service packs, and device drivers.

If you use a distribution share, it should contain the Windows Server 2016 operating system image and the answer file to respond to installation configuration queries. The target computer must be able to connect to the distribution share over the network. After the distribution share and target computers are connected, you can initiate the installation process. Figure 2.12 illustrates the unattended installation process.

**FIGURE 2.12** Unattended installation with distribution share and a target computer

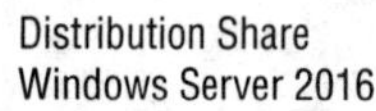


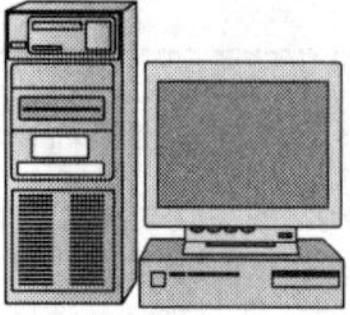

## Advantages of Unattended Installation

In a midsize or large organization, it just makes sense to use automated setups. As stated earlier, it is nearly impossible to install Windows Server 2016 one at a time on hundreds of machines. But there are many advantages to using unattended installations as a method for automating Windows Server 2016:

- Unattended installation saves time and money because users do not have to interactively respond to each installation query.

- It can be configured to provide an automated query response while still selectively allowing users to provide specified input during installations.
- It can be used to install clean copies of Windows Server 2016 or upgrade an existing operating system (providing it is on the list of permitted operating systems) to Windows Server 2016.
- It can be expanded to include installation instructions for applications, additional language support, service packs, and device drivers.
- The physical media for Windows Server 2016 does not need to be distributed to all computers on which it will be installed.

### Disadvantages of Unattended Installation

As stated earlier, a manual installation is not practical for mass installations. But one of the biggest disadvantages to performing an unattended installation is that an administrator does not physically walk through the installation of Windows Server 2016. A client operating system is one of the most important items that you will install onto a machine. As an IT manager and consultant, I have always felt better physically installing a client operating system. This way, if there are any glitches, I can see and deal with them immediately. If something happens during an unattended install, you may never know it, but the end user may experience small issues throughout the lifetime of the machine.

Two other disadvantages of using unattended installations as a method for automating Windows Server 2016 installations are listed here:

- They require more initial setup than a standard installation of Windows Server 2016.
- Someone must have access to each client computer and must initiate the unattended installation process on the client side.

## An Overview of the System Preparation Tool and Disk Imaging

The *System Preparation Tool,* or *Sysprep* (`Sysprep.exe`), is used to prepare a computer for disk imaging, and the disk image can then be captured using any image capturing software including DISM or third-party imaging software.

Sysprep is a free utility that comes on all Windows operating systems. By default, the Sysprep utility can be found on Windows Server 2016 and Windows Server 2016 operating systems in the `\Windows\system32\sysprep` directory.

*Disk imaging* is the process of taking a checkpoint of a computer and then using those checkpoints to create new computers, thus allowing for automated deployments. The reference, or source, computer has Windows Server 2016 installed and is configured with the settings and applications that should be installed on the target computers. The image (checkpoints) is then created and can be transferred to other computers, thus installing the operating system, settings, and applications that were defined on the reference computer.

### Using Imaging Software

Using the System Preparation Tool and disk imaging is a good choice (and the one most commonly used in the real world) for automatic deployment when you have a large number of computers with similar configuration requirements or machines that need to be rebuilt frequently.

For example, StormWind Studios, an online computer education company, reinstalls the same software every few week for new classes. Imaging is a fast and easy way to simplify the deployment process.

Most organizations use images to create new machines quickly and easily, but they also use them to reimage end users' machines that crash.

In most companies, end users will have space on a server (home folders) to allow them to store data. We give our end users space on the server because this way we need to back up only the servers at night and not the end users' machines. If your end users place all of their important documents on the server, that information gets backed up.

Now, if we are also using images in our company and an end user's machine crashes, we just reload the image and they are back up and running in minutes. Since their documents are being saved on the server, they do not lose any of their information.

Many organizations use third-party imaging software (such as Ghost) instead of using `Sysprep.exe` and Image Capture Wizard. This is another good way of imaging your Windows Server 2016 machines. Just make sure your third-party software supports the Windows Server 2016 operating system.

To perform an unattended installation, the System Preparation Tool prepares the reference computer by stripping away any computer-specific data, such as the security identifier (SID), which is used to uniquely identify each computer on the network; any event logs; and any other unique system information. The System Preparation Tool also detects any Plug and Play devices that are installed can adjust dynamically for any computers that have different hardware installed.

When the client computer starts an installation using a disk image, you can customize what is displayed on the Windows Welcome screen and the options that are displayed through the setup process. You can also fully automate when and how the Windows Welcome screen is displayed during the installation process by using the `/oobe` option with the System Preparation Tool and an answer file named `Oobe.xml`.

Sysprep is a utility that is good only for setting up a new machine. You do not use Sysprep to image a computer for upgrading a current machine. There are a few switches that you can use in conjunction with Sysprep to configure the Sysprep utility for your specific needs. Table 2.1 shows you the important Sysprep switches and what they will do for you when used.

**TABLE 2.1** Sysprep switches

| Switch | Explanation |
|---|---|
| `/pnp` | Forces a mini-setup wizard to start at reboot so that all Plug and Play devices can be recognized. |
| `/generalize` | This allows Sysprep to remove all system-specific data from the Sysprep image. If you're running the GUI version of Sysprep, this is a checkbox option. |
| `/oobe` | Initiates the Windows Welcome screen at the next reboot. |
| `/audit` | Initiates Sysprep in audit mode. |
| `/nosidgen` | Sysprep does not generate a new SID on the computer restart. Forces a mini-setup on restart. |
| `/reboot` | Stops and restarts the computer system. |
| `/quiet` | Runs without any confirmation dialog messages being displayed. |
| `/mini` | Tells Sysprep to run the mini-setup on the next reboot. |

**Real World Scenario**

### The SID Problem with Deployment Software

For many years, when you had to create many machines that each had a Microsoft operating system on it, you would have to use files to help deploy the multiple systems.

Then, multiple third-party companies came out with software that allowed you to take a picture of the Microsoft operating system, and you could deploy that picture to other machines. One advantage of this is that all the software that is installed on the system could also be part of that picture. This was a great way to copy all the software on a machine over to another machine.

There was one major problem for years—*security identifier (SID)* numbers. All computers get assigned a unique SID that represents them on a domain network. The problem for a long time was that when you copied a machine to another machine, the SID number was also copied.

Microsoft released Sysprep many years ago, and that helped solve this problem. Sysprep would allow you to remove the SID number so that a third-party software package could image it to another machine. Many third-party image software products now also remove the SID numbers, but Sysprep was one of the first utilities to help solve this problem.

When you decide to use Sysprep to set up your images, there are a few rules that you must follow for Sysprep to work properly:

- You can use images to restart the Windows activation clock. The Windows activation clock starts to decrease as soon as Windows starts for the first time. You can restart the Windows activation clock only three times using Sysprep.
- The computer on which you're running Sysprep has to be a member of a workgroup. The machine can't be part of a domain. If the computer is a member of the domain, when you run Sysprep, the computer will automatically be removed from the domain.
- It simplifies the addition of user-specific or computer-specific configuration information.
- When installing the image, the system will prompt you for a product key. During the install you can use an answer file, which in turn will have all the information needed for the install, and you will not be prompted for any information.
- A third-party utility or Image Capture Wizard is required to deploy the image that is created from Sysprep.
- If you are using Sysprep to capture an NTFS partition, any files or folders that are encrypted will become corrupt and unreadable.

One advantage to Sysprep and Windows Server 2016 is that you can use Sysprep to prepare a new machine for duplication. You can use Sysprep to image a Windows Server 2016 machine. The following steps are necessary to image a new machine:

1. Install the Windows Server 2016 operating system.
2. Install all components on the OS.
3. Run `Sysprep /generalize` to create the image.

When you image a computer using the Windows Sysprep utility, a Windows image (`.wim`) file is created. Most third-party imaging software products can work with the Windows image file.

## Advantages of the System Preparation Tool

The following are advantages of using the System Preparation Tool as a method for automating Windows Server 2016 installations:

- For large numbers of computers with similar hardware, it greatly reduces deployment time by copying the operating system, applications, and Desktop settings from a reference computer to an image, which can then be deployed to multiple computers.
- Using disk imaging facilitates the standardization of Desktops, administrative policies, and restrictions throughout an organization.
- Reference images can be copied across a network connection or through DVDs that are physically distributed to client computers.

### Disadvantages of the System Preparation Tool

There are some disadvantages of using the System Preparation Tool as a method for automating Windows Server 2016 installations:

- Image Capture Wizard, third-party imaging software, or hardware disk-duplication devices must be used for an image-based setup.
- The version of the System Preparation Tool that shipped with Windows Server 2016 must be used. An older version of Sysprep cannot be used on a Windows Server 2016 image.
- The System Preparation Tool will not detect any hardware that is not Plug and Play compliant.

## Overview of the Windows Assessment and Deployment Kit

Another way to install Windows Server 2016 is to use the *Windows Assessment and Deployment Kit (ADK)*. The Windows (ADK) is a set of utilities and documentation that allows an administrator to configure and deploy Windows operating systems. An administrator can use the Windows (ADK) to do the following:

- Windows Imaging and Configuration Designer (ICD)
- Windows Assessment Toolkit
- Windows Performance Toolkit

The Windows (ADK) can be installed and configured on the following operating systems:

- Windows Server 2016
- Windows 7 / 8 / 8.1 / 10
- Windows Server 2012 R2
- Windows Server 2012

The Windows (ADK) is a good solution for organizations that need to customize the Windows deployment environments. The Windows (ADK) allows an administrator to have the flexibility needed for mass deployments of Windows operating systems. Since every organization's needs are different, the Windows (ADK) allows you to use all or just some of the deployment tools available. It allows you to manage deployments by using some additional tools.

**Windows Imaging and Configuration Designer (ICD)** The tools included with this part of the Windows (ADK) will allow an administrator to easily deploy and configure Windows operating systems and images.

**Windows Assessment Toolkit** When new Windows operating systems are installed, applications that ran on the previous version of Windows may not work properly. The Application Compatibility Toolkit allows an administrator to help solve these issues before they occur.

**Windows Performance Toolkit** The Windows Performance Toolkit is a utility that will locate computers on a network and then perform a thorough inventory of them. This inventory can then be used to determine which machines can have Windows Server 2016 installed.

## Windows Imaging and Configuration Designer

The Windows Imaging and Configuration Designer (ICD) allows an administrator to work with images. The ICD allows an IT Department to do the following;

- View and configure all of the settings and policies for a Windows Server 2016 image or provisioning package.
- Create Windows provisioning answer files.
- Allow an answer file to add third-party drivers, apps, or other assets.
- Create variants and specify the settings that apply to each variant.
- Build and flash a Windows image.
- Build a provisioning package.

The Windows (ICD) gives an IT department many options on how to deploy and setup Windows Server 2016 clients. Here are some of the following tools included with the Windows (ICD).

- Configure and edit images by using the Deployment Image Servicing and Management (DISM) utility
- Create Windows Preinstallation Environment (Windows PE) images
- Migrate user data and profiles using the User State Migration Tool (USMT)
- Windows Imaging and Configuration Designer (Windows ICD)

## Summary of Windows Server 2016 Deployment Options

Table 2.2 summarizes the installation tools and files that are used with unattended, automated installations of Windows Server 2016, the associated installation method, and a description of each tool.

**TABLE 2.2** Summary of Windows Server 2016 unattended deployment utilities

| Tool or File | Automated Installation Option | Description |
|---|---|---|
| WDS | Unattended or attended installations | Program installed onto a Windows Server 2016 server (discussed in Chapter 1 "Installing Windows Server 2016"). |

| Tool or File | Automated Installation Option | Description |
|---|---|---|
| `Setup.exe` | Unattended installation | Program used to initiate the installation process. |
| `Autounattend.xml` | Unattended installation | Answer file used to customize installation queries. |
| Windows System Image Manager | Unattended installation | Program used to create answer files to be used for unattended installations. |
| `Windows Deployment Services Image Capture Wizard` | Sysprep | Utility that is initiated by using the F8 button at startup. This utility can work in conjunction with Sysprep to create and manage Windows Server 2016 image files for deployment. |
| `Sysprep.exe` | Sysprep | System Preparation Tool, which prepares a source reference computer that will be used in conjunction with a distribution share or with disk duplication through Image Capture Wizard, third-party software, or hardware disk-duplication devices. |

The Windows Server 2016 installation utilities and resources relating to automated deployment are found in a variety of locations. Table 2.3 provides a quick reference for each utility or resource and its location.

**TABLE 2.3** Location of Windows Server 2016 deployment utilities and resources

| Utility | Location |
|---|---|
| `Sysprep.exe` | Included with Windows Server 2016; installed to `%WINDIR%\system32\sysprep`. |
| `Image Configuration Designer` | Installed with the WAIK; installed to `C:\ProgramFiles(x86)\Windows Kits\10\Assessment and Deployment Kits\ Imaging and Configuration Designer\x86\ICD.exe`. |
| Windows System Image Manager | Installed with WAIK; installed to `C:\ProgramFiles(x86)\Windows Kits\10\Assessment and Deployment Kits\Imaging and Configuration Designer\x86\ICD.exe`. |

# Deploying Unattended Installations

You can deploy Windows Server 2016 installations or upgrades through a Windows Server 2016 distribution DVD or through a distribution server that contains Windows Server 2016 images and associated files, such as `Autounattend.xml` for unattended installations. Using a DVD can be advantageous if the computer on which you want to install Windows Server 2016 is not connected to the network or is connected via a low-bandwidth network. It is also typically faster to install a Windows Server 2016 image from DVD than to use a network connection.

Unattended installations rely on options configured in an answer file that is deployed with the Windows Server 2016 image. Answer files are XML files that contain the settings that are typically supplied by the installer during attended installations of Windows Server 2016. Answer files can also contain instructions for how programs and applications should be run.

The Windows Setup program is run to install or upgrade to Windows Server 2016 from computers that are running compatible versions of Windows, as discussed in Chapter 1. In fact, Windows Setup is the basis for the other types of installation procedures I'll be discussing in this chapter, including unattended installations, WDS, and image-based installations.

The Windows Setup program (`Setup.exe`) replaces `Winnt32.exe` and `Winnt.exe`, which are the setup programs used in versions of Windows prior to Windows 7 / 8. Although it's a graphical tool, Windows Setup can be run from the command line. For example, you can use the following command to initiate an unattended installation of Windows Server 2016:

```
setup.exe /unattend:answerfile
```

The Windows Setup program has several command-line options that can be applied. Table 2.4 describes the `Setup.exe` command-line options.

**TABLE 2.4** `Setup.exe` command-line options and descriptions

| **Setup.exe Option** | **Description** |
|---|---|
| `/1394debug:` *channel* `[baudrate:`*baudrate*`]` | Enables kernel debugging over a FireWire (IEEE 1394) port for troubleshooting purposes. The [baudrate] optional parameter specifies the baud rate for data transfer during the debugging process. |
| `/debug:`*port* *[baudrate:baudrate]* | Enables kernel debugging over the specified port for troubleshooting purposes. The [baudrate] optional parameter specifies the baud rate for data transfer during the debugging process. |

| `Setup.exe` Option | Description |
|---|---|
| `/emsport:{com1\|com 2\|usebiossettings\|off} [/emsbaudrate:`*baudrate*`]` | Configures EMS to be enabled or disabled. The `[baudrate]` optional parameter specifies the baud rate for data transfer during the debugging process. |
| `/m:`*folder_name* | Used with Setup to specify that replacement files should be copied from the specified location. If the files are not present, Setup will use the default location. |
| `/noreboot` | Normally, when the down-level phase of `Setup.exe` is complete, the computer restarts. This option specifies that the computer should not restart so that you can execute another command prior to the restart. |
| `/tempdrive:`*drive letter* | Specifies the location that will be used to store the temporary files for Windows Server 2016 and the installation partition for Windows Server 2016. |
| `/unattend:[`*answerfile*`]` | Specifies that you will be using an unattended installation for Windows Server 2016. The `answerfile` variable points to the custom answer file you will use for installation. |

Next we'll look at the System Preparation Tool (Sysprep); using it is one of many ways to install Windows Server 2016 automatically.

## Using the System Preparation Tool to Prepare an Installation for Imaging

You can use disk images to install Windows Server 2016 on computers that have similar hardware configurations. Also, if a computer is having technical difficulties, you can use a disk image to quickly restore it to a baseline configuration.

To create a disk image, you install Windows Server 2016 on the source computer with the configuration that you want to copy and use the System Preparation Tool to prepare the installation for imaging. The source computer's configuration should also include any applications that should be installed on target computers.

Once you have prepared the installation for imaging, you can use imaging software such as Image Capture Wizard to create an image of the installation.

The System Preparation Tool (`Sysprep.exe`) is included with Windows Server 2016, in the `%WINDIR%\system32\sysprep` directory. When you run this utility on the source computer, it strips out information that is unique for each computer, such as the SID. Table 2.5 defines the command options that you can use to customize the `Sysprep.exe` operation.

**TABLE 2.5** System Preparation Tool command-line options

| Switch | Description |
|---|---|
| `/audit` | Configures the computer to restart into audit mode, which allows you to add drivers and applications to Windows or test the installation prior to deployment. |
| `/generalize` | Removes any unique system information from the image, including the SID and log information. |
| `/oobe` | Specifies that the Windows Welcome screen should be displayed when the computer reboots. |
| `/quiet` | Runs the installation with no user interaction. |
| `/quit` | Specifies that the System Preparation Tool should quit after the specified operations have been completed. |
| `/reboot` | Restarts the target computer after the System Preparation Tool completes. |
| `/shutdown` | Specifies that the computer should shut down after the specified operations have been completed. |
| `/unattend` | Indicates the name and location of the answer file to use. |

In the following sections, you will learn how to create a disk image and how to copy and install from it.

## Preparing a Windows Server 2016 Installation

To run the System Preparation Tool and prepare an installation for imaging, take the following steps:

1. Install Windows Server 2016 on a source computer. The computer should have a similar hardware configuration to that of the destination computer(s). The source computer should not be a member of a domain. (See Chapter 1 for instructions on installing Windows Server 2016.)
2. Log on to the source computer as Administrator and, if desired, install and configure any applications, files (such as newer versions of Plug and Play drivers), or custom settings (for example, a custom Desktop) that will be applied to the target computer(s).
3. Verify that your image meets the specified configuration criteria and that all applications are properly installed and working.
4. Select Start ➢ Computer, and navigate to `C:\%WINDIR%\System32\sysprep`. Double-click the Sysprep application icon.

5. The Windows System Preparation Tool dialog box appears. Select the appropriate options for your configuration.
6. If configured to do so, Windows Server 2016 will be rebooted into setup mode, and you will be prompted to enter the appropriate setup information.
7. You will now be able to use imaging software to create an image of the computer to deploy to other computers.

In Exercise 2.3, you will use the System Preparation Tool to prepare the computer for disk imaging. The Sysprep utility must be run on a machine with a clean version of Windows Server 2016. If you upgraded a Windows Server 2012 R2 machine to Windows Server 2016, you will not be able to run the Sysprep utility.

**EXERCISE 2.3**

**Prepare a System for Imaging by Using the System Preparation Tool**

1. Log on to the source computer as Administrator and, if desired, install and configure any applications that should also be installed on the target computer.
2. Select Start ➢ Computer, and navigate to `C:\%WINDIR%\System32\sysprep`. Double-click the Sysprep application icon.
3. In the System Preparation Tool dialog box, select Enter System Out-Of-Box Experience (OOBE) in the system cleanup action.
4. Under the shutdown options, depending on the options selected, the System Preparation Tool will quit, the computer will shut down, or the computer will be rebooted into setup mode, where you will need to configure the setup options. Choose the Reboot option. Click OK.
5. After you configure the Sysprep utility, you can use an imaging tool like DISM to capture the image.

After creating the Sysprep image, you need to use some type of third-party software to capture it. Windows includes a utility called Image Capture Wizard for just that purpose.

## Using Windows Imaging and Configuration Designer (Windows ICD) to Create a Disk Image

After you've run the System Preparation Tool on the source computer, you can create an image from the installation, and you can then install the image on target computers. To create an image, you can use Image Capture Wizard, which is a utility that can be used to create and manage Windows image (`.wim`) files.

At the time this book was written, The Windows ICD supports disk images for Windows 10 Desktop editions, Windows 10, Mobile editions, and Windows 10 IoT Core images. Windows ICD Does not support the configuration of Windows Server 2016 editions.

To run the Image Capture Wizard utility to create a disk image of a Windows Server 2016 installation, follow these steps:

To install Windows ICD and configure images for Windows 10, you must install the Windows Assessment and Deployment Kit (ADK) for Windows 10.

1. From the Windows ICD Start page, select Simple Provisioning.
2. In the Enter Project Details window, specify a Name and Location for your project. Optionally, you can also enter a brief Description to describe your project.
3. Click Next.
4. In the Enter Project Details window, you need to enter the Name of your project and the location of the project. You can also enter a description. Click Next.
5. In the Choose which settings to view and configure window, select the Windows edition that you want to do a provision package. Then click Next.
6. Optional. If you have a provisioning package that contains customizations already configured in a different project and you want to reuse the customizations from this package, click Browse in the Import a provisioning package screen to locate the provisioning package that was exported from another project.
7. Click Finish.

There is also a Command Line version of the Windows (ICD) tool (C:\Program Files(x86)\Windows Kits\10\Assessment and Deployment Kit\Imaging and Configuration Designer\x86) that you can use. The Microsoft exams have started using a lot of command line utilities on their tests. So let us take a look at the Windows (ICD) command line utility. The command that we use for this is icd.exe:

```
icd.exe <command> <parameters>
```

Table 2.6 shows you the `icd.exe` command and some of the switches that you can use to configure the images.

To see a list of all ICD switches and commands, please visit Microsoft's website at:

`https://msdn.microsoft.com/en-us/library/windows/hardware/dn916115(v=vs.85).aspx`

**TABLE 2.6** ICD.exe Switches

| Switch | Description |
|---|---|
| `/CustomizationXML` | This command identifies the location of the Windows provisioning XML file. This file holds the information for customization assets and settings. |
| `/PackagePath` | Identifies the location and the built provisioning package name where the package will be saved. |
| `/StoreFile` | This command allows IT administrators to use their own settings store instead of the default store used by Windows ICD. If an IT administrator does not determine their own store, a default store that's common to all Windows editions will be loaded by Windows ICD. |
| `/MSPackageRoot` | Identifies the location of the root directory that holds the Microsoft packages that you downloaded from the Windows Portal. |
| `/OEMInputXML` | Identifies the location to the `OEMInput.xml` file. This file defines a subset of settings that can be designed based on the image type. |
| `/Variables` | Identifies a macro pair that is separated by semicolon <name> and <value>. |
| `Encrypted` | Indicates if the provisioning package should be created with encryption or not. Windows ICD will then automatically generate a decryption password that is included with the output. |
| `Overwrite` | Indicates whether or not to overwrite the existing provisioning package. |
| `/?` | This command is used to access the ICD help. The help lists the switches and their descriptions for the ICD command-line tool. |

After you create the disk image, the next step is to install it. In the next section, you'll learn how to install the disk image on a new machine.

## Installing from a Disk Image

After you've run the System Preparation Tool and Image Capture Wizard on the source computer, you can copy the image and then install it on the target computer.

Once the image is copied, you should boot the destination computer into the Windows PE. If the computer has been used previously, it may be necessary to reformat the hard drive, which you can do using the `diskpart` command in Windows PE. If the image is stored over the network, you should then copy the image to the destination computer by using the `net use` *[dir] [network share]* and `copy` *[file] [dir]* commands. Then, you should use the `/apply` option of the Image Capture Wizard utility to apply the image to the local computer. If an answer file has not been deployed along with the image, you may have to apply such information as regional settings, the product key, the computer name, and the password to the new computer after the destination computer is rebooted.

In Exercise 2.4, you will use the stripped image that was created in Exercise 2.3 to simulate the process of continuing an installation from a disk image.

**EXERCISE 2.4**

**Installing Windows Server 2016 from a Disk Image**

1. Boot the target computer into Windows PE.
2. Copy the image created in Exercise 2.3 to the local computer by using the following commands:

```
net use z: \\Server\Images
copy  Z:\Images\image.wim C:
```

3. Apply the image to the target computer using the following Image Capture Wizard command:

```
D:\ICD.exe /apply C:\Images\image.wim C:
```

When you install Windows Server 2016, the installation wizard asks you questions such as your username and computer name. There is a way to answer these questions without actually being in front of the computer. As you'll see in the next section, you can do this by using an answer file.

# Using the Deployment Image Servicing and Management Tool

Deployment Image Servicing and Management (`DISM.exe`) is a PowerShell and command-line utility that allows you to manipulate a Windows image. DISM also allows you to prepare a Windows PE image. DISM replaces multiple programs that were included with Windows 7/8. These programs include Package Manager (`Pkgmgr.exe`), PEimg, and Intlcfg. These tools have been consolidated into one tool (`DISM.exe`), and new functionality has been added to improve the experience for offline servicing.

DISM provides additional functionality when used with Windows Server 2016 and Windows Server 2012/2012 R2. You can use DISM to do the following:

- Add, remove, and enumerate packages
- Add, remove, and enumerate drivers

- Enable or disable Windows features
- Apply changes to an `Unattend.xml` answer file
- Configure international settings
- Upgrade a Windows image to a different edition
- Prepare a Windows PE 3.0 image
- Works with all platforms (32-bit, 64-bit, and Itanium)
- Allows for the use of Package Manager scripts

## DISM and Command-Line Commands

As stated above, DISM can work as a command line utility or a PowerShell utility. In this first section, I will show you how to use DISM with command line switches. Table 2.7 shows the different commands that can be used with `DISM.exe`. To see all DISM commands, type DISM in a command prompt.

**TABLE 2.7** `DISM.exe` command-line commands

| Command | Description |
|---|---|
| `/Split-Image` | Splits an existing .wim or .ffu file into multiple files. |
| `/Apply-Image` | Applies an image. |
| `/Get-MountedImageInfo` | Displays basic information about mounted WIM and VHD images. |
| `/Get-ImageInfo` | Displays information about images in a WIM or VHD file. |
| `/commit-Image` | Saves changes to a mounted WIM or VHD image. |
| `/Unmount-Image` | Unmounts a mounted WIM or VHD image. |
| `/mount-image` | Mounts an image from a WIM or VHD file. |
| `/Remount-Image` | Recovers an orphaned image mount directory. |
| `/List-Image` | Displays a list of files and folders in a specific image. |
| `/Delete-Image` | Deletes the specified image. |
| `/Append-Image` | Adds another image to a WIM file. |
| `/Capture-Image` | Captures an image of a drive into a new WIM file. Captures all directories, including folders and subfolders. |

## DISM and PowerShell

Now that we had a chance to see how DISM works in the command-line application, we need to now examine how DISM works with PowerShell. DISM has evolved over the last few years and it has become a much more powerful tool than when it was first released. To show this, Table 2.8 will show just some of the PowerShell commands that can be used to configure and manipulate images.

The table I used for this section was from Microsoft's website. To see the complete list of DISM PowerShell cmdlets, please visit `https://technet.microsoft.com/en-us/library/dn376474.aspx`.

**TABLE 2.8** DISM and PowerShell

| PowerShell cmdlet | Description |
|---|---|
| `Add-AppxProvisionedPackage` | This cmdlet allows an administrator to add an app package (.appx) that will install for each new user to a Windows image. |
| `Add-WindowsDriver` | Administrators can use this cmdlet to add a driver to an offline Windows image. |
| `Add-WindowsImage` | This allows an administrator to add an additional image to an existing image (.wim) file. |
| `Add-WindowsPackage` | Allows an administrator to add a single .cab or .msu file to an existing Windows image. |
| `Disable-WindowsOptionalFeature` | Administrators can use this cmdlet to disable a feature in a Windows image. |
| `Enable-WindowsOptionalFeature` | Administrators can use this cmdlet to enable a feature in a Windows image. |
| `Expand-WindowsImage` | This cmdlet allows an admin to expand an image to a specified location. |
| `Export-WindowsImage` | Allows an administrator to export a copy of the specified image to another file. |
| `Get-WindowsCapability` | Shows the Windows capabilities for an image or a running operating system. |
| `Get-WindowsDriver` | Allows you to see information about drivers in a Windows image. |

| PowerShell cmdlet | Description |
|---|---|
| Get-WindowsEdition | Administrators can view edition information about a Windows image. |
| Get-WindowsImage | Allows an admin to see information about a Windows image in a WIM or VHD file. |
| Get-WindowsImageContent | Used to display a list of the files and folders in a specified image. |
| Get-WindowsOptionalFeature | This shows you information about optional features in a Windows image. |
| New-WindowsImage | Allows an administrator to capture an image of a drive to a new WIM file. |
| Remove-WindowsDriver | Allows you to remove a driver from an offline Windows image. |
| Remove-WindowsImage | Administrators can remove a specified volume image from a WIM file that has multiple volume images. |
| Remove-WindowsPackage | Allows you to remove a package from a Windows image. |
| Repair-WindowsImage | Allows an administrator to repair a Windows image in a WIM or VHD file. |
| Save-WindowsImage | Allows you to apply changes made to a mounted image to its WIM or VHD file. |
| Set-WindowsEdition | Allows an administrator to change a Windows image to a higher Windows edition. |
| Set-WindowsProductKey | An administrator can set the product key for the Windows image. |
| Split-WindowsImage | Allows an administrator to split an existing .wim file into multiple read-only split .wim files. |

## Using Windows System Image Manager to Create Answer Files

Answer files are automated installation scripts used to answer the questions that appear during a normal Windows Server 2016 installation. You can use answer files with Windows Server 2016 unattended installations, disk image installations, or WDS installations. Setting up answer files allows you to easily deploy Windows Server 2016 to computers that may not be configured in the same manner, with little or no user intervention. Because answer files are associated with image files, you can validate the settings within an answer file against the image file.

You can create answer files by using the Windows System Image Manager (Windows SIM) utility. There are several advantages to using Windows SIM to create answer files:

- You can easily create and edit answer files through a graphical interface, which reduces syntax errors.
- You can validate existing answer files against newly created images.
- You can include additional application and device drivers in the answer file.

In the following sections, you will learn about options that can be configured through Windows SIM, how to create answer files with Windows SIM, how to format an answer file, and how to manually edit answer files.

## Configuring Components through Windows System Image Manager

You can use Windows SIM to configure a wide variety of installation options. The following list defines which components can be configured through Windows SIM and gives a short description of each component:

**auditSystem** Adds additional device drivers, specifies firewall settings, and applies a name to the system when the image is booted into audit mode. Audit mode is initiated by using the `sysprep/audit` command.

**auditUser** Executes `RunSynchronous` or `RunAsynchronous` commands when the image is booted into audit mode. Audit mode is initiated by using the `sysprep/audit` command.

**generalize** Removes system-specific information from an image so that the image can be used as a reference image. The settings specified in the generalize component will be applied only if the `sysprep/generalize` command is used.

**offlineServicing** Specifies the language packs and packages to apply to an image prior to the image being extracted to the hard disk.

**oobeSystem** Specifies the settings to apply to the computer the first time the computer is booted into the Windows Welcome screen, which is also known as the Out-Of-Box Experience (OOBE). To boot to the Welcome screen, the `sysprep/oobe` command should be used.

**specialize** Configures the specific settings for the target computer, such as network settings and domain information. This configuration pass is used in conjunction with the generalize configuration pass.

**Windows PE** Sets the Windows PE–specific configuration settings, as well as several Windows Setup settings, such as partitioning and formatting the hard disk, selecting an image, and applying a product key.

## Microsoft Assessment and Planning (MAP) Toolkit

This chapter is all about installing Windows Server 2016 the easiest way possible. One utility that you can use to help design your network is the *Microsoft Assessment and Planning (MAP) Toolkit*. MAP is a utility that will locate computers on a network and then perform a thorough inventory of these computers. To obtain this inventory, MAP uses multiple utilities like the Windows Management Instrumentation (WMI), the Remote Registry Service, or the Simple Network Management Protocol (SNMP).

Having this information will allow an administrator to determine if the machines on their network will be able to load Microsoft Windows clients (including Vista, Windows 7/8/10, or Windows Server 2008/2008 R2/2012/2012 R2/2016, Microsoft Office, and Microsoft Application Virtualization. One advantage of using MAP when determining the needs for Windows is that MAP will also advise you of any hardware upgrades needed for a machine or device driver availability.

Anyone who has been in the industry for a while can see the potential of using MAP. Having a utility go out and discover your network hardware and then advise you of needed resources to allow the operating system to operate properly is a tool that should be in every administrator's arsenal.

When deciding to locate the computers on your network, you have multiple ways to do this. The following are your discovery options and how they try to discover the computers:

- Use Active Directory Domain Services
  - Select this check box to find computer objects in Active Directory.
- Use The Windows Networking Protocols.
  - Select this check box to find computers in workgroups and Windows NT 4.0 domains.
- Import Computer Names From A File
  - Select this check box to import computer names from a file.
- Scan An IP Address Range
  - Select this check box to find computers within a specified IP address range.
- Manually Enter Computer Names And Credentials
  - Select this check box to enter computer names individually.

As a network administrator, one thing that is always difficult to determine is how many servers are needed for your Windows end users and where to place them on your network. An included feature with MAP is the ability to obtain performance metric data from the computers. MAP will also generate a report that recommends which machines can be used for Windows clients.

MAP generates your report in both Microsoft Excel and Microsoft Word. These reports can provide information to you in both summary and full detail modes. MAP can generate reports for you for some of the following scenarios:

- Identify currently installed client operating systems and their requirements for migrating to Windows 10.

- Identify currently installed Windows Server systems and their requirements for migrating to Windows Server 2016.
- Identify currently installed Microsoft Office software and their requirements for migrating to Microsoft Office 2016.
- Server performance by using the Performance Metrics Wizard.
- Hyper-V server consolidation and placement.
- Assessment of machines (Clients, Servers) for installation of Microsoft Application Virtualization (formally known as SoftGrid).

To install MAP, we must first take a look at the system requirements.

## MAP System Requirements

- **Supported Operating Systems:** Windows Server 2012 or above and/or Windows 7 and above.
- **CPU Architecture:** One advantage to the Microsoft Assessment and Planning Solution Accelerator is that it can be installed on both the 32-Bit and 64-bit versions of any of the operating systems listed above.
- **Hardware Requirements:**
  - 1.6 GHz or faster processor minimum or dual-core for Windows 7
  - 2.0GB for Windows 7
  - Minimum 1 GB of available hard-disk space
  - Network card that supports 10/100 Mbps

Microsoft Assessment and Planning Toolkit is free to use but it must be downloaded from Microsoft's website or installed from the Windows AIK installation disk. In Exercise 2.5 will walk you through the steps to install the Microsoft Assessment and Planning Toolkit from the Windows AIK installation utility. You can download the newest MAP toolkit at `https://www.microsoft.com/en-in/download/details.aspx?id=7826`.

**EXERCISE 2.5**

### Installing the Microsoft Assessment and Planning Toolkit

1. Download the MAP Toolkit (`MapSetup.exe`).
2. When you get the message "Do you want to run MapSetup.exe," click the Run button.
3. The Welcome to the Setup Wizard for Microsoft Assessment and Planning Toolkit. Click Next.
4. Accept the License Agreement and click Next.
5. At the Installation Folder screen, just accept the default location by clicking Next.

6. You will be asked to Join the Customer Experience. Click the Do not Join the program at this time radio button and click Next.
7. At the Begin to Install screen, click the Install button.
8. After the installation is complete, the Installation Successful screen will appear. Click the Finish button.

---

Now that we have installed the Microsoft Assessment and Planning toolkit, it's now time to configure and test our server. In Exercise 2.6, we will create our database for testing.

**EXERCISE 2.6**

### Configuring MAP

1. Start the Microsoft Assessment and Planning toolkit by clicking Start, Recently added and then Microsoft Planning and Assessment Toolkit.
2. The first thing we need to do is select our database. We are going to create our database at this time. To accomplish this, click on select a database in either the center or right window panes.
3. The Create or select a database screen will appear. Make sure that the Create an inventory database radio button is clicked. In the Name Field, type in **Windows 10** and click the OK button.

---

After your database is created, you now have the ability to run the different options to test the machines and servers. This is where you decide which scenarios you would like to test for your network.

As a consultant and system administrator for many years, it is very useful to have a utility like MAP to help you not only detect your network and its operating systems, but also recommend enhancements.

# Understanding Hyper-V

In the following sections, I'll introduce you to Hyper-V. In Chapter 4 "Understanding Hyper-V" I will show you how to completely install and configure Hyper-V. But to understand Hyper-V images and deploying servers using these images, I need to give you a brief understanding of how Hyper-V works.

Hyper-V is very easy to understand. Hyper-V allows you to run multiple operating systems on the same hardware. The Windows Server 2016 machine with the Hyper-V role installed is called the Hyper-V Host. The Windows operating systems that run within Hyper-V are referred to as Hyper-V guests (also called Virtual Machines).

## What Is Virtualization?

*Virtualization* is a method for abstracting physical resources from the way they interact with other resources. For example, if you abstract the physical hardware from the operating system, you get the benefit of being able to move the operating system between different physical systems.

This is called *server virtualization*. But there are also other forms of virtualization available, such as presentation virtualization, desktop virtualization, and application virtualization. I will now briefly explain the differences between these forms of virtualization:

**Server Virtualization** This basically enables multiple operating systems to run on the same physical server. Hyper-V is a server virtualization tool that allows you to move physical machines to virtual machines and manage them on a few physical servers. Thus, you will be able to consolidate physical servers.

**Presentation Virtualization** When you use *presentation virtualization*, your applications run on a different computer and only the screen information is transferred to your computer. An example of presentation virtualization is Microsoft Remote Desktop Services in Windows Server 2016.

**Desktop Virtualization** *Desktop virtualization* provides you with a virtual machine on your desktop, comparable to server virtualization. You run your complete operating system and applications in a virtual machine so that your local physical machine just needs to run a very basic operating system. An example of this form of virtualization is Microsoft Windows 10 Hyper-V.

**Application Virtualization** *Application virtualization* helps prevent conflicts between applications on the same PC. Thus it helps you to isolate the application running environment from the operating system installation requirements by creating application-specific copies of all shared resources, and it helps reduce application-to-application incompatibility and testing needs. An example of an application virtualization tool is Microsoft Application Virtualization (App-V).

Now that I have given you a brief understanding of virtualization, let's look at how we can install Hyper-V. In Chapter 4, "Understanding Hyper-V," I will have exercises showing you how to do full installations of Hyper-V on a Windows Server 2016.

There are multiple ways that you can install Hyper-V onto a Windows Server 2016 system. The first and easiest way to install Hyper-V is to use Server Manager and choose the Hyper-V role. Another way is to install Hyper-V role is by using PowerShell. The following is the command that is run while in Windows PowerShell to install Hyper-V:

```
Enable-WindowsOptionalFeature -Online -FeatureName Microsoft-Hyper-V -All
```

## Linux and FreeBSD Image Deployments

One of the new features of Windows 2016 is the ability for Hyper-V to support Linux and FreeBSD virtual machines. Hyper-V now can support these new virtual machines because Hyper-V has the ability to emulate Linux and FreeBSD devices. Because Hyper-V now has the ability to emulate these two devices, no additional software needs to be installed on Hyper-V.

Unfortunately, because Hyper-V has to emulate these devices, you lose some of the Hyper-V functionality like high performance and full management of the virtual machines. So it's a trade-off. You get to run Linux and FreeBSD type Hyper-V virtual machines but you lose some of the benefits of Hyper-V.

But wait. There is a way to get your Hyper-V functionality back. This issue can be resolved as long as you install Hyper-V on machines that can support Linux and FreeBSD operating systems. The drivers that are needed on Hyper-V are called Linux Integration Services (LIS) and FreeBSD Integrated Services (FIS). By putting these drivers on a device that can handle Linux and FreeBSD, you can then have Hyper-V with all of the features Microsoft offers.

To get these drivers and make Hyper-V work will all of its functionality, you must make sure that you install a newer release of Linux that includes LIS. To get the most out of FreeBSD, you must get a version after 10.0. For FreeBSD versions that are older than 10.0, Microsoft offers ports that work with BIS drivers that need to be installed. Hyper-V will work with Linux and FreeBSD without the need of any additional drivers or equipment. By having drivers and equipment that supports Linux and FreeBSD, you just get all of the Hyper-V features that your origination may need.

# Summary

In this chapter, we discussed automated installation of Windows Server 2016. Installing Windows Server 2016 through an automated process is an effective way to install the Windows Server 2016 operating system on multiple computers.

There are several methods for automated installation: unattended installations, Windows Assessment and Deployment Kit (ADK), third-party applications, unattended installations, and using the System Preparation Tool along with DISM.

The Windows (ADK) is a set of utilities and documentation that allows an administrator to configure and deploy Windows operating systems.

You can use unattended answer files to automatically respond to the queries that are generated during the normal installation process.

You can also prepare an installation for imaging by using the System Preparation Tool (`Sysprep.exe`) and creating a disk image by using the Image Capture Wizard utility or a third-party utility.

Microsoft Deployment Toolkit (MDT) 2013 Update 2 is a way of automating desktop and server deployment. With the MDT, an administrator can deploy desktops and servers through the use of a common console, which allows for quicker deployments, having standardized desktop and server images and security and zero-touch deployments of Windows Server 2016, Windows 8, Windows 7, Windows Server 2008, Windows Server 2008 R2, Windows Server 2012, Windows Server 2012 R2, and Windows Server 2016.

# Video Resources

There are no videos available for this chapter.

# Exam Essentials

**Know the difference between the various unattended installation methods.** Understand the various options available for unattended installations of Windows Server 2016 and when it is appropriate to use each installation method.

**Be able to use disk images for unattended installations.** Know how to perform unattended installations of Windows Server 2016 using the System Preparation Tool and disk images.

**Know how to use Windows System Image Manager to create and edit answer files.** Understand how to access and use Windows System Image Manager to create answer files. Be able to edit the answer files and know the basic options that can be configured for them.

**Understand the Microsoft Deployment Toolkit (MDT) 2013 Update 2.** Know that the MDT is a way of automating desktop and server deployment. Understand that the MDT allows an administrator to deploy desktops and servers through the use of a common console.

# Review Questions

1. You are the network administrator for your organization. You have a reference computer that runs Windows Server 2016. You need to create and deploy an image of the Windows Server 2016 computer. You create an answer file named `answer.xml`. You have to make sure that the installation applies the answer file after you deploy the image. Which command should you run before you capture the image?

   A. ICD.exe /append answer.xml/check

   B. ICD.exe /mount answer.xml/verify

   C. Sysprep.exe/reboot/audit/unattend:answer.xml

   D. Sysprep.exe/generalize/oobe/unattend:answer.xml

2. You have a Windows Server 2016 Windows Image (WIM) that is mounted. You need to display information about the image. What should you do?

   A. Run DISM and specify the `/get-ImageInfo` parameter.

   B. Run `Driverquery.exe` and use the `/si` parameter.

   C. From Device Manager, view all hidden drivers.

   D. From Windows Explorer, open the `mount` folder.

3. You are a network technician for your company, and you need to deploy Windows Server 2016 to multiple computers. You want to automate the installation of Windows Server 2016 so that no user interaction is required during the installation process. Which of the following utilities could you use?

   A. Windows SIM

   B. Image Capture Wizard

   C. System Preparation Tool

   D. WDSUTIL

4. Will is the network manager for a large company. He has been tasked with creating a deployment plan to automate installations for 100 computers that need to have Windows Server 2016 installed. Will wants to use WDS for the installations. To fully automate the installations, he needs to create an answer file. Will does not want to create the answer files with a text editor. What other program can he use to create unattended answer files via a GUI interface?

   A. Image Capture Wizard

   B. Answer Manager

   C. Windows System Image Manager

   D. System Preparation Tool

5. You want to initiate a new installation of Windows Server 2016 from the command line. You plan to accomplish this by using the `Setup.exe` command-line setup utility. You want to use an answer file with this command. Which command-line option should you use?
   - **A.** `/unattend`
   - **B.** `/apply`
   - **C.** `/noreboot`
   - **D.** `/generalize`
6. You run a training department that needs the same software installed from scratch on the training computers each week. You decide to use Image Capture Wizard to deploy disk images. Which Windows Server 2016 utility can you use in conjunction with Image Capture Wizard to create these disk images?
   - **A.** UAF
   - **B.** Answer Manager
   - **C.** Setup Manager
   - **D.** System Preparation Tool
7. You are trying to decide whether you want to use WDS as a method of installing Windows Server 2016 within your company. Which of the following options is *not* an advantage to using a WDS automated installation?
   - **A.** The Windows Server 2016 security is retained when you restart the computer.
   - **B.** Windows Server 2016 installation media does not need to be deployed to each computer.
   - **C.** Unique information is stripped out of the installation image so that it can be copied to other computers.
   - **D.** You can quickly recover the operating system in the event of a system failure.
8. You are the network manager of XYZ Corporation. You are in charge of developing an automated deployment strategy for rolling out new Windows Server 2016 computers. You want to install a WDS server and are evaluating whether an existing server can be used as a WDS server for Windows Server 2016 deployment. Which of the following is *not* a requirement for configuring the WDS server?
   - **A.** The remote installation folder must be NTFS version 3.0 or later.
   - **B.** The remote installation folder must reside on the system partition.
   - **C.** RIS must be installed on the server.
   - **D.** The existing server must run Windows Server 2003 with Service Pack 1 installed.

9. You are planning on deploying a new Windows Server 2016 image to 100 client computers that are similarly configured. You are using the Windows SIM tool to create an answer file that will be used to automate the installation process. You want each computer to contain two partitions, one for the system partition and one that will function as a data partition. You need to modify the answer file to support this configuration. Which component of the answer file will you need to modify?

   A. oobeSystem

   B. auditSystem

   C. Windows PE

   D. specialize

10. You want to install a group of 25 computers using disk images created in conjunction with the System Preparation Tool. Your plan is to create an image from a reference computer and then copy the image to all the machines. You do not want to create an SID on the destination computer when you use the image. Which `Sysprep.exe` command-line option should you use to set this up?

   A. `/specialize`

   B. `/generalize`

   C. `/oobe`

   D. `/quiet`

# Configuring Storage and Replication

## THE FOLLOWING 70-740 EXAM OBJECTIVES ARE COVERED IN THIS CHAPTER:

✓ **Configure disks and volumes**

- This objective may include but is not limited to: Configure sector sizes appropriate for various workloads; configure GUID partition table (GPT) disks; create VHD and VHDX files using Server Manager or Windows PowerShell Storage module cmdlets; mount virtual hard disks; determine when to use NTFS and ReFS file systems; configure NFS and SMB shares using Server Manager; configure SMB share and session settings using Windows PowerShell; configure SMB server and SMB client configuration settings using Windows PowerShell; configure file and folder permissions.

✓ **Implement server storage**

- This objective may include but is not limited to: Configure storage pools; implement simple, mirror, and parity storage layout options for disks or enclosures; expand storage pools; configure Tiered Storage; configure iSCSI target and initiator; configure iSNS; configure Datacenter Bridging (DCB); configure Multi-Path IO (MPIO).

✓ **Implement data deduplication**

- This objective may include but is not limited to: Implement and configure deduplication; determine appropriate usage scenarios for deduplication; monitor deduplication; implement a backup and restore solution with deduplication.

This chapter explains how to set up your servers so that your network users have something to access. Before you can set up a server, you have to determine the purpose of it. Is it going to be a print server, a file storage server, a remote access server, or a domain controller?

After you have decided how the machine is going to help your network, you must implement your decision. In this chapter, I'll show you how to set up a print server and a file server. In addition, I will discuss how to set up permissions and security for these servers and how you can limit the amount of space your users can have on a server.

Finally in the chapter, I will show you how to setup and use data duplication. I will explain the benefits of duplication and how to use data duplication for backups. I will also show you how to monitor the data that is being duplicated.

But I am going to start the chapter by introducing you to the different Windows File Systems. So let's begin.

# Understanding File Systems

When we start the discussion about understanding Windows files systems, we have to first think about how the Windows Server 2016 machine will be used. There are four (4) supported file systems: FAT, FAT32, NTFS, and ReFS. FAT and FAT32 partitions may not always be an available option. As you can see in Figure 3.1, all 4 file systems are available because the partition is under 4 GB.

**FIGURE 3.1** Format options on Windows Server 2016

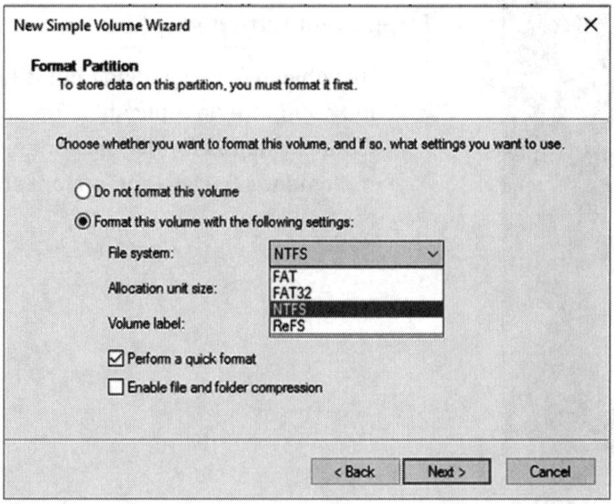

FAT has a max partition size of 4GB and FAT32 has a max partition size of 32 GB. In Figure 3.1, since it's a 3 GB partition, all four options are available. But since most drives today are much larger than 32 GB, we will continue our focus on just NTFS and ReFS.

When you're planning your Active Directory deployment, the file system that the operating system uses is an important concern for two reasons. First, the file system can provide the ultimate level of security for all the information stored on the server itself. Second, it is responsible for managing and tracking all of this data. The Windows Server 2016 platform supports two main file systems:

- Windows NT File System (NTFS)
- Resilient File System (ReFS)

Although ReFS was new to Windows Server 2012, NTFS has been around for many years, and NTFS in Windows Server 2016 has been improved for better performance.

## Resilient File System (ReFS)

Windows Server 2016 includes a file system called *Resilient File System (ReFS)*. ReFS was created to help Windows Server 2016 maximize the availability of data and online operation. ReFS allows the Windows Server 2016 system to continue to function despite some errors that would normally cause data to be lost or the system to go down. ReFS uses data integrity to protect your data from errors and also to make sure that all of your important data is online when that data is needed.

One of the issues that IT members have had to face over the years is the problem of rapidly growing data sizes. As we continue to rely more and more on computers, our data continues to get larger and larger. This is where ReFS can help an IT department. ReFS was designed specifically with the issues of scalability and performance in mind, which resulted in some of the following ReFS features:

**Availability** If your hard disk becomes corrupt, ReFS has the ability to implement a salvage strategy that removes the data that has been corrupted. This feature allows the healthy data to continue to be available while the unhealthy data is removed. All of this can be done without taking the hard disk offline.

**Scalability** One of the main advantages of ReFS is the ability to support volume sizes up to 2^78 bytes using 16 KB cluster sizes, while Windows stack addressing allows 2^64 bytes. ReFS also supports file sizes of 2^64-1 bytes, 2^64 files in a directory, and the same number of directories in a volume.

**Robust Disk Updating** ReFS uses a disk updating system referred to as an *allocate-on-write transactional model* (also known as *copy on write*). This model helps to avoid many hard disk issues while data is written to the disk because ReFS updates data using disk writes to multiple locations in an atomic manner instead of updating data in place.

**Data Integrity** ReFS uses a check-summed system to verify that all data that is being written and stored is accurate and reliable. ReFS always uses allocate-on-write for updates to the data, and it uses checksums to detect disk corruption.

**Application Compatibility** ReFS allows for most NTFS features and also supports the Win32 API. Because of this, ReFS is compatible with most Windows applications.

## NTFS

Let's start with some of the features of NTFS. There are many benefits to using NTFS, including support for the following:

**Disk Quotas** To restrict the amount of disk space used by users on the network, system administrators can establish *disk quotas*. By default, Windows Server 2016 supports disk quota restrictions at the volume level. That is, you can restrict the amount of storage space that a specific user uses on a single disk volume. Third-party solutions that allow more granular quota settings are also available.

**File System Encryption** One of the fundamental problems with network operating systems (NOSs) is that system administrators are often given full permission to view all files and data stored on hard disks, which can be a security and privacy concern. In some cases, this is necessary. For example, to perform backup, recovery, and disk management functions, at least one user must have all permissions. Windows Server 2016 and NTFS address these issues by allowing for *file system encryption*. Encryption essentially scrambles all of the data stored within files before they are written to the disk. When an authorized user requests the files, they are transparently decrypted and provided. By using encryption, you can prevent the data from being used in case it is stolen or intercepted by an unauthorized user—even a system administrator.

**Dynamic Volumes** Protecting against disk failures is an important concern for production servers. Although earlier versions of Windows NT supported various levels of Redundant Array of Independent Disks (RAID) technology, software-based solutions had some shortcomings. Perhaps the most significant was that administrators needed to perform server reboots to change RAID configurations. Also, you could not make some configuration changes without completely reinstalling the operating system. With Windows Server 2016 support for *dynamic volumes*, system administrators can change RAID and other disk configuration settings without needing to reboot or reinstall the server. The result is greater data protection, increased scalability, and increased uptime. Dynamic volumes are also included with ReFS.

**Mounted Drives** By using *mounted drives*, system administrators can map a local disk drive to an NTFS directory name. This helps them organize disk space on servers and increase manageability. By using mounted drives, you can mount the `C:\Users` directory to an actual physical disk. If that disk becomes full, you can copy all of the files to another, larger drive without changing the directory path name or reconfiguring applications.

**Remote Storage** System administrators often notice that as soon as they add more space, they must plan the next upgrade. One way to recover disk space is to move infrequently used files to external hard drives. However, backing up and restoring these files can be quite difficult and time-consuming. System administrators can use the *remote storage* features supported by NTFS to off-load seldom-used data automatically to a backup system or other devices. The files, however, remain available to users. If a user requests an archived file,

Windows Server 2016 can automatically restore the file from a remote storage device and make it available. Using remote storage like this frees up system administrators' time and allows them to focus on tasks other than micromanaging disk space.

**Self-healing NTFS** In previous versions of the Windows Server operating system, if you had to fix a corrupted NTFS volume, you used a tool called `Chkdsk.exe`. The disadvantage of this tool is that the Windows Server's availability was disrupted. If this server was your domain controller, that could stop domain logon authentication.

To help protect the Windows Server 2016 NTFS file system, Microsoft now uses a feature called self-healing NTFS. *Self-healing NTFS* attempts to fix corrupted NTFS file systems without taking them offline. Self-healing NTFS allows an NTFS file system to be corrected without running the `Chkdsk.exe` utility. New features added to the NTFS kernel code allow disk inconsistencies to be corrected without system downtime.

**Security** NTFS allows you to configure not only folder-level security but also file-level security. NTFS security is one of the biggest reasons most companies use NTFS. ReFS also allows folder- and file-level security.

## Setting Up the NTFS Partition

Although the features mentioned in the previous section likely compel most system administrators to use NTFS, additional reasons make using it mandatory. The most important reason is that the Active Directory data store must reside on an NTFS partition. Therefore, before you begin installing Active Directory, make sure you have at least one NTFS partition available. Also, be sure you have a reasonable amount of disk space available (at least 4 GB). Because the size of the Active Directory data store will grow as you add objects to it, also be sure that you have adequate space for the future.

Exercise 3.1 shows you how to use the administrative tools to view and modify disk configuration.

Before you make any disk configuration changes, be sure you completely understand their potential effects; then perform the test in a lab environment and make sure you have good, verifiable backups handy. Changing partition sizes and adding and removing partitions can result in a total loss of all information on one or more partitions.

If you want to convert an existing partition from FAT or FAT32 to NTFS, you need to use the `CONVERT` command-line utility. For example, the following command converts the `C:` partition from FAT to NTFS:

```
CONVERT c: /fs:ntfs
```

**EXERCISE 3.1**

### Viewing Disk Configurations

1. Right-click the Start button and then choose Disk Management (shown in Figure 3.2).

**FIGURE 3.2** Disk Management

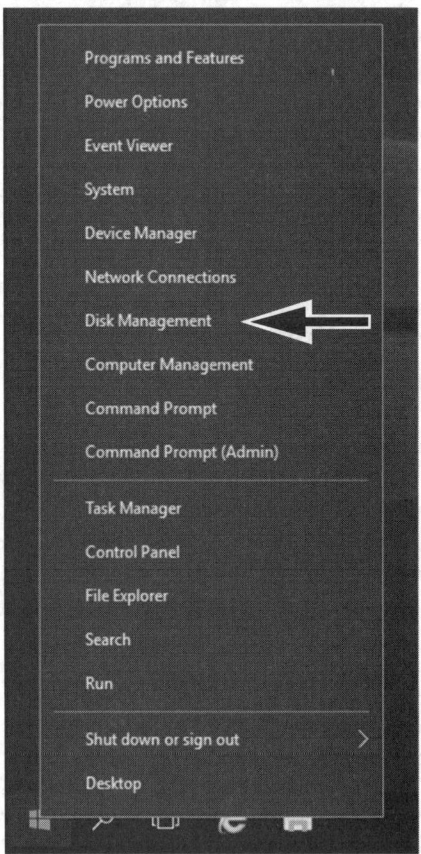


The Disk Management program shows you the logical and physical disks that are currently configured on your system. Note that information about the size of each partition is also displayed (in the Capacity column).

2. To see the available options for modifying partition settings, right-click any of the disks or partitions and choose Properties. This step is optional.

3. Close Disk Management.

# Storage in Windows Server 2016

As an IT administrator, you'll need to ask many questions before you start setting up a server. What type of disks should be used? What type of RAID sets should be made? What type of hardware platform should be purchased? These are all questions you must ask when planning for storage in a Windows Server 2016 server. In the following sections, I will answer these questions so that you can make the best decisions for storage in your network's environment.

## Initializing Disks

To begin, I must first discuss how to add disk drives to a server. Once a disk drive has been physically installed, it must be initialized by selecting the type of partition. Different types of partition styles are used to initialize disks: *Master Boot Record (MBR)* and *GUID Partition Table (GPT)*.

MBR has a partition table that indicates where the partitions are located on the disk drive, and with this particular partition style, only volumes up to 2 TB (2,048 GB) are supported. An MBR drive can have up to four primary partitions or can have three primary partitions and one extended partition that can be divided into unlimited logical drives.

Windows Server 2016 can only boot off an MBR disk unless it is based on the Extensible Firmware Interface (EFI); then it can boot from GPT. An Itanium server is an example of an EFI-based system. GPT is not constrained by the same limitations as MBR. In fact, a GPT disk drive can support volumes of up to 18EB (18,874,368 million terabytes) and 128 partitions. As a result, GPT is recommended for disks larger than 2TB or disks used on Itanium-based computers. Exercise 3.2 demonstrates the process of initializing additional disk drives to an active computer running Windows Server 2016. If you're not adding a new drive, then stop after step 4. I am completing this exercise using Computer Management, but you also can do this exercise using Server Manager.

**EXERCISE 3.2**

### Initializing Disk Drives

1. Open Computer Management under Administrative Tools.
2. Select Disk Management.
3. After disk drives have been installed, right-click Disk Management and select Rescan Disks.
4. A pop-up box appears indicating that the server is scanning for new disks. If you did not add a new disk, go to step 9.
5. After the server has completed the scan, the new disk appears as Unknown.
6. Right-click the Unknown disk, and select Initialize Disk.

**EXERCISE 3.2 *(continued)***

7. A pop-up box appears asking for the partition style. For this exercise, choose MBR.
8. Click OK.
9. Close Computer Management.

The disk will now appear online as a basic disk with unallocated space.

## Configuring Basic and Dynamic Disks

Windows Server 2016 supports two types of disk configurations: basic and dynamic. Basic disks are divided into partitions and can be used with previous versions of Windows. Dynamic disks are divided into volumes and can be used with Windows 2000 Server and newer releases.

When a disk is initialized, it is automatically created as a basic disk, but when a new fault-tolerant (RAID) volume set is created, the disks in the set are converted to dynamic disks. Fault-tolerance features and the ability to modify disks without having to reboot the server are what distinguish dynamic disks from basic disks.

Fault tolerance (RAID) is discussed in detail later in this chapter in the "Redundant Array of Independent Disks" section.

A basic disk can simply be converted to a dynamic disk without loss of data. When a basic disk is converted, the partitions are automatically changed to the appropriate volumes. However, converting a dynamic disk back to a basic disk is not as simple. First, all the data on the dynamic disk must be backed up or moved. Then, all the volumes on the dynamic disk have to be deleted. The dynamic disk can then be converted to a basic disk. Partitions and logical drives can be created, and the data can be restored.

The following are actions that can be performed on basic disks:

- Formatting partitions
- Marking partitions as active
- Creating and deleting primary and extended partitions
- Creating and deleting logical drives
- Converting from a basic disk to a dynamic disk

The following are actions that can be performed on dynamic disks:

- Creating and deleting simple, striped, spanned, mirrored, or RAID-5 volumes
- Removing or breaking a mirrored volume
- Extending simple or spanned volumes
- Repairing mirrored or RAID-5 volumes
- Converting from a dynamic disk to a basic disk after deleting all volumes

In Exercise 3.3, you'll convert a basic disk to a dynamic disk.

EXERCISE 3.3

### Converting a Basic Disk to a Dynamic Disk

1. Open Computer Management under Administrative Tools.
2. Select Disk Management.
3. Right-click a basic disk that you want to convert and select Convert To Dynamic Disk, as shown in Figure 3.3.

**FIGURE 3.3** Converting a disk

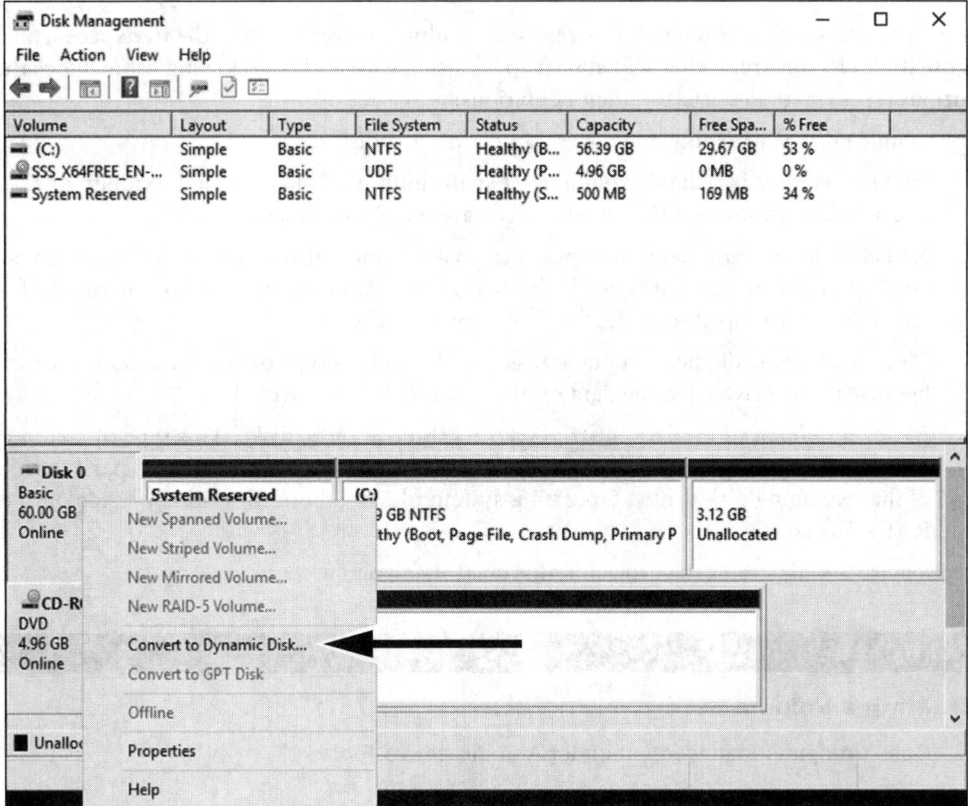

4. The Convert To Dynamic Disk dialog box appears. From here, select all of the disks that you want to convert to dynamic disks. In this exercise, only one disk will be converted.
5. Click OK.
6. The Convert To Dynamic Disk dialog box changes to the Disks To Convert dialog box and shows the disk/disks that will be converted to dynamic disks.
7. Click Convert.

**EXERCISE 3.3 *(continued)***

8. Disk Management will warn that if you convert the disk to dynamic, you will not be able to start the installed operating system from any volume on the disk (except the current boot volume). Click Yes.
9. Close Computer Management.

The converted disk will now show as Dynamic in Disk Management.

## Managing Volumes

A *volume set* is created from volumes that span multiple drives by using the free space from those drives to construct what will appear to be a single drive. The following list includes the various types of volume sets and their definitions:

- *Simple volume* uses only one disk or a portion of a disk.
- *Spanned volume* is a simple volume that spans multiple disks, with a maximum of 32. Use a spanned volume if the volume needs are too great for a single disk.
- *Striped volume* stores data in stripes across two or more disks. A striped volume gives you fast access to data but is not fault tolerant, nor can it be extended or mirrored. If one disk in the striped set fails, the entire volume fails.
- *Mirrored volume* duplicates data across two disks. This type of volume is fault tolerant because if one drive fails, the data on the other disk is unaffected.
- *RAID-5 volume* stores data in stripes across three or more disks. This type of volume is fault tolerant because if a drive fails, the data can be re-created from the parity off of the remaining disk drives. Operating system files and boot files cannot reside on the RAID-5 disks.

Exercise 3.4 illustrates the procedure for creating a volume set.

**EXERCISE 3.4**

### Creating a Volume Set

1. Open Computer Management under Administrative Tools.
2. Select Disk Management.
3. Select and right-click a disk that has unallocated space. If there are no disk drives available for a particular volume set, that volume set will be grayed out as a selectable option. In this exercise, you'll choose a spanned volume set, but the process after the volume set selection is the same regardless of which kind you choose. The only thing that differs is the number of disk drives chosen.

4. The Welcome page of the New Spanned Volume Wizard appears and explains the type of volume set chosen. Click Next.
5. The Select Disks page appears. Select the disk that will be included with the volume set and click Add. Repeat this process until all of the desired disks have been added. Click Next.
6. The Assign Drive Letter Or Path page appears. From here you can select the desired drive letter for the volume, mount the volume in an empty NTFS folder, or choose not to assign a drive letter. The new volume is labeled as E. Click Next.
7. The Format Volume page appears. Choose to format the new volume. Click Next.
8. Click Finish.
9. If the disks have not been converted to dynamic, you will be asked to convert the disks. Click Yes.

The new volume will appear as a healthy spanned dynamic volume with the new available disk space of the new volume set.

## Storage Spaces in Windows Server 2016

Windows Server 2016 includes a technology called *Storage Spaces*. Windows Server 2016 allows an administrator to virtualize storage by grouping disks into storage pools. These storage pools can then be turned into virtual disks called *storage spaces*.

The Storage Spaces technology allows an administrator to have a highly available, scalable, low-cost, and flexible solution for both physical and virtual installations. Storage Spaces allows you to set up this advantage on either a single server or in scalable multinode mode. So, before going any further, let's look at these two terms that you must understand.

**Storage Pools** *Storage pools* are a group of physical disks that allows an administrator to delegate administration, expand disk sizes, and group disks together.

**Storage Spaces** *Storage spaces* allow an administrator to take free space from storage pools and create virtual disks called storage spaces. Storage spaces give administrators the ability to have precise control, resiliency, and storage tiers.

Storage spaces and storage pools can be managed by an administrator through the use of the Windows Storage Management API, Server Manager, or Windows PowerShell.

One of the advantages of using the Storage Spaces technology is the ability to set up resiliency. There are three types of Storage Space resiliency: mirror, parity, and simple (no resiliency).

Fault tolerance (RAID) is discussed in detail in the "Redundant Array of Independent Disks" section.

Now that you understand what storage spaces and storage pools do, let's take a look at some of the other advantages of using these features in Windows Server 2016.

**Availability** One advantage to the Storage Spaces technology is the ability to fully integrate the storage space with failover clustering. This advantage allows administrators to achieve service deployments that are continuously available. Administrators have the ability to set up storage pools to be clustered across multiple nodes within a single cluster.

**Tiered Storage** The Storage Spaces technology allows virtual disks to be created with a two-tier storage setup. For data that is used often, you have an SSD tier; for data that is not used often, you use an HDD tier. The Storage Spaces technology will automatically transfer data at a subfile level between the two different tiers based on how often the data is used. Because of tiered storage, performance is greatly increased for data that is used most often, and data that is not used often still gets the advantage of being stored on a low-cost storage option.

**Delegation** One advantage of using storage pools is that administrators have the ability to control access by using access control lists (ACLs). What is nice about this advantage is that each storage pool can have its own unique access control lists. Storage pools are fully integrated with Active Directory Domain Services.

## Redundant Array of Independent Disks

The ability to support drive sets and arrays using *Redundant Array of Independent Disks (RAID)* technology is built into Windows Server 2016. RAID can be used to enhance data performance, or it can be used to provide fault tolerance to maintain data integrity in case of a hard disk failure. Windows Server 2016 supports three types of RAID technologies: RAID-0, RAID-1, and RAID-5.

**RAID-0 (Disk Striping)** *Disk striping* is using two or more volumes on independent disks created as a single striped set. There can be a maximum of 32 disks. In a striped set, data is divided into blocks that are distributed sequentially across all of the drives in the set. With RAID-0 disk striping, you get very fast read and write performance because multiple blocks of data can be accessed from multiple drives simultaneously. However, RAID-0 does not offer the ability to maintain data integrity during a single disk failure. In other words, RAID-0 is not fault tolerant; a single disk event will cause the entire striped set to be lost, and it will have to be re-created through some type of recovery process, such as a tape backup.

**RAID-1 (Disk Mirroring)** *Disk mirroring* is two logical volumes on two separate identical disks created as a duplicate disk set. Data is written on two disks at the same time; that way, in the event of a disk failure, data integrity is maintained and available. Although this fault tolerance gives administrators data redundancy, it comes with a price because it diminishes the amount of available storage space by half. For example, if an administrator wants to create a 300GB mirrored set, they would have to install two 300GB hard drives into the server, thus doubling the cost for the same available space.

**RAID-5 Volume (Disk Striping with Parity)** With a RAID-5 volume, you have the ability to use a minimum of three disks and a maximum of 32 disks. RAID-5 volumes allow data to be striped across all of the disks with an additional block of error-correction called parity. *Parity* is used to reconstruct the data in the event of a disk failure. RAID-5 has slower write performance than the other RAID types because the OS must calculate the parity information for each stripe that is written, but the read performance is equivalent to a stripe set, RAID-0, because the parity information is not read. Like RAID-1, RAID-5 comes with additional cost considerations. For every RAID-5 set, roughly an entire hard disk is consumed for storing the parity information. For example, a minimum RAID-5 set requires three hard disks, and if those disks are 300GB each, approximately 600GB of disk space is available to the OS and 300GB is consumed by parity information, which equates to 33.3 percent of the available space. Similarly, in a five-disk RAID-5 set of 300GB disks, approximately 1,200GB of disk space is available to the OS, which means that 20 percent of the total available space is consumed by the parity information. The words *roughly* and *approximately* are used when calculating disk space because a 300GB disk will really be only about 279GB of space. This is because vendors define a gigabyte as 1 billion bytes, but the OS defines it as $2^{30}$ (1,073,741,824) bytes. Also, remember that file systems and volume managers have overhead as well.

Software RAID is a nice option for a small company, but hardware RAID is definitely a better option if the money is available.

Table 3.1 breaks down the various aspects of the supported RAID types in Windows Server 2016.

**TABLE 3.1** Supported RAID-level properties in Windows Server 2016

| RAID Level | RAID Type | Fault Tolerant | Advantages | Minimum Number of Disks | Maximum Number of Disks |
|---|---|---|---|---|---|
| 0 | Disk striping | No | Fast reads and writes | 2 | 32 |
| 1 | Disk mirroring | Yes | Data redundancy and faster writes than RAID-5 | 2 | 2 |
| 5 | Disk striping with parity | Yes | Data redundancy with less overhead and faster reads than RAID-1 | 3 | 32 |

## Creating RAID Sets

Now that you understand the concepts of RAID and how to use it, you can look at the creation of RAID sets in Windows Server 2016. The process of creating a RAID set is the same as the process for creating a simple or spanned volume set, except for the minimum disk requirements associated with each RAID type.

Creating a mirrored volume set is basically the same as creating a volume set except that you will select New Mirrored Volume. It is after the disk select wizard appears that you'll begin to see the difference. Since a new mirrored volume is being created, the volume requires two disks.

During the disk select process, if only one disk is selected, the Next button will be unavailable because the disk minimum has not been met. Refer to Figure 3.4 to view the Select Disks page of the New Mirrored Volume Wizard during the creation of a new mirrored volume, and notice that the Next button is not available.

**FIGURE 3.4** Select Disks page of the New Mirrored Volume Wizard

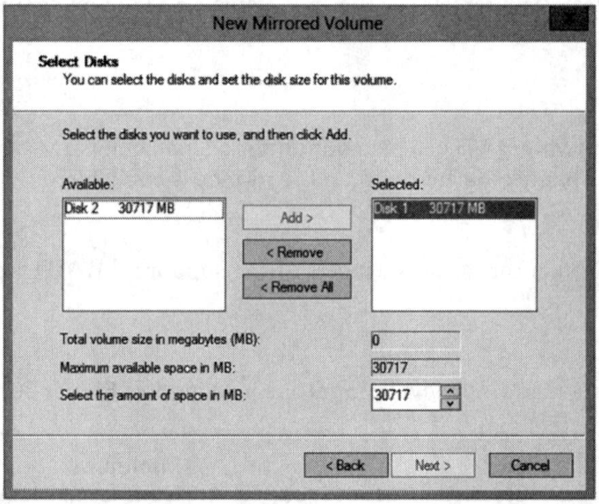

To complete the process, you must select a second disk by highlighting the appropriate disk and adding it to the volume set. Once the second disk has been added, the Next button is available to complete the mirrored volume set creation.

A drive letter will have to be assigned, and the volume will need to be formatted. The new mirrored volume set will appear in Disk Management. In Figure 3.5, notice that the capacity of the volume equals one disk even though two disks have been selected.

To create a RAID-5 volume set, you use the same process that you use to create a mirrored volume set. The only difference is that a RAID-5 volume set requires that a minimum of three disks be selected to complete the volume creation. The process is simple: Select New RAID-5 Volume, select the three disks that will be used in the volume set, assign a drive letter, and format the volume.

**FIGURE 3.5** Newly created mirrored volume set

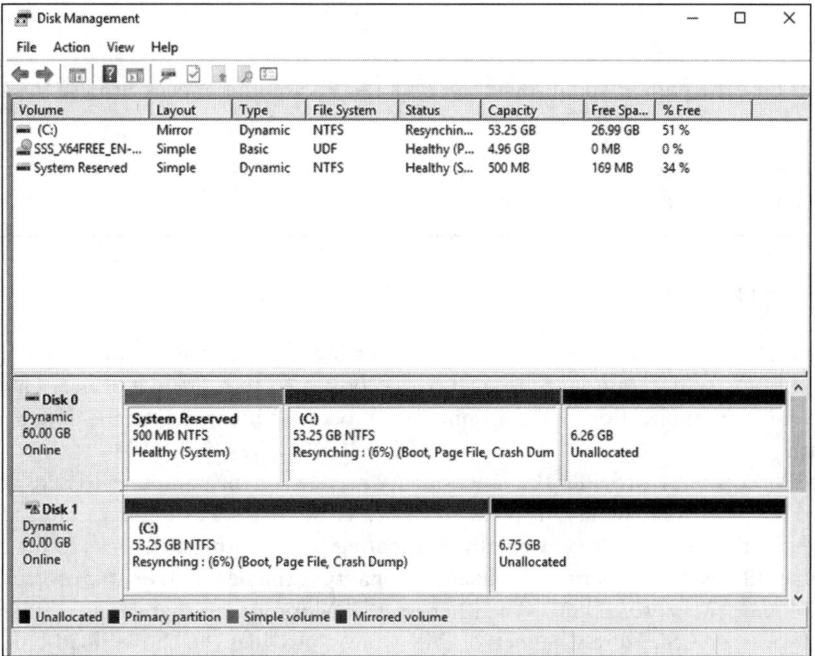


## Mount Points

With the ever-increasing demands of storage, mount points are used to surpass the limitation of 26 drive letters and to join two volumes into a folder on a separate physical disk drive. A *mount point* allows you to configure a volume to be accessed from a folder on another existing disk.

Through Disk Management, a mount point folder can be assigned to a drive instead of using a drive letter, and it can be used on basic or dynamic volumes that are formatted with NTFS. However, mount point folders can be created only on empty folders within a volume. Additionally, mount point folder paths cannot be modified; they can be removed only once they have been created. Exercise 3.5 shows the steps to create a mount point.

**EXERCISE 3.5**

### Creating Mount Points

1. Right click the Start button and select Disk Management.
2. Right-click the volume where the mount point folder will be assigned, and select Change Drive Letter And Paths.

**EXERCISE 3.5 *(continued)***

3. Click Add.
4. Either type the path to an empty folder on an NTFS volume or click Browse to select or make a new folder for the mount point.

When you explore the drive, you'll see the new folder created. Notice that the icon indicates that it is a mount point.

## Microsoft MPIO

*Multipath I/O (MPIO)* is associated with high availability because a computer will be able to use a solution with redundant physical paths connected to a storage device. Thus, if one path fails, an application will continue to run because it can access the data across the other path.

The MPIO software provides the functionality needed for the computer to take advantage of the redundant storage paths. MPIO solutions can also load-balance data traffic across both paths to the storage device, virtually eliminating bandwidth bottlenecks to the computer. What allows MPIO to provide this functionality is the new native *Microsoft Device Specific Module (Microsoft DSM)*. The Microsoft DSM is a driver that communicates with storage devices—iSCSI, Fibre Channel, or SAS—and it provides the chosen load-balancing policies. Windows Server 2016 supports the following load-balancing policies:

**Failover** In a failover configuration, there is no load balancing. There is a primary path that is established for all requests and subsequent standby paths. If the primary path fails, one of the standby paths will be used.

**Failback** This is similar to failover in that it has primary and standby paths. However, with failback you designate a preferred path that will handle all process requests until it fails, after which the standby path will become active until the primary reestablishes a connection and automatically regains control.

**Round Robin** In a round-robin configuration, all available paths will be active and will be used to distribute I/O in a balanced round-robin fashion.

**Round Robin with a Subset of Paths** In this configuration, a specific set of paths will be designated as a primary set and another as standby paths. All I/O will use the primary set of paths in a round-robin fashion until all of the sets fail. Only at this time will the standby paths become active.

**Dynamic Least Queue Depth** In a dynamic least queue depth configuration, I/O will route to the path with the least number of outstanding requests.

**Weighted Path** In a weighted path configuration, paths are assigned a numbered weight. I/O requests will use the path with the least weight—the higher the number, the lower the priority.

Exercise 3.6 demonstrates the process of installing the Microsoft MPIO feature for Windows Server 2016.

**EXERCISE 3.6**

## Installing Microsoft MPIO

1. Choose Server Manager by clicking the Server Manager icon on the Taskbar.
2. Click number 2, Add Roles And Features.
3. Choose role-based or feature-based installation and click Next.
4. Choose your server and click Next.
5. Click Next on the Roles screen.
6. On the Select Features screen, choose the Multipath I/O check box (see Figure 3.6). Click Next.

**FIGURE 3.6** Multipath I/O

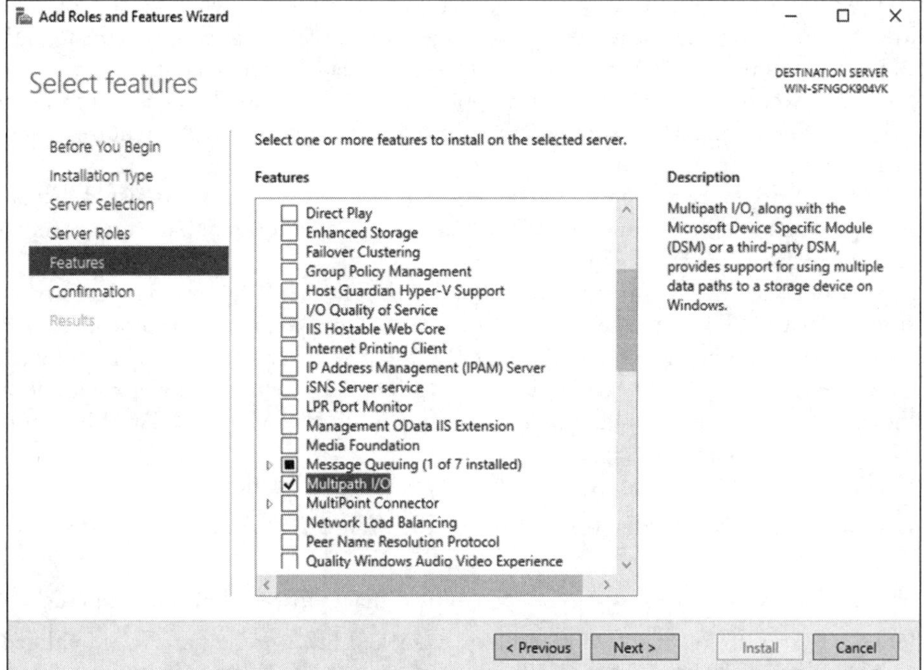


7. On the Confirm Installation Selections page, verify that Multipath I/O is the feature that will be installed. Click Install.
8. After the installation completes, the Installation Results page appears stating that the server must be rebooted to finish the installation process.
9. Click Close.
10. Restart the system.

Typically, most storage arrays work with the Microsoft DSM. However, some hardware vendors require DSM software that is specific to their products. Third-party DSM software is installed through the MPIO utility as follows:

1. Open Administrative Tools ➢ MPIO.
2. Select the DSM Install tab.
3. Add the path of the INF file and click Install.

## Configuring iSCSI Target

*Internet Small Computer System Interface (iSCSI)* is an interconnect protocol used to establish and manage a connection between a computer (initiator) and a storage device (target). It does this by using a connection through TCP port 3260, which allows it to be used over a LAN, a WAN, or the Internet. Each initiator is identified by its iSCSI Qualified Name (iqn), and it is used to establish its connection to an iSCSI target.

iSCSI was developed to allow block-level access to a storage device over a network. This is different from using a network attached storage (NAS) device that connects through the use of Common Internet File System (CIFS) or Network File System (NFS).

Block-level access is important to many applications that require direct access to storage. Microsoft Exchange and Microsoft SQL are examples of applications that require direct access to storage.

By being able to leverage the existing network infrastructure, iSCSI was also developed as an alternative to Fibre Channel storage by alleviating the additional hardware costs associated with a Fibre Channel storage solution.

iSCSI also has another advantage over Fibre Channel in that it can provide security for the storage devices. iSCSI can use Challenge Handshake Authentication Protocol (CHAP or MS-CHAP) for authentication and Internet Protocol Security (IPsec) for encryption. Windows Server 2016 is able to connect an iSCSI storage device out of the box with no additional software needing to be installed. This is because the Microsoft iSCSI initiator is built into the operating system.

Windows Server 2016 supports two different ways to initiate an iSCSI session.

- Through the native Microsoft iSCSI software initiator that resides on Windows Server 2016
- Using a hardware iSCSI host bus adapter (HBA) that is installed in the computer

Both the Microsoft iSCSI software initiator and iSCSI HBA present an iSCSI qualified name that identifies the host initiator. When the Microsoft iSCSI software initiator is used, the CPU utilization may be as much as 30 percent higher than on a computer with a hardware iSCSI HBA. This is because all of the iSCSI process requests are handled within the operating system. Using a hardware iSCSI HBA, process requests can be offloaded to the adapter, thus freeing the CPU overhead associated with the Microsoft iSCSI software initiator. However, iSCSI HBAs can be expensive, whereas the Microsoft iSCSI software initiator is free.

It is worthwhile to install the Microsoft iSCSI software initiator and perform load testing to see how much overhead the computer will have prior to purchasing an iSCSI HBA or HBAs, depending on the redundancy level. Exercise 3.7 explains how to install and configure an iSCSI connection.

**EXERCISE 3.7**

**Configuring iSCSI Storage Connection**

1. Right-click the Start button ➢ Control Panel ➢ Administrative Tools ➢ iSCSI Initiator.
2. If a dialog box appears, click Yes to start the service.
3. Click the Discovery tab.
4. In the Target Portals portion of the page, click Discover Portal.
5. Enter the IP address of the target portal and click OK.
6. The IP address of the target portal appears in the Target Portals box.
7. Click OK.

## Internet Storage Name Service

*Internet Storage Name Service (iSNS)* allows for central registration of an iSCSI environment because it automatically discovers available targets on the network. The purpose of iSNS is to help find available targets on a large iSCSI network.

The Microsoft iSCSI initiator includes an iSNS client that is used to register with the iSNS. The iSNS feature maintains a database of clients that it has registered either through DCHP discovery or through manual registration. iSNS DHCP is available after the installation of the service, and it is used to allow iSNS clients to discover the location of the iSNS. However, if iSNS DHCP is not configured, iSNS clients must be registered manually with the `iscsicli` command.

To execute the command, launch a command prompt on a computer hosting the Microsoft iSCSI and type **`iscsicli addisnsserver server_name`**, where **`server_name`** is the name of the computer hosting iSNS. Exercise 3.8 walks you through the steps required to install the iSNS feature on Windows Server 2016, and then it explains the different tabs in iSNS.

**EXERCISE 3.8**

**Installing the iSNS Feature**

1. Choose Server Manager by clicking the Server Manager icon on the Taskbar.
2. Click number 2 ➢ Add Roles And Features.

**EXERCISE 3.8 *(continued)***

3. Choose role-based or featured-based installation and click Next.
4. Choose your server and click Next.
5. Click Next on the Roles screen.
6. On the Select Features screen, choose the iSNS Server Service check box. Click Next.
7. On the Confirmation screen, click the Install button.
8. Click the Close button. Close Server Manager and reboot.
9. Log in and open the iSNS server under Administrative Tools.
10. Click the General tab. This tab displays the list of registered initiators and targets. In addition to their iSCSI qualified name, it lists storage node type (Target or Initiator), alias string, and entity identifier (the Fully Qualified Domain Name [FQDN] of the machine hosting the iSNS client).
11. Click the Discovery Domains tab (see Figure 3.7). The purpose of Discovery Domains is to provide a way to separate and group nodes. This is similar to zoning in Fibre Channel. The following options are available on the Discovery Domains tab:
    - *Create* is used to create a new discovery domain.
    - *Refresh* is used to repopulate the Discovery Domain drop-down list.
    - *Delete* is used to delete the currently selected discovery domain.
    - *Add* is used to add nodes that are already registered in iSNS to the currently selected discovery domain.
    - *Add New* is used to add nodes by entering the iSCSI Qualified Name (iQN) of the node. These nodes do not have to be currently registered.
    - *Remove Used* is used to remove selected nodes from the discovery domain.
12. Click the Discovery Domain Sets tab. The purpose of discovery domain sets is to separate further discovery domains. Discovery domains can be enabled or disabled, giving administrators the ability to restrict further the visibility of all initiators and targets. The options on the Discovery Domain Sets tab are as follows:
    - The *Enable* check box is used to indicate the status of the discovery domain sets and to turn them off and on.
    - *Create* is used to create new discovery domain sets.
    - *Refresh* is used to repopulate the Discovery Domain Sets drop-down list.
    - *Delete* is used to delete the currently selected discovery domain set.
    - *Add* is used to add discovery domains to the currently selected discovery domain set.
    - *Remove* is used to remove selected nodes from the discovery domain sets.

**FIGURE 3.7** Discovery Domain Tab

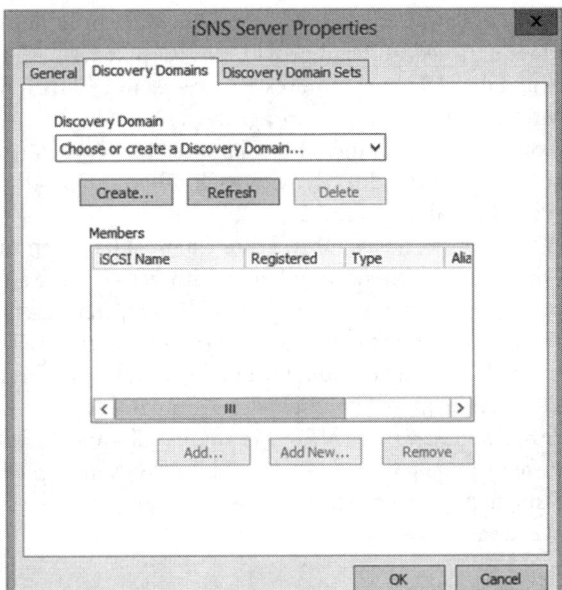


13. Close the iSNS server.

## Implement Thin Provisioning and Trim

Thin provisioning and trim can be useful features that allow organizations to get the most out of their storage arrays. These solutions apply directly to a virtualized environment using virtual disks that are thin provisioned.

*Thin provisioning* is a way of providing what is known as just-in-time allocations. Blocks of data are written to disk only as they are used instead of zeroing out all of the blocks of data that have been allocated to the virtual disk configuration. Thin provisioning is tricky to manage properly because you could easily find yourself in a position where you have an over-provisioned environment because of over-allocation.

For example, you have 100 VMs that are all provisioned with 40GB thin-provisioned virtual disks. Each VM is currently utilizing only 20GB of the total 40GB that has been allocated. The problem is that you have only 2TB worth of storage. Without realizing it, you've over-provisioned your environment by 200 percent because of thin provisioning.

This is where trim comes in to help us manage thin provisioning. *Trim* automatically reclaims free space that is not being used. In addition to trim, Windows Server 2016 provides standardized notifications that will alert administrators when certain storage thresholds are crossed.

## Fibre Channel

*Fibre Channel* storage devices are similar to iSCSI storage devices in that they both allow block-level access to their data sets and can provide MPIO policies with the proper hardware configurations. However, Fibre Channel requires a Fibre Channel HBA, fiber-optic cables, and Fibre Channel switches to connect to a storage device.

A *World Wide Name (WWN)* from the Fibre Channel HBA is used from the host and device so that they can communicate directly with each other, similar to using a NIC's MAC address. In other words, a logical unit number (LUN) is presented from a Fibre Channel storage device to the WWN of the host's HBA. Fibre Channel has been the preferred method of storage because of the available connection bandwidth between the storage and the host.

Fibre Channel devices support 1Gb/s, 2Gb/s, and 4Gb/s connections, and they soon will support 8Gb/s connections, but now that 10Gb/s Ethernet networks are becoming more prevalent in many datacenters, iSCSI can be a suitable alternative. It is important to consider that 10Gb/s network switches can be more expensive than comparable Fibre Channel switches.

*N-Port Identification Virtualization (NPIV)* is a Fibre Channel facility allowing multiple N-port IDs to share a single physical N-Port. This allows multiple Fibre Channel initiators to occupy a single physical port. By using a single port, this eases hardware requirements in storage area network (SAN) design.

## Network Attached Storage

The concept of a *network attached storage (NAS)* solution is that it is a low-cost device for storing data and serving files through the use of an Ethernet LAN connection. A NAS device accesses data at the file level via a communication protocol such as NFS, CIFS, or even HTTP, which is different from iSCSI or FC Fibre Channel storage devices that access the data at the block level. NAS devices are best used in file-storing applications, and they do not require a storage expert to install and maintain the device. In most cases, the only setup that is required is an IP address and an Ethernet connection.

## Virtual Disk Service

*Virtual Disk Service (VDS)* was created to ease the administrative efforts involved in managing all of the various types of storage devices. Many storage hardware providers used their own applications for installation and management, and this made administering all of these various devices very cumbersome.

VDS is a set of application programming interfaces (APIs) that provides a centralized interface for managing all of the various storage devices. The native VDS API enables the management of disks and volumes at an OS level, and hardware-vendor-supplied APIs manage the storage devices at a RAID level. These are known as software and hardware providers.

A *software provider* is host based, and it interacts with Plug and Play Manager because each disk is discovered and operates on volumes, disks, and disk partitions. VDS includes two software providers: basic and dynamic. The basic software provider manages basic disks with no fault tolerance, whereas the dynamic software providers manage dynamic disks with fault management. A hardware provider translates the VDS APIs into instructions specific to the storage hardware. This is how storage management applications are able to communicate with the storage hardware to create LUNs or Fibre Channel HBAs to view the WWN. The following are Windows Server 2016 storage management applications that use VDS:

- The *Disk Management snap-in* is an application that allows you to configure and manage the disk drives on the host computer. You have already seen this application in use when you initialized disks and created volume sets.
- `DiskPart` is a command-line utility that configures and manages disks, volumes, and partitions on the host computer. It can also be used to script many of the storage management commands. `DiskPart` is a robust tool that you should study on your own because it is beyond the scope of this book. Figure 3.8 shows the various commands and their function in the `DiskPart` utility.

**FIGURE 3.8** DiskPart commands

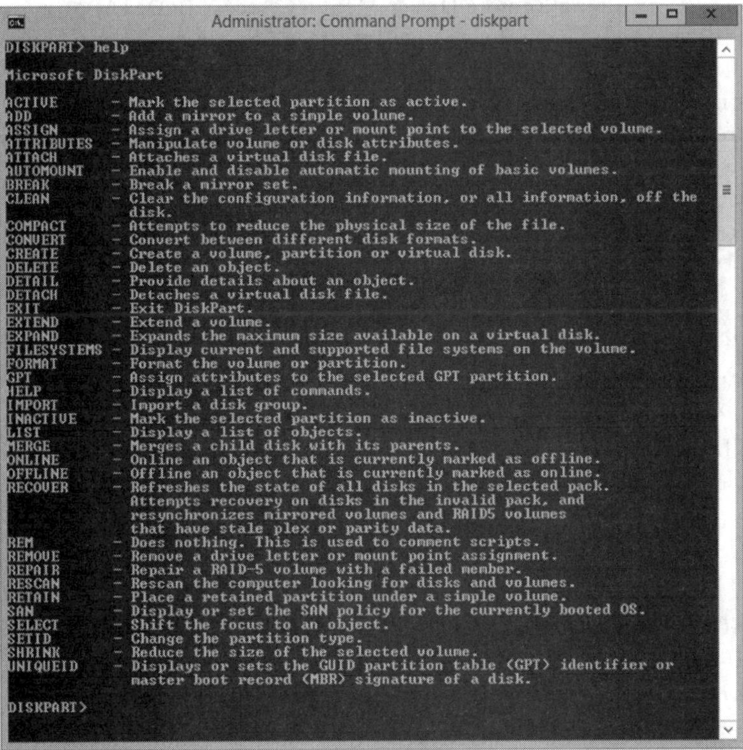


- `DiskRAID` is also a scriptable command-line utility that configures and manages hardware RAID storage systems. However, at least one VDS hardware provider must be installed for `DiskRAID` to be functional. `DiskRAID` is another useful utility that you should study on your own because it's beyond the scope of this book.

# Understanding Data Center Bridging

I think the easiest way to understanding Data Center Bridging (DCB) is to understand NIC bridging. Many of us who have used laptops have used both the Wireless and Wired networks at the same time. This is bridging network adapter cards to work as one. Well, Data Center Bridging is the same thing but just done on a larger scale.

The Institute of Electrical and Electronic Engineers (IEEE) created a suite of standards called Data Center Bridging. DCB allows the same ethernet infrastructure to work throughout the datacenter. This means that all of the network servers, clusters, and datacenter will share the same ethernet infrastructure. DCB works through the use of hardware based bandwidth allocation. This means that the hardware controls the flow of data through DCB.

DCB is nice because when you setup the hardware based flow control, you can determine which type of traffic gets a higher priority to the allocated bandwidth. This can be very useful for data that bypasses the operating system and accesses the network adapters directly (like virtualization can). DCB can work with different types of network adapters including Remote Direct Memory Access (RDMA) over Converged Ethernet, Internet Small Computer System Interface (iSCSI), or Fiber Channel over Ethernet (FCoE).

The reason that the IEEE has developed the DCB standard is because many third party and hardware manufacturers do not work together well. By having an industry standard of hardware based flow control protocol, many IT datacenters can use DCB to make different vendors work together. Also, Windows Server 2016 makes it very easy to deploy and manage DCB. There are a couple of requirements that are needed when deploying DCB through Windows Server 2016:

- The Ethernet adapters installed into the Windows Server 2016 systems must be DCB compatible.
- The Hardware switches that are deployed to your infrastructure must also be DCB compatible.

DCB can be installed onto a Windows Server two ways: through Server Manager or through PowerShell. Here are the steps for both ways.

## Installing DCB Using PowerShell

If you would like to install and use DCB through PowerShell, you need to complete the following steps:

1. Click the Start button, then right-click Windows PowerShell ➢ More ➢ Run As Administrator.
2. In the Windows PowerShell console, enter the following command followed by the Enter key:

```
Install-WindowsFeature "data-center-bridging"
```

### Installing DCB Using Server Manager

If you would like to install and use DCB through Server Manager, you need to complete the following steps:

1. On the Windows Server 2016 system, open Server Manager.
2. Click the Add Roles And Features link.
3. At the Before You Begin screen, click Next.
4. At the Select Installation Type screen, choose Role-based or feature-based installation and then click Next.
5. The Select Destination Server screen will be next. Make sure the server that you want to install DCB on is selected and then click Next.
6. On the Select Server Roles screen, just click Next.
7. On the Select Features screen, check the box for Data Center Bridging. If a dialog box appears asking to install additional features, click the Add Feature button. Then click Next.
8. At the Confirmation screen, verify that everything is OK and then click the Install button.

# Configuring Permissions

Before I can dive into how permissions work, let's first talk about how clients and servers talk to each other. In the Microsoft Windows world, clients and servers talk to each other using the Server Message Block (SMB) protocol. So let's start our discussion there.

## Understanding SMB

Server Message Block (SMB) is a network-sharing protocol that allows Windows machines (either client- or server-based operating systems) that are running applications to read and write data to files. SMB also allows systems to request services or resources that are running on remote servers. The one advantage to SMB is that it doesn't matter what network protocol you are using (TCP/IP, etc.), SMB runs on top of the network protocol that is being used on your corporate infrastructure.

It's important to understand what protocols work with client- and server-based systems because it can affect your network's performance. For example, when Microsoft released Windows Server 2012, it released SMB 3.0. The issue that many users had was that SMB 3.0 was not compatible with Macintosh-based systems. So if you were running Apple Macintosh on your network and upgraded to Windows Server 2012, your Apple-based systems would not communicate properly. This issue was eventually resolved, but this is why it's important to understand that SMB file sharing is used between Windows client and server systems.

I will show you how to use Windows PowerShell for configuring SMB shares in the section called "Windows PowerShell" later in this chapter. For a complete list of SMB PowerShell commands, visit Microsoft's website at `https://technet.microsoft.com/en-us/library/jj635726(v=wps.630).aspx`.

Now that you understand how Windows clients and servers communicate with each other, let's look at how we can protect the files and folders that clients access. You can add security to a folder in two ways: NTFS security or shared permissions. But when it comes to securing files, you can secure files in only one way: NTFS Security. So let's take a look at these methods and how they work independently and then together.

## Understanding NTFS

NTFS is an option that you have when you are formatting a hard drive. You can format a hard drive for a Microsoft operating system in three ways:

- File Allocation Table (FAT) is supported on older operating systems only (Server 2003, Server 2000, XP, and so on).
- FAT32 is supported in Windows Server 2016.
- NTFS is supported in Windows Server 2016.

NTFS has many advantages over FAT and FAT32. They include the following:

**Compression** Compression helps compact files or folders to allow for more efficient use of hard drive space. For example, a file that usually takes up 20 MB of space might use only 13 MB after compression. To enable compression, just open the Advanced Attributes dialog box for a folder and check the Compress Contents To Save Disk Space box (see Figure 3.9).

**FIGURE 3.9** Setting up compression on a folder

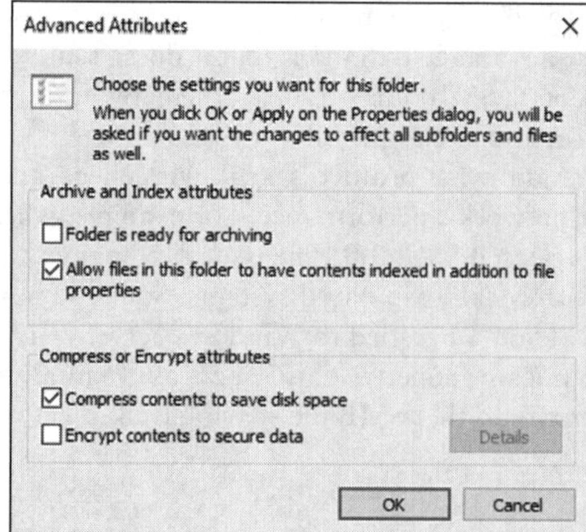

**Quotas** *Quotas* allow you to limit how much hard drive space users can have on a server. Quotas are discussed in greater detail in the section "Configuring Disk Quotas."

**Encryption** *Encrypting File System (EFS)* allows a user or administrator to secure files or folders by using encryption. Encryption employs the user's security identification (SID) number to secure the file or folder. To implement encryption, open the Advanced Attributes dialog box for a folder and check the Encrypt Contents To Secure Data box (see Figure 3.10).

**FIGURE 3.10** Setting up encryption on a folder

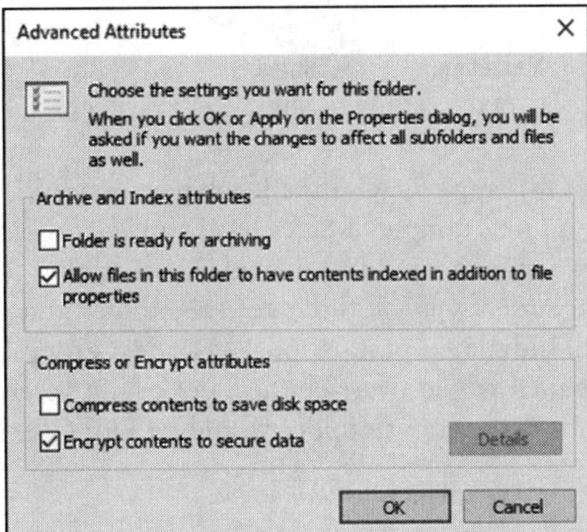


If files are encrypted using EFS and an administrator has to unencrypt the files, there are two ways to do this. First, you can log in using the user's account (the account that encrypted the files) and unencrypt the files. Second, you can become a recovery agent and manually unencrypt the files.

If you use EFS, it's best not to delete users immediately when they leave a company. Administrators have the ability to recover encrypted files, but it is much easier to gain access to the user's encrypted files by logging in as the user who left the company and unchecking the encryption box.

**Security** One of the biggest advantages of NTFS is security. Security is one of the most important aspects of an IT administrator's job. An advantage of NTFS security is that the security can be placed on individual files and folders. It does not matter whether you are local to the share (in front of the machine where the data is stored) or remote to the share (coming across the network to access the data); the security is always in place with NTFS.

The default security permission is `Users = Read` on new folders or shares.

NTFS security is *additive*. In other words, if you are a member of three groups (Marketing, Sales, and R&D) and these three groups have different security settings, you get the highest level of permissions. For example, let's say you have a user by the name of wpanek who belongs to all three groups (Marketing, Sales, and R&D). Figure 3.11 shows this user's permissions. The Marketing group has Read and Execute permissions to the `StormWind Documents` folder. The Sales group has Read and Write, and the R&D group has Full Control. Since wpanek is a member of all three groups, wpanek would get Full Control (the highest level).

**FIGURE 3.11** Security settings on the `StormWind Documents` folder

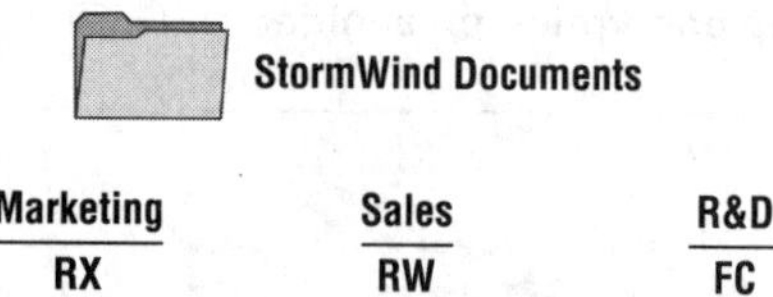


The only time this does not apply is with the Deny permission. Deny overrides any other group setting. Taking the same example, if Sales has Deny permission for the `StormWind Documents` folder, the user wpanek would be denied access to that folder. The only way around this Deny is if you added wpanek directly to the folder and gave him individual permissions (see Figure 3.12). Individual permissions override a group Deny. In this example, the individual right of wpanek would override the Sales group's Deny. The user's security permission for the `StormWind Documents` folder would be Full Control.

**FIGURE 3.12** Individual permissions

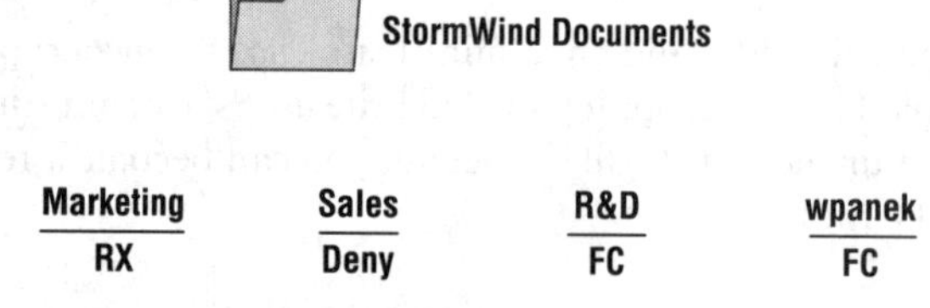

Give users only the permissions necessary to do their jobs. Do not give them higher levels than they need.

## Understanding Shared Permissions

When you set up a folder to be shared, you have the ability to assign that folder's permissions. *Shared permissions* can be placed only on the folder and not on individual files. Files have the ability to inherit their permissions from the parent folder.

Shared folder permissions are in effect only when users are remote to the shared data. In other words, if computer A shares a folder called `Test Share` and assigns that folder shared permissions, those permissions would apply only if you connected to that share from a machine other than computer A. If you were sitting in front of computer A, the shared permissions would not apply.

Like NTFS permissions (discussed in the previous section), shared permissions are additive, so users receive the highest level of permissions granted by the groups of which they are members.

Also, as with NTFS permissions, the Deny permission (see Figure 3.13) overrides any group permission, and an individual permission overrides a group Deny.

**FIGURE 3.13** Setting up permissions on a shared folder

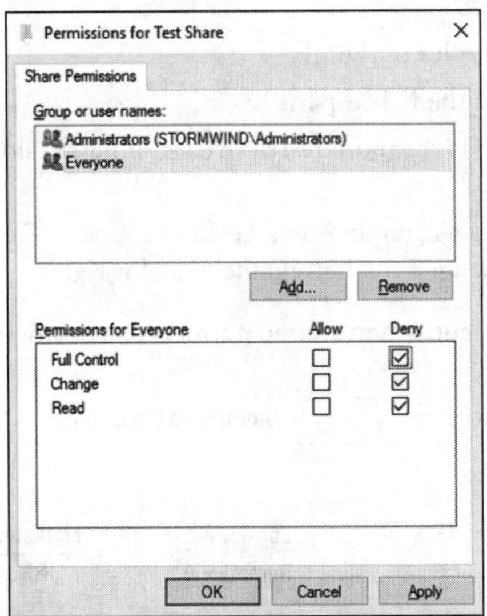


The default shared permission is `Administrators = Full Control`. The shared permissions going from lowest to highest are Read, Change, Full Control, and Deny. Table 3.2 compares the two different types of permissions and security.

**TABLE 3.2** NTFS security vs. shared permissions

| Description | NTFS | Shared |
|---|---|---|
| Folder-level security. | Yes | Yes |
| File-level security. | Yes | No |
| In effect when local to the data. | Yes | No |
| In effect when remote to the data. | Yes | Yes |
| Permissions are additive. | Yes | Yes |
| Group Deny overrides all other group settings. | Yes | Yes |
| Individual settings override group settings. | Yes | Yes |

## How NTFS Security and Shared Permissions Work Together

When you set up a shared folder, you need to set up shared permissions on that folder. If you're using NTFS, you will also need to set up NTFS security on the folder. Since both shared permissions and NTFS security are in effect when the user is remote, what happens when the two conflict?

These are the two basic rules of thumb:

- The local permission is the NTFS permission.
- The remote permission is the more restrictive set of permissions between NTFS and shared.

This is easy to do as long as you do it in steps. Let's look at Figure 3.14 and walk through the process of figuring out what wpanek has for rights.

**FIGURE 3.14** NTFS security and shared permissions example

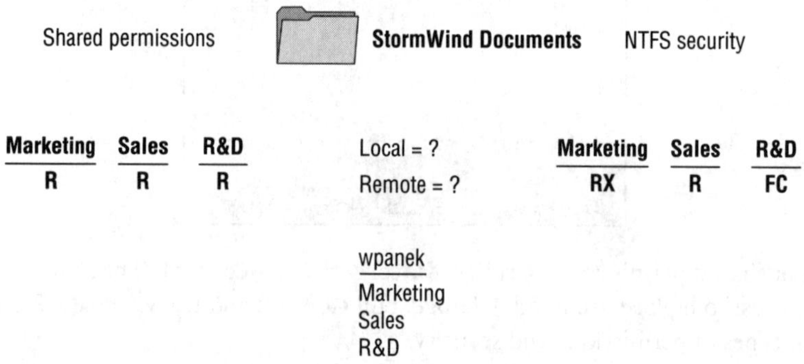

As you can see, wpanek belongs to three groups (Marketing, Sales, and R&D), and all three groups have settings for the `StormWind Documents` folder. In the figure, you will notice that there are two questions: Remote = ? and Local = ? That's what you need to figure out—what are wpanek's effective permissions when he is sitting at the computer that shares the folder, and what are his effective permissions when he connects to the folder from another computer (remotely)? To figure this out, follow these steps:

1. Add up the permissions on each side separately.

   Remember, permissions and security are *additive*. You get the highest permission. So, if you look at each side, the highest shared permission is the Read permission. The NTFS security side should add up to equal Full Control. Thus, now you have Read permission on shared and Full Control on NTFS.

2. Determine the local permissions.

   Shared permissions do not apply when you are local to the data. Only NTFS would apply. Thus, the local permission would be Full Control.

3. Determine the remote permissions.

   Remember, the remote permission is the most restrictive set of permissions between NTFS and shared. Since Read is more restrictive than Full Control, the remote permission would be Read.

Let's try another. Look at Figure 3.15, and see whether you can come up with wpanek's local and remote permissions.

**FIGURE 3.15** NTFS security and shared permissions

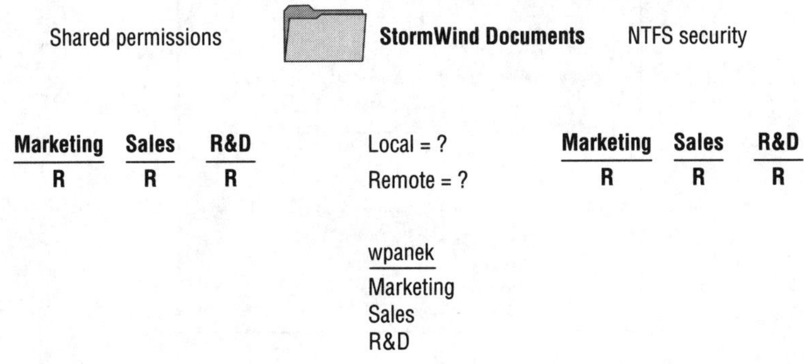


Your answer should match the following:

Local = Read

Remote = Read

Remember, first you add up each side to get the highest level of rights. NTFS would be Read, and shared would be Full Control. The local permission is always just NTFS (shared does not apply to local permissions), and remote permission is whichever permission (NTFS or shared) is the most restrictive (which would be Read on the NTFS side).

Exercise 3.9 walks you through the process of setting both NTFS and shared permissions. This exercise assumes that you have Active Directory installed on the server and you have some groups created. If you do not, go to Computer Management (right-click Start ➢ Computer Management) and under Local Users and Groups, create a new group that can be used in this exercise.

**EXERCISE 3.9**

### Configuring Shared and NTFS Settings

1. Create a new folder in the root directory of your `C:` partition and name it Test Share.
2. Right-click the `Test Share` folder you created and choose Properties.
3. Click the Sharing tab and then click the Advanced Sharing button. Click the box Share This Folder. Make sure the share name is Test Share (see Figure 3.16).

**EXERCISE 3.9 *(continued)***

**FIGURE 3.16** Advanced Sharing

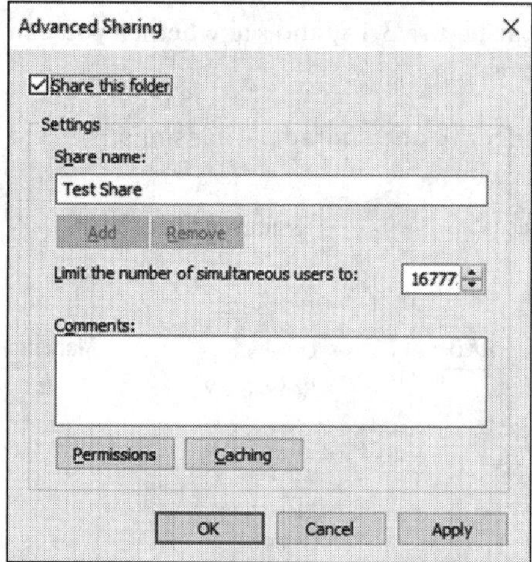


4. Click the Permissions button. Click the Add button. When the Select User page appears, choose a group from Active Directory or from the local group you created. (I used the Sales group.) Once you find your group, click OK.
5. The Permissions dialog box appears. With your group highlighted, click the Allow check box next to Full Control and click OK. (All of the other Allow check boxes will automatically become checked.)
6. On the Advanced Sharing page, click OK. Now click the Security tab. (This allows you to set the NTFS security settings.)
7. Click the Edit button. That takes you to the Permissions page. Now click the Add button. When the Select User page appears, choose a group from Active Directory. (I used the Everyone group.) Once you find your group, choose OK.
8. The Permissions dialog box appears. With your group highlighted, click the Allow check box next to Modify, and click OK. (All of the check boxes below Modify will automatically become checked.)
9. Click Close.

## Understanding NFS Shares

The NFS role service and feature set gives IT administrators the ability to integrate a Windows Server–based environment with Unix-based operating systems. Most corporate environments today consist of a mixed operating system infrastructure to some extent. Using a

Windows NFS file server, you can configure file shares for use by multiple operating systems throughout the environment.

Windows Server 2016 takes those capabilities even further by enabling you to integrate with platforms such as ESXi. ESXi is VMware's exclusive operating system–independent hypervisor. ESXi is referred to as a *bare-metal* operating system because once it is installed on server virtualization hardware, guest virtual machines can be installed without requiring the use of any other underlying operating system. With Windows Server 2016, you can use an NFS share efficiently as an ESXi data store to house all of your guest virtual machines. Let's take a look at configuring an NFS data store in Exercise 3.10.

For this exercise, you will need the following:

- A Windows Server 2016 server
- A VMware ESXi 5 server

**EXERCISE 3.10**

### Configure the NFS Data Store

1. Open Server Manager on your Windows Server 2016 machine.
2. Launch the Add Roles And Features Wizard from the dashboard.
3. Install the Server for NFS role on the server. A reboot is not required.
4. Create a new folder on your server named `NFS_Datastore`, right-click and select Properties, and then navigate to the NFS Sharing tab.
5. Click the Manage NFS Sharing button to open the NFS Advanced Sharing page and then check the Share This Folder box. Notice how enabling the share also enables the share's default settings. The share settings let you configure share authentication and user access further if the need arises. The default settings will work just fine for this exercise.
6. Click the Permissions tab to open the NFS Share Permissions page. This is where you will configure the type of access that will be allowed by machines accessing this NFS data store. By default, the NFS share permissions are set to Read-Only and do not include root access. For this exercise, you will need to change the type of access to Read-Write and check the box to allow root access.
7. Click OK to close the NFS Share Permissions page and then click Apply and OK on the NFS Advanced Sharing page. Your new NFS share is now built, ready to be presented as an NFS data store to a VMware ESXi host. Be sure to record the network path displayed on the NFS Sharing tab of the share's Properties page. You will need that information to perform a proper mount on the ESXi host.
8. Switch to your ESXi host and launch the Add Storage Wizard from the Configuration tab.
9. On the Select Storage Type page of the wizard, select the Network File System storage type; click Next to continue to the Locate Network File System page.

**EXERCISE 3.10 *(continued)***

10. On this page of the wizard, you will fill in the server and folder information for the NFS share that you will be using as a vSphere data store. Using the information recorded from step 7, properly fill out the server and folder fields and then name your new data store.

11. Click Next to continue to the Ready To Complete page of the wizard. Review the information and click Finish. Once the Create NAS data store task completes on the ESXi host, you are ready to use your Windows Server 2016 shared folder as a vSphere ESXi data store.

The previous exercise shows how versatile Windows Server 2016 shares can be. The same principles can be applied to making Windows Server shares available to other Unix-based operating systems such as ESXi.

I will show you how to use Windows PowerShell for configuring NFS shares in the section below called "Windows PowerShell." If you would like to see a more complete list of NFS PowerShell commands, please visit Microsoft's website at `https://technet.microsoft.com/en-us/library/jj603081(v=wps.630).aspx`.

# Configuring Disk Quotas

In this chapter so far, you have learned how to set up permissions and security and how NTFS and shared permissions work with each other. It's time to learn how to limit users' hard drive space on the servers.

*Disk quotas* give administrators the ability to limit how much storage space a user can have on a hard drive. As mentioned earlier in this chapter, disk quotas are an advantage of using NTFS over FAT32. If you decide to use FAT32 on a volume or partition, quotas will not be available.

You have a few options available to you when you set up disk quotas. You can set up disk quotas based on volume or on users.

A good rule of thumb is to set up an umbrella quota policy that covers the entire volume and then let individual users exceed the umbrella as needed.

**Setting Quotas by Volume** One way to set up disk quotas is by setting the quota by volume, on a per-volume basis. This means that if you have a hard drive with `C:`, `D:`, and `E:` volumes, you would have to set up three individual quotas—one for each volume. This is your umbrella. This is where you set up an entire disk quota based on the volume for all users.

**Setting Quotas by User** You have the ability to set up quotas on volumes by user. Here is where you would individually let users have independent quotas that exceed your umbrella quota.

**Specifying Quota Entries** You use quota entries to configure the volume and user quotas. You do this on the Quotas tab of the volume's Properties dialog box. (See Exercise 3.11.)

**Creating Quota Templates** Quota templates are predefined ways to set up quotas. Templates allow you to set up disk quotas without needing to create a disk quota from scratch. One advantage of using a template is that when you want to set up disk quotas on multiple volumes (`C:`, `D:`, and `E:`) on the same hard drive, you do not need to re-create the quota on each volume.

Exercise 3.11 will show you how to set up an umbrella quota for all users and then have an individual account in your Active Directory exceed this quota.

## EXERCISE 3.11

### Configuring Disk Quotas

1. Open Windows Explorer.
2. Right-click the local disk (`C:`) and choose Properties.
3. Click the Quotas tab.
4. Check the Enable Quota Management check box. Also check the Deny Disk Space To Users Exceeding Quota Limit box.
5. Click the Limit Disk Space To option and enter **1000MB** in the box.
6. Enter **750MB** in the Set Warning Level To boxes.
7. Click the Apply button. If a warning box appears, click OK. This warning is just informing you that the disk may need to be rescanned for the quota.
8. Now that you have set up an umbrella quota to cover everyone, you'll set up a quota that exceeds the umbrella. Click the Quota Entries button.
9. The Quotas Entries for (`C:`) window appears. You will see some users already listed. These are users who are already using space on the volume. Click the Quota menu at the top and choose New Quota Entry.
10. Notice the N/A entry in the Percent Used column. This belongs to the administrator account, which by default has no limit.
11. On the Select User page, choose a user that you want to allow to exceed the quota (for this example, I used the wpanek account). Click OK.
12. This opens the Add New Quota Entry dialog box. Click the Do Not Limit Disk Usage option and click OK.
13. You will notice that the new user has no limit. Close the disk quota tool.

# Windows PowerShell

*Windows PowerShell* is a task-based, command-line scripting utility that allows you to execute commands locally or remotely on a Windows Server 2016 machine. It was specifically designed for system administrators to allow for local or remote administration.

Microsoft asks a lot of questions on the exam about Windows PowerShell. Therefore, I will be discussing PowerShell throughout this book because of its importance on all of the Windows Server 2016 exams.

Most operating system shells, including `Cmd.exe` and the SH, KSH, CSH, and BASH Unix shells, work by running a command or utility in a new process and then presenting the results to the user as text. These system shells also have commands that are built into the shell and execute in the shell process. In most system shells, because there are only a few built-in commands, many utilities have been created over the years to complete tasks.

Windows PowerShell contains an interactive prompt and a scripting environment that can be used independently or in combination. Unlike the previously mentioned system shells, which accept and return text, Windows PowerShell is built using the *.NET Framework common language runtime (CLR)* and the .NET Framework. Because of this, Windows PowerShell accepts and returns .NET Framework objects. This important change in the shell allows you to use entirely new tools and methods to manage and configure Windows.

Windows PowerShell introduced the concept of using cmdlets (pronounced "command-lets"). Cmdlets are simple, single-function command-line tools built into the shell. Administrators can use the cmdlets independently, or they can combine these tools to execute complex tasks and harness the true power of PowerShell. Windows PowerShell includes more than a hundred core cmdlets, but the true advantage of PowerShell is that anyone can write their own cmdlets and share them with other users.

Administrators often automate the management of their multicomputer environments by running sequences of long-running tasks, or *workflows*, which can affect multiple managed computers or devices at the same time. Windows PowerShell can help administrators accomplish workflows in a more effective way. Windows PowerShell includes some of the following advantages:

**Windows PowerShell Scripting Syntax** Administrators can use Windows PowerShell scripting expertise to create script-based tasks by using the extensible Windows PowerShell language. Windows PowerShell script-based tasks are easy to create, and IT members can share them easily by entering them into an email or publishing them on a web page.

**Day-to-Day Management Tasks** Windows PowerShell allows administrators to configure and maintain servers. PowerShell allows you to pre-create scripts or use ready-to-use scripts to handle day-to-day tasks. This way, an administrator can just run a script to complete server configurations or management.

**Multiserver Management** Administrators can concurrently apply workflow tasks to hundreds of managed servers and computers. Windows PowerShell includes common parameters to set workflows automatically, such as `PSComputerName`, to enable multicomputer administrative scenarios. You can also use PowerShell to help you create new servers by creating new virtual hard drive (`.vhd`) files.

**Single Task to Manage Complex, End-to-End Processes** Administrators can combine related scripts or commands that act upon an entire scenario into a single workflow. The status of activities within the workflow can be viewed at any time.

**Automated Failure Recovery** Using Windows PowerShell allows workflows to survive both planned and unplanned interruptions, such as computer restarts. Administrators have the ability to suspend workflow operations and then restart or resume the workflow from the exact point at which it was suspended. Administrators can then create checkpoints as part of their workflow process so that they can resume the workflow from the last persisted task (or checkpoint) instead of restarting the workflow from the beginning.

**Activity Retries** Administrators can create workflows that also specify activities that must rerun if the activity does not get completed on one or more managed computers (for example, if a target node was not online at the time the activity was running).

**Connect and Disconnect** Administrators can connect and disconnect from the node that is executing the workflow, but the workflow will continue to run.

**Configuring Non-Domain Servers** Another advantage of PowerShell is the ability to configure non-domain servers from a Windows Server 2016 server (domain member). When you are running commands on the non-domain machine, you must have access to the non-domain machine's system administrator account. Another way to configure a non-domain server is to connect through remote desktop into the non-domain server and then configure the machine or run PowerShell commands while connected through remote desktop.

**Task Scheduling** Workflow tasks have the ability to be scheduled and started when specific conditions are met. This is also true for any other Windows PowerShell cmdlet or script.

Table 3.3 defines a few of the cmdlets available in Windows PowerShell. Again, there are hundreds of cmdlets, and the ones listed in the table are just some of the more common ones. You can retrieve a list of all the cmdlets starting here:

`http://technet.microsoft.com/en-us/scriptcenter/dd772285.aspx`

**TABLE 3.3** Windows PowerShell cmdlets

| Cmdlet | Definition |
|---|---|
| `Add-VMHardDiskDrive` | Allows you to add a .vhd file to a virtual machine. |
| `Block-SmbShareAccess` | This cmdlet allows an administrator to add a deny access control entry (ACE) to the security descriptor for the Server Message Block (SMB) share. |

**TABLE 3.3** Windows PowerShell cmdlets *(continued)*

| Cmdlet | Definition |
|---|---|
| `Clear-History` | Deletes entries from the command history. |
| `Close-SmbOpenFile` | This allows an administrator to forcibly close an open file by one of the clients of the Server Message Block (SMB) server. |
| `Close-SmbSession` | This allows an administrator to forcibly kill a Server Message Block (SMB) session. |
| `Format-table` | Shows the results in a table format. |
| `Get-Date` | Shows the date and time. |
| `Get-event` | Shows an event in the event queue. |
| `Get-Help Install-WindowsFeature` | Shows the syntax and accepted parameters for the `Install-WindowsFeature cmdlet`. |
| `Get-NetIPAddress` | Shows information about IP address configuration. |
| `Get-NfsClientConfiguration` | Shows configuration settings for an NFS client. |
| `Get-NfsMappedIdentity` | Shows an NFS mapped identity. |
| `Get-NfsMappingStore` | Shows the configuration settings for the identity mapping store. |
| `Get-NfsNetgroup` | Shows the netgroup. |
| `Get-NfsSession` | Shows the information about client systems that are currently connected to a shares on an NFS server. |
| `Get-NfsShare` | Shows an NFS share on the NFS server. |
| `Get-NfsSharePermission` | Shows you the NFS shares permissions that are on a NFS server. |
| `Get-Package` | This command allows an administrator to view a list of all software packages that have been installed by using Package Management. |
| `Get-ShieldedVMProvisioningStatus` | This command allows you to view the provisioning status of a shielded virtual machine. |

| Cmdlet | Definition |
|---|---|
| Get-SmbOpenFile | Allows an admin to see basic information about the files that are open on the Server Message Block (SMB) server. |
| Get-SmbShare | Allows an administrator to see the Server Message Block (SMB) shares on the computer. |
| Get-WindowsFeature | Shows a list of available and installed roles and features on the local server. |
| Get-WindowsFeature -ServerName | Shows a list of available and installed roles and features on a remote server. |
| Import-Module | Adds modules to the current session. |
| Install-Windowsfeature | This command allows you to installs a role, role service, or feature on the local or a specified remote server that is running Windows Server 2016. |
| Invoke-command | Runs commands on local or remote computers. |
| New-NfsShare | Allows you to create an NFS file share. |
| New-event | Creates a new event. |
| New-SmbShare | Allows an admin to create a new SMB share. |
| New-VHD | Allows you to create a new .vhd file. |
| Optimize-VHD | This command allows an administrator to optimize the allocation of space in virtual hard disk files, except for fixed virtual hard disks. |
| Out-file | Sends the job results to a file. |
| Receive-job | Gets the results of a Windows PowerShell background job. |
| Remove-job | Deletes a Windows PowerShell background job. |
| Remove-NfsShare | Allows you to delete an NFS file share. |
| Remove-SmbShare | Allows an admin to delete an SMB share. |
| Set-Date | Sets the system time and date on a computer. |

**TABLE 3.3** Windows PowerShell cmdlets *(continued)*

| Cmdlet | Definition |
|---|---|
| `Set-NetIPAddress` | Modifies IP address configuration properties of an existing IP address. |
| `Set-NetIPv4Protocol` | Modifies information about the IPv4 protocol configuration. |
| `Set-SmbShare` | Allows an administrator to modify the properties of the Server Message Block (SMB) share. |
| `Set-VM` | This command allows you to configure some virtual machine settings, like configuring the locations for snap shot storage and smart paging. |
| `Set-VMDvdDrive` | Allows you to set a virtual machine to use a DVD or .ISO file. |
| `Set-VMHost` | This command allows an administrator to configure a Hyper-V host. |
| `Set-VMMemory` | This command allows you to set the RAM for a virtual machine. |
| `Set-VMNetworkAdapter` | This command allows an administrator to configure features of the virtual network adapter in a virtual machine or the management operating system. |
| `Set-VMProcessor` | This command allows an admin to configure the processors of a virtual machine. This command is also used for nested virtualization. While the virtual machine is OFF, run the Set-VMProcessor command on the physical Hyper-V host to enable nested virtualization for the virtual machine. |
| `Set-VMSwitch` | This command allows an administrator to configure a virtual switch. |
| `Start-job` | Starts a Windows PowerShell background job. |
| `Stop-job` | Stops a Windows PowerShell background job. |
| `Trace-command` | Configures and starts a trace of a command on a machine. |
| `Uninstall-WindowsFeature` | Removes a role or feature. |

**Windows PowerShell Commands**

I will show you Windows PowerShell commands throughout this book. If I show you how to install a role or feature in Server Manager, I will also try to include the Windows PowerShell equivalent.

Another advantage of Windows PowerShell is that it allows you to gain access to a file system on a computer and to access the Registry, digital certificate stores, and other data stores.

Complete Exercise 3.12 to start the Windows PowerShell utility in the Windows Server 2016 Server Core machine.

**EXERCISE 3.12**

### Starting the Windows PowerShell Utility

1. Type **`Start PowerShell`** at the Windows Server 2016 Server Core command prompt.
2. When the Windows PowerShell utility starts, type **`Help`** and press Enter. This will show you the Windows PowerShell syntax and some of the commands included in Windows PowerShell.
3. At the Windows PowerShell command prompt, type **`Get-Date`**. This will show you the system's date and time.
4. At the Windows command prompt, type **`Help *`**. This will show you all of the cmdlets you can use.
5. Close the Windows PowerShell utility by typing **`Exit`**.

# Using Server Manager

Server Manager is a very powerful MMC snap-in. If you want to install any features using a GUI interface, you will be using Server Manager. But what a lot of users don't know is that you can use Server Manager to configure and manage the features that are installed on a server.

This also includes configuring disks. The one advantage of using Server Manager is that it is included with every GUI version of Windows Server 2016. When it comes to hard disks, Server Manager allows you to manage and create disks from within the Server Manager program (see Figure 3.17).

**FIGURE 3.17** Using Server Manager

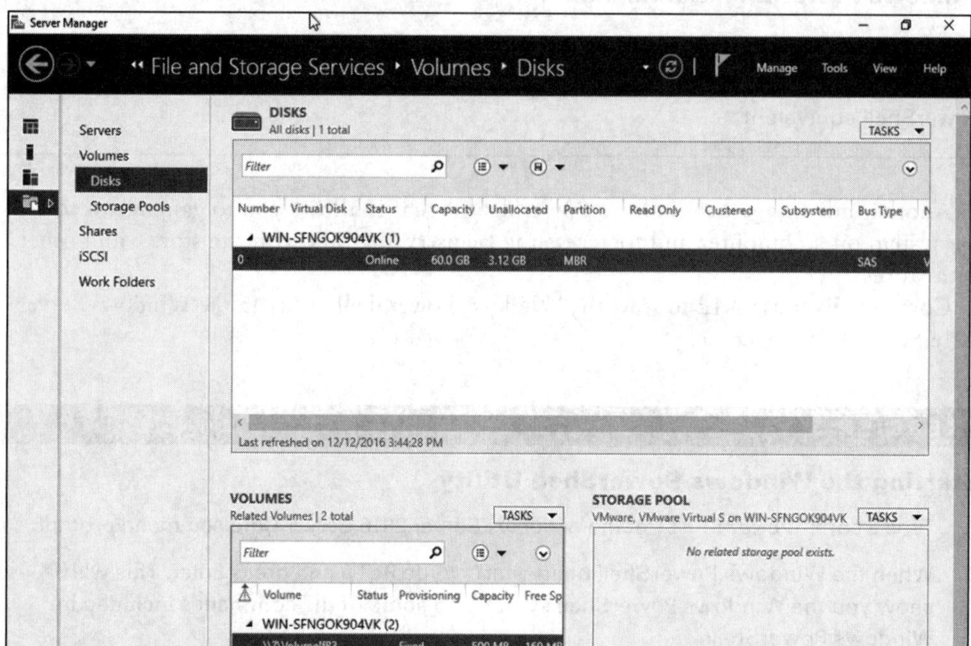


Once you are in the Server Manager application, click the File and Storage Services link on the left side. Once you are in the File and Storage Services section, you can create volumes, .vhd files, storage pools, shares, iSCSI targets, and work folders. You can also manage disk quotas from Server Manager.

One of the nice advantages of Server Manager is that you can configure and manage other Windows Servers from Server Manager. You need to add the server to Server Manager but once this is done, you can configure those servers. This is very helpful for machines that are running Server Core. If you need to install a Windows Serve without the GUI installed, you can still configure that server by using Server Manager.

## Booting from a VHD

Now that I have shown you how to create a .VHD file by using PowerShell or by using Server Manager (Disk Administrator), I need to show you how to boot a machine up using that .VHD. To do this, we will work with the Boot Configuration Data store.

The Boot Configuration Data (BCD) store contains boot information parameters that were previously found in `boot.ini` in older versions of Windows (Windows Server 2003 and previous). To edit the boot options in the BCD store, use the `bcdedit` utility, which can be launched only from a command prompt. To open a command prompt window, do the following:

1. Launch `\Windows\system32\cmd.exe`.
2. Open the Run command by pressing the Windows key plus the R key and then entering **`cmd`**.
3. Type **`cmd.exe`** in the Search Programs And Files box and press Enter.

After the command prompt window is open, type **`bcdedit`** to launch the `bcdedit` utility. You can also type **`bcdedit /?`** to see all of the different `bcdedit` commands. To boot from a VHD file, you can use the following command:

```
bcdedit /set {GUID} description="Windows 2016 VHD"
```

You can also use the `bcdboot` command to change how the Boot Configuration Data store boots from another Windows directory or VHD. So, for example, let's say that you copied the bootable VHD drive to the `V:` drive. You would then use the following command to boot from the VHD file:

```
bcdboot V:\Windows.vhd
```

# Understanding Data Deduplication

Data deduplication involves finding and removing duplicate data within the company network without compromising its integrity. The object is to store more data in less space by segmenting files into small chunks, identifying duplicate chunks, and maintaining a single copy of each chunk.

Data deduplication allows redundant copies of data chunks and then it references those multiple copies into a single copy. The data is first compressed and then the data is configured into a file system container in the System Volume Information folder.

After the data deduplication is completed, the data files will no longer be stored as independent files. The data files are replaced with markers that direct the computer system to the data blocks within the data store. Because the duplicate files are now migrated into a single data point, the data is only stored once and thus saves space on the servers.

When the files are then accessed, the data blocks are transparently re-assembled to fulfill the data request. This is all done without the users or applications having any knowledge that the data has been transformed into a single spot. This is a nice advantage to administrators because they do not have to worry that the data will be impacted in any negative way by using data deduplication.

To enable data deduplication, you enable a volume for duplication and then the data is automatically optimized. After this happens, the volume will contain the following:

**Optimized Files** The volume will contain files that are optimized, and that means that these files will have pointers to map the data to its respective areas of the chunk store.

**Unoptimized files** Some files will not meet the standards for data deduplication. These files will remain as Unoptimized files. For example, encrypted files are not eligible to be optimized. So these encrypted files will remain Unoptimized on the volume.

**Chunk Store** This is the location that the data duplicated files will be stored and optimized.

**Free Space** Because data files are optimized and require less space, your volumes will have additional free space that the administrator can use for users or applications.

## Backup and Restoring Deduplicated Volumes

One issue that every administrator has faced in their career has to do with how we are going to protect our data by using backups. Backups are a million dollar industry because every backup company knows the importance of protecting your data. Well the issue that we, as IT administrators, deal with is backup space.

This is where data deduplication can help us out. Because the files are optimized, the files will require less space used on backups. This doesn't matter if its cloud-based or tape-based backups. The backups will use less space and this in turn will allow us to retain the data longer without requiring more space. Also, because the data is optimized (thus being smaller), the backups will be quicker, and if any restores are needed, they will also be faster.

Any backup system that uses block-based backup applications should work without any modifications to the backup systems. File-based backups may be an issue because file-based backups normally copy the files in their original data form. If you are using file-based backups, you must have enough backup space available to handle the files in their original form.

If your organization is using the Windows Server 2016 backup software, your backups will have the ability to back up the files as optimized files and no other changes will be needed. Since most of us don't use Windows backup, make sure your backup can handle data deduplication if you are planning on using it.

If you decide to use Windows backup, the following steps will help you backup and restore data duplicated files.

1. You will need to install Windows Server Backup on the machines running data deduplication. This can be done through Server Manager or by running the following PowerShell command:

   ```
   Add-WindowsFeature -name Windows-Server-Backup
   ```

2. Administrators can then run a backup by using the following PowerShell command (this command is backing up the E: volume to the F: drive):

   ```
   wbadmin start backup -include:E: -backuptarget:F:
   ```

3. You will then want to get the version ID of the backup you just created. You can do this by running the following command:

   ```
   wbadmin get versions
   ```

4. After you run the wbadmin get version command, you will be given the date and time of the backup. This will be needed if you are going to do a restore. The following is an example of the output: 04/24/2017-14:30. To restore the volume you would run the following command:

   ```
   Wbadmin start recovery -version:04/24/2017-14:30 -itemtype:
   Volume  -items:E: -recoveryTarget:E:
   ```

   To restore just a part of a volume or folder, you would run the following command (for example, the `E:\WPanek` folder):

   ```
   Wbadmin start recovery -version:04/24/2017-14:30 -itemtype:
   File  -items:E:\WPanek  -recursive
   ```

## Installing and Enabling Data Deduplication

To install data deduplication, there are two ways to do the install. You can install data deduplication through Server Manager or through PowerShell. Let's take a look at each way.

To install data deduplication by using Server Manager:

1. On the Windows Server 2016 system, open Server Manager.
2. Click the Add Roles and Features link.
3. At the Before You Begin screen, click Next.
4. At the Select Installation Type screen, choose Role-based or feature-based installation and then click Next.
5. Choose the server where you want to install Data Deduplication and click Next.
6. On the Select Server Roles screen, select File And Storage Services ➢ File And iSCSI Services and then select the Data Deduplication check box (shown in Figure 3.18). Click Next.
7. Click Next on the Selected Features screen.
8. Then click the Install button once you confirmed that all options are correct.
9. Once completed, close Server Manager.

To install data deduplication by using PowerShell:

1. Click the Start button, then right-click Windows PowerShell ➢ More ➢ Run As Administrator.
2. In the Windows PowerShell console, enter the following commands (one at a time) followed by the Enter key:
    1. `Import-Module ServerManager`
    2. `Add-WindowsFeature -name FS-Data-Deduplication`
    3. `Import-Module Deduplication`

**FIGURE 3.18** Selecting Data Deduplication

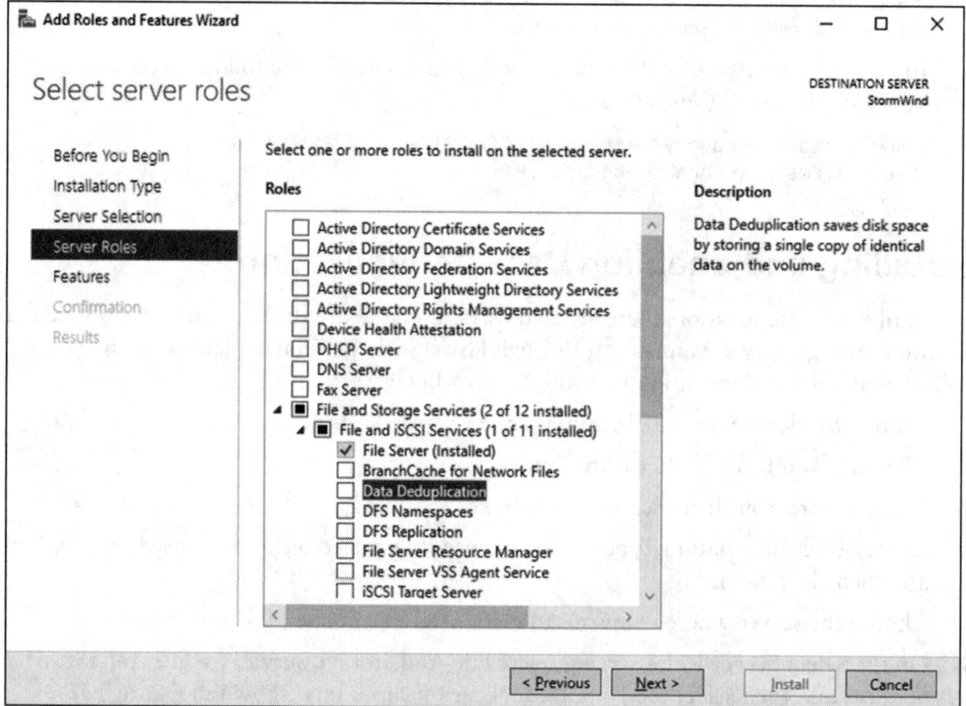


After you have installed data deduplication, you must then enable it on the servers. To enable data deduplication in Server Manager, you would need to complete the following steps:

1. In Server Manager, click File And Storage Services.

2. Click Volumes. On the right side, click the volume on which you want to set up Data Deduplication. Right-click the volume and choose Configure Data Deduplication (see Figure 3.19).

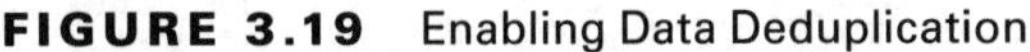

**FIGURE 3.19** Enabling Data Deduplication

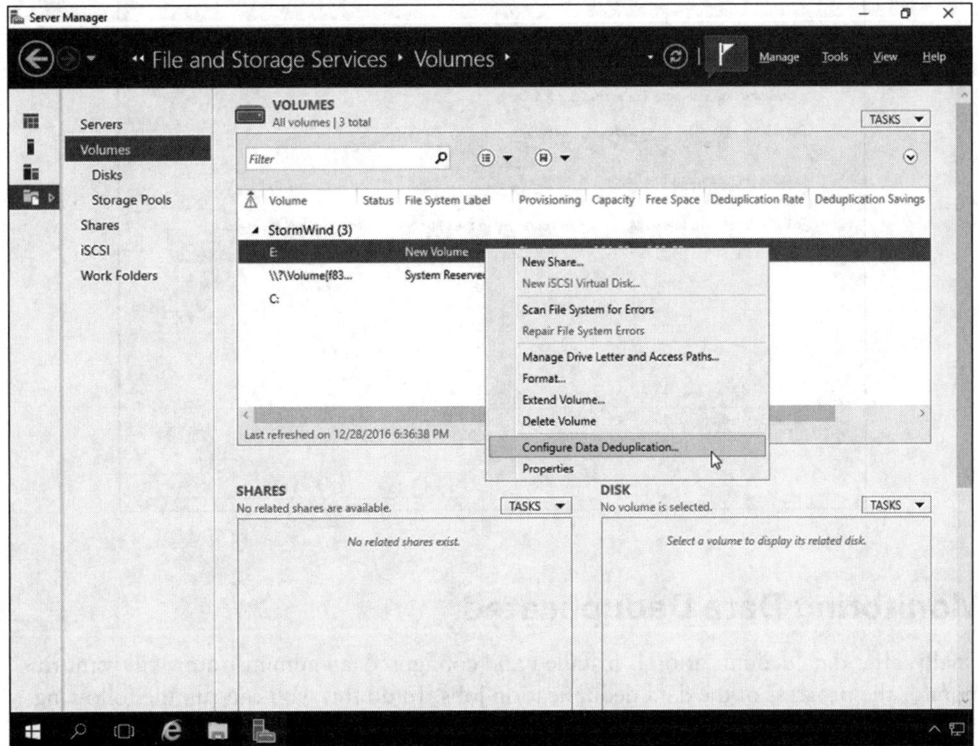


3. The New Volume Deduplication Settings Wizard will start. Under the Data Deduplication pulldown, choose General Purpose File Server (shown in Figure 3.20). Enter the number of days that should elapse from the date of file creation until files are duplicated (I used 3 days), enter the extensions of any file types that should not be duplicated (I used `.exe`), and then click Add to browse to any folders with files that should not be duplicated (I included \test share). Click OK once completed. You can also set a Deduplication Schedule by clicking the Set Deduplication Schedule button.

**FIGURE 3.20** Data Deduplication setup

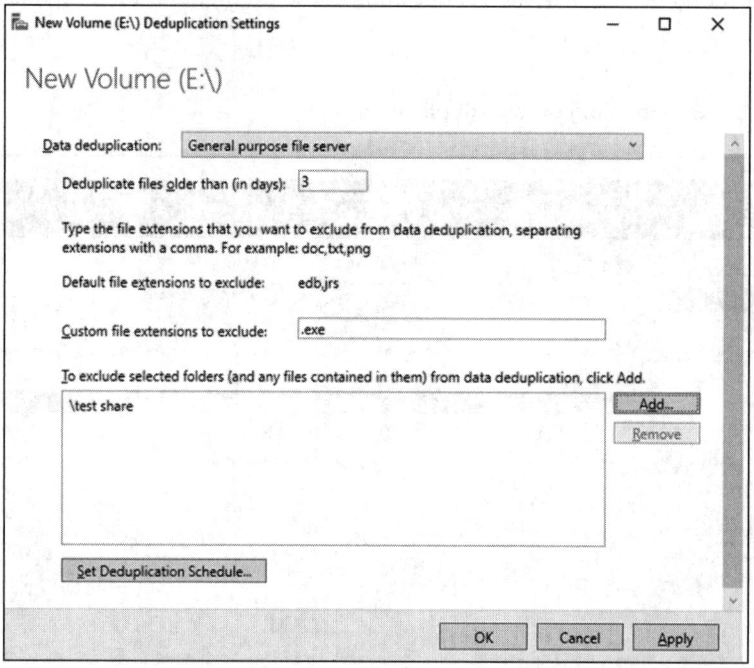

## Monitoring Data Deduplicated

Finally, after data deduplication is installed and configured, an administrator will want to monitor the progress of the data deduplication jobs. To do this, you can run the following PowerShell commands (this command will show you the status of the deduplication process):

```
Get-DedupStatus
Get-DedupVolume
```

# Summary

In this chapter, I discussed file servers and how they can be effective on your network. I also discussed sharing folders for users to access, and then I discussed how to publish those shared folders to Active Directory.

You learned about NTFS security versus shared folder permissions and how to limit users' hard drive space by setting up disk quotas. The chapter also covered the Encrypting File System (EFS) and how users can encrypt and compress files.

I also discussed how configuring file and storage solutions can be highly effective within your organization. You now have a better understanding of how Windows Server 2016 can provide you with extended functionality for effectively controlling corporate data.

Finally, I finished the chapter by talking about data deduplication and how data deduplication can help protect your corporate data and also provide a company with a backup solution.

# Video Resources

There are videos available for the following exercises:

3.3

3.6

3.12

You can access the videos at `http://sybextestbanks.wiley.com` on the Other Study Tools tab.

# Exam Essentials

**Know storage technologies.** Understand how to use the Fibre Channel, iSCSI, and NAS storage technologies. Know how to configure an iSCSI initiator and how to establish a connection to a target. Practice configuring tiered storage and using thin provisioning and trim.

**Know how to configure NTFS security.** One of the major advantages of using NTFS over FAT32 is access to additional security features. NTFS allows you to put security at the file and folder layers. NTFS security is in effect whether the user is remote or local to the computer with the data.

**Know how to configure shared permissions.** Shared permissions allow you to determine the access a user will receive when connecting to a shared folder. Shared permissions are allowed only at the folder layer and are in effect only when the user is remote to the computer with the shared data.

**Understand how NTFS and shared permissions work together.** NTFS and shared permissions are individually additive—you get the highest level of security and permissions within each type. NTFS is always in effect, and it is the only security available locally. Shared permissions are in effect only when connecting remotely to access the shared data. When the two types of permissions meet, the most restrictive set of permissions applies.

**Know how to configure disk quotas.** Disk quotas allow an organization to determine the amount of disk space that users can have on a volume of a server. An administrator can set up disk quotas based on volumes or by users. Each volume must have its own separate set of disk quotas.

**Understand Windows PowerShell.** Understanding Windows PowerShell is not only important for the exam, it will also allow you to configure Server Core more efficiently. Windows PowerShell is a command-line utility that allows you run single cmdlets as well as run complex tasks to exploit the full power from PowerShell.

**Understand data deduplication.** Understand that data deduplication involves finding and removing duplicate data within the company network without compromising its integrity. Understand that the goal is to store more data in less space by segmenting files into small chunks, identifying duplicate chunks, and maintaining a single copy of each chunk.

# Review Questions

1. What is the default TCP port for iSCSI?
   - **A.** 3260
   - **B.** 1433
   - **C.** 21
   - **D.** 3389
2. You have a Windows Server 2016 Hyper-V host named Jupiter. You want to deploy several shielded virtual machines on Jupiter. You deploy a Host Guardian on a new server. You need to view the process of the shielded virtual machines installation. What should you run to see the progress of the shielded VM?
   - **A.** `Get-ShieldedVMProvisioningStatus` cmdlet
   - **B.** the `Diskpart` command
   - **C.** the `Set-VHD` cmdlet
   - **D.** the `Set-VM` cmdlet
3. You are the administrator of a mid-size network. You have a Hyper-V host that runs Windows Server 2016. The host contains a virtual machine named Virtual1. Virtual1 has resource metering enabled. You need to use resource metering to track the amount of network traffic that Virtual1 sends to the 10.10.16.0/20 network. Which command would you run?
   - **A.** `Add-VMNetworkAdapteiAd`
   - **B.** `Set-VMNetworkAdapter`
   - **C.** `New-VMResourcePool`
   - **D.** `Set-VMNetworkAdapterRoutingDomamMapping`
4. You are the administrator for an organization that has started using Hyper-V. You have a Hyper-V host named Server1 that runs Windows Server 2016. Server1 contains a virtual machine named Earth. You need to make sure that you can use nested virtualization on Earth. What should you run on Server1?
   - **A.** The `Mount-VHD` cmdlet
   - **B.** The `DiskPart` command
   - **C.** The `Set-VMProcessor` cmdlet
   - **D.** The `Set-VM` cmdlet
5. You need to ensure that VM1 and VM2 can communicate with each other only. The solution must prevent VM1 and VM2 from communicating with Server1. Which cmdlet should you use?
   - **A.** `Set-NetNeighbor`
   - **B.** `Remove-VMSwitchTeamMember`
   - **C.** `Set-VMSwitch`
   - **D.** `Enable-VMSwitchExtension`

6. You are the admin for a mid-size company. You have a Hyper-V host named Server1 that runs Windows Server 2016. Server1 has a dynamically expanding virtual hard disk (VHD) file that is 950 GB. The VHD currently contains around 450 GB of free space. You want to reduce the amount of disk space used by the VHD. What command should you run?

   A. The `Mount-VHD` cmdlet

   B. The `DiskPart` command

   C. The `Set-VHD` cmdlet

   D. The `Optimize-VHD` cmdlet

7. You have a Nano Server named Nano1. Which cmdlet should you use to identify whether the DNS Server role is installed on Nano1?

   A. `Find-ServerPackage`

   B. `Get-Package`

   C. `Find-Package`

   D. `Get-WindowsOptionalFeature`

8. You are working on a Windows Server 2016 Datacenter Server system. You need to view which roles and services are installed on the machine. Which PowerShell cmdlet can you use to see this?

   A. `Get-event`

   B. `New-event`

   C. `Trace-command`

   D. `Get-WindowsFeature`

9. What command would be used to register an iSCSI initiator manually to an iSNS server?

   A. `iscsicli refreshisnsserver server_name`

   B. `iscsicli listisnsservers server_name`

   C. `iscsicli removeisnsserver server_name`

   D. `iscsicli addisnsserver server_name`

10. You are an administrator who has set up two Hyper-V servers named Server1 (Windows Server 2016) and Server2 (Windows Server 2012 R2). Each Hyper-V server has multiple network cards. Each network card is connected to a different TCP/IP subnet. Server1 contains a dedicated migration network. Server2 contains a virtual machine named VM1. You plan to perform a live migration of VM1 to Server1. You need to ensure that Server1 uses all of the available networks to perform the live migration of VM1. What should you run to complete this task?

    A. The `Mount-VHD` cmdlet

    B. The `DiskPart` command

    C. The `Set-VHD` cmdlet

    D. The `Set-VMHost` cmdlet

# Understanding Hyper-V

## THE FOLLOWING 70-740 EXAM OBJECTIVES ARE COVERED IN THIS CHAPTER:

✓ **Install and configure Hyper-V**

- This objective may include but is not limited to: Determine hardware and compatibility requirements for installing Hyper-V; install Hyper-V; install management tools; upgrade from existing versions of Hyper-V; delegate virtual machine management; perform remote management of Hyper-V hosts; configure virtual machines using Windows PowerShell Direct; implement nested virtualization.

✓ **Configure virtual machine (VM) settings**

- This objective may include but is not limited to: Add or remove memory in running a VM; configure dynamic memory; configure Non-Uniform Memory Access (NUMA) support; configure smart paging; configure Resource Metering; manage Integration Services; create and configure Generation 1 and 2 VMs and determine appropriate usage scenarios; implement enhanced session mode; create Linux and FreeBSD VMs; install and configure Linux Integration Services (LIS); install and configure FreeBSD Integration Services (BIS); implement Secure Boot for Windows and Linux environments; move and convert VMs from previous versions of Hyper-V to Windows Server 2016 Hyper-V; export and import VMs; implement Discrete Device Assignment (DDA).

✓ **Configure Hyper-V storage**

- This objective may include but is not limited to: Create VHDs and VHDX files using Hyper-V Manager; create shared VHDX files; configure differencing disks; modify virtual hard disks; configure pass-through disks; resize a virtual hard disk; manage checkpoints; implement production checkpoints; implement a virtual Fibre Channel adapter; configure storage Quality of Service (QoS).

✓ **Configure Hyper-V networking**

- This objective may include but is not limited to: Add and remove virtual network interface cards (vNICs); configure Hyper-V virtual switches; optimize network performance; configure MAC addresses; configure network isolation; configure synthetic and legacy virtual network adapters; configure NIC teaming in VMs; configure virtual machine queue (VMQ); enable Remote Direct Memory Access (RDMA) on network adapters bound to a Hyper-V virtual switch using Switch Embedded Teaming (SET); configure Bandwidth Management.

One of the greatest improvements to Microsoft's servers over the past few versions is its implementation of their Virtual Server called Hyper-V.

*Hyper-V* is a server role in Windows Server 2016 that allows you to virtualize your environment and therefore run multiple virtual operating system instances simultaneously on a physical server. This not only helps you to improve server utilization but also helps you to create a more cost-effective and dynamic system.

Hyper-V allows an organization of any size to act and compete with other organizations of any size. A small company can buy a single server and then virtualize that server into multiple servers. Hyper-V gives a small company the ability to run multiple servers on a single box and compete with a company of any size.

For the large organizations, an administrator can consolidate multiple servers onto Hyper-V servers thus saving an organization time and money by using less physical boxes but still having all the servers needed to run the business.

In this chapter, you will learn the basic concepts and features of Hyper-V that a Windows Server 2016 technical specialist must know. You will also get a solid understanding of what is important in virtualization and in what areas of your work life you can use it.

# Hyper-V Overview

In the following sections, I'll introduce you to Hyper-V. To begin, you'll take a look at virtualization and what types of virtualization exist. I will then discuss Hyper-V features and the Hyper-V architecture before finishing up with the Hyper-V requirements for software and hardware.

## What Is Virtualization?

*Virtualization* is a method for abstracting physical resources from the way that they interact with other resources. For example, if you abstract the physical hardware from the operating system, you get the benefit of being able to move the operating system between different physical systems.

This is called *server virtualization*. But there are also other forms of virtualization available, such as presentation virtualization, desktop virtualization, and application virtualization. I will now briefly explain the differences between these forms of virtualization:

**Server Virtualization** This basically enables multiple servers to run on the same physical server. Hyper-V is a server virtualization tool that allows you to move physical machines to virtual machines and manage them on a few physical servers. Thus, you will be able to consolidate physical servers.

**Presentation Virtualization** When you use *presentation virtualization*, your applications run on a different computer, and only the screen information is transferred to your computer. An example of presentation virtualization is Microsoft Remote Desktop Services in Windows Server 2016.

**Desktop Virtualization** *Desktop virtualization* provides you with a virtual machine on your desktop, comparable to server virtualization. You run your complete operating system and applications in a virtual machine so that your local physical machine just needs to run a very basic operating system. An example of this form of virtualization is Microsoft Virtual PC.

**Application Virtualization** *Application virtualization* helps prevent conflicts between applications on the same PC. Thus, it helps you to isolate the application running environment from the operating system installation requirements by creating application-specific copies of all shared resources. It also helps reduce application-to-application incompatibility and testing needs. An example of an application virtualization tool is Microsoft Application Virtualization (App-V).

# Hyper-V Features

As a lead-in to the virtualization topic and Hyper-V, I will start with a list of key features, followed by a list of supported guest operating systems. This should provide you with a quick, high-level view of this feature before you dig deeper into the technology.

## Key Features of Hyper-V

The following are just some of the key features of Hyper-V:

The following features are just some of the new and improved features for Windows Server 2016 Hyper-V. To see a complete list of features, please visit Microsoft's website at:

`https://technet.microsoft.com/en-us/windows-server-docs/compute/hyper-v/what-s-new-in-hyper-v-on-windows?f=255&MSPPError=-2147217396`

**Architecture** The hypervisor-based architecture, which has a 64-bit micro-kernel, provides a new array of device support as well as performance and security improvements.

**Operating System Support** Both 32-bit and 64-bit operating systems can run simultaneously in Hyper-V. Also, different platforms like Windows, Linux, and others are supported.

**Support for Symmetric Multiprocessors** Support for up to 64 processors in a virtual machine environment provides you with the ability to run applications as well as multiple virtual machines faster.

**Compatible with Connected Standby** If an administrator installs the Hyper-V role on a computer that has the Always On/Always Connected (AOAC) power model configured, the

Connected Standby power state is now available. The Connected Standby power state is a low-power state that allows Windows to function more like a tablet than a PC.

**Encryption Support for Generation 1 VMs** Administrators now have the ability to encrypt the operating system disk in generation 1 virtual machines by using BitLocker drive encryption. This is possible because of a new Hyper-V feature called key storage. Key storage creates a small, dedicated drive to store the system drive's BitLocker key. When you want to decrypt the disk and start the virtual machine, the Hyper-V host will need to be either a part of an authorized guarded fabric or use a private key from one of the virtual machine's guardians. Version 8 virtual machines must be used for key storage to function properly.

**Host Resource Protection** Administrators can enable this feature to ensure that a virtual machine does not use more than its share of the host machine's system resources. Enabling this feature ensures that no one virtual machine can cause a performance issue on the host or on any other virtual machines. This feature is off by default. To enable this feature, an administrator will need to run the following Windows PowerShell command:

```
Set-VMProcessor -EnableHostResourceProtection $true
```

**Network Load Balancing** Hyper-V provides support for *Windows Network Load Balancing (NLB)* to balance the network load across virtual machines on different servers.

**Hardware Architecture** Hyper-V's architecture provides improved utilization of resources such as networking, memory, and disks.

**Quick Migration** Hyper-V's *quick migration* feature provides you with the functionality to run virtual machines in a clustered environment with switchover capabilities when there is a failure. Thus, you can reduce downtime and achieve higher availability of your virtual machines.

**Virtual Machine Checkpoint** You can take checkpoints of running virtual machines, which provides you with the capability to recover to any previous virtual machine checkpoint state quickly and easily.

**Resource Metering** Hyper-V *resource metering* allows an organization to track usage within the businesses departments. It allows an organization to create a usage-based billing solution that adjusts to the provider's business model and strategy.

**Scripting** Using the Windows Management Instrumentation (WMI) interfaces and APIs, you can easily build custom scripts to automate processes in your virtual machines.

**RemoteFX** Windows Server 2016 Hyper-V RemoteFX allows for an enhanced user experience for RemoteFX desktops by providing a 3D virtual adapter, intelligent codecs, and the ability to redirect USB devices in virtual machines.

**Fibre Channel** The virtual Fibre Channel feature allows you to connect to the Fibre Channel storage unit from within the virtual machine. *Virtual Fibre Channel* allows an administrator to use their existing Fibre Channel to support virtualized workloads. Hyper-V users have the ability to use Fibre Channel storage area networks (SANs) to virtualize the workloads that require direct access to SAN logical unit numbers (LUNs).

**Enhanced Session Mode** *Enhanced Session Mode* enhances the interactive session of the Virtual Machine Connection for Hyper-V administrators who want to connect to their virtual machines. It gives administrators the same functionality as a remote desktop connection when the administrator is interacting with a virtual machine.

In previous versions of Hyper-V, the virtual machine connection gave you limited functionality while you connected to the virtual machine screen, keyboard, and mouse. An administrator could use an RDP connection to get full redirection abilities, but that would require a network connection to the virtual machine host.

Enhanced Session Mode gives administrators the following benefits for local resource redirection:

- Display configuration
- Audio
- Printers
- Clipboard
- Smart cards
- Drives
- USB devices
- Supported Plug and Play devices

**Shared Virtual Hard Disk** Windows Server 2016 Hyper-V has a feature called Shared Virtual Hard Disk. *Shared Virtual Hard Disk* allows an administrator to cluster virtual machines by using Shared Virtual Hard Disk (VHDX) files.

Shared virtual hard disks allow an administrator to build a high availability infrastructure, which is important if you are setting up either a private cloud deployment or a cloud-hosted environment for managing large workloads. Shared virtual hard disks allow two or more virtual machines to access the same virtual hard disk (VHDX) file.

**Automatic Virtual Machine Activation (AVMA)** *Automatic Virtual Machine Activation (AVMA)* is a feature that allows administrators to install virtual machines on a properly activated Windows Server 2016 system without the need to manage individual product keys for each virtual machine. When using AVMA, virtual machines get bound to the licensed Hyper-V server as soon as the virtual machine starts.

**Network Isolation** One nice feature of using Microsoft Hyper-V network virtualization is the ability of Hyper-V to keep virtual networks isolated from the physical network infrastructure of the hosted system. Because administrators can set up Hyper-V software–defined virtualization policies, you are no longer limited by the IP address assignment or VLAN isolation requirements of the physical network. Hyper-V allows for built-in network isolation to keep the virtual network separated from the virtual network.

**Discrete Device Assignment** One feature of Windows Server 2016 is the ability to use Discrete Device Assignment (DDA). DDA allows an administrator to take full advantage of performance and application compatibility improvements in the user experience by allowing the system's graphic cards to be directly assigned to a virtual machine. This allows the graphic card processor to be fully available to the virtual desktops that are utilizing the native driver of the graphics card processor.

**Non-Uniform Memory Access** Non-Uniform Memory Access (NUMA) is a multiprocessor memory architecture that allows a processor to access its local memory quicker than memory located on another processor. NUMA allows a system to access memory quickly by providing separate memory on each processor. Processor can access their local assigned memory thus speeding the system performance. Normally a multi-processor system runs into performance issues when multiple processors access the same memory at the same time. NUMA helps prevent this by allowing processors to access their own memory. Memory that is dedicated to a processor is referred to as a NUMA node.

**Dynamic Memory** *Dynamic Memory* is a feature of Hyper-V that allows it to balance memory automatically among running virtual machines. Dynamic Memory allows Hyper-V to adjust the amount of memory available to the virtual machines in response to the needs of the virtual machines. It is currently available for Hyper-V in Windows Server 2016.

**Virtual Machine Queue** Windows Server 2016 Hyper-V includes a feature called Virtual machine queue (VMQ) as long as the hardware is VMQ compatible network hardware. VMQ uses packet filtering to provide data from an external virtual machine network directly to virtual machines. This helps reduce the overhead of routing packets from the management operating system to the virtual machine.

Once VMQ is enabled on Hyper-V, a dedicated queue is created on the physical network adapter for each virtual network adapter to use. When data arrives for the virtual network adapter, the physical network adapter places that data in a queue and once the system is available, all of the data in the queue is delivered to the virtual network adapter.

To enable the virtual machine queue on a specific virtual machine, enter the settings for the virtual machine and expand Network Adapter. Click Hardware Acceleration and on the right hand window, check the box for Enable virtual machine queue.

**Hyper-V Nesting** Windows Server 2016 has introduced a new feature of Hyper-V called Hyper-V nesting. Hyper-V nesting allows you to run a virtual machine in a virtual machine. So let's say that you build a new 2016 Hyper-V server. You install Windows Server 2016 into a virtual machine. Then in that virtual machine, you can install Hyper-V and build other virtual machines within the first virtual machine. This is new to Windows Server 2016 and can be very useful in training situations. You can install a Windows Server 2016 virtual machine and still show others how to install and create virtual machines in the original virtual machine. To enable Hyper-V nesting, you would run the following PowerShell command on the Hyper-V Host. The virtual machines must be in the OFF State when this command is run (this means the virtual machines must be turned off):

```
Set-VMProcessor -VMName <VMName> -ExposeVirtualizationExtensions $true
```

## Supported Guest Operating Systems

The following guest operating systems have been successfully tested on Hyper-V and are hypervisor-aware. Table 4.1 shows all of the guest server operating systems and the maximum number of virtual processors. Table 4.2 shows all of the guest client operating systems and the maximum number of virtual processors.

**TABLE 4.1** Hyper-V guest server operating systems

| Guest Operating System (Server) | Maximum Number of Virtual Processors |
|---|---|
| Windows Server 2016 | 64 |
| Windows Server 2012 and Server 2012 R2 | 64 |
| Windows Server 2008 R2 with Service Pack 1 (SP1) | 64 |
| Windows Server 2008 R2 | 64 |
| Windows Server 2008 with Service Pack 2 (SP2) | 8 |
| Windows Home Server 2011 | 4 |
| Windows Small Business Server 2011 | Essentials edition: 2<br>Standard edition: 4 |
| Windows Server 2003 R2 with Service Pack 2 (SP2) | 2 |
| Windows Server 2003 with Service Pack 2 (SP2) | 2 |
| Red Hat Enterprise Linux 5.7 and 5.8 | 64 |
| Red Hat Enterprise Linux 6.0–6.3 | 64 |
| SUSE Linux Enterprise Server 11 SP2 | 64 |
| Open SUSE 12.1 | 64 |
| Ubuntu 12.04 | 64 |

**TABLE 4.2** Hyper-V guest client operating systems

| Guest Operating System (Client) | Maximum Number of Virtual Processors |
|---|---|
| Windows 10 | 32 |
| Windows 8 / 8.1 | 32 |
| Windows 7 with Service Pack 1 (SP1) | 4 |
| Windows 7 | 4 |
| Windows Vista with Service Pack 2 (SP2) | 2 |
| Windows XP with Service Pack 3 (SP3) | 2 |
| Windows XP x64 Edition with Service Pack 2 (SP2) | 2 |
| CentOS 5.7 and 5.8 | 64 |
| CentOS 6.0–6.3 | 64 |
| Red Hat Enterprise Linux 5.7 and 5.8 | 64 |
| Red Hat Enterprise Linux 6.0–6.3 | 64 |
| SUSE Linux Enterprise Server 11 SP2 | 64 |
| Open SUSE 12.1 | 64 |
| Ubuntu 12.04 | 64 |

The list of supported guest operating systems may always be extended. Please check the official Microsoft Hyper-V site to obtain a current list of supported operating systems: `www.microsoft.com/virtualization`.

## Hyper-V Architecture

This section will provide you with an overview of the Hyper-V architecture (see Figure 4.1). I'll explain the differences between a hypervisor-aware and a non-hypervisor-aware child partition.

**FIGURE 4.1** Hyper-V architecture

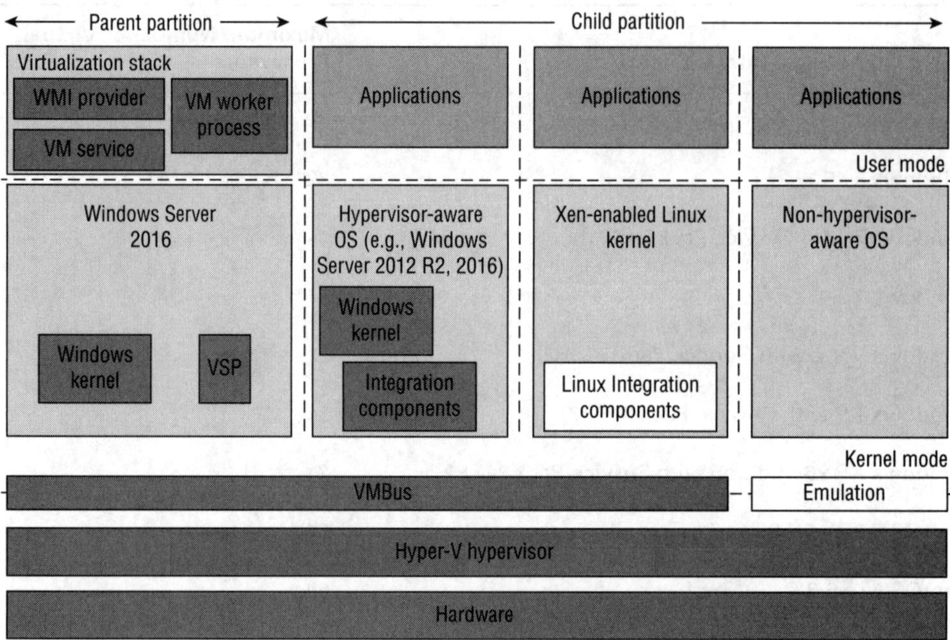


As you can see, Hyper-V is based on the microkernel architecture. Hyper-V provides a virtualization layer called a *hypervisor* that runs directly on the system hardware. You can see that the hypervisor is similar to what the kernel is to Windows. It is a software layer responsible for the interaction with the core hardware and works in conjunction with an optimized instance of Windows Server 2016 that allows running multiple operating systems on a physical server simultaneously. The Hyper-V architecture consists of the hypervisor and parent and child partitions.

The Windows Server 2016 operating system runs in the parent partition, and it delivers the WMI provider for scripting as well as the VM service.

Virtual machines each run in their own child partitions. Child partitions do not have direct access to hardware resources; instead, they have a virtual view of the resources, which are called *virtual devices*.

If you're running a hypervisor-aware operating system like Windows Server 2003, Windows Server 2008, Windows Server 2008 R2, Windows Server 2012, or Windows Server 2016 in your virtual machine, any request to the virtual devices is redirected via the high-speed bus to the devices in the parent partition, which will manage the requests.

By default, only Windows Server 2008 R2, Server 2012, and Server 2012 R2 are hypervisor-aware operating systems. Once you install Hyper-V Integration Components on an operating system other than Windows Server 2008 R2 and newer, it will be hypervisor-aware. Microsoft provides a hypervisor adapter to make Linux hypervisor aware.

Non-hypervisor-aware operating systems (for example, Windows NT 4.0) use an emulator to communicate with the Windows hypervisor, which is slower than molasses in the winter.

## Hyper-V Requirements

The following sections will describe the hardware and software requirements for installing the Hyper-V server role. It is important to understand these requirements for obtaining your software license as well as for planning for server hardware. When you understand the requirements, you can design and configure a Hyper-V solution that will meet the needs of your applications.

### Hardware Requirements

In addition to the basic hardware requirements for Windows Server 2016, there are requirements for running the Hyper-V server role on your Windows server. They are listed in Table 4.3.

**TABLE 4.3** Hardware requirements for Hyper-V

| Requirement Area | Definition |
|---|---|
| CPU | x64-compatible processor with Intel VT or AMD-V technology enabled. Hardware Data Execution Prevention (DEP), specifically Intel XD bit (execute disable bit) or AMD NX bit (no execute bit), must be available and enabled. Minimum: 1.4 GHz. Recommended: 2 GHz or faster. |
| Memory | Minimum: 1 GB RAM. Recommended: 2 GB RAM or greater. (Additional RAM is required for each running guest operating system.) Maximum: 1 TB. |
| Hard disk | Minimum: 8 GB. Recommended: 20 GB or greater. (Additional disk space needed for each guest operating system.) |

The Add Roles Wizard in Server Manager additionally verifies the hardware requirements. A good starting point is to check your hardware against the Microsoft hardware list to make sure that Windows Server 2016 supports your hardware. If you try to install the Hyper-V server role on a computer that does not meet the CPU requirements, you'll get a warning window that looks like Figure 4.2.

**FIGURE 4.2** Warning window that Hyper-V cannot be installed

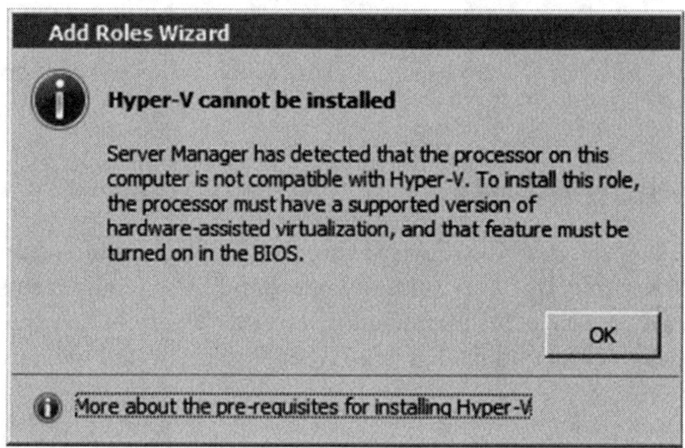


### Software Requirements

To use virtualization in Windows Server 2016, you need to consider the basic software requirements for Hyper-V. Hyper-V runs only on the following editions of the Windows Server 2016 operating system:

- Windows Server 2016 Standard edition
- Windows Server 2016 Datacenter edition
- Microsoft Hyper-V Server 2012 R2 edition
- Windows Server 2016 Hyper-V edition

# Hyper-V Installation and Configuration

The following sections explain how to install the Hyper-V role using Server Manager in Windows Server 2016 Full installation mode or the command-line mode in Windows Server 2016 Server Core. We will then take a look at Hyper-V as part of Server Manager before discussing how to use the Hyper-V Manager. Finally, we will look at the Hyper-V server settings and then cover two important areas for Hyper-V: virtual networks and virtual hard disks.

## Install the Hyper-V Role

Now it's time to see how to install the Hyper-V server role on the two installation options of Windows Server 2016, namely, a Full installation and a Server Core installation.

### Installing Hyper-V in Full Installation Mode

You can install the Hyper-V server role on any Windows Server 2016 installation for which the Full option was chosen. In addition, the server must meet both the hardware and software requirements. The installation process is simple, as Exercise 4.1 demonstrates.

**EXERCISE 4.1**

### Installing Hyper-V in Full Installation Mode

1. Open Server Manager.
2. In Server Manager, choose option 2, Add Roles And Features.
3. At the Select Installation Type page, choose the role-based or feature-based installation. Click Next.
4. On the Select Destination Server screen, choose Select A Server From The Server Pool and choose the server to which you want to add this role. Click Next.
5. On the Select Server Roles screen, click the check box next to Hyper-V (see Figure 4.3). When the Add Features dialog box appears, click the Add Features button. Then click Next.

**FIGURE 4.3** Server Manager Add Features

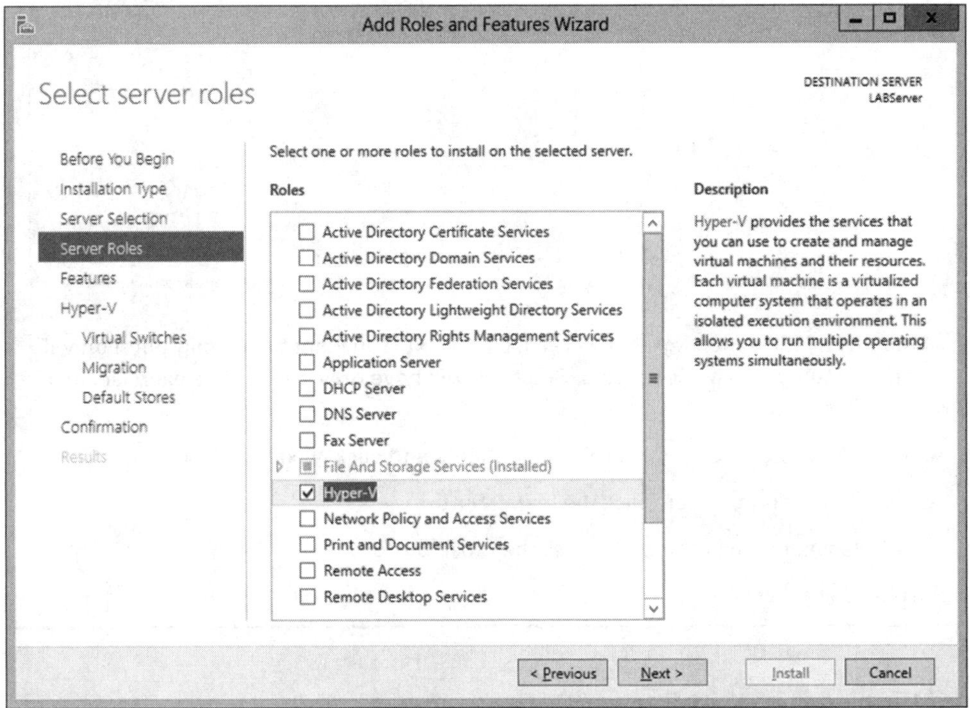


6. At the Select Features screen, click Next.
7. At the Hyper-V introduction screen, click Next.
8. At the Create Virtual Switches screen, choose your adapter and click Next (see Figure 4.4).

**EXERCISE 4.1 (continued)**

**FIGURE 4.4** Virtual switch screen

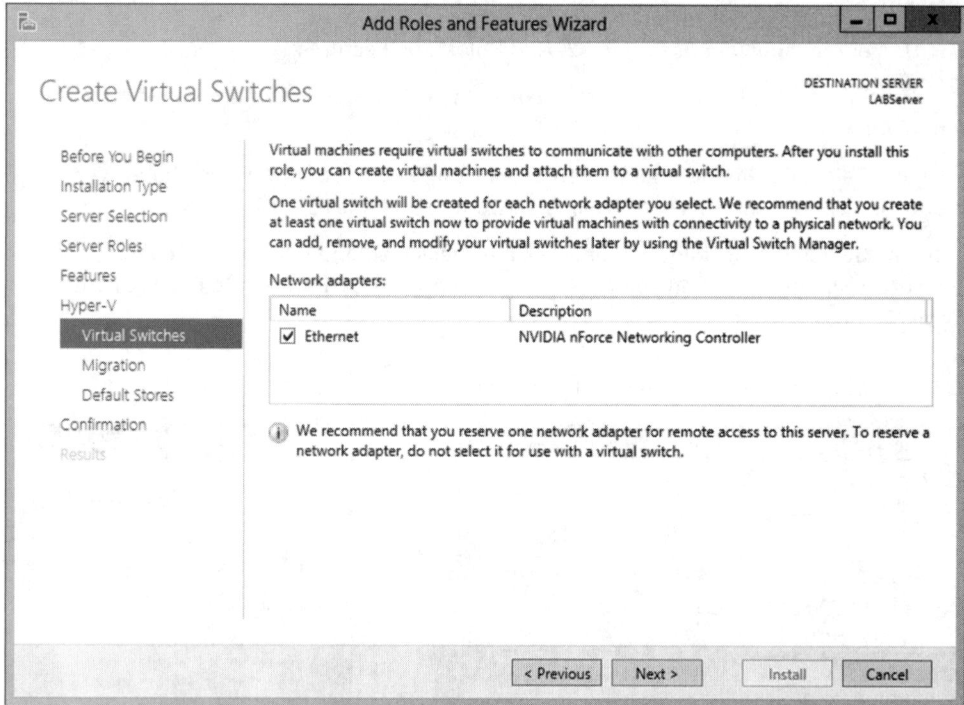


9. At the Virtual Machine Migration screen, click Next. You want to use migration only if you have multiple Hyper-V servers. Since we will have only one for this exercise, just skip this screen.
10. At the Default Stores screen, accept the defaults and click Next.
11. At the Confirmation screen, click the Install button.
12. After the installation is complete, click the Close button.
13. Restart your server.

## Installing Hyper-V in Server Core

The Server Core installation option is introduced in Windows Server 2008. It creates an operating system installation without a GUI shell. You can either manage the server remotely from another system or use the Server Core's command-line interface.

This installation option provides the following benefits:

- Reduces attack surface (because fewer applications are running on the server)
- Reduces maintenance and management (because only the required options are installed)

- Requires less disk space and produces less processor utilization
- Provides a minimal parent partition
- Reduces system resources required by the operating system as well as the attack surface

By using Hyper-V on a Server Core installation, you can fundamentally improve availability because the attack surface is reduced and the downtime required for installing patches is optimized. It will thus be more secure and reliable with less management.

To install Hyper-V for a Windows Server 2016 installation, you must execute the following command in the command-line interface:

```
Dism /online /enable-feature /featurename:Microsoft-Hyper-V
```

## Hyper-V in Server Manager

As with all of the other Windows Server 2016 roles, the Hyper-V role neatly integrates into Server Manager. Server Manager filters the information just for the specific role and thus displays only the required information. As you can see in Figure 4.5, the Hyper-V Summary page shows related event log entries, the state of the system services for Hyper-V, and useful resources and support.

**FIGURE 4.5** Hyper-V in Server Manager

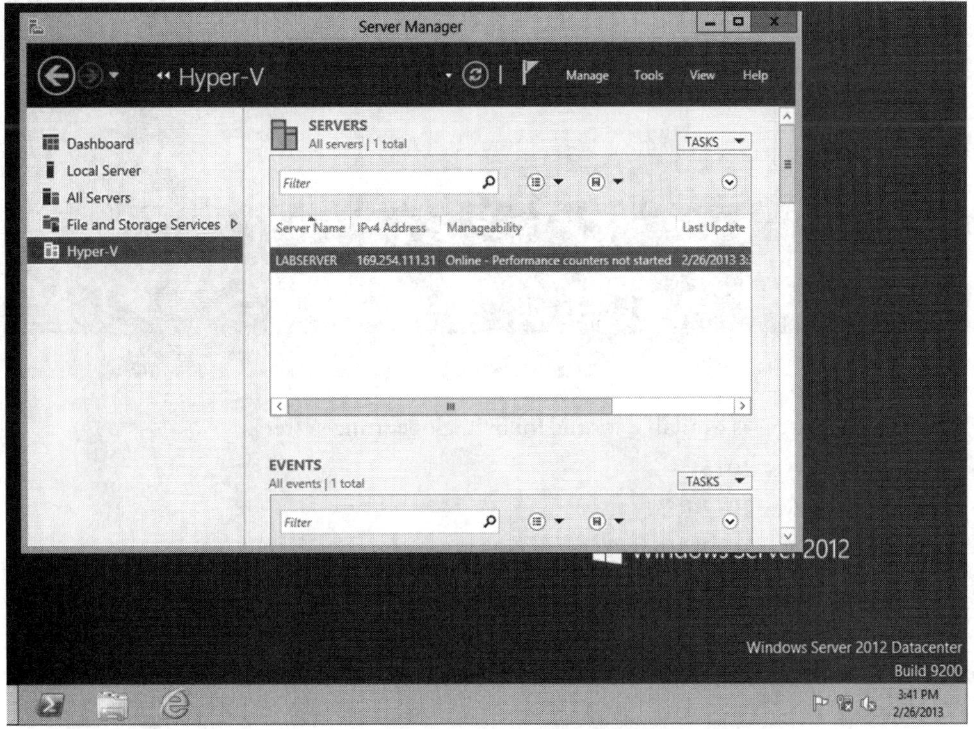

## Using Hyper-V Manager

*Hyper-V Manager* is the central management console to configure your server and create and manage your virtual machines, virtual networks, and virtual hard disks. Hyper-V Manager is managed through a Microsoft Management Console (MMC) snap-in. You can access it either in Server Manager or by using Administrative Tools ➢ Hyper-V Manager. Figure 4.6 shows how Hyper-V Manager looks once you start it.

**FIGURE 4.6** Hyper-V Manager

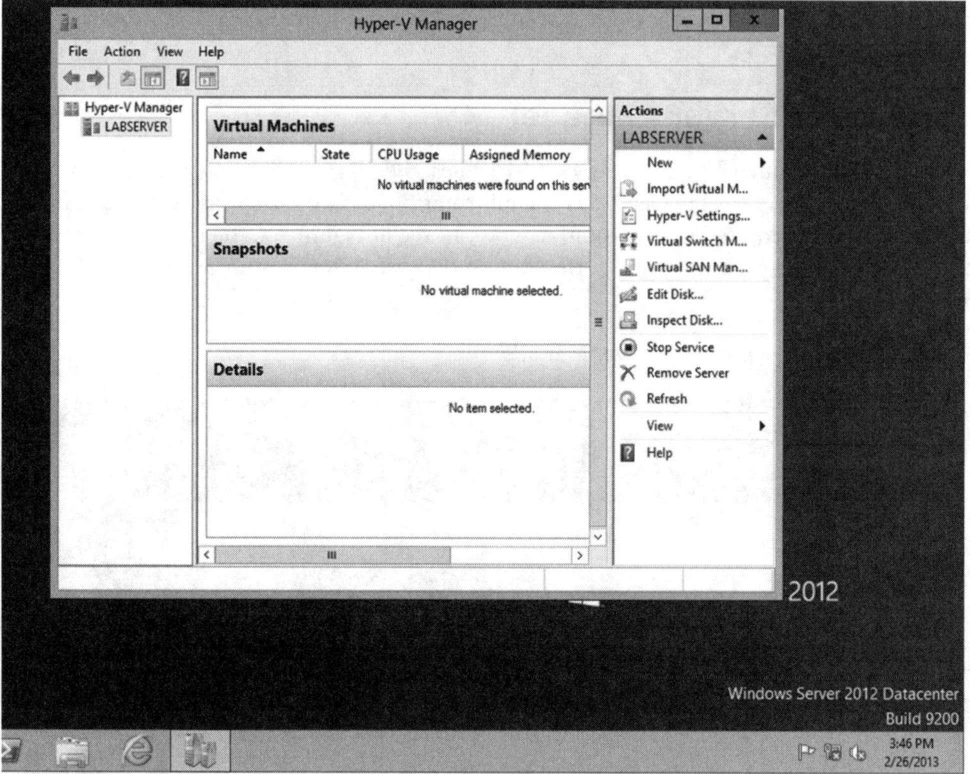


Hyper-V Manager is available for the following operating systems:

- Windows Server 2016
- Windows Server 2012 R2
- Windows Server 2012
- Windows Server 2008 R2
- Windows Server 2008
- Windows 8
- Windows 10
- Windows 8.1

- Windows 7
- Windows Vista with Service Pack 1 (SP1)

Hyper-V Manager is installed on a Windows Server 2016 machine only when you install Hyper-V on it. On Windows Server 2012 R2/2012/2008/2008 R2/ 2003, Windows 10/8/7, or Windows Vista, you will need to install the Hyper-V Manager MMC using the Remote Server Administration Tools (RSAT).

You can use Hyper-V Manager to connect to any Full or Server Core installation remotely. Besides Hyper-V Manager, you can use the WMI interface for scripting Hyper-V.

## Configure Hyper-V Settings

In this section, you will get an overview of the available Hyper-V settings for the server. You configure all server-side default configuration settings like default locations of your configuration files or the release key. You can open the Hyper-V Settings page (see Figure 4.7) in Hyper-V Manager by clicking Hyper-V Settings in the Actions pane.

**FIGURE 4.7** Hyper-V Settings

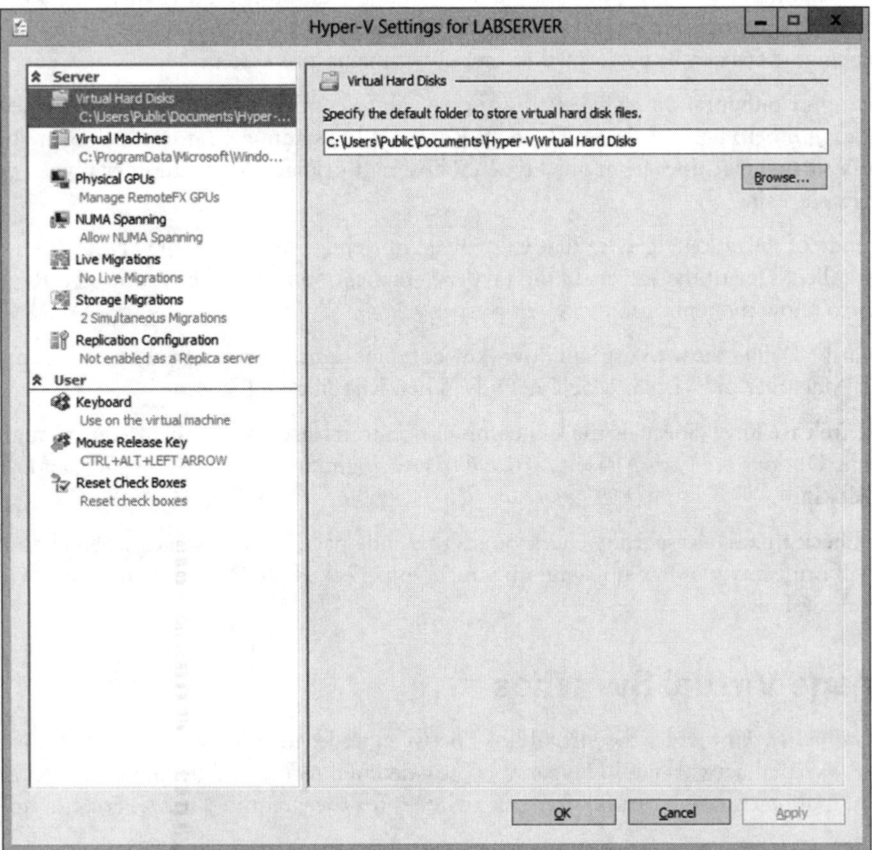

The Hyper-V Settings page includes the following settings:

**Virtual Hard Disks** Specifies the default location of your virtual hard disk files (`.vhd` and `.vhdx`).

**Virtual Machines** Specifies the default location of your virtual machine configuration files. It includes the Virtual Machine XML configuration files (part of the `Virtual Machines` folder) as well as related checkpoints (part of the `Checkpoints` folder).

**Physical GPUs** This feature allows for graphical processing unit (GPU) accelerated video within a virtual machine. The GPU will allow you to support 3D GPU accelerated graphics.

**NUMA Spanning** An administrator can configure Hyper-V to allow virtual machines to span nonuniform memory architecture (NUMA) nodes. When the physical computer has NUMA nodes, this setting provides virtual machines with additional computing resources. Spanning NUMA nodes can help you run more virtual machines at the same time. However, using NUMA can decrease overall performance.

**Live Migrations** *Live migration* allows a Hyper-V administrator to relocate running virtual machines easily from one node of the failover cluster to another node in the same cluster.

**Storage Migrations** *Storage Migration* allows an administrator to move their virtual machine storage from one location to another. This setting allows you to specify how many storage migrations can be performed at the same time on this system.

**Replication Configuration** This setting allows you to configure this computer as a Replica Server to another Hyper-V server. Hyper-V Replica allows administrators to replicate their Hyper-V virtual machines from one Hyper-V host at a primary site to another Hyper-V host at the Replica site.

Each node of the failover cluster that is involved in Replica must have the Hyper-V server role installed. One of the servers in the Hyper-V replication needs to be set up as a Replica Broker to allow the replication to work properly.

**Keyboard** Defines how to use Windows key combinations. Options are Physical Computer, Virtual Machine, and Virtual Machine Only When Running Full Screen.

**Mouse Release Key** Specifies the key combination to release the mouse in your virtual machine. Options are Ctrl+Alt+left arrow, Ctrl+Alt+right arrow, Ctrl+Alt+space, and Ctrl+Alt+Shift.

**Reset Check Boxes** Resets any check boxes that hide pages and messages when checked. This will bring any window up again on which you checked the Do Not Show This Window Again check box.

## Manage Virtual Switches

A *virtual network* provides the virtual links between nodes in either a virtual or physical network. Virtual networking in Hyper-V is provided in a secure and dynamic way because you can granularly define virtual network switches for their required usage. For example, you can define a private or internal virtual network if you don't want to allow your virtual machines to send packages to the physical network.

To allow your virtual machines to communicate with each other, you need virtual networks. Just like normal networks, virtual networks exist only on the host computer and allow you to configure how virtual machines communicate with each other, with the host, and with the network or the Internet. You manage virtual networks in Hyper-V using Virtual Switch Manager, as shown in Figure 4.8.

**FIGURE 4.8** Virtual Network Manager

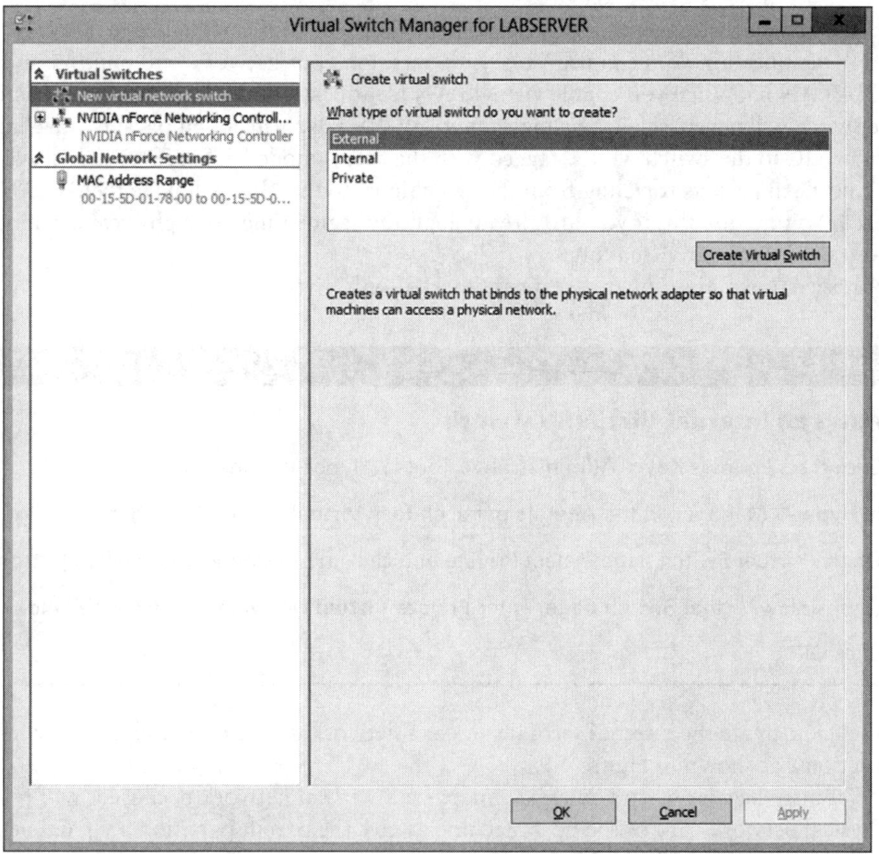


Using *Virtual Switch Manager*, you can create, manage, and delete virtual switches. You can define the network type as external, internal only, or private.

**External** Any virtual machine connected to this virtual switch can access the physical network. You would use this option if you want to allow your virtual machines to access, for example, other servers on the network or the Internet. This option is used in production environments where your clients connect directly to the virtual machines.

**Internal** This option allows virtual machines to communicate with each other as well as the host system but not with the physical network. When you create an internal network, it also creates a local area connection in Network Connections that allows the host machine to communicate with the virtual machines. You can use this if you want to separate your host's network from your virtual networks.

**Private** When you use this option, virtual machines can communicate with each other but not with the host system or the physical network; thus, no network packets are hitting the wire. You can use this to define internal virtual networks for test environments or labs, for example.

On the external and internal-only virtual networks, you also can enable virtual LAN (VLAN) identification. You can use VLANs to partition your network into multiple subnets using a VLAN ID. When you enable virtual LAN identification, the NIC that is connected to the switch will never see packets tagged with VLAN IDs. Instead, all packets traveling from the NIC to the switch will be tagged with the access mode VLAN ID as they leave the switch port. All packets traveling from the switch port to the NIC will have their VLAN tags removed. You can use this if you are already logically segmenting your physical machines and also use it for your virtual ones.

Exercise 4.2 explains how to create an internal-only virtual switch.

**EXERCISE 4.2**

### Creating an Internal Virtual Network

1. Click the Windows Key > Administrative Tools > Hyper-V Manager.
2. In Hyper-V Manager, in the Actions pane, choose Virtual Switch Manager.
3. On the Virtual Switch page, select Private and click the Create Virtual Switch button.
4. On the New Virtual Switch page, enter **Private Virtual Network** in the Name field.
5. Click OK.

When you create the internal virtual switch, a network device is created in Network Connections, as shown in Figure 4.9.

This is also the case when you create an external virtual network because it will replace the physical network card of the host machine to give the parent partition a virtual network card that is also used in the child partitions.

Hyper-V binds the virtual network service to a physical network adapter only when an external virtual network is created. The benefit of this is that the performance is better if you do not use the external virtual network option. The downside, however, is that there will be a network disruption when you create or delete an external virtual network.

**FIGURE 4.9** Virtual network card

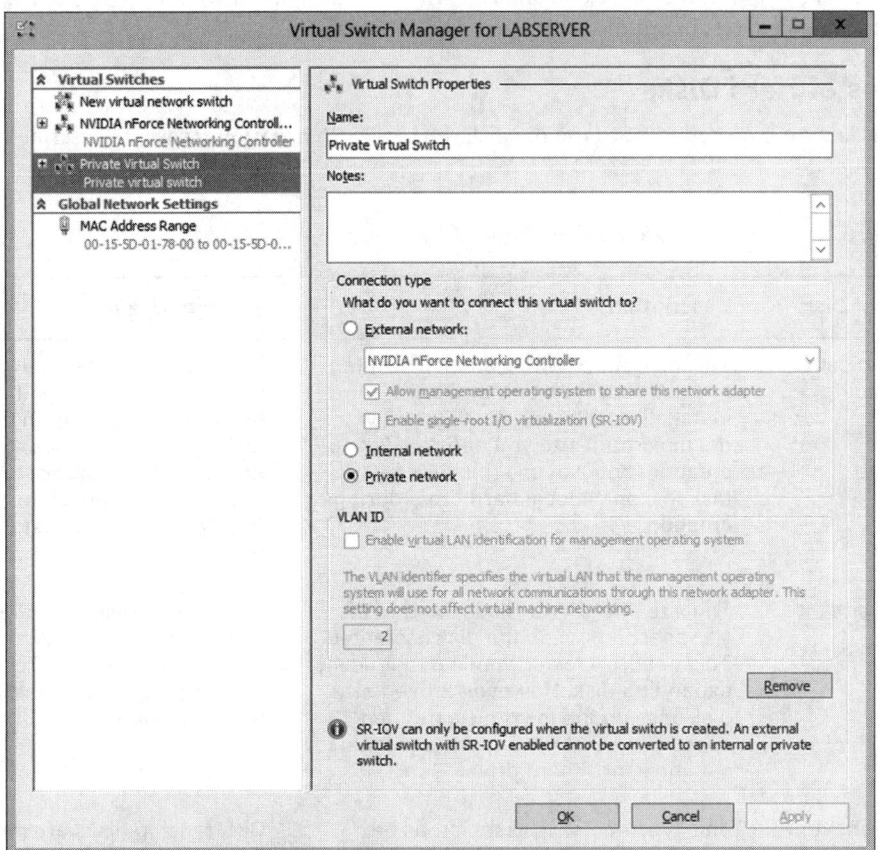

Communication between the virtual machine and the local host computer is not configured automatically. Once you install a virtual machine, you need to make sure that the TCP/IP settings are in agreement with the settings you define in the virtual network card. Start with a successful ping from your host machine to the virtual machines to verify that communication is working.

## Managing Virtual Hard Disks

In addition to virtual networks, you need to manage virtual hard disks that you attach to your virtual machines. A virtual hard disk in Hyper-V, apart from a pass-through disk, is a VHD or VHDX file that basically simulates a hard drive on your virtual machine.

The following sections will first show you what types of virtual hard disks are available and then show you how to create them. You will also learn about what options are available to manage virtual hard disks.

## Types of Hard Disks

Depending on how you want to use the disk, Hyper-V offers various types, as described in Table 4.4.

**TABLE 4.4** Virtual hard disks in Hyper-V

| Type of Disk | Description | When to Use It |
|---|---|---|
| Dynamically expanding | This disk starts with a small VHD file and expands it on demand once an installation takes place. It can grow to the maximum size you defined during creation. You can use this type of disk to clone a local hard drive during creation. | This option is effective when you don't know the exact space needed on the disk and when you want to preserve hard disk space on the host machine. Unfortunately, it is the slowest disk type. |
| Fixed size | The size of the VHD file is fixed to the size specified when the disk is created. This option is faster than a dynamically expanding disk. However, a fixed-size disk uses up the maximum defined space immediately. This type is ideal for cloning a local hard drive. | A fixed-size disk provides faster access than dynamically expanding or differencing disks, but it is slower than a physical disk. |
| Differencing | This type of disk is associated in a parent-child relationship with another disk. The differencing disk is the child, and the associated virtual disk is the parent. Differencing disks include only the differences to the parent disk. By using this type, you can save a lot of disk space in similar virtual machines. This option is suitable if you have multiple virtual machines with similar operating systems. | Differencing disks are most commonly found in test environments and should not be used in production environments. |
| Physical (or pass-through disk) | The virtual machine receives direct pass-through access to the physical disk for exclusive use. This type provides the highest performance of all disk types and thus should be used for production servers where performance is the top priority. The drive is not available for other guest systems. | This type is used in high-end datacenters to provide optimum performance for VMs. It's also used in failover cluster environments. |

## Creating Virtual Hard Disks

To help you gain practice in creating virtual hard disks, the following three exercises will teach you how to create a differencing hard disk, how to clone an existing disk by creating a new disk, and how to configure a physical or pass-through disk to your virtual machine. First, in Exercise 4.3, you will learn how to create a differencing virtual hard disk.

**EXERCISE 4.3**

### Creating a Differencing Hard Disk

1. Open Hyper-V Manager.
2. In Hyper-V Manager, on the Actions pane, choose New ➢ Hard Disk.
3. In the New Virtual Hard Disk Wizard, click Next on the Before You Begin page.
4. At the Choose Disk Format screen, choose VHDX and click Next. The size of your VHDs depends on which format you choose. If you're going to have a VHD larger than 2,040 GB, use VHDX. If your VHD is less than 2,040 GB, then you should use VHD.
5. On the Choose Disk Type page, select Fixed Size and click Next.
6. On the Specify Name And Location page, enter the new name of the child disk (for example, **newvirtualharddisk.vhdx**). You can also modify the default location of the new VHDX file if you want. Click Next to continue.
7. Next, on the Configure Disk page, you need to specify the size of the VHDX file. Choose a size based on your hard disk and then click Next to continue. I used 60 GB as our test size.
8. On the Completing The New Virtual Hard Disk Wizard page, verify that all settings are correct and click Finish to create the hard disk.

The process to add a physical or pass-through disk to a virtual machine is quite different. For this, first you need to create the virtual machine, and then you open the virtual machine settings to configure the physical disk. If you want to add a physical disk to a virtual machine, the physical disk must be set as Offline in Disk Management, as shown in Figure 4.10.

To access Disk Management, click the Windows key, choose Administrative Tools ➢ Computer Management, expand Storage in the left pane, and click Disk Management.

You cannot share a physical disk among multiple virtual machines or with the host system.

**FIGURE 4.10** In Disk Management, you can set disks as Offline.

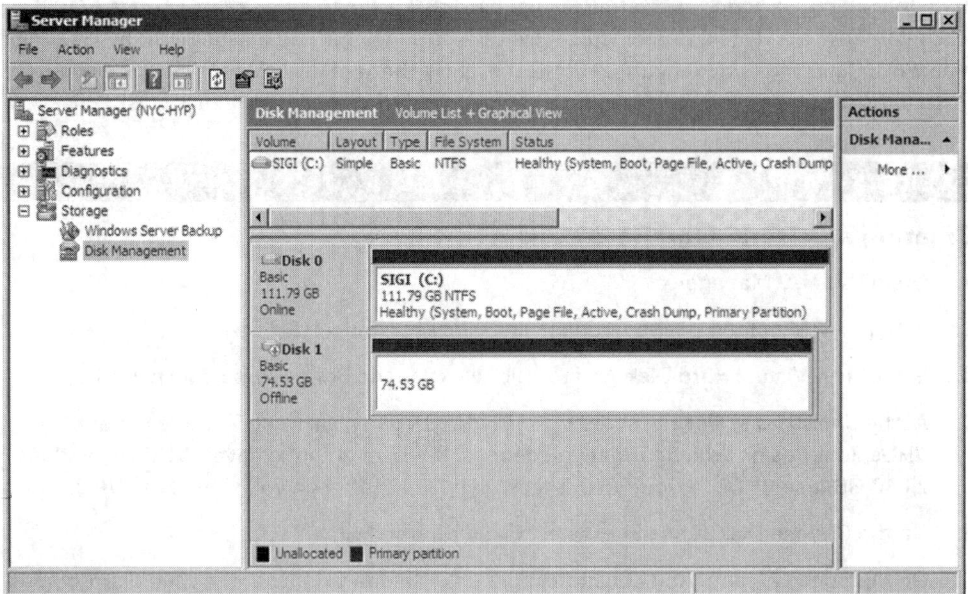


Physical or pass-through disks might not be that important if your use of virtualization is based on test environments, but they become crucial when you need to plan for highly available virtual datacenters. This is especially true if you consider using failover clusters to provide the Quick Migration feature, which is when you should consider matching one logical unit number (LUN) from your enterprise storage system or storage area network (SAN) as one physical disk. This provides you with the optimum performance you need in such an environment.

## Managing Virtual Hard Disks

Hyper-V also provides two tools to manage virtual hard disks: Inspect Disk and Edit Disk. These tools are available on the Actions pane in Hyper-V Manager.

**Inspect Disk** This provides you with information about the virtual hard disk. It shows you not only the type of the disk but also information such as the maximum size for dynamically expanding disks and the parent VHD for differencing disks.

**Edit Disk** This provides you with the Edit Virtual Hard Disk Wizard, which you can use to compact, convert, expand, merge, or reconnect hard disks. Figure 4.11 shows you the wizard's options when you select a dynamically expanding disk.

**FIGURE 4.11** The Edit Virtual Hard Disk Wizard

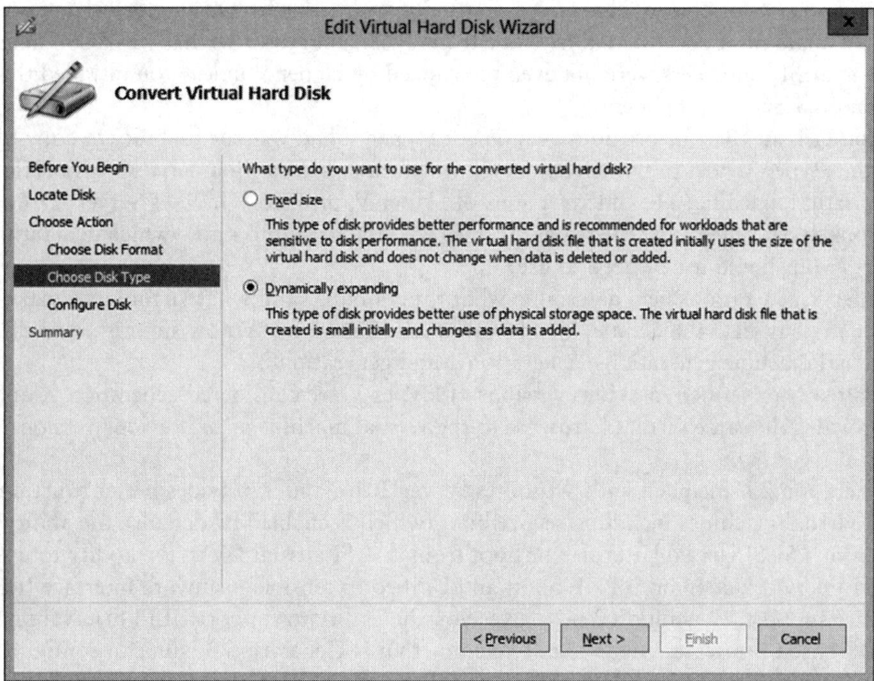


Table 4.5 provides you with an overview of what you can do with the wizard.

**TABLE 4.5** Edit Disk overview

| Action | Description |
|---|---|
| Compact | Reduces the size of a dynamically expanding or differencing disk by removing blank space from deleted files. |
| Convert | Converts a dynamically expanding disk to a fixed disk or vice versa. |
| Expand | Increases the storage capacity of a dynamically expanding disk or a fixed virtual hard disk. |
| Merge | Merges the changes from a differencing disk into either the parent disk or another disk (applies to differencing disks only!). |
| Reconnect | If a differencing disk no longer finds its referring parent disk, this option can reconnect the parent to the disk. |

## Generation 1 vs. Generation 2 VHDs

Previous versions of Hyper-V had some pretty major drawbacks. One big drawback was that Hyper-V could not boot a virtual machine from a virtual hard drive that was SCSI. Believe it or not, SCSI controllers were not even recognized by Hyper-V unless you installed the Integration Services component.

Another issue that the previous versions of Hyper-V had was the inability to copy files from the Hyper-V host to the virtual machines without the use of a network connection in the virtual machine. The older versions of Hyper-V, prior to Windows Server 2016, are now considered generation 1 versions. Why is it so important to know which generations of Hyper-V you should use or need to use?

Hyper-V generations help determine what functionality and what virtual hardware you can use in your virtual machine. Windows Server 2016 Hyper-V now supports two different virtual machine generations: generation 1 and generation 2.

As already explained, previous versions of Hyper-V are considered generation 1, and this provides the same virtual hardware to the virtual machine as in previous versions of Hyper-V.

Generation 2 is included with Windows Server 2016, and it provides better functionality on the virtual machines including secure boot (which is enabled by default), the ability to boot from a SCSI virtual hard disk or boot from a SCSI virtual DVD, the ability to use a standard network adapter to PXE boot, and Unified Extensible Firmware Interface (UEFI) firmware support. Generation 2 now gives you the ability to support UEFI firmware instead of BIOS-based firmware. On a virtual machine that is Generation 2, you can configure Secure Boot, Enable TPM, and set security policies by clicking on the Security section of the virtual machines properties.

So when you create VHDs in Windows Server 2016, one of your choices will be the ability to create the VHDs as a generation 1 or generation 2 VHD. If you need the ability to have your VHDs run on older versions of Hyper-V, make them a generation 1 VHD. If they are going to run only on Windows Server 2016, make your VHDs generation 2 and take advantage of all the new features and functionality.

# Configuring Virtual Machines

The following sections cover the topics of creating and managing virtual machines as well as how to back up and restore virtual machines using features such as Import and Export and Checkpoint. You'll also briefly look at Hyper-V's Live Migration feature.

## Creating and Managing Virtual Machines

It is important to learn how to create a virtual machine, how to change its configuration, and how to delete it. You will take a look at the Virtual Machine Connection tool and install the Hyper-V Integration Components onto a virtual machine.

## Virtual Machines

Virtual machines define the child partitions in which you run operating system instances. Each virtual machine is separate and can communicate with the others only by using a virtual network. You can assign hard drives, virtual networks, DVD drives, and other system components to it. A virtual machine is similar to an existing physical server, but it no longer runs on dedicated hardware—it shares the hardware of the host system with the other virtual machines that run on the host.

Exercise 4.4 shows you how to create a new virtual machine. Before completing this exercise, download an eval copy of Windows Server from Microsoft's website (`www.microsoft.com/downloads`). Make sure the file downloaded is an image file (.iso). You will use this image to install the operating system into the virtual machine.

**EXERCISE 4.4**

### Creating a New Virtual Machine

1. Open Hyper-V Manager (see Figure 4.12).

**FIGURE 4.12** Hyper-V Manager

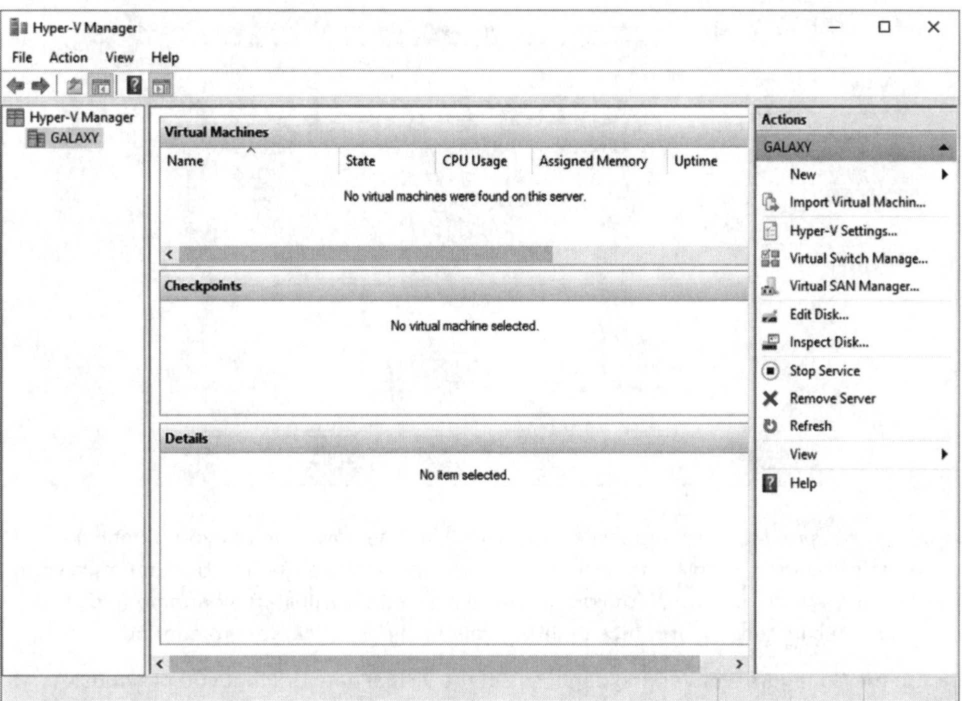

**EXERCISE 4.4 *(continued)***

2. In Hyper-V Manager, on the Actions pane, choose New ➢ Virtual Machine.
3. In the New Virtual Machine Wizard, click Next on the Before You Begin page.
4. On the Specify Name And Location page, give your virtual machine a name and change the default location of the virtual machine configuration files. Click Next to continue.
5. The Specify Generation screen is next. Choose Generation 2 (see Figure 4.13) and click Next.

**FIGURE 4.13** Specify Generation screen

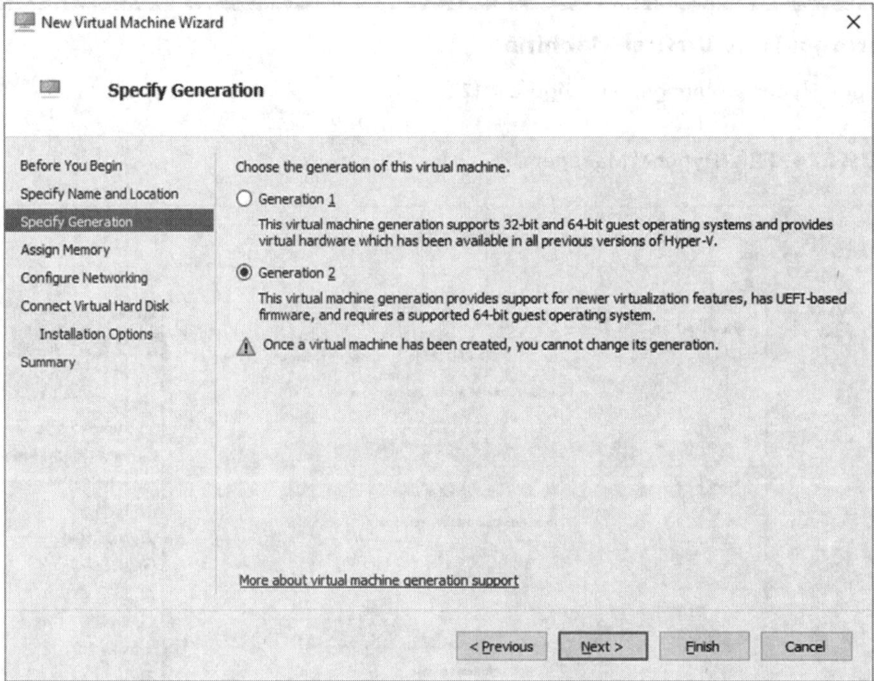


6. On the Assign Memory page (see Figure 4.14), define how much of your host computer's memory you want to assign to this virtual machine. Remember that once your virtual machine uses up all of your physical memory, it will start swapping to disk, thus reducing the performance of all virtual machines. Click Next to continue.
7. On the Configure Networking page, select the virtual network that you previously configured using Virtual Network Manager (see Figure 4.15). Click Next to continue.

**FIGURE 4.14** VM RAM

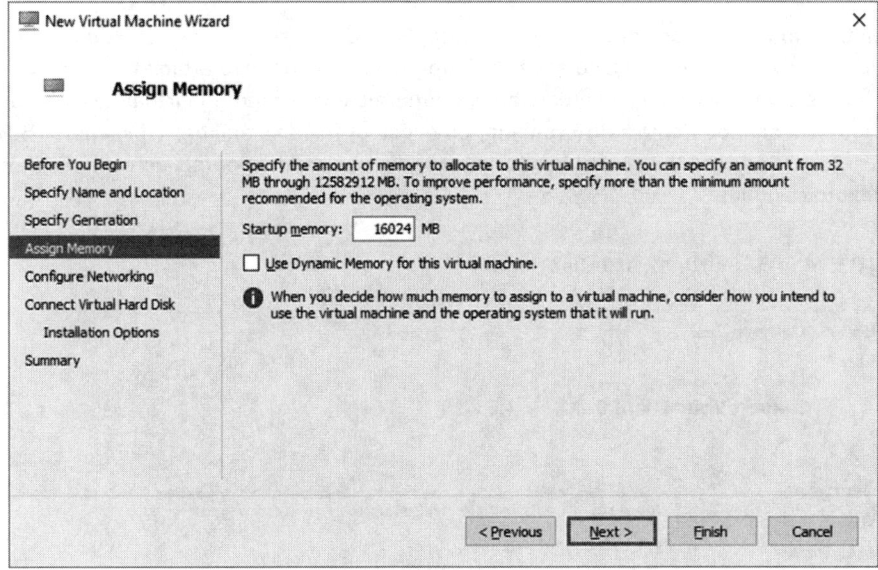


**FIGURE 4.15** Networking page

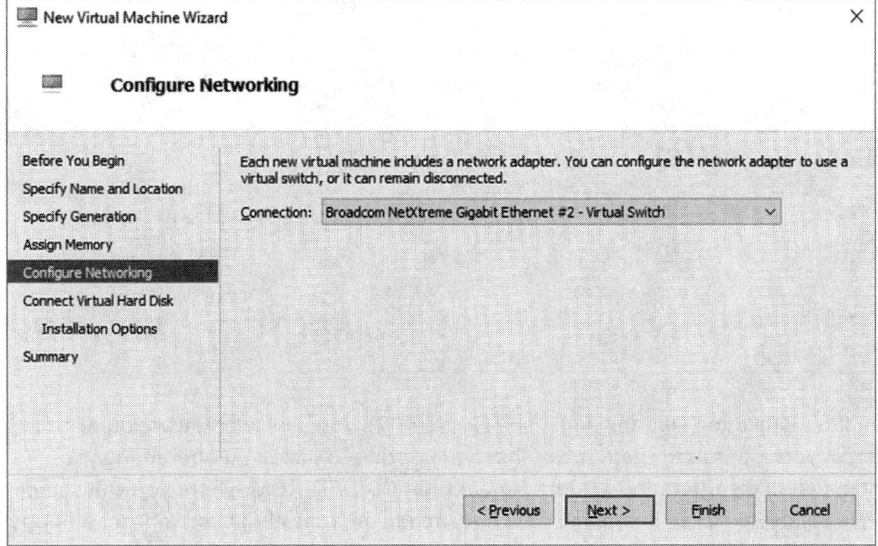

**EXERCISE 4.4 *(continued)***

8. On the next page, you configure your virtual hard disk (see Figure 4.16). You can create a new virtual hard disk, select an existing disk, or choose to attach the hard disk later. Be aware that you can create only a dynamically expanding virtual disk on this page; you cannot create a differencing, physical, or fixed virtual hard disk there. However, if you created the virtual hard disk already, you can, of course, select it. Click Next to continue.

**FIGURE 4.16** Virtual Hard Disk page

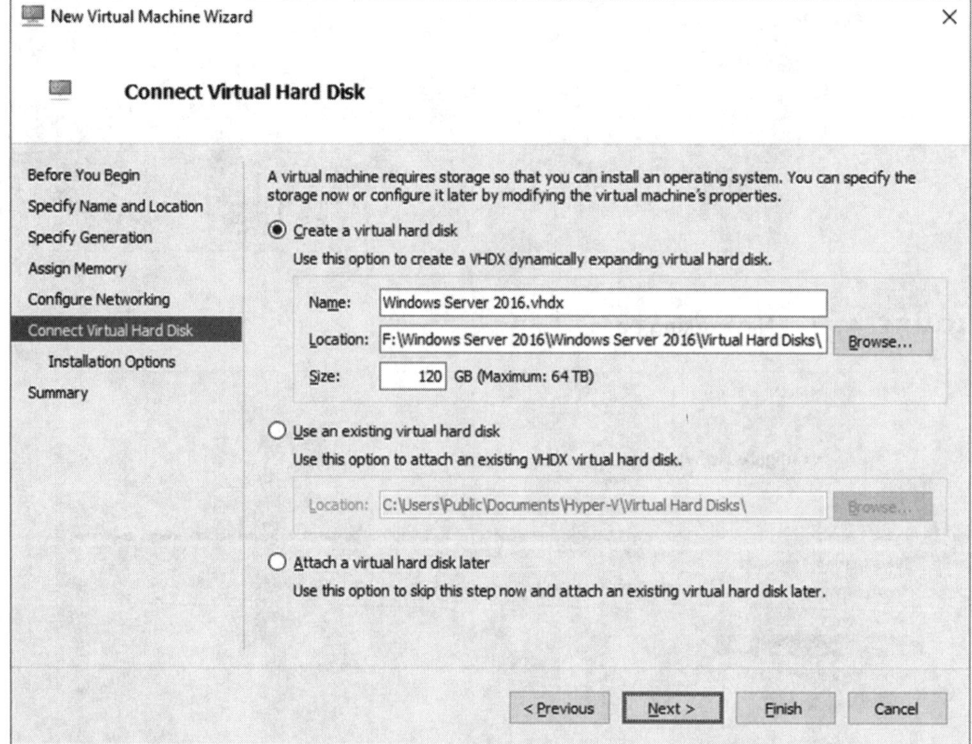


9. On the Installation Options page (see Figure 4.17), you can select how you want to install your operating system. You have the option to install an operating system later, install the operating system from a boot CD/DVD-ROM where you can select a physical device or an image file (ISO file), install an operating system from a floppy disk image (VFD file, or a virtual boot floppy disk), or install an operating system from a network-based installation server. The last option will install a legacy network adapter to your virtual machine so that you can boot from the network adapter. Select Install An Operating System from a bootable CD/DVD-ROM and choose Image File (.iso). Then click Next.

**FIGURE 4.17** Installing OS screen

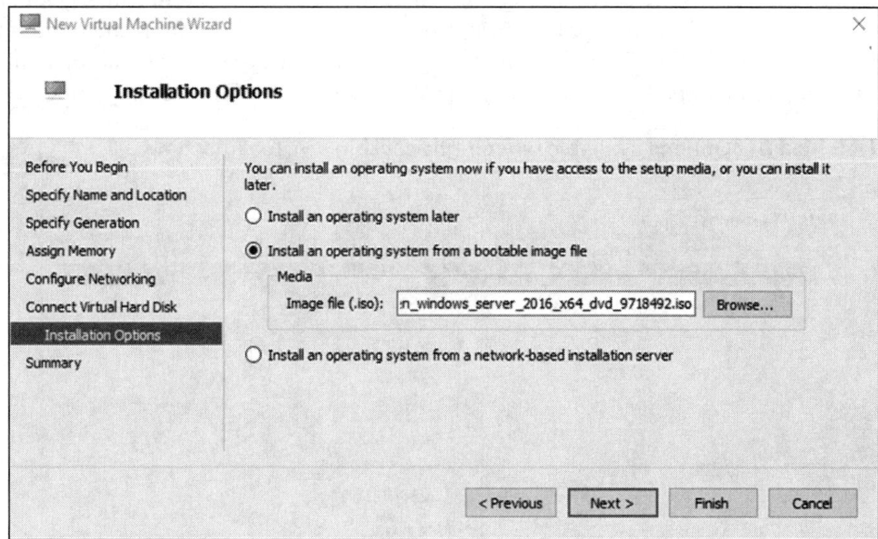


10. On the Completing The New Virtual Machine Wizard summary page, verify that all settings are correct (see Figure 4.18). You also have the option to start the virtual machine immediately after creation. Click Next to create the virtual machine.

**FIGURE 4.18** Completing the New Virtual Machine Wizard screen

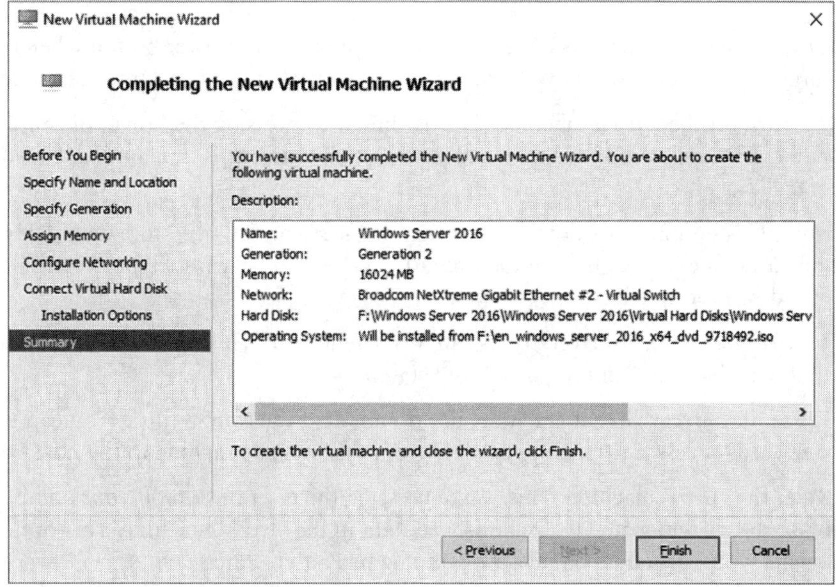


11. Repeat this process and create a few more virtual machines.

After completing Exercise 4.4, you will have a virtual machine available in Hyper-V Manager. Initially, the state of the virtual machine will be Off. Virtual machines can have the following states: Off, Starting, Running, Paused, and Saved. You can change the state of a virtual machine in the Virtual Machines pane by right-clicking the virtual machine's name, as shown in Figure 4.19, or by using the Virtual Machine Connection window.

**FIGURE 4.19** Options available when right-clicking a virtual machine

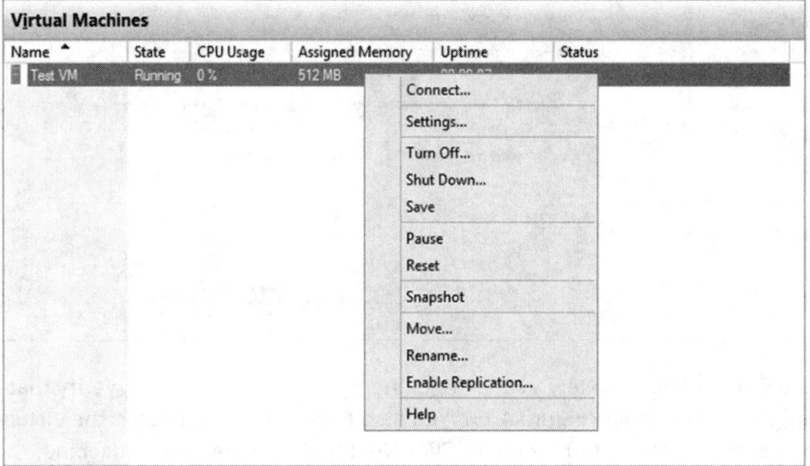


Here is a list of some of the state options (when the VM is running) available for a virtual machine:

**Start** Turn on the virtual machine. This is similar to pressing the power button when the machine is turned off. This option is available when your virtual machine is Off or in Saved state.

**Turn Off** Turn off the virtual machine. This is similar to pressing the power-off button on the computer. This option is available when your virtual machine is in Running, Saved, or Paused state.

**Shut Down** This option shuts down your operating system. You need to have the Hyper-V Integration Components installed on the operating system; otherwise, Hyper-V will not be able to shut down the system.

**Save** The virtual machine is saved to disk in its current state. This option is available when your virtual machine is in Running or Paused state.

**Pause** Pause the current virtual machine, but do not save the state to disk. You can use this option to release processor utilization quickly from this virtual machine to the host system.

**Reset** Reset the virtual machine. This is like pressing the reset button on your computer. You will lose the current state and any unsaved data in the virtual machine. This option is available when your virtual machine is in Running or Paused state.

**Resume** When your virtual machine is paused, you can resume it and bring it online again.

## Changing Configuration on an Existing Virtual Machine

To change the configuration settings on an existing virtual machine, you right-click your virtual machine's name in the Virtual Machines pane in Hyper-V Manager and choose Settings. You can change settings such as memory allocation and hard drive configuration. All items that you can configure are described in the following list:

**Add Hardware** Add devices to your virtual machine, namely, a SCSI controller, a network adapter, or a legacy network adapter. A legacy network adapter is required if you want to perform a network-based installation of an operating system.

**Firmware** This is the replacement of the virtual machine's BIOS. Because you can no longer enter the BIOS during startup, you need to configure it with this setting. You can turn Num Lock on or off and change the basic startup order of the devices.

**Security** This setting allows an administrator to set up the Secure Boot option along with enabling the Trusted Platform Module (TPM). TPM is a special-purpose microprocessor which provides cryptographic services. You can also set virtual machine shielding in the security section.

**Memory** Change the amount of random access memory (RAM) allocated to the virtual machine.

**Processor** Change the number of logical processors this virtual machine can use and define resource control to balance resources among virtual machines by using a relative weight.

**SCSI Controller** Configure all hard drives that are connected to the SCSI controller. You can add up to 63 hard drives to each SCSI controller, and you can have multiple SCSI controllers available.

**Hard Drive** Select a controller to attach to this device as well as to specify the media to use with your virtual hard disk. The available options are Virtual Hard Disk File (with additional buttons labeled New, Edit, Inspect, and Browse that are explained in the virtual hard disk section) and Physical Hard Disk. You can also remove the device here.

**DVD Drive** Select a controller to attach to this device and specify the media to use with your virtual CD/DVD drive. The available options are None, Image File (ISO Image), and Physical CD/DVD Drive Connected To The Host Computer. You also can remove the device here.

**Network Adapter** Specify the configuration of the network adapter or remove it. You can also configure the virtual network and MAC address for each adapter and enable virtual LAN identification. The network adapter section also allows you to control Bandwidth Management.

Bandwidth Management allows an administrator to specify how the network adapter will utilize network bandwidth. Administrators have the ability to set a minimum network bandwidth that a network adapter can use and a maximum bandwidth. This gives administrators greater control over how much bandwidth a virtual network adapter can use.

**Name** Edit the name of the virtual machine and provide some notes about it.

**Integration Services** Define what integration services are available to your virtual machine. Options are Operating System Shutdown, Time Synchronization, Data Exchange, Heartbeat, and Backup (Volume Checkpoint).

**Checkpoints** Define the default file location of your checkpoint files. Virtual machine checkpoints allow an administrator to restore a virtual machine to a previous state. After checkpoints are created, an administrator would use the "Recover action" to restore a virtual machine back to the time the checkpoint was created.

**Smart Paging File Location** This area allows you to set up a paging file for your virtual machine. Windows Server 2016 has a Hyper-V feature called *Smart Paging*. If you have a virtual machine that has a smaller amount of memory than what it needs for startup memory, when the virtual machine gets restarted, Hyper-V then needs additional memory to restart the virtual machine. Smart Paging is used to bridge the memory gap between minimum memory and startup memory. This allows your virtual machines to restart properly.

**Automatic Start** Define what this virtual machine will do when the physical computer starts. Options are Nothing, Automatically Start If The Service Was Running, and Always Start This Virtual Machine. You also can define a start delay here.

**Automatic Stop** Define what this virtual machine will do when the physical computer shuts down. Options are Save State, Turn Off, and Shut Down.

Please be aware that only some settings can be changed when the virtual machine's state is Running. It is best practice to shut down the virtual machine before you modify any setting.

## Deleting Virtual Machines

You can also delete virtual machines using Hyper-V Manager. This deletes all of the configuration files, as shown in Figure 4.20.

**FIGURE 4.20** Delete Virtual Machine warning window

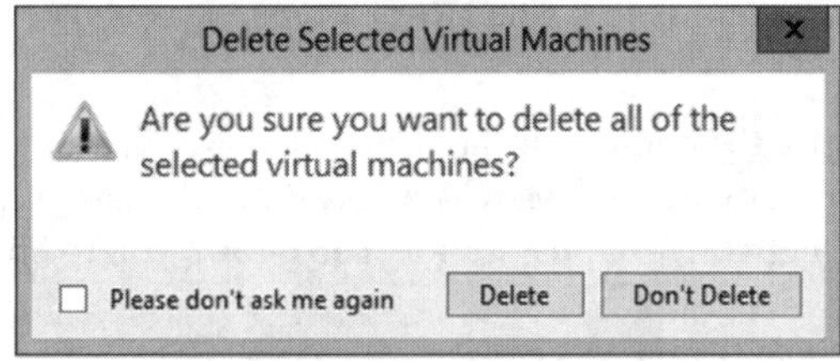


Make sure you manually delete any virtual disks that were part of the virtual machines to free up disk space. Virtual disks are *not* deleted when you delete a virtual machine.

## Virtual Machine Connection

Hyper-V comes with Virtual Machine Connection to connect to virtual machines that run on a local or remote server. You can use it to log onto the virtual machine and use your computer's mouse and keyboard to interact with the virtual machine. You can open Virtual Machine Connection in Hyper-V Manager by double-clicking a virtual machine or by right-clicking a virtual machine and selecting Connect. If your virtual machine is turned off, you might see a window similar to the one in Figure 4.21.

**FIGURE 4.21** Virtual Machine Connection window when the machine is turned off

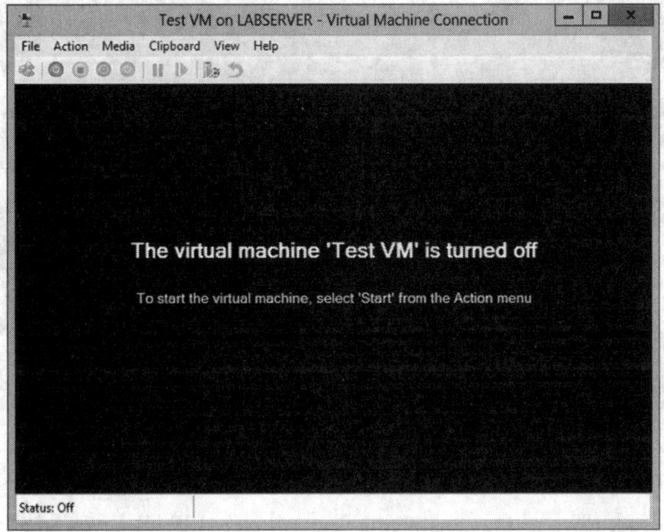


Virtual Machine Connection not only provides you with functionality similar to that of Hyper-V Manager, such as being able to change the state of a virtual machine, but it also provides you with additional features that are especially useful when you want to work with a virtual machine.

**File Access Settings or Exit Virtual Machine Connection** Change the state of a virtual machine and create or revert a checkpoint. Additionally, you have the options to send Ctrl+Alt+Delete to your virtual machine and Insert Integration Services Setup Disk.

**Context-Sensitive Buttons Provide Quick Access to Key Features** These buttons are available under the menu bar to provide you with fast access to the most important features, as you can see in Figure 4.22. It shows the connection of a running VM, but the VM has not had an operating system installed yet, so the figure shows the Windows Server 2016 Setup screen.

**FIGURE 4.22** Virtual Machine Connection window showing a running Windows Server 2016 virtual machine

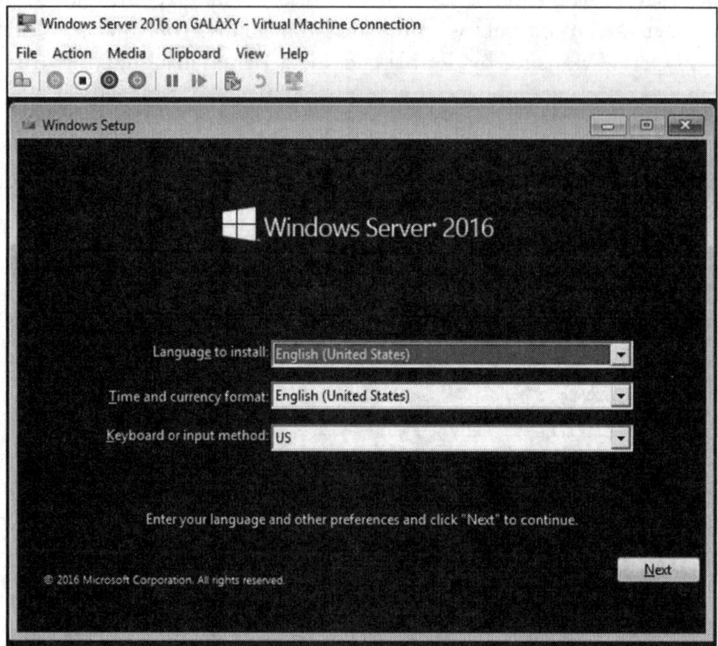


## NIC Teaming

NIC Teaming, also known as load balancing and failover (LBFO), gives an administrator the ability to allow multiple network adapters on a system to be placed into a team. Independent hardware vendors (IHVs) have required NIC Teaming, but until Windows Server 2012, NIC Teaming was *not* part of the Windows Server operating system.

To be able to use NIC Teaming, the computer system must have at least one Ethernet adapter. If you want to provide fault protection, an administrator must have a minimum of two Ethernet adapters. One advantage of Windows Server 2016 is that an administrator can set up 32 network adapters in a NIC team.

NIC Teaming is a common practice when setting up virtualization. This is one way that you can have load balancing with Hyper-V.

NIC Teaming gives an administrator the ability to allow a virtual machine to use virtual network adapters in Hyper-V. The advantage of using NIC Teaming in Hyper-V is that the administrator can use NIC Teaming to connect to more than one Hyper-V switch. This allows Hyper-V still to have connectivity even if the network adapter under the Hyper-V switch gets disconnected.

An administrator can configure NIC Teaming in either Server Manager or PowerShell. NIC Teaming can be configured in different configuration models including Switch Independent or Switch Dependent. Switch Independent means that each NIC adapter is connected into a different switch. Switch Dependent means that all NIC adapters are connected into the same switch. If you use Switch Independent NIC Teaming then you must connect your NICs to different switches but both switches must be on the same subnet.

## Remote Direct Memory Access

When most of us think of Hyper-V, we think of a group of virtual machines sharing access to a systems resource. With Windows Server 2016, Hyper-V includes Remote Direct Memory Access (RDMA).

RDMA allows one computer to directly access memory from the memory of another computer without the need of interfacing with either one's operating system. This gives systems the ability to have high throughput and low-latency networking. This is very useful when it comes to clustering systems (including Hyper-V).

Windows Server 2012 R2 RDMA services couldn't be bound to a Hyper-V Virtual Switch and because of this, Remote Direct Memory Access and Hyper-V had to be on the same computer as the network adapters. Because of this, there was a need for a higher number of physical network adapters that were required to be installed on the Hyper-V host.

Because of the improvements of RDMA on Windows Server 2016, administrators can use less network adapters while using RDMA.

## Switch Embedded Teaming

Earlier we discussed NIC Teaming but we also have the ability to do Switch Embedded Teaming (SET). SET can be an alternative to using NIC Teaming in environments that include Hyper-V and the Software Defined Networking (SDN) stack in Windows Server 2016. SET is available in all versions of Windows Server 2016 that include Hyper-V and SDN stack.

SET does use some of the functionality of NIC Teaming into the Hyper-V Virtual Switch but SET allows an administrator to combine a group of physical adapters (minimum of 1 adapter and a maximum of 8 adapters) into software based virtual adapters.

By using virtual adapters, you get better performance and greater fault tolerance in the event of a network adapter going bad. For SET to be enabled, all of the physical network adapters must be installed on the same physical Hyper-V host.

One of the requirements of SET is that all network adapters that are members of the SET group be identical adapters. This means that they need to be the same adapter types from the same manufacturers.

One main difference between NIC Teaming and Set is that SET only supports Switch Independent mode setups. Again this means that the NIC adapters are connected to different switches.

Administrators need to create a SET team at the same time that they create the Hyper-V Virtual Switch. Administrators can do this by using the Windows PowerShell command `New-VMSwitch`.

At the time an administrator creates a Hyper-V Virtual Switch, the administrator needs to include the EnableEmbeddedTeaming parameter in their command syntax. The following example shows a Hyper-V switch named StormSwitch.

```
New-VMSwitch -Name StormSwitch -NetAdapterName "NIC 1","NIC 2"
-EnableEmbeddedTeaming $true
```

Administrators also have the ability to remove a SET team by using the following PowerShell command. This example removes a Virtual Switch named StormSwitch.

```
Remove-VMSwitch [StormSwitch]
```

## Storage Quality of Service

Windows Server 2016 Hyper-V includes a feature called *Storage Quality of Service (QoS)*. Storage QoS allows a Hyper-V administrator to manage how virtual machines access storage throughput for virtual hard disks.

Storage QoS gives an administrator the ability to guarantee that the storage throughput of a single VHD cannot adversely affect the performance of another VHD on the same host. It does this by giving administrators the ability to specify the maximum and minimum I/O loads based on I/O operations per second (IOPS) for each virtual disk in your virtual machines.

To configure Storage QoS, you would set the maximum IOPS values (or limits) and set the minimum values (or reserves) on virtual hard disks for virtual machines.

If you are using shared virtual hard disks, Storage QoS will not be available.

## Installing Hyper-V Integration Components

Hyper-V *Integration Components*, also called *Integration Services*, are required to make your guest operating system hypervisor-aware. These components improve the performance of the guest operating system once they are installed. From an architectural perspective, virtual devices are redirected directly via the VMBus; thus, quicker access to resources and devices is provided.

If you do not install the Hyper-V Integration Components, the guest operating system uses emulation to communicate with the host's devices, which of course makes the guest operating system slower.

Exercise 4.5 shows you how to install Hyper-V Integration Components on one of your virtual machines running Windows Server 2016.

**EXERCISE 4.5**

### Installing Hyper-V Integration Components

1. Open Hyper-V Manager.
2. In Hyper-V Manager, in the Virtual Machines pane, right-click the virtual machine on which you want to install Hyper-V Integration Components and click Start.

3. Right-click the virtual machine again and click Connect. Meanwhile, your virtual machine should already be booting.
4. If you need to log into the operating system of your virtual machine, you should do so.
5. Once the Windows Desktop appears, you need to select Insert Integration Services Setup Disk from the Actions menu of your Virtual Machine Connection window.
6. Once the Hyper-V Integration Components are installed, you are asked to perform a reboot.

After the reboot, Hyper-V Integration Components are installed on your operating system, and you will be able to use them.

---

## Linux and FreeBSD Image Deployments

One of the features of Windows 2016 is the ability for Hyper-V to support Linux and FreeBSD virtual machines. Hyper-V now can support these new virtual machines because Hyper-V has the ability to emulate Linux and FreeBSD devices. Because Hyper-V now has the ability to emulate these two devices, no additional software needs to be installed on Hyper-V.

Unfortunately, because Hyper-V has to emulate these devices, you lose some of the Hyper-V functionality like high performance and full management of the virtual machines. So it's a tradeoff. You get to run Linux and FreeBSD type Hyper-V virtual machines but you lose some of the benefits of Hyper-V.

But wait; there is a way to get your Hyper-V functionality back. This issue can be resolved as long as you install Hyper-V on machines that can support Linux and FreeBSD operating systems. The drivers that are needed on Hyper-V are called Linux Integration Services (LIS) and FreeBSD Integrated Services (FIS). By putting these drivers on a device that can handle Linux and FreeBSD, you can then have Hyper-V with all of the features Microsoft offers.

To get these drivers and make Hyper-V work will all of its functionality, you must make sure that you install a newer release of Linux that includes LIS. To get the most out of FreeBSD you must get a version after 10.0. For FreeBSD versions that are older than 10.0, Microsoft offers ports that work with BIS drivers that need to be installed. Hyper-V will work with Linux and FreeBSD without the need of any additional drivers or equipment. By having drivers and equipment that supports Linux and FreeBSD, you just get all of the Hyper-V features that your organization may need.

In Exercise 4.6, I will show you how to install Linux into a virtual machine. I will then walk you through a full installation of a Linux Server. Before you complete this lab, you must download a copy of Linux. For this exercise, I downloaded a free copy of Linux Ubuntu Server as an image file (.iso). If you choose a different version of Linux, the installation screens during the exercise may be different.

**EXERCISE 4.6**

### Creating a Linux Virtual Machine

1. Open Hyper-V Manager.
2. In the right hand window under Actions, click New ➢ Virtual Machine (see Figure 4.23).

**FIGURE 4.23** New Virtual Machine

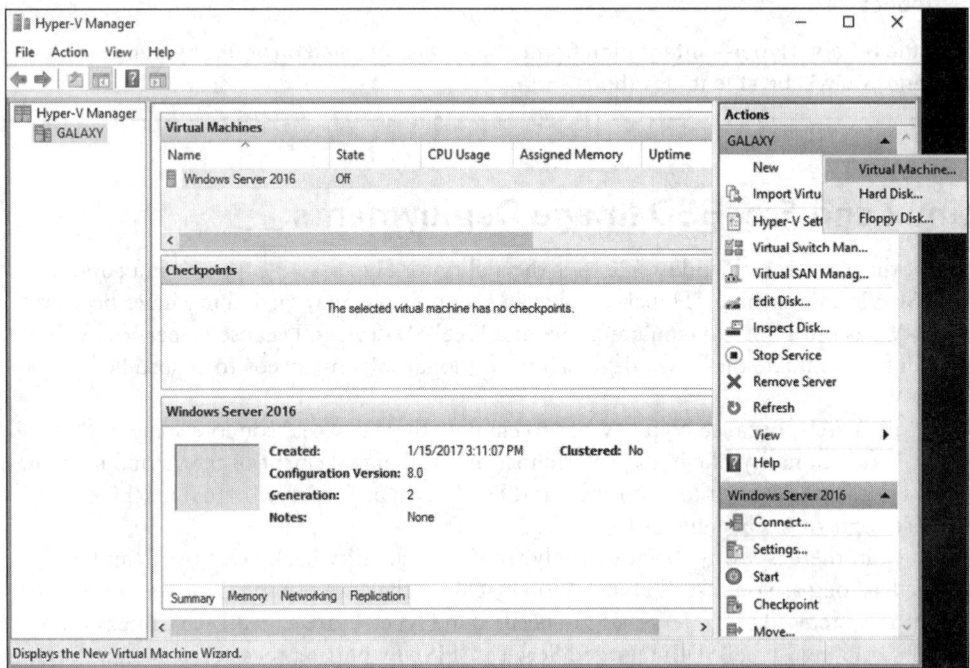


3. At the Before you Begin screen, just choose Next.
4. At the Specify Name and Location screen, enter in the name of the Linux virtual machine and the location you would like to store the virtual machine files. Then click Next.
5. At the Generation screen, choose Generation 2 and click Next.
6. At the Assign Memory screen, enter in the amount of memory you want to allocate to this virtual machine. I am using 12GB (12000MB). Click Next.
7. Choose which network connection you want to use and click Next.
8. At the Connect Virtual Hard Disk screen, choose Create a virtual hard disk. Set the location of where you want the files to reside and also how much space you want to use (I chose 127GB). Click Next.
9. At the Installation Options screen, choose Install an Operating system from a bootable image file and point to your Linux .iso download. Click Next.

10. At the Completing the New Virtual Machine Wizard screen, make sure all of the settings are correct and choose Finish.
11. After the virtual machine was created, click the virtual machine and on the right side under Linux, click Start.
12. When the Linux install starts, click your Language.
13. At the Ubuntu menu, choose Install Ubuntu Server.
14. Again, you will need to choose your language for the install.
15. Choose your country.
16. On the detect keyboard layout, choose No. Choose your keyboard (ours is US Normal). The installation will Continue.
17. Next you will choose a hostname. I am keeping the default of Ubuntu. Click Continue.
18. Enter your user account (full name) and click Continue.
19. Enter your username. First name is fine and click Continue.
20. Type in your password and click Continue. Do not choose to show your password in clear. You will then be asked to re-enter your password and click Continue.
21. When it asks you to encrypt your home directory, choose No.
22. The install will try to figure out your time zone. If it picks correctly, chose Yes. If it doesn't, choose No and enter your time zone.
23. The next screen will ask you about setting up a Partition disk. I am going to allow Linux to configure the disk (Guided) and I will allow it to use the entire drive with a Logical Volume Manager (LVM). So I am choosing Guided—use entire disk and set up LVM.
24. It will then ask about partition type. I am choosing SCSI3.
25. The next screen will verify your choices for partitioning. Choose Yes.
26. It will then verify your disk size and then if you want to continue. Choose the disk size and then choose Yes to continue.
27. The next screen will ask you if you use a Proxy server for Internet access. If you use a Proxy, put it in and if you don't, just click Continue.
28. You will be asked about updates for Linux. Choose how you want to do your updates. Since this is a test virtual machine, I am choosing No automatic updates.
29. At the Software selection screen, choose what software you want installed during this process. I chose DNS, Samba File Server, and standard system utilities. Click Continue.
30. At the GRUB boot screen, click Yes to install the GRUB boot loader. This is OK since we have no other operating system on this virtual machine.
31. Once the installation is complete, choose Continue. At this point, Linux will restart and ask you for your login and password. After you enter them, you will be at a Linux prompt.
32. Type `shutdown` at the prompt to shut down the virtual machine.

Now that we have installed Linux (or FreeBSD), the next step is to help improve the Hyper-V performance. As I stated earlier, this issue will be resolved as long as we install the drivers that are needed on Hyper-V called Linux Integration Services (LIS) and FreeBSD Integrated Services (FIS). By putting these drivers on a device that can handle Linux and FreeBSD, you can then have Hyper-V with all of the features Microsoft offers.

Depending on what version of Linux or FreeBSD that you installed, you will need to download some additional updates to get the best performance out of Hyper-V. The following Microsoft website has a list of links for the different versions of Linux and FreeBSD updates: `https://technet.microsoft.com/windows-server-docs/compute/hyper-v/supported-linux-and-freebsd-virtual-machines-for-hyper-v-on-windows?f=255&MSPPError=-2147217396`.

In Exercise 4.7, I will show you how to install the additional updates needed for the Linux Ubuntu version (16.10) that I installed in Exercise 4.6.

**EXERCISE 4.7**

### Updating Linux Ubuntu 16.10

1. Open Hyper-V Manager.
2. Start the Linux virtual machine by clicking on the Linux virtual machine and clicking Start on the right hand menu.
3. At the Ubuntu login, enter the login and password that you created in Exercise 4.6.
4. Since we are using Ubuntu 16.10, we need to install the latest virtual kernel to have up-to-date Hyper-V capabilities. To install the virtual HWE kernel, run the following command as root (or sudo):
   `sudo apt-get update`
5. You will be asked for your password. Enter your password.
6. Next type in the following command:
   `sudo apt-get install linux-image-virtual`
7. You will be asked to confirm your choice by typing Y and hit enter.
8. Type in the following command:
   `sudo apt-get install linux-tools-virtual linux-cloud-tools-virtual`
9. You will be asked to confirm your choice by typing Y and hit enter.
10. After everything is installed, you are ready to go. You can clear the screen by typing `Clear` and hit enter. To shut down the system, type `shutdown`.

Finally, if you want to setup the Linux or FreeBSD virtual machines to use the advantages of secure boot, you would need to run the following PowerShell command on the Hyper-V server:

```
Set-VMFirmware -VMName "VMname" -EnableSecureBoot Off
```

# PowerShell Commands

One of the things that Microsoft has stated is that the exams are going to be more PowerShell intensive. So, I wanted to add a PowerShell section showing the different PowerShell commands that you can use for Hyper-V. This table has been taken directly from Microsoft's websites. Table 4.6 explains just some of the PowerShell commands that you can use with Hyper-V.

Table 4.6 shows you just some of the PowerShell commands for Hyper-V. To see a more comprehensive list, please visit Microsoft's website at `https://technet.microsoft.com/en-us/library/hh848559.aspx`.

**TABLE 4.6** Hyper-V PowerShell commands

| Command | Explanation |
|---|---|
| `Add-VMDvdDrive` | Adds a DVD drive to a virtual machine. |
| `Add-VMHardDiskDrive` | Adds a hard disk drive to a virtual machine. |
| `Add-VMMigrationNetwork` | Adds a network for virtual machine migration on one or more virtual machine hosts. |
| `Add-VMNetworkAdapter` | Adds a virtual network adapter to a virtual machine. |
| `Add-VMSwitch` | Adds a virtual switch to an Ethernet resource pool. |
| `Checkpoint-VM` | Creates a checkpoint of a virtual machine. |
| `Convert-VHD` | Converts the format, version type, and block size of a virtual hard disk file. |
| `Copy-VMFile` | Copies a file to a virtual machine. |
| `Debug-VM` | Debugs a virtual machine. |

**TABLE 4.6** Hyper-V PowerShell commands *(continued)*

| Command | Explanation |
|---|---|
| `Disable-VMConsoleSupport` | Disables keyboard, video, and mouse for virtual machines. |
| `Disable-VMMigration` | Disables migration on one or more virtual machine hosts. |
| `Dismount-VHD` | Dismounts a virtual hard disk. |
| `Enable-VMConsoleSupport` | Enables keyboard, video, and mouse for virtual machines. |
| `Enable-VMMigration` | Enables migration on one or more virtual machine hosts. |
| `Enable-VMReplication` | Enables replication of a virtual machine. |
| `Enable-VMResourceMetering` | Collects resource utilization data for a virtual machine or resource pool. |
| `Export-VM` | Exports a virtual machine to disk. |
| `Export-VMSnapshot` | Exports a virtual machine checkpoint to disk. |
| `Get-VHD` | Gets the virtual hard disk object associated with a virtual hard disk. |
| `Get-VHDSet` | Gets information about a VHD set. |
| `Get-VHDSnapshot` | Gets information about a checkpoint in a VHD set. |
| `Get-VM` | Gets the virtual machines from one or more Hyper-V hosts. |
| `Get-VMDvdDrive` | Gets the DVD drives attached to a virtual machine or checkpoint. |
| `Get-VMHardDiskDrive` | Gets the virtual hard disk drives attached to one or more virtual machines. |
| `Get-VMMemory` | Gets the memory of a virtual machine or checkpoint. |
| `Get-VMNetworkAdapter` | Gets the virtual network adapters of a virtual machine, checkpoint, or management operating system or of a virtual machine and management operating system. |
| `Get-VMProcessor` | Gets the processor of a virtual machine or checkpoint. |

| Command | Explanation |
|---|---|
| `Get-VMReplication` | Gets the replication settings for a virtual machine. |
| `Get-VMSwitch` | Gets virtual switches from one or more virtual Hyper-V hosts. |
| `Merge-VHD` | Merges virtual hard disks. |
| `Mount-VHD` | Mounts one or more virtual hard disks. |
| `Move-VM` | Moves a virtual machine to a new Hyper-V host. |
| `New-VHD` | Creates one or more new virtual hard disks. |
| `New-VM` | Creates a new virtual machine. |
| `New-VMGroup` | Creates a virtual machine group. |
| `New-VMSwitch` | Creates a new virtual switch on one or more virtual machine hosts. |
| `Remove-VHDSnapshot` | Removes a checkpoint from a VHD set file. |
| `Remove-VM` | Deletes a virtual machine. |
| `Remove-VMHardDiskDrive` | Deletes one or more virtual hard disks (VHDs) from a virtual machine (VM). |
| `Remove-VMNetworkAdapter` | Removes one or more virtual network adapters from a virtual machine. |
| `Remove-VMReplication` | Removes the replication relationship of a virtual machine. |
| `Remove-VMSan` | Removes a virtual storage area network (SAN) from a Hyper-V host. |
| `Remove-VMSwitch` | Deletes a virtual switch. |
| `Rename-VM` | Renames a virtual machine. |
| `Rename-VMGroup` | Renames virtual machine groups. |
| `Resize-VHD` | Resizes a virtual hard disk. |
| `Restart-VM` | Restarts a virtual machine. |

**TABLE 4.6** Hyper-V PowerShell commands *(continued)*

| Command | Explanation |
|---|---|
| Save-VM | Saves a virtual machine. |
| Set-VHD | Sets properties associated with a virtual hard disk. |
| Set-VM | Configures a virtual machine. |
| Set-VMBios | Configures the BIOS of a Generation 1 virtual machine. |
| Set-VMMemory | Configures the memory of a virtual machine. |
| Set-VMNetworkAdapter | Configures features of the virtual network adapter in a virtual machine or the management operating system. |
| Set-VMProcessor | Configures one or more processors of a virtual machine. The Set-VMProcessor command also allows an administrator to configure nested virtualization. While the virtual machine is in the OFF state, run the Set-VMProcessor command on the physical Hyper-V host. This will enable nested virtualization for the virtual machine. |
| Set-VMReplicationServer | Configures a host as a Replica server. |
| Set-VMSan | Configures a virtual storage area network (SAN) on one or more Hyper-V hosts. |
| Set-VMSwitch | Configures a virtual switch. |
| Stop-VM | Shuts down, turns off, or saves a virtual machine. |
| Suspend-VM | Suspends, or pauses, a virtual machine. |

# Summary

Virtualization is quickly becoming a hot topic in information technology. The potential for consolidation is tremendous, and thus it will become more and more important.

After reading this chapter, you should have a good understanding of the Hyper-V architecture and what is required to install Hyper-V.

The section about installation and configuration covered various basic aspects of configuring the virtualization environment. You learned about the different types of virtual networks that are available, the options for installing the Hyper-V role, and the various types of virtual hard disks that you can use to optimize virtualization for your specific scenario.

You also learned how to configure virtual machines using the Hyper-V environment and how to create your own virtual datacenter on top of your Hyper-V machines. I showed you how to create and manage virtual machines, how to use Virtual Machine Connection to control a virtual machine remotely, and how to install Hyper-V Integration Components. You also learned how to export and import virtual machines as well as how to do checkpoints of your virtual machine.

If you have never worked with virtualization software before, the information in this chapter may have been completely new to you. You should now be well prepared to try Hyper-V in your own environment.

# Video Resources

There are videos available for the following exercises:

4.1

4.4

You can access the videos at `http://sybextestbanks.wiley.com` on the Other Study Tools tab.

# Exam Essentials

**Understand Hyper-V's architecture.** When you have a good understanding of Hyper-V's architecture, especially when an operating system in a virtual machine is hypervisor-aware versus non-hypervisor-aware, you have a solid understanding of what is important from an architectural perspective.

You should know about the Hyper-V Integration Components and how they change the behavior of a virtual machine. Also know for which operating systems the integration components are available.

**Know Hyper-V's requirements and how to install it.** Know the hardware and software requirements as well as how to install Hyper-V. Hyper-V requires an x64-based processor and Data Execution Protection (DEP). Hardware-assisted virtualization must be enabled—don't forget this! Also remember that you can install Hyper-V two ways: using Server Manager or using the command line in Server Core.

**Understand virtual networks and virtual hard disks.** Virtual networks and hard disks are the two most tested topics. You definitely should know the types of virtual networks available (that is, external, internal only, and private virtual network) as well as all types of virtual hard disks (namely, dynamically expanding, fixed size, differential, and physical or pass-through). You should be able to apply the correct one when needed. Don't forget the Edit Virtual Hard Disk Wizard, which is also a good source for questions in the exam.

**Know how to create and manage virtual machines.** You should be able to explain how to create a virtual machine, what options are available to install an operating system in a virtual machine, and how to install the Hyper-V Integration Components on a virtual machine. Don't forget about the virtual machine states and the virtual machine settings!

**Understand how to back up and restore virtual machines.** Have a good understanding of the concept of exporting and importing virtual machines, how checkpoints work, and what lies behind a quick migration. Understand how you can export a virtual machine, what you should consider when moving it to a new host machine, and what happens after importing it to the import folder. The same applies to checkpoints: You need to know what options you have available and what each option will do. Especially recognize the difference between applying and reverting a checkpoint.

# Review Questions

1. On which of the following x64 editions of Windows Server 2016 does Hyper-V run? (Choose all that apply.)
    - **A.** Windows Server 2016 Web Edition
    - **B.** Windows Server 2016 Standard Edition
    - **C.** Windows Server 2016 Itanium Edition
    - **D.** Windows Server 2016 Datacenter Edition
2. You want to build a test environment based on virtual machines on a single Windows Server 2016 machine, but you also want to make sure the virtual machines communicate with only each other. What type of virtual network do you need to configure?
    - **A.** External
    - **B.** Internal only
    - **C.** Private virtual machine network
    - **D.** Public virtual machine network
3. Andy wants to change the memory of a virtual machine that is currently powered up. What does he need to do?
    - **A.** Shut down the virtual machine, use the virtual machine's settings to change the memory, and start it again.
    - **B.** Use the virtual machine's settings to change the memory.
    - **C.** Pause the virtual machine, use the virtual machine's settings to change the memory, and resume it.
    - **D.** Save the virtual machine, use the virtual machine's settings to change the memory, and resume it.
4. You want to make sure the hard disk space for your virtual machines is occupied only when needed. What type of virtual hard disk would you recommend?
    - **A.** Dynamically expanding disk
    - **B.** Fixed-size disk
    - **C.** Differencing disk
    - **D.** Physical or pass-through disk
5. How do you add a physical disk to a virtual machine?
    - **A.** Use the Virtual Hard Disk Wizard.
    - **B.** Use the Edit Virtual Hard Disk Wizard.
    - **C.** Use the virtual machine's settings.
    - **D.** Use the New Virtual Machine Wizard.

6. Rich bought a new server with an Itanium IA-64 processor, 4 GB RAM, and a SAN that provides 1 TB hard disk space. After installing Windows Server 2016 for Itanium-based systems, he wants to install Hyper-V on this server. Can Hyper-V be installed on this system?
   A. Yes
   B. No
7. What are the minimum CPU requirements for running Hyper-V on a machine? (Choose all that apply.)
   A. An x64-based processor (Intel or AMD).
   B. Hardware Data Execution Protection (DEP) must be enabled.
   C. Hardware-assisted virtualization must be enabled.
   D. The processor must at least have a dual core.
8. What is the command to install Hyper-V on a Windows Server 2016 machine that was installed in Server Core?
   A. `start /w ocsetup Hyper-V`
   B. `start /w ocsetup microsoft-hyper-v`
   C. `start /w ocsetup Microsoft-Hyper-V`
   D. `start /w ocsetup hyper-v`
9. On what operating systems can you install the Hyper-V Manager MMC? (Choose all that apply.)
   A. Windows Server 2012 R2
   B. Windows Server 2003
   C. Windows 10
   D. Windows 7, Windows 8
10. What statement is correct for an external virtual network?
   A. The virtual machines can communicate with each other and with the host machine.
   B. The virtual machines can communicate with each other only.
   C. The virtual machines can communicate with each other, with the host machine, and with an external network.
   D. The virtual machines cannot communicate with each other.

# Configuring High Availability

## THE FOLLOWING 70-740 EXAM OBJECTIVES ARE COVERED IN THIS CHAPTER:

✓ **Implement high availability and disaster recovery options in Hyper-V**

- This objective may include, but is not limited to: Implement Hyper-V Replica; implement Live Migration; implement Shared Nothing Live Migration; configure CredSSP or Kerberos authentication protocol for Live Migration; implement storage migration.

✓ **Implement Network Load Balancing (NLB)**

- This objective may include, but is not limited to: Install NLB nodes; configure NLB prerequisites; configure affinity; configure port rules; configure cluster operation mode; upgrade an NLB cluster.

✓ **Manage VM movement in clustered nodes**

- This objective may include but is not limited to: Perform a live migration; perform a quick migration; perform a storage migration; import, export, and copy VMs; configure VM network health protection; configure drain on shutdown.

It is now time to start talking about keeping our servers up and running as much as possible. So with this in mind, this chapter and Chapter 6, "Understanding Clustering," work hand in hand together.

In this chapter, I will start introducing you to some of the techniques and components of high availability. I will explain how to set up high availability using Network Load Balancing. I will talk about some of the reasons why you would choose to use Network Load Balancing over using a failover cluster and which applications or servers work better with Network Load Balancing. I will also show you how to use PowerShell for NLB.

I will continue the chapter by explaining how to keep your Hyper-V servers up and running by implementing high availability and disaster recovery options in Hyper-V. Finally, I will show you the PowerShell commands for Hyper-V high availability.

# Components of High Availability

*High availability* is a buzzword that many application and hardware vendors like to throw around to get you to purchase their products. Many different options are available to achieve high availability, and there also seem to be a number of definitions and variations that help vendors sell their products as high-availability solutions.

When it comes right down to it, however, high availability simply means providing services with maximum uptime by avoiding unplanned downtime. Often, *disaster recovery (DR)* is also closely lumped into discussions of high availability, but DR encompasses the business and technical processes that are used to recover once a disaster has happened.

Defining a high availability plan usually starts with a *service level agreement (SLA)*. At its most basic, an SLA defines the services and metrics that must be met for the availability and performance of an application or service. Often, an SLA is created for an IT department or service provider to deliver a specific level of service. An example of this might be an SLA for a Microsoft Exchange server. The SLA for an Exchange server might have uptime metrics on how much time during the month the mailboxes need to be available to end users, or it might define performance metrics for the amount of time it takes for email messages to be delivered.

When determining what goes into an SLA, two other factors need to be considered. However, you will often see them discussed only in the context of disaster recovery, even though they are important for designing a highly available solution. These factors are the *recovery point objective (RPO)* and the *recovery time objective (RTO)*.

An RTO is the length of time an application can be unavailable before service must be restored to meet the SLA. For example, a single component failure would have an RTO of less than five minutes, and a full-site failure might have an RTO of three hours. An RPO is essentially the amount of data that must be restored in the event of a failure. For example, in a single server or component failure, the RPO would be 0, but in a site failure, the RPO might allow for up to 20 minutes of lost data.

SLAs, on the other hand, are usually expressed in percentages of the time the application is available. These percentages are also often referred to by the number of nines the percentage includes. So if someone told you that you need to make sure that the router has a rating of Five 9s, that would mean that the router could only be down for 5.26 minutes a year. Table 5.1 shows you some of the different nines rating and what each rating allows for downtime.

**TABLE 5.1** Availability percentages

| Availability Rating | Allowed Unplanned Downtime/Year |
|---|---|
| 99 (two nines) percent | 3.65 days |
| 99.9 (three nines) percent | 8.76 hours |
| 99.99 (four nines) percent | 52.56 minutes |
| 99.999 (five nines) percent | 5.26 minutes |
| 99.9999 (six nines) percent | 31.5 seconds |
| 99.99999 (seven nines) percent | 3.15 seconds |

Two important factors that affect an SLA are the *mean time between failure (MTBF)* and the *mean time to recovery (MTTR)*. To be able to reduce the amount of unplanned downtime, the time between failures must be increased, and the time it takes to recover must be reduced. Modifying these two factors will be addressed in the next several sections of this chapter.

# Achieving High Availability

Windows Server 2016 is the most secure and reliable Windows version to date. It also is the most stable, mature, and capable of any version of Windows. Although similar claims have been made for previous versions of Windows Server, you can rest assured that Windows Server 2016 is much better than previous versions for a variety of reasons.

An honest look at the feature set and real-world use should prove that this latest version of Windows provides the most suitable foundation for creating a highly available solution. However, more than just good software is needed to be able to offer high availability for applications.

## High Availability Foundation

Just as a house needs a good foundation, a highly available Windows server needs a stable and reliable hardware platform on which to run. Although Windows Server 2016 will technically run on desktop-class hardware, high availability is more easily achieved with server-class hardware. What differentiates desktop-class from server-class hardware? *Server-class hardware* has more management and monitoring features built into it so that the health of the hardware is capable of being monitored and maintained.

Another large difference is that server-class hardware has redundancy options. Server-class hardware often has options to protect from drive failures, such as RAID controllers, and to protect against power supply failures, such as multiple power supplies. Enterprise-class servers have even more protection.

More needs to be done than just installing Windows Server 2016 to ensure that the applications remain running with the best availability possible. Just as a house needs maintenance and upkeep to keep the structure in proper repair, so too does a server. In the case of a highly available server, this means *patch management*.

### Installing Patches

Microsoft releases monthly updates to fix security problems with its software, both for operating system fixes and for applications. To ensure that your highly available applications are immune to known vulnerabilities, these patches need to be applied in a timely manner during a scheduled maintenance window. Also, to address stability and performance issues, updates and service packs are released regularly for many applications, such as Microsoft SQL Server, Exchange Server, and SharePoint Portal Server. Many companies have a set schedule—daily, weekly, or monthly—to apply these patches and updates after they are tested and approved.

Desired Configuration Manager (DCM), an option in Microsoft System Center Configuration Manager, is a great tool for helping to validate that your cluster nodes are patched. It can leverage the SCCM client to collect installed patches and help reporting within the enterprise on compliancy with desired system states based on the software installed.

To continue with the house analogy, if you were planning to have the master bath remodeled, would you rather hire a college student on spring break looking to make some extra money to do the job or a seasoned artisan? Of course, you would want someone with experience and a proven record of accomplishment to remodel your master bath.

Likewise, with any work that needs to be done on your highly available applications, it's best to hire only decidedly qualified individuals. This is why obtaining a Microsoft certification is definitely an excellent start to becoming qualified to configure a highly available server properly. There is no substitute for real-life and hands-on experience. Working with highly available configurations in a lab and in production will help you know not only what configurations are available but also how the changes should be made.

For example, it may be possible to use Failover Clustering for a DNS server, but in practice DNS replication may be easier to support and require less expensive hardware in order to provide high availability. This is something you would know only if you had enough experience to make this decision.

As with your house, once you have a firm and stable foundation built by skilled artisans and a maintenance plan has been put into place, you need to ascertain what more is needed. If you can't achieve enough uptime with proper server configuration and mature operational processes, a cluster may be needed.

Windows Server 2016 provides two types of high availability: *Failover Clustering* and *Network Load Balancing (NLB)*. Failover clustering is used for applications and services such as SQL Server and Exchange Server. Network Load Balancing is used for network-based services such as web and FTP servers. The remaining sections of this chapter will cover NLB and Hyper-V high availability in depth. Chapter 6 "Understanding Clustering" will cover all of the clustering aspects.

# Understanding Network Load Balancing

So the first thing we have to discuss is why an administrator would choose to use NLB. NLB allows an administrator to configure two or more servers as a single virtual cluster. NLB is designed for high availability and scalability of Internet server applications. So this means that Windows Server 2016 NLB is designed to work with web servers, FTP servers, firewalls, proxy servers, and virtual private networks (VPNs).

Administrators can use NLB for other mission-critical servers, but you can also use failover clusters on many of these servers. So after these two chapters are done, hopefully you will be able to choose the appropriate high availability server setup for your network and applications.

Network Load Balancing is a form of clustering where the nodes are highly available for a network-based service. This is typically a port listener configuration where a farm of, say, Microsoft Internet Information Services servers all listen on ports 80 and 443 for incoming web traffic from client endpoints. These nodes, while not fully clustered in a technical sense, are load balanced, where each node handles some of the distributed network traffic.

The NLB feature uses the TCP/IP networking protocol to distribute traffic. For web servers and other necessary servers, NLB can provide performance and consistency when two or more computers are combined into a single virtual cluster.

Hosts are servers that make up an NLB cluster. Each host runs their own individual copy of the server applications. The incoming client requests are distributed by NLB to each of the hosts in the cluster. The administrator can configure the load so that it is handled by each host. Hosts can be added to the cluster to increase the load. If NLB has all traffic directed to a specific single host, then it is called a default host.

With the use of NLB, all the computers in a cluster can use the same set of IP addresses while each host maintains its own exclusive IP address. When a host fails for load-balanced applications, the computers still in operation will receive the workload automatically. When the down computer is ready to rejoin the cluster, it comes back online and will regain its share of the workload. This allows the rest of the computers in the cluster to handle less traffic.

NLB is beneficial in that stateless applications (for example, web servers) are available with little downtime and it allows for scalability.

Scalability is the capability of a system, network, or process to handle a growing amount of work, or its potential to be enlarged in order to accommodate growth. Scalability, when used for NLB clusters, is the ability to add one or more systems to an existing cluster when the need arises. An administrator can do the following with NLB to support scalability:

- A single cluster can support up to 32 computers.
- Handle multiple server load requests from across multiple hosts in a cluster.
- For single TCP/IP services, balance load requests across the NLB cluster.
- As the workload grows, be able to add hosts to the NLB cluster without failure.
- When the workload declines, be able to remove hosts from the cluster.
- Allow higher performance and lower overhead by utilizing a pipelined implementation. Pipelining allows requests to be sent to the NLB cluster without waiting for a response.
- Use NLB Manager or Windows PowerShell cmdlets to manage and configure NLB clusters and hosts from a single computer.
- Determine port rules for each website. Port rules allow you to configure which ports are going to be enabled or disabled. Ports are doorways that applications can use to access resources. For example, DNS traffic uses port 53 for all DNS traffic. Here are some of the more common port numbers:
    - FTP uses ports 20/21.
    - Secure Shell uses port 22.
    - SMTP (mail) uses port 25.
    - DNS uses port 53.
    - HTTP uses port 80.
    - POPv3 uses port 110.
    - HTTPS uses port 443.

- Determine load-balancing behavior using port management rules for an IP port or group of ports.
- Use an optional, single-host rule that will direct all client requests to a single host. NLB will route client requests to a specific host that is running particular applications.
- Allow certain IP ports to block unwanted network access.
- When operating in multicast mode, enable Internet Group Management Protocol (IGMP) support on the cluster host. This will control switch port flooding (when all incoming network packets are sent to all ports on the switch).
- Use Windows PowerShell to start, stop, and control NLB actions remotely.
- Check NLB events using Windows Event Log. All NLB actions and cluster changes are logged in the Event Log.

## NLB Requirements

The NLB cluster hardware requirements are as follows:

- All hosts must be on the same subnet.
- For each host, there is no limitation to the number of network adapters.
- All network adapters must be multicast or unicast within the cluster. Mixed environments, within a single cluster, are NOT supported.
- If using unicast mode, the network adapter used to handle client-to-cluster traffic must support media access control (MAC) address changing.

NLB cluster software requirements:

- The adapter on which NLB is enabled can only support TCP/IP.
- Must have a static IP address on the servers in the cluster.

## Installing NLB Nodes

You can install NLB nodes like any other server build. Administrators can install NLB by using either Server Manager or the Windows PowerShell commands for NLB.

Administrators should first make sure that all NLB servers have the most current updates, provisioned with appropriate resources (typically with multiple network interface cards for capacity and responsiveness), and monitored for health and reliability. In Exercise 5.1, I will walk you through the installation of your NLB nodes.

**EXERCISE 5.1**

### Installing NLB Nodes

1. Once you have multiple hosts ready for the installation of NLB, simply run the Add roles and features Wizard and select Network Load Balancing in the Features area of the wizard. If the Add Features dialog box appears, click the Add Features button.

**EXERCISE 5.1** ***(continued)***

2. Click the Next button. At the Confirmation screen, click the Install button. After the installation is finished, click the Close button and then close Server Manager.
3. This wizard places a new application in your Start menu under Windows Administrative Tools, the Network Load Balancing Manager (see Figure 5.1).

**FIGURE 5.1** Network Load Balancing

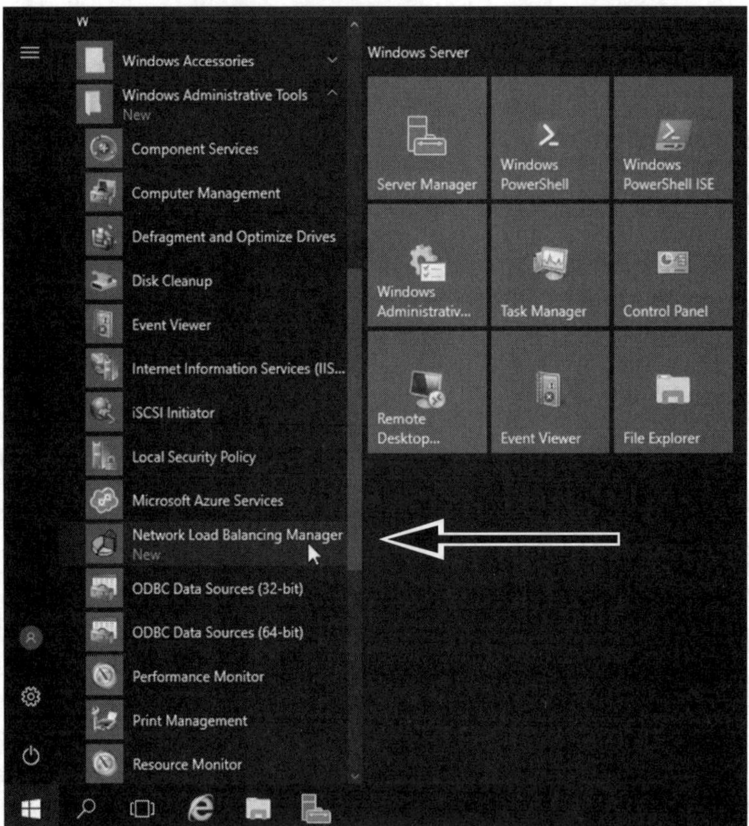


4. Right-click Network Load Balancing Clusters and select New Cluster (see Figure 5.2).
5. You are then presented with the New Cluster: Connect wizard where you can specify the name of one of your hosts. Type in the name of one of your cluster nodes and hit connect (see Figure 5.3). After the connection is made the TCP/IP address will be shown. Click Next.

**FIGURE 5.2** New Cluster

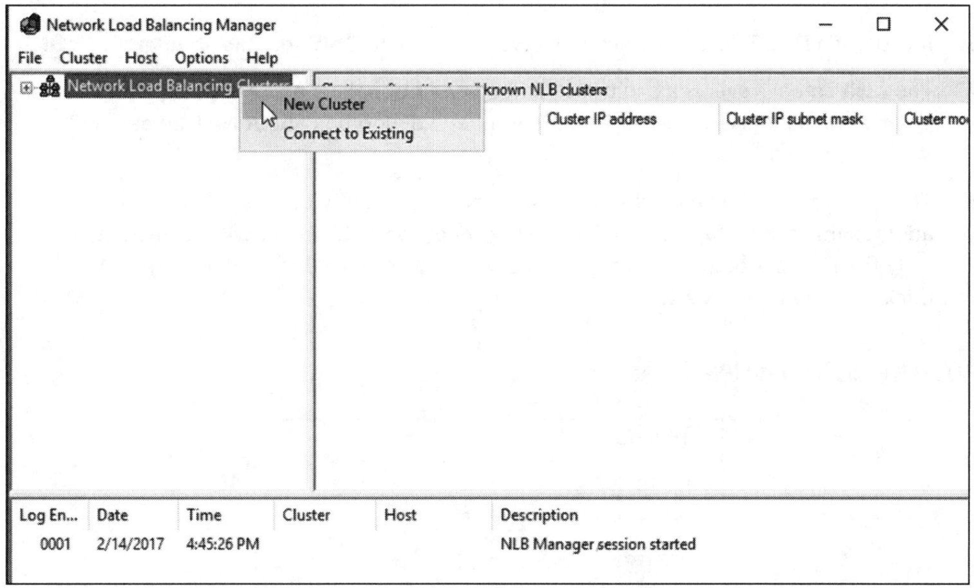


**FIGURE 5.3** Host Name setup

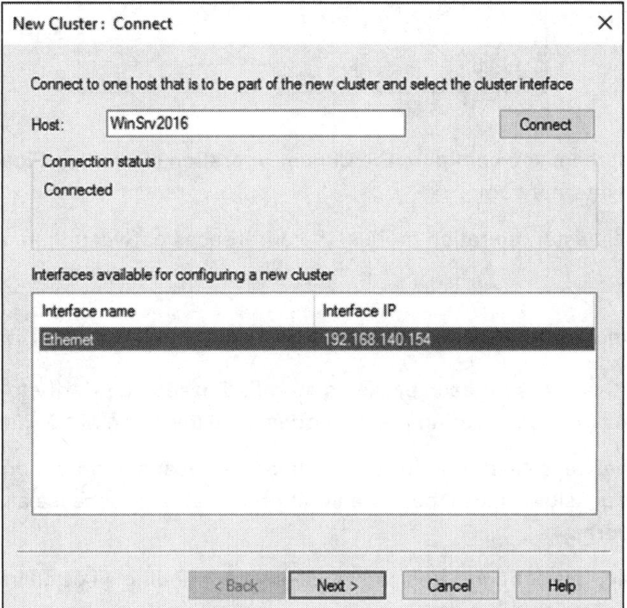

**EXERCISE 5.1** ***(continued)***

6. If you get a DHCP dialog box, you will want to disable DHCP on this adapter. Click OK.
7. The next screen reveals a prompt to add any additional IPs and assign a priority level. You can do all this later, so hit Next. If you get a dialog box about No Dedicated IP Addresses, click Yes.
8. The next wizard screen is where you specify the cluster IP address. This is the address that the endpoints or clients or users of the NLB cluster will contact. Typically the network team will assign a cluster IP address for this use (see Figure 5.4). Click OK. Then Click Next.

**FIGURE 5.4** Add IP address

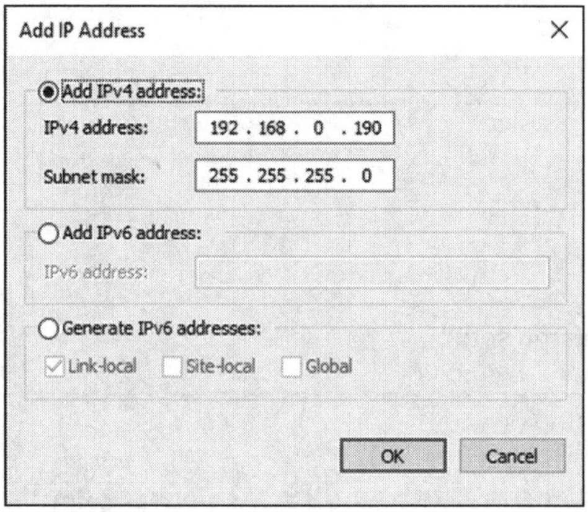

9. On the next screen, you configure the Cluster operation mode (see Figure 5.5) and specify a Full internet name.

With regard to the cluster operation modes, the differences between them are as follows:

**Unicast**

The cluster adapters for all nodes are assigned the same MAC address.

The outgoing MAC address for each packet is modified based on priority to prevent upstream switches from discovering that all nodes have the same MAC address.

Communication between cluster nodes (other than heartbeat and other administrative NLB traffic) is not possible unless there are additional adapters (because all nodes have the same MAC address).

Depending on load, this configuration can cause switch flooding since all inbound packets are sent to all ports on the switch.

**FIGURE 5.5** Cluster Parameters

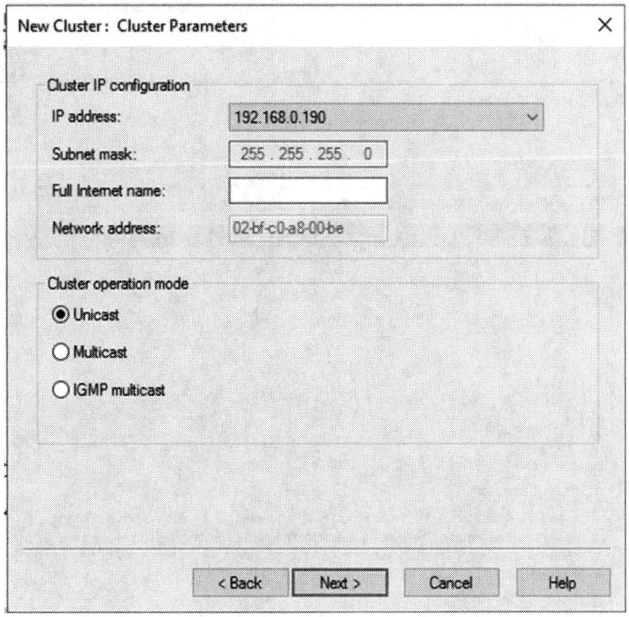

### Multicast

The cluster adapters for all nodes are assigned their own MAC unicast address.

The cluster adapters for all nodes are assigned a multicast MAC address (derived from the IP of the cluster).

Non-NLB network traffic between cluster nodes works fine since they all have their own MAC address.

### IGMP Multicast

This is much like multicast, but the MAC traffic goes only to the switch ports of the NLB cluster, preventing switch flooding.

10. After selecting the appropriate settings, the next page is where port rules (see Figure 5.6) are configured. By default, it is set up to be wide open. Most implementations will limit NLB ports to just the ports needed for the application. For example, a web server would need port 80 enabled. It is also in this area where you can configure filtering mode.

    The affinity sets a client's preference to a particular NLB host. It is not recommended to set affinity to None when UDP is an expected traffic type.

**EXERCISE 5.1 *(continued)***

**FIGURE 5.6** Port Rules

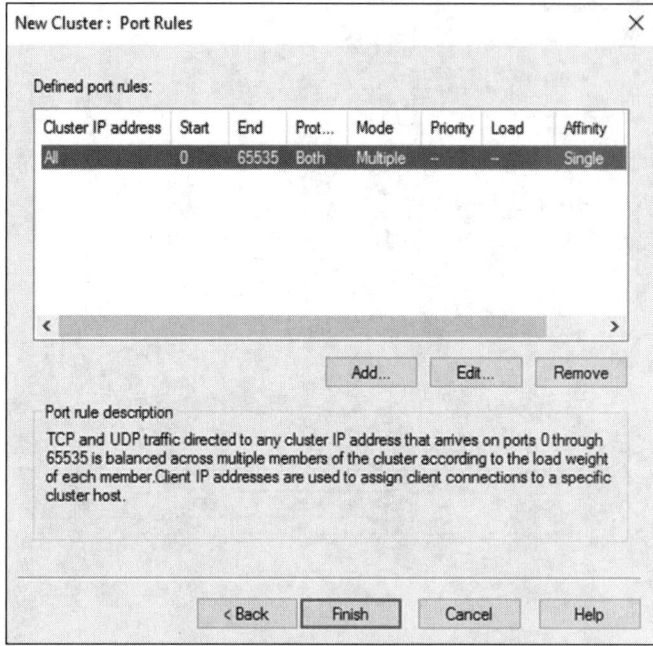


11. Click the Finish button. Close the NLB Manager.

If you decide that you want to install NLB using Windows PowerShell commands, you would open an elevated Windows PowerShell prompt and type in the following command:

```
Install-WindowsFeature NLB -IncludeManagementTools
```

## Upgrading an NLB Cluster

Upgrading an NLB cluster is a fairly straightforward process. The first thing that you have to do is stop the NLB cluster. There are two ways to stop a NLB cluster: stop or drainstop.

If an administrator decides to use the `stop` command, the cluster stops immediately. This also means that any current connections to the NLB cluster are killed.

If an administrator decides to use the `drainstop` command, the cluster stops after answering all of the current NLB connections. So the current NLB connections are finished but no new connections to that node are accepted.

So to do your upgrade, you should execute a `stop` or `drainstop` on the NLB cluster node that you want to upgrade or remove existing connections to the application on the local host. After the NLB cluster is stopped you then perform an in-place upgrade in a rolling manner.

If you want to stop the entire cluster from running, while in the NLB manager (type `NLBmgr in Run` command), you would right click on the cluster, point to Control Hosts, and then choose Stop.

If you want to stop a single node in the cluster from running, while in the NLB manager (type `NLBmgr in Run` command), you would right click on the node, point to Control Hosts, and then choose Stop.

## PowerShell Commands for a NLB Cluster

In Table 5.2, I will show you some of the different PowerShell commands that you can use to manage the NLB cluster.

**TABLE 5.2** PowerShell Commands for NLB

| PowerShell Command | Description |
|---|---|
| `Add-NlbClusterNode` | This command adds a new node to the NLB cluster. |
| `Add-NlbClusterNodeDip` | This command will add a dedicated IP address to a cluster. |
| `Add-NlbClusterPortRule` | This command adds a new port rule to a cluster. |
| `Add-NlbClusterVip` | This command adds a virtual IP address to a cluster. |
| `Disable-NlbClusterPortRule` | This command disables a port rule on a Network Load Balancing (NLB) cluster. |
| `Enable-NlbClusterPortRule` | This command enables a port rule on a cluster. |
| `Get-NlbCluster` | This command allows you to view information about the Network Load Balancing (NLB) cluster. |
| `Get-NlbClusterDriverInfo` | This command allows you to see information about the NLB drivers on a machine. |
| `Get-NlbClusterNode` | This command gets the information about the cluster object. |
| `Get-NlbClusterPortRule` | This command gets the port rule objects. |
| `New-NlbCluster` | This command creates a cluster on the specified interface. |
| `New-NlbClusterIpv6Address` | This command generates IPv6 addresses to create cluster virtual IP addresses. |

**TABLE 5.2** PowerShell Commands for NLB *(continued)*

| PowerShell Command | Description |
|---|---|
| `Remove-NlbCluster` | This command deletes a cluster. |
| `Remove-NlbClusterNode` | This command removes a node from a cluster. |
| `Remove-NlbClusterPortRule` | This command deletes a port rule from a cluster. |
| `Resume-NlbCluster` | This command resumes all nodes in the cluster. |
| `Set-NlbCluster` | This command allows you to edit the configuration of an NLB cluster. |
| `Set-NlbClusterNode` | This command allows an administrator to edit the NLB cluster node settings. |
| `Set-NlbClusterPortRule` | This command allows you to edit the NLB port rules. |
| `Start-NlbCluster` | This command will start all of the nodes in a cluster. |
| `Start-NlbClusterNode` | This command will start one of the nodes in a cluster. |
| `Stop-NlbCluster` | This command stops all nodes in the cluster. |
| `Stop-NlbClusterNode` | This command will stop one of the nodes in a cluster. |

# Achieving High Availability with Hyper-V

One of the nice advantages of using Hyper-V is the ability to run an operating server within another server. Virtualization allows you to run multiple servers on top of a single Hyper-V server. But we need to make sure that these servers stay up and running.

That is where Hyper-V high availability comes into play. Having the ability to ensure that your Hyper-V servers are going to continue to run even if there is a hardware issue is an important step in guaranteeing the success of your network.

There are many ways that you can ensure that your virtual machines will continue to operate. One is to set up clustering (discussed in Chapter 6) and another is to set up Hyper-V high availability without clustering.

To set up reliability without clustering requires that your Hyper-V servers have replica copies that can automatically start up if the virtual machine errors out. This is referred to as Live Migration and replica servers.

## Implementing a Hyper-V Replica

Hyper-V Replica is an important part of the Hyper-V role. It replicates the Hyper-V virtual machines from the primary site to the replica secondary sites simultaneously.

Once an administrator enables Hyper-V Replica for a particular virtual machine on the primary Hyper-V host server, the Hyper-V Replica will begin to create an exact copy of the virtual machine for the secondary site. After this replication, Hyper-V Replica creates a log file for the virtual machine VHDs. This log file is rerun in reverse order to the replica VHD. This is done using replication frequency. The log files and reverse order helps ensure that the latest changes are stored and copied asynchronously. If there is an issue with the replication frequency then the administrator will receive an alert.

On the virtual machine, an administrator can establish resynchronization settings. This can be setup to be done manually, automatically or automatically on an explicit schedule. To fix constant synchronization issues an administrator may choose to set up automatic resynchronization.

Hyper-V Replica will aid in a disaster recovery strategy by replicating virtual machines from one host to other while keeping workloads accessible. Hyper-V Replica can create a copy of a running virtual machine to a replica offline virtual machine.

### Hyper-V Hosts

With replication over a WAN link the primary and secondary host servers can be located in the same physical location or at different geographical locations. Hyper-V hosts can be standalone, clustered or a combination of both. Hyper-V hosts are not dependent upon Active Directory and there is no need to be domain members.

### Replication and Change Tracking

When an administrator enables Hyper-V Replica on a particular virtual machine an identical copy of the virtual machine is created on a secondary host server. Once this happens, the Hyper-V Replica will create a log file that will track changes made on a virtual machine VHD. The log file is rerun in reverse order to the replica VHD. This is based on the replication frequency settings. This ensures that the latest changes are created and replicated asynchronously. This can be done over HTTP or HTTPS.

### Extended (Chained) Replication

Extended (chained) Replication allows an administrator to replicate a virtual machine from a primary host to a secondary host and then replicate the secondary host to a third host. It is not possible to replicate from the primary host directly to the second and third hosts.

Extended (Chained) Replication aids in disaster recovery in that an administrator can recover from both the primary and extended replica. Extended Replication will also aid if the primary and secondary locations go offline. It must be noted that the extended replica does not support application-consistent replication and it must use the same VHD that the secondary replica uses.

## Setting the Affinity

NLB allows an administrator to configure three types of affinity settings to help response times between NLB clients. Each affinity setting determines a method of distributing NLB client requests. There are three different affinity settings: None, Single, and Class C. The New Cluster Wizard sets the default affinity to Single.

**No Affinity (None)** When setting the affinity to No Affinity (None), NLB will not assign a NLB client with any specific member. When a request is sent to the NLB, the requests are balanced among all of the nodes. The No Affinity provides greater performance but there may be issues with clients establishing sessions. This happens because the request may be load balanced between NLB nodes and session information may not be present.

**Single Affinity** Setting the cluster affinity to Single will send all traffic from a specific IP address to a single cluster node. This will keep a client on a specific node where the client should not have to authenticate again. Setting the affinity mode to Single would remove the authentication problem but would not distribute the load to other servers unless the initial server was down. Setting the affinity to Single allows a client's IP address to always connect to the same NLB node. This setting allows clients using an intranet to get the best performance.

**Class C Affinity** When setting the affinity to Class C, NLB links clients with a specific member based on the Class C part of the client's IP address. This allows an administrator to setup NLB so that clients from the same Class C address range can access the same NLB member. This affinity is best for NLB clusters using the internet.

## Failover

If the primary or the secondary (extended) host server locations goes offline an administrator can manually initiate failover. Failover is not automatic. There are several different types of manually initiating failover:

**Test Failover** Use Test Failover to verify that the replica virtual machine can successfully start in the secondary site. It will create a copy test virtual machine during failover and does not affect standard replication. After the test failover, if the administrator selects Failover on the replica test virtual machine the test failover will be deleted.

**Planned Failover** Use Planned Failover during scheduled downtime. The administrator will have to turn off the primary machine before performing a planned failover. Once the machine fails over the Hyper-V Replica will start replicating changes back to the primary server. The changes are tracked and sent to ensure that there is no data lost. Once the planned failover is complete, the reverse replication begins so that the primary virtual machine become the secondary and vice versa. This ensures that the hosts are synchronized.

**Unplanned Failover** Use Unplanned Failover during unforeseen outages. Unplanned failover is started on the replica virtual machine. This should only be used if the primary machine goes offline. A check will confirm whether the primary machine is running. If the administrator has recovery history enabled then it is possible to recover to an earlier point in time. During failover an administrator should ensure that the recovery point is acceptable and then finish the failover to ensure that recovery points are combined.

## Virtual Machine Advanced Features

One nice feature of virtual machines is the ability to setup advanced features. In the Advanced Features section (see Figure 5.7), there are multiple settings that you can configure.

**FIGURE 5.7** VM Advanced Features

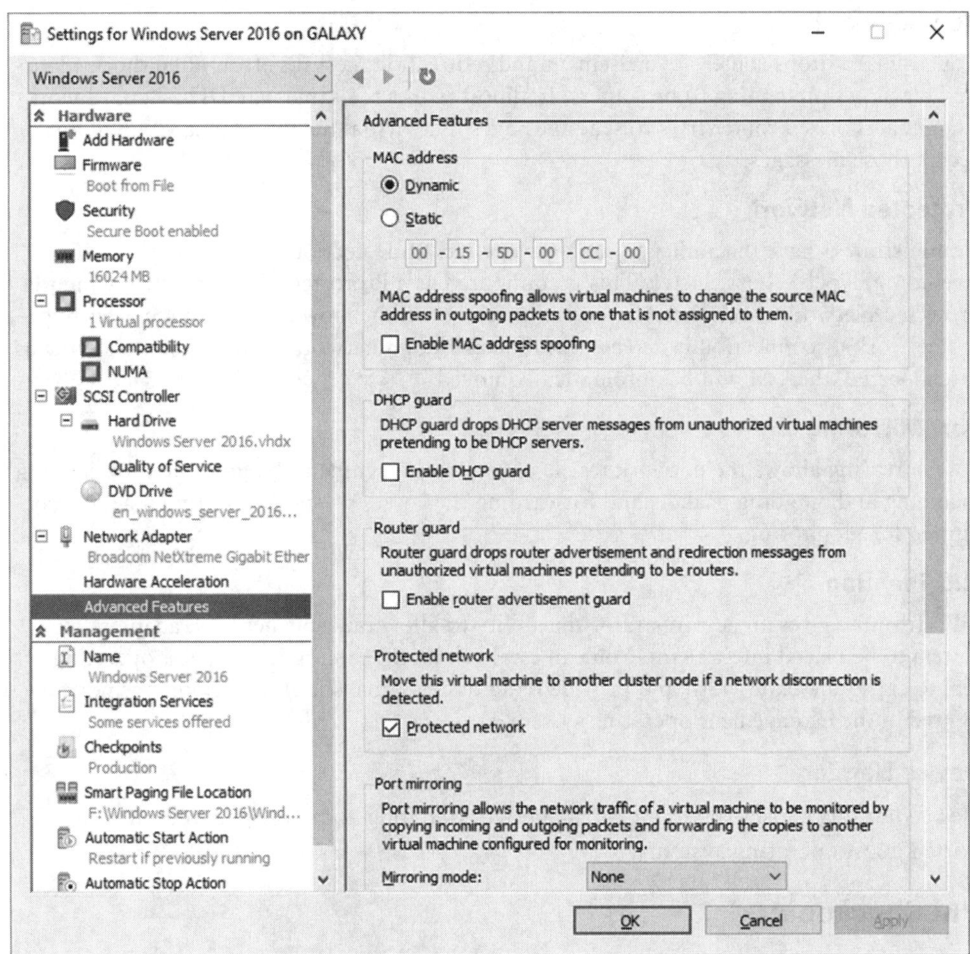

### MAC Addressing

The first thing that you can configure in the Advanced Features section is setting a MAC address. The MAC address is a physical address that is associated to the NIC adapter. Administrators have the ability to set the MAC address to Dynamic (creates its own MAC addresses) or Static (this is where you can set a MAC address).

You also have the ability to do MAC spoofing. This is where a VM can change the source MAC address in outgoing packets to one that is not assigned to the NIC adapters.

### DHCP Guard

DHCP guard drops DHCP server messages from unauthorized virtual machines pretending to be a DHCP server. So what does this mean to you? If a server tries to pretend to be a DHCP server, your virtual machine will drop any messages that are sent by that DHCP server.

### Router Guard

Router guard drops router advertisement and redirection messages from unauthorized virtual machines pretending to be routers. It almost works the same way DHCP guard works. If an unauthorized router tries to send messages to a virtual machine, that VM will not accept those messages.

### Protected Network

Administrators have the ability to set Network Health Detection at the virtual machine level for a Hyper-V host cluster. This is configured as a Protected Network. By setting the Protected Network check box, the virtual machine will be moved to another cluster node if a network disconnection is detected. If the health of a network connection is showing as disconnected, the VM will be automatically moved.

### Port Mirroring

Port mirroring allows the network traffic of a virtual machine to be monitored by copying incoming and outgoing packets and forwarding the copies to another virtual machine configured for monitoring.

### NIC Teaming

NIC Teaming gives an administrator the ability to allow multiple network adapters on a system to be placed into a team. You can establish NIC Teaming in the guest operating system to aggregate bandwidth and provide redundancy. This is useful if teaming is not configured in the management operating system.

### Device Naming

Device naming causes the name of the network adapter to be propagated into supported guest operating systems.

## VM Checkpoints

One thing that you may want to setup on your Hyper-V server is recovery points or checkpoints. A checkpoint is a snapshot in time from when an administrator can recover a virtual machine. It's like taking a picture of the virtual machine and using that picture to recover the VM. Administrators can create multiple checkpoints of a VM and then recover back to any of those checkpoints if there is an issue. Using a more recent recovery point will result in less data lost. Checkpoints can be accessed from up to 24 hours ago.

If you want to enable these checkpoints in time for Hyper-V, you just need to follow the steps below:

1. In Hyper-V Manager, right-click on the virtual machine and then click Settings.
2. Under the Management section, choose Checkpoints.
3. To enable checkpoints for a VM, check the box Enable checkpoints. If you want to disable checkpoints, just clear box.
4. Once finished, Click Apply. Once you are finished, click OK and close the Hyper-V Manager.

### Software Load Balancing

Windows Server 2016 Hyper-V also allows an administrator to distribute virtual network traffic using Software Load Balancing (SLB). Software Load Balancing allows administrators to have multiple servers hosting the same virtual networking workload in a multitenant environment. This allows an administrator to setup high availability.

Using SLB allows an organization to load balance virtual machines on the same Hyper-V server. So let's take a look at how SLB works. SLB is possible because it sets up a virtual IP address (VIP) that is automatically mapped to the dynamic IP addresses (DIP) of the virtual machines. The DIP addresses are the IP addresses of the virtual machines that are part of the load balancing setup.

So when someone tries to access the resources in the load balancing setup, they access it by using the VIP address. The VIP request then gets sent to the DIP address of the virtual machines. So users use the single VIP address and that address gets sent to the load balancing virtual machines.

## Understanding Live Migration

Before we can implement Live Migration, first you need to understand what Live Migration does for Hyper-V. Hyper-V live migration transfers a running virtual machine from one physical server to another. The real nice advantage of Live Migration is that during the move of the virtual machine, there is no impact on the network's users. The virtual machine will continue to operate even during the move. This is different from using Quick Migrations. Quick Migrations require a pause in the Hyper-V VM while it's being moved.

Live Migrations allow administrators to move virtual machines between servers. This is very useful when a Hyper-V server starts having issues. For example, if a Hyper-V machine is starting to have hardware issues, you can move the virtual machines from that Hyper-V server to another server that is running properly.

When setting up VM migrations, you have a few options. You can Live Migrate a VM, Quick Migrate a VM, or just move a VM. As stated before, Live Migration requires no interruption of the VM. Quick Migration requires that you first pause the VM, then save the VM, then move the VM and finally re-start the VM. Moving a virtual machine means that you are going to copy a VM from one Hyper-V server to another while the virtual machine is turned off.

So if you decide to setup and use Live Migrations, there are a few things that you should understand before setting it up. So let's take a look at some of the configuration settings that you can configure.

## Configure CredSSP or Kerberos authentication

When choosing to setup Live Migrations, one of the settings that you get to manipulate is the type of authentication you can use. Choosing the authentication type is a feature listed under the Advanced Features of Live Migration. Administrators can choose two types of authentication (as shown in Figure 5.8): Kerberos or Credential Security Support Provider (CredSSP).

**FIGURE 5.8** Live Migration Advanced Features

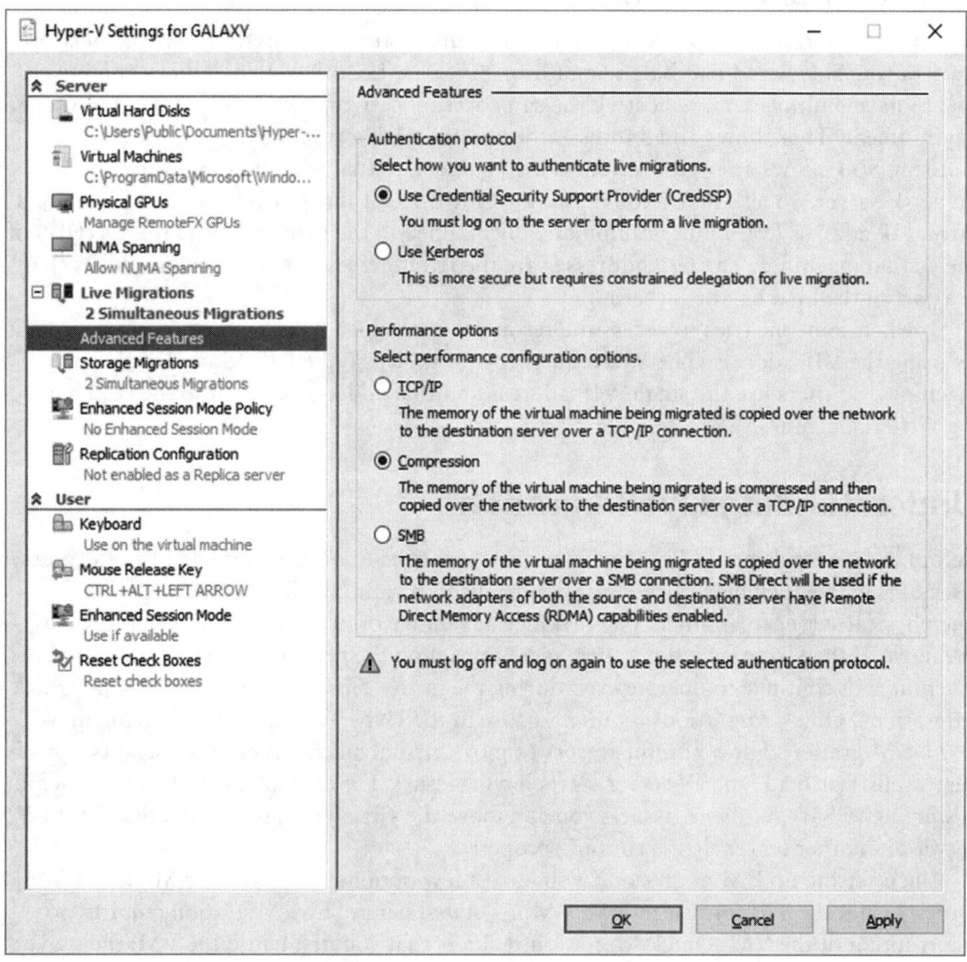

Authentication is choosing which protocol you will use to guarantee that live migration traffic between the source and destination servers are verified. Let's take a look at both options.

- Use Credential Security Support Provider (CredSSP)
    - This option allows an administrator to setup better security but requires constrained delegation for Live Migration. Administrators have the ability to sign in to the source server. Administrators can sign in to the source server by using a local console session, a Remote Desktop session, or a remote Windows PowerShell session.
- Use Kerberos
    - This option allows an administrator to avoid having to sign in to the server, but requires constrained delegation to be set up.

Another section that you setup in the Advanced Features of Live Migrations is the Performance options. This section allows you to choose how the network traffic for Live Migrations will be configured. There are three options that you can choose from:

**TCP/IP** The memory of the virtual machine being migrated is copied over the network to the destination server over a TCP/IP connection.

**Compression** The memory of the virtual machine being migrated is compressed and then copied over the network to the destination server over a TCP/IP connection.

**SMB** The memory of the virtual machine is copied over the network to the destination server over a SMB (Server Message Block) connection. SMB Direct will be used if the network adapters of both the source and destination server have Remote Direct Memory Access (RDMA) capabilities enabled.

## Implementing Live Migration

You will need the following to set up non-clustered hosts for live migration:

- A user account in the local Hyper-V Administrators group or the Administrators group on both the source and destination computers. Membership in the Domain Administrators group.
- The Hyper-V role in Windows Server 2016 or Windows Server 2012 R2 installed on both the source and destination servers. Live migration can be done if the virtual machine is at least version 5.
- The source and destination computers must belong to the same Active Directory domain or belong to trusted domains.
- The Hyper-V management tools installed on the server. Computer must be running Windows Server 2016 or Windows 10.

If an administrator wants to setup the source and destination of the live migration, they would need to use the following steps in Hyper-V Manager:

1. Open Hyper-V Manager. (click Start ➢ Administrative Tools ➢ Hyper-V Manager.)
2. In the navigation pane, click on one of the servers. Right click on the server ➢ Hyper-V Settings ➢ Live Migrations.

3. Click on the Live Migrations pane. Check the box Enable incoming and outgoing live migrations.
4. Under the section Simultaneous live migrations, specify the number of Simultaneous live migrations (the default is 2).
5. Under Incoming live migrations, administrators can choose to accept any network for live migrations or specify the IP address you want to use for live migration. If you want to use an IP address, click the Add button and type in the IP address information. Click OK once you're finished.
6. For Kerberos and performance options, expand Live Migrations (click the plus sign next to Live Migrations) and then select Advanced Features.
   - Under Authentication protocol, select either Use CredSSP or Use Kerberos.
   - Under Performance options, Select performance configuration options (either TCP/IP, Compression, or SMB).
7. Click OK.
8. If you have any other servers that you want to setup for Live Migrations, select the server and repeat the steps.

### Implement Shared Nothing Live Migration

Administrators can now Live Migrate virtual machines even if the Hyper-V host is not part of a cluster. Before using Live Migrate without a Windows Cluster an administrator will need to configure the servers. Either choose Kerberos or Credential Security Support Provider (CredSSP) to authenticate the Live Migration.

To trigger a Shared Nothing Live Migration remotely, the administrator will need to enable Kerberos constrained delegation.

Constrained delegation is configured through Active Directory Users and Computers in the Delegation tab for each computer taking part in the Shared Nothing Live Migration.

## Implementing Storage Migration

Hyper-V supports moving virtual machine storage without downtime by allowing the administrator to move storage while the virtual machine is running. This can be performed by using Hyper-V Manager or Windows PowerShell.

An administrator can add storage to a Hyper-V cluster or a stand-alone computer, and then move virtual machines to the new storage while the virtual machines continue to run.

An administrator can move virtual machine storage between physical storage devices to respond to a decrease in performance that results from bottlenecks.

### Storage Migration Requirements

The following will be needed to utilize Hyper-V functionality of moving virtual machine storage:

- One or more installations of Windows Server 2016 with the Hyper-V role installed.

- A server that is capable of running Hyper-V.
- Virtual machines that are configured to use only virtual hard disks for storage.

Storage Migration allows administrators to move the virtual hard disks of a virtual machine while the virtual hard disks are still able to be used by the running virtual machine (see Figure 5.9). When an administrator moves a running virtual machine's virtual hard disks, Hyper-V performs the following steps:

1. Disk reads and writes utilize the source virtual hard disk.
2. When reads and writes occur on the source virtual hard disk, the disk data is copied to the new destination virtual hard disk.
3. Once the initial disk copy is complete, the disk writes are mirrored to both the source and destination virtual hard disks while outstanding disk changes are replicated.
4. After the source and destination virtual hard disks are entirely synchronized, the virtual machine changes over to using the destination virtual hard disk.
5. The source virtual hard disk is deleted.

**FIGURE 5.9** Storage Migration Settings

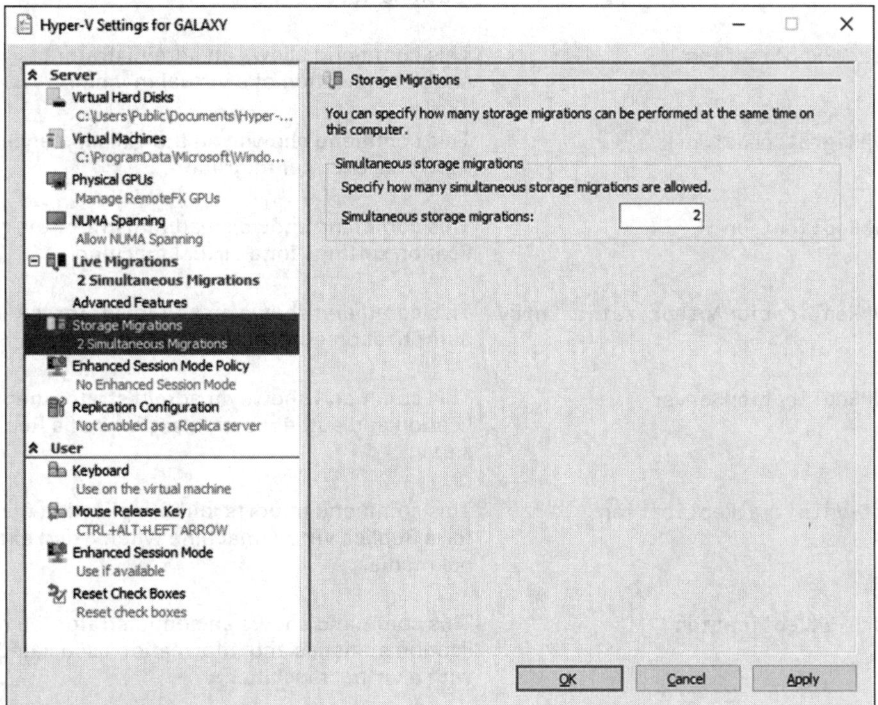

## PowerShell Commands for Hyper-V High Availability

When configuring Hyper-V high availability, you may want to setup some of the components using PowerShell. Table 5.3 shows you some of the available PowerShell commands available for setting up Hyper-V high availability.

**TABLE 5.3** PowerShell Commands for High Availability

| PowerShell Command | Description |
|---|---|
| `Complete-VMFailover` | This command helps finish a virtual machine's failover process on the Replica server. |
| `Disable-VMMigration` | This command allows an administrator to disable virtual machine migration on a virtual machine host. |
| `Enable-VMMigration` | This command allows an administrator to enable virtual machine migration on a virtual machine host. |
| `Enable-VMReplication` | This command allows an administrator to enable replication of a virtual machine. |
| `Get-VMMigrationNetwork` | This command shows you the virtual machine networks used for migration. |
| `Get-VMReplication` | This command shows an administrator the replication settings for a virtual machine. |
| `Get-VMReplicationAuthorizationEntry` | This command shows an administrator the authorization entries of a Replica server. |
| `Get-VMReplicationServer` | This command shows an administrator the replication and authentication settings of a Replica server. |
| `Import-VMInitialReplication` | This command imports initial replication files for a Replica virtual machine when using external media. |
| `Measure-VMReplication` | This command shows an administrator the replication statistics and information associated with a virtual machine. |
| `New-VMReplicationAuthorizationEntry` | This command allows you to create an authorization entry to replicate data to a specified Replica server. |

| PowerShell Command | Description |
|---|---|
| Remove-VMMigrationNetwork | This command allows an administrator to remove a network from use in migration. |
| Remove-VMReplication | This command removes the replication from a specific virtual machine. |
| Reset-VMReplicationStatistics | This command allows an administrator to reset the replication statistics of a virtual machine. |
| Resume-VMReplication | This command allows an administrator to resume virtual machine replication after an error, a pause, a suspension, or a resynchronization is required. |
| Set-VMProcessor | This command allows an administrator to configure which processors are used for a virtual machine. |
| Set-VMReplication | This command allows an administrator to modify the replication settings of a virtual machine. |
| Set-VMReplicationServer | This command allows an admin to configure a host as a Replica server. |
| Start-VMInitialReplication | This command starts replication of a virtual machine. |
| Stop-VMReplication | This command stops replication of a virtual machine. |
| Suspend-VMReplication | This command suspends replication of a virtual machine. |
| Test-VMReplicationConnection | This command allows an administrator to test the connection of a primary server and a Replica server. |

# Summary

High availability is more than just clustering. It is achieved through improved hardware, software, and processes. This chapter focused on how to configure Failover Clustering and Network Load Balancing in order to achieve high availability and scalability.

High availability should be approached through proper hardware configuration, training, and operational discipline. Failover Clustering provides a highly available base for many applications, such as databases and mail servers.

Network load-balanced clusters are used to provide high availability and scalability for network-based applications, such as VPNs and web servers. Network load-balanced clusters can be configured with any edition of Windows Server 2016 except for the Windows Server 2016 Hyper-V Edition.

Windows Server 2016 Hyper-V can also have high availability set up on it without using clustering. Administrators have the ability to set up Live Migrations on Hyper-V virtual machines.

Live Migration allows you to move a virtual machine from one server to another without any impact on the users. This can be very useful if you have a Hyper-V server that is starting to show hardware issues. Administrators can move the virtual machine from the server with issues to a server without any issues.

# Video Resources

There are no videos available for this chapter.

# Exam Essentials

**Know the hardware requirements for Network Load Balancing.** Network Load Balancing has distinct hardware requirements. Know the requirements for NLB.

**Know the PowerShell commands for NLB.** Make sure you know the different PowerShell commands for Network Load Balancing. Understand which command is used to create, manage, and stop NLB clusters.

**Understanding Live Migration.** Understand how Live Migrations work and why we use them. Understand that Live Migrations allow an administrator to move a virtual machine from one server to another without any impact on the users.

**Know PowerShell for VM Replication** Make sure you know the different PowerShell commands for Virtual Machine Replication. Understand which commands are used to create, manage, and stop VM Replication.

# Review Questions

1. You are the administrator for a mid-size organization. You have been asked by the owner to set up a NLB cluster. You want to use PowerShell to set up the cluster. What command would you use?

   A. `New-NlbCluster`

   B. `Create-NlbCluster`

   C. `Setup-NlbCluster`

   D. `Set-NlbCluster`

2. You are the administrator for your company. You have an application named AppA. AppA is distributed in a multitenant setup across multiple Hyper-V virtual machines. You need to ensure that the traffic is distributed evenly among the virtual machines that host AppA. What should you include in the environment?

   A. Router and Windows Server Network Load Balancing (NLB) nodes

   B. Router and Windows Server Software Load Balancing (SLB) nodes

   C. RAS Gateway and Windows Server Network Load Balancing (NLB) nodes

   D. RAS Gateway and Windows Server Software Load Balancing (SLB) nodes

3. What is the maximum number of nodes that can participate in a Windows Server 2016 NLB single cluster?

   A. 32

   B. 4

   C. 16

   D. 64

4. Which of the following actions should be performed against an NLB cluster node if maintenance needs to be performed while not terminating current connections?

   A. Evict

   B. Drainstop

   C. Pause

   D. Stop

5. Which of the following actions should be performed against an NLB cluster node if maintenance needs to be performed and all connections must be terminated immediately?

   A. Evict

   B. Drainstop

   C. Pause

   D. Stop

6. You are the network administrator for your organization and you want to stop virtual machine replication. What PowerShell command would you use?
   - A. `Stop-VMReplication`
   - B. `Terminate-VMReplication`
   - C. `Kill-VMReplication`
   - D. `Drainstop-VMReplication`
7. You are the network administrator for a company that has a Windows Server 2016 Hyper-V failover cluster. This cluster contains two nodes named ServerA and ServerB. On ServerA, you create a virtual machine named VirtualMachineA by using Hyper-V Manager. You need to configure VirtualMachineA to move to ServerB automatically if ServerA becomes unavailable. What should you do?
   - A. In the Failover Cluster manager, run the configure Role actions.
   - B. In the Hyper-V Manager, click VirtualMachineA and click Enable Replication.
   - C. In the Hyper-V Manager, click ServerA and modify the hyper-V settings.
   - D. Using Windows PowerShell, run the `Enable-VMReplication` cmdlet.
8. To configure an NLB cluster with unicast, what is the minimum number of network adapters required in each node?
   - A. One
   - B. Two
   - C. Three
   - D. Six
9. Users who are connecting to an NLB cluster have been complaining that after using the site for a few minutes they are prompted to log in using their username. What should you do to fix the problem and retain scalability?
   - A. Create a port rule to allow only ports 80 and 443.
   - B. Set the cluster affinity to None.
   - C. Set the filtering mode to Single Host.
   - D. Set the cluster affinity to Single.
10. Users who are connecting to an NLB cluster through the Internet are complaining that they keep connecting to different NLB nodes in different locations. You want to keep Internet users connecting to the same NLB members each time they connect. What should you do to fix the problem?
    - A. Create a port rule to allow only ports 80 and 443.
    - B. Set the cluster affinity to None.
    - C. Set the cluster affinity to Class C.
    - D. Set the cluster affinity to Single.

Chapter 6

# Understanding Clustering

## THE FOLLOWING 70-740 EXAM OBJECTIVES ARE COVERED IN THIS CHAPTER:

✓ **Implement failover clustering**

- This objective may include but is not limited to: Implement Workgroup, Single, and Multi-Domain clusters; configure quorum; configure cluster networking; restore single node or cluster configuration; configure cluster storage; implement Cluster-Aware Updating; implement Cluster Operating System Rolling Upgrade; configure and optimize clustered shared volumes (CSVs); configure clusters without network names; implement Scale-Out File Server (SoFS); determine different scenarios for the use of SoFS vs. clustered File Server; determine usage scenarios for implementing guest clustering; implement a Clustered Storage Spaces solution using Shared SAS storage enclosures; implement Storage Replica; implement Cloud Witness; implement VM resiliency; implement shared VHDX as a storage solution for guest clusters.

✓ **Implement Storage Spaces Direct**

- This objective may include but is not limited to: Determine scenario requirements for implementing Storage Spaces Direct; enable Storage Spaces direct using Windows PowerShell; implement a disaggregated Storage Spaces Direct scenario in a cluster; implement a hyper-converged Storage Spaces Direct scenario in a cluster.

✓ **Manage failover clustering**

- This objective may include but is not limited to: Configure role-specific settings, including continuously available shares; configure VM monitoring; configure failover and preference settings; implement stretch and site-aware failover clusters; enable and configure node fairness.

As I started to explain in the last chapter, keeping servers up and running 24/7 is one of the most important jobs that we have in IT. There are many ways that we can be sure that our servers are always going to be available. I started explaining one way in the last chapter with NLB and keeping servers highly available.

Well now I am going to keep that discussion going with clustering. There are different ways that you can set up clustering. You can set up high availability clusters and you can also set up failover clusters.

In this chapter, I will show you the different types of clusters that you can set up and configure. I will also explain some of the different situations in which each cluster would be best used. So let's continue our discussion on keeping our servers up and running 24/7 with clustering.

# Achieving High Availability with Failover Clustering

Taking high availability to the next level for enterprise services often means creating a failover cluster. In a failover cluster, all of the clustered application or service resources are assigned to one node or server in the cluster. Commonly clustered applications are SQL Server and Exchange Server; commonly clustered services are File and Print. Since the differences between a clustered application and a clustered service are primarily related to the number of functions or features, for simplicity's sake I will refer to both as *clustered applications*. Another, more frequently, clustered resource is a Hyper-V virtual machine.

If there is a failure of the primary node or if the primary node is taken offline for maintenance, the clustered application is started on another cluster node. The client requests are then automatically redirected to the new cluster node to minimize the impact of the failure.

How does Failover Clustering improve availability? By increasing the number of server nodes available on which the application or virtual machine can run, you can move the application or virtual machine to a healthy server if there is a problem, if maintenance needs to be completed on the hardware or the operating system, or if patches need to be applied. The clustered application being moved will have to restart on the new server regardless of whether the move was intentional. This is why the term *highly available* is used instead of *fault tolerant*. Virtual machines, however, can be moved from one node to another node using a process known as *live migration*. Live migration is where one or more virtual machines are intentionally moved from one node to another with their current memory state intact through the cluster network with no indicators to the virtual machine consumer that the virtual machine has moved from one server to another. However, in the event of a cluster node or virtual machine failure, the virtual machine will still fail and will then be brought online again on another healthy cluster node.

Figure 6.1 shows an example of SQL Server running on the first node of a Windows Server 2016 failover cluster.

**FIGURE 6.1** Using Failover Clustering to cluster SQL Server

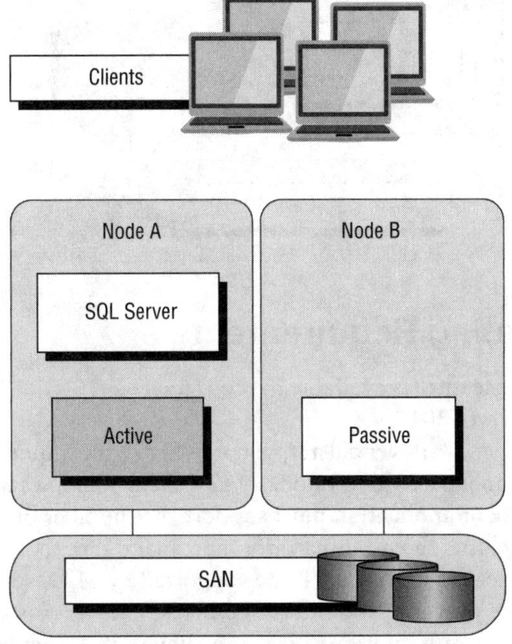


The clustered SQL Server in Figure 6.2 can be failed over to another node in the cluster and still service database requests. However, the database will be restarted.

Failover clustering is notorious for being complicated and expensive. Windows Server 2016 makes strides in removing both of these concerns. Troubleshooting and other advanced concepts are outside of the scope of the Microsoft MCSA exams and thus this book, so I will cover only the basic requirements and concepts needed to configure a failover cluster.

**FIGURE 6.2** Failing the SQL Server service to another node

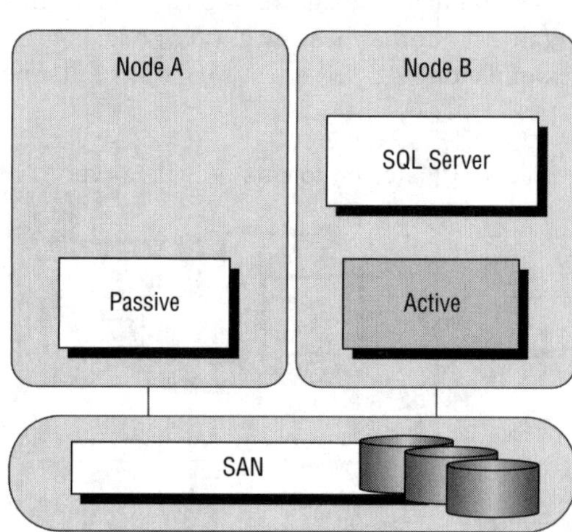


## Failover Clustering Requirements

The Failover Clustering feature is available in the Datacenter, Standard, and Hyper-V editions of Windows Server 2016.

To be able to configure a failover cluster, you must have the required components. A single failover cluster can have up to 64 nodes when using Windows Server 2016, however, and the clustered service or application must support that number of nodes.

To create a failover cluster, an administrator must make sure that all the hardware involved meets the cluster requirements. To be supported by Microsoft, all hardware must be certified for Windows Server 2016, and the complete failover cluster solution must pass all tests in the Validate a Configuration Wizard. Although the exact hardware will depend on the clustered application, a few requirements are standard:

- Server components must be marked with the "Certified for Windows Server 2016" logo.
- Although not explicitly required, server hardware should match and contain the same or similar components.
- All of the Validate a Configuration Wizard tests must pass.

The requirements for Failover Clustering storage have changed from previous versions of Windows. For example, Parallel SCSI is no longer a supported storage technology for any of the clustered disks. There are, however, additional requirements that need to be met for the storage components:

- Disks available for the cluster must be Fibre Channel, iSCSI, or Serial Attached SCSI.
- Each cluster node must have a dedicated network interface card for iSCSI connectivity. The network interface card you use for iSCSI should not be used for network communication.
- Multipath software must be based on Microsoft's Multipath I/O (MPIO).
- Storage drivers must be based on `storport.sys`.
- Drivers and firmware for the storage controllers on each server node in the cluster should be identical.
- Storage components must be marked with the "Certified for Windows Server 2016" logo.

In addition, there are network requirements that must be met for Failover Clustering:

- Cluster nodes should be connected to multiple networks for communication redundancy.
- Network adapters should be the same make, use the same driver, and have the firmware version in each cluster node.
- Network components must be marked with the "Certified for Windows Server 2016" logo.

There are two types of network connections in a failover cluster. These should have adequate redundancy because total failure of either could cause loss of functionality of the cluster. The two types are as follows:

**Public Network** This is the network through which clients are able to connect to the clustered service application.

**Private Network** This is the network used by the nodes to communicate with each other.

To provide redundancy for these two network types, additional network adapters would need to be added to the node and configured to connect to the networks.

In previous versions of Windows Server, support was given only when the entire cluster configuration was tested and listed on the Hardware Compatibility List. The tested configuration listed the server and storage configuration down to the firmware and driver versions. This proved to be difficult and expensive from both a vendor and a consumer perspective to deploy supported Windows clusters.

When problems did arise and Microsoft support was needed, it caused undue troubleshooting complexity as well. With Windows Server 2016 Failover Clustering and simplified requirements, including the "Certified for Windows Server 2016" logo program and the Validate a Configuration Wizard, it all but eliminates the guesswork of getting the cluster components configured in a way that follows best practices and allows Microsoft support to assist you easily when needed.

## Workgroup and Multi-Domain Clusters

One nice new advantage of using Windows Server 2016 is the ability to set up a cluster on systems not part of the same domain. In Window Server 2012 R2 and previous versions, clusters could only be created on machines that were part of the same domain. Windows

Server 2016 allows you to set up a cluster without using Active Directory dependencies. Administrators can create clusters in the following situations:

**Single-Domain Cluster** All nodes in cluster are part of the same domain.

**Multi-Domain Cluster** Nodes in cluster are part of a different domain.

**Workgroup Cluster** Nodes are member servers and part of a workgroup.

## Site-Aware, Stretched, or Geographically Dispersed Clusters (Geoclustering)

One nice advantage of Windows Server 2016 clustering is that you can set up site-aware failover clusters. Site-Aware clustering allows an administrator to expand clustered nodes to different geographic locations (sites). Site-aware failover clusters allow you to setup clusters in remote locations for failover, placement policies, Cross-Site Heartbeating, and for quorum placement.

One of the issues with previous clusters was the heartbeat. The cluster heartbeat is a signal sent between servers so that they know that the machines are up and running. Servers send heartbeats and if after 5 non-responsive heartbeats, the cluster would assume that the node was offline. So if you had nodes in remote locations, the heartbeats would not get the response they needed.

But now Windows Server 2016 includes Cross-Site Heartbeating and it allows you to setup delays so that remote nodes can answer the heartbeat within time. The following two PowerShell commands allow you to setup the delay necessary for Cross-Site Heartbeating.

```
(Get-Cluster).CrossSiteDelay = <value>
(Get-Cluster).CrossSiteThreshold = <value>
```

The first PowerShell command (`CrossSiteDelay`) is what is used to set the amount of time between each heartbeat sent to nodes. This value is done in milliseconds (default is 1000).

The second PowerShell command (`CrossSiteThreshold`) is the value that you set for the number of missed heartbeats (default is 20) before the node is considered offline.

One issue you may face is if you have multiple sites or if the cluster is geographically dispersed. If the failover cluster does not have a shared common disk, data replication between nodes might not pass the cluster validation "storage" tests.

Setting up a cluster in a site-aware, stretched, or geocluster (these terms can be used interchangeably) configuration is a common practice. As long as the cluster solution does not require external storage to fail over, it will not need to pass the storage test to function properly.

## Cluster Quorum

When a group of people set out to accomplish a single task or goal, a method for settling disagreements and for making decisions is required. In the case of a cluster, the goal is to provide a highly available service in spite of failures. When a problem occurs and a cluster node loses communication with the other nodes because of a network error, the functioning nodes are supposed to try to bring the redundant service back online.

How, though, is it determined which node should bring the clustered service back online? If all the nodes are functional despite the network communications issue, each one might try. Just like a group of people with their own ideas, a method must be put in place to determine which idea, or node, to grant control of the cluster. Windows Server 2016 Failover Clustering, like other clustering technologies, requires that a quorum exist between the cluster nodes before a cluster becomes available.

A *quorum* is a consensus of the status of each of the nodes in the cluster. Quorum must be achieved in order for a clustered application to come online by obtaining a majority of the votes available (see Figure 6.3). Windows Server 2016 has four models, or methods, for determining the quorum and for adjusting the number and types of votes available:

- Node majority (no witness)
- Node majority with witness (disk or file share)
- Node and file share majority
- No majority (disk witness only)

**FIGURE 6.3** Majority needed

When a majority of the nodes are communicating, the cluster is functional.

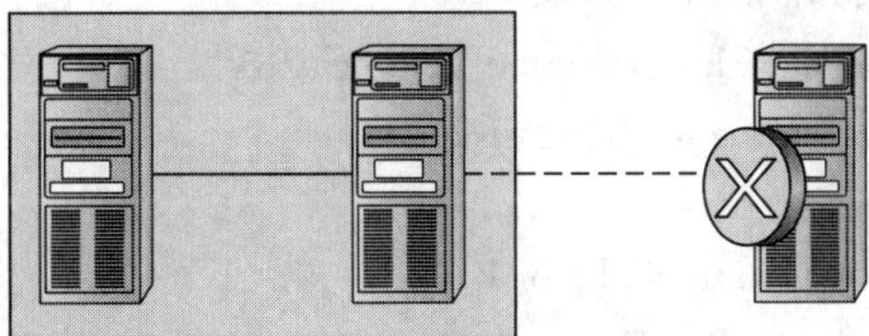

When a majority of the nodes are not communicating, the cluster stops.

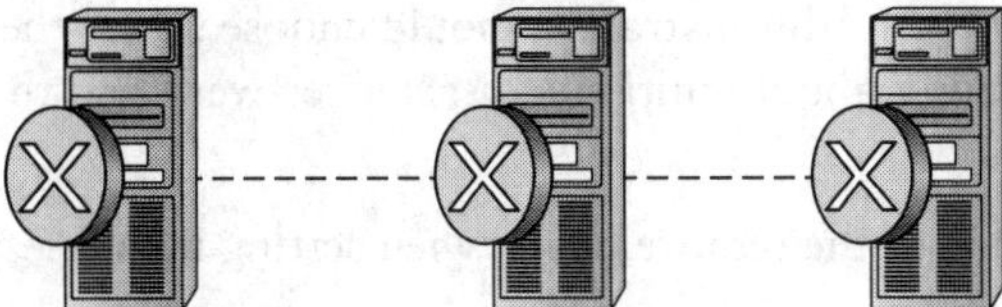

## Witness Configuration

Most administrators follow some basic rules. For example, when you configure a quorum, the voting components in the cluster should be an odd number. For example, if I set up a quorum for five elements and I lose one element, I continue to work. If I lose two elements, I continue to work. If I lose three elements, the cluster stops—as soon as it hits half plus 1, the cluster stops. This works well with an odd number.

If the cluster contains an even number of voting elements, an administrator should then configure a disk witness or a file share witness. The advantage of using a witness (disk or file share) is that the cluster will continue to run even if half of the cluster nodes simultaneously go down or are disconnected. The ability to configure a disk witness is possible only if the storage vendor supports read-write access from all sites to the replicated storage.

One of the advantages of Windows Server 2016 is the advanced quorum configuration option. This option allows you to assign or remove quorum votes on a per-node basis. Administrators now have the ability to remove votes from nodes in certain configurations. For example, if your organization uses a site-aware cluster, you may choose to remove votes from the nodes in the backup site. This way, those backup nodes would not affect your quorum calculations.

There are different ways that you can setup quorum witnesses. Here are some of the options that you can choose from:

**Configure a Disk Witness** Choosing the quorum disk witness is normally setup if all nodes can see the disks. To set this disk witness up, the cluster must be able to see the Dedicated LUN. The LUN needs to store a copy of the cluster database and it's most useful for clusters that are using shared storage. The following list is just some of the requirements when setting up a Disk Witness:

- LUN needs to be at least 512 MB minimum.
- The disk must be dedicated to cluster use only.
- Must pass disk storage validation tests.
- The disk can't be used is a Cluster Shared Volume (CSV).
- You must use a single volume for Basic disks.
- No drive letter needed.
- Drive must be formatted using NTFS or ReFS.
- Can be used with hardware RAID.
- Should not be used with Antivirus or backup software

**Configure a File Share Witness** Administrators should choose to use the File Share Witness when you need to think about multi-site disaster recovery and the file server must be using the SMB file share.

The following list is just some of the requirements when setting up a File Share Witness:

- Minimum of 5 MB of free space required.
- File share must be dedicated to the cluster and not used to store user data or application data.

**Configure a Cloud Witness** Windows Server 2016 Cloud Witness is a new type of Failover Cluster quorum witness that leverages Microsoft Azure as the intercession point. The Cloud Witness gets a vote just like any other quorum witness. Administrators can setup the cloud witness as a quorum witness using the Configure a Cluster Quorum Wizard.

### Dynamic Quorum Management

Another advantage in Windows Server 2016 is dynamic quorum management. *Dynamic quorum management* automatically manages the vote assignment to nodes. With this feature enabled, votes are automatically added or removed from nodes when that node either joins or leaves a cluster. In Windows Server 2016, dynamic quorum management is enabled by default.

## Validating a Cluster Configuration

Configuring a failover cluster in Windows Server 2016 is much simpler than in previous versions of Windows Server. Before a cluster can be configured, the Validate A Configuration Wizard should be run to verify that the hardware is configured in a fashion that is supportable. Before you can run the Validate A Configuration Wizard, however, the Failover Clustering feature needs to be installed using Server Manager. The account that is used to create a cluster must have administrative rights on each of the cluster nodes and have permissions to create a cluster name object in Active Directory. Follow these steps:

1. Prepare the hardware and software perquisites.
2. Install the Failover Clustering feature on each server.
3. Log in with the appropriate user ID and run the Validate A Configuration Wizard.
4. Create a cluster.
5. Install and cluster applications and services.

To install the Failover Clustering feature on a cluster node, follow the steps outlined in Exercise 6.1.

**EXERCISE 6.1**

#### Installing the Failover Cluster Feature

1. Press the Windows key and select Administrative Tools > Server Manager.
2. Select number 2, Add Roles And Features.
3. At the Select Installation Type screen, choose a role-based or feature-based installation.
4. At the Select Destination Server screen, choose Select A Server From The Server Pool and click Next.
5. At the Select Server Roles screen, click Next.
6. At the Select Features screen, click the Failover Clustering (see Figure 6.4) check box. If the Add Features dialog box appears, click the Add Features button. Click Next.
7. At the confirmation screen (see Figure 6.5), click the Install button.

**EXERCISE 6.1 *(continued)***

**FIGURE 6.4** Failover Cluster feature

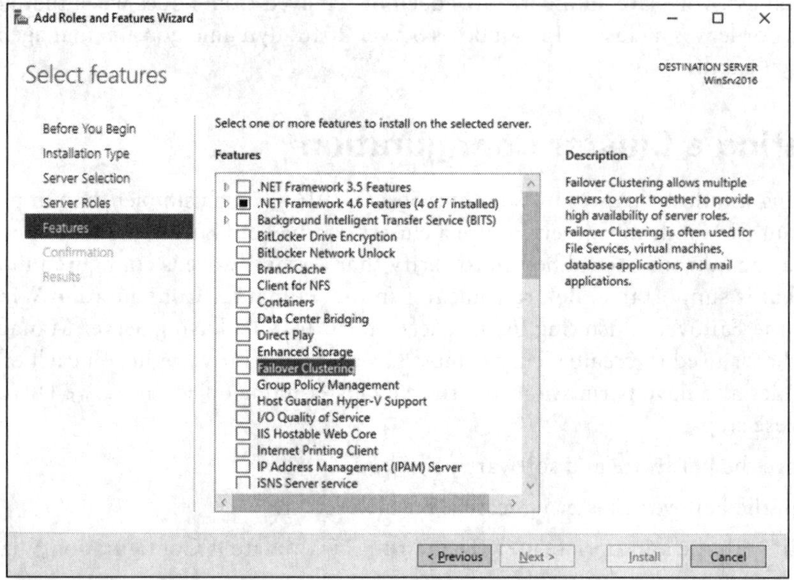


**FIGURE 6.5** Confirmation screen

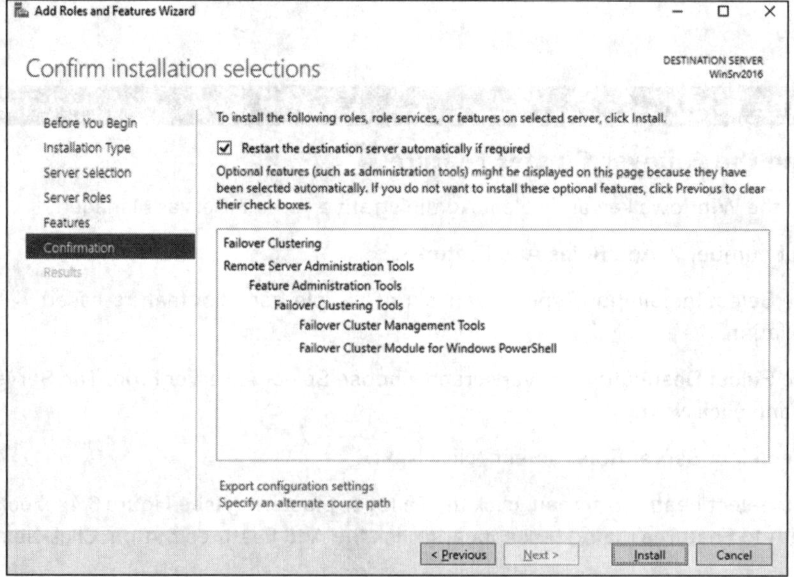


8. Once the installation is complete, click the Close button.
9. Close Server Manager.

Using the Validate A Configuration Wizard before creating a cluster is highly recommended. This wizard validates that the hardware configuration and the software configuration for the potential cluster nodes are in a supported configuration. Even if the configuration passes the tests, take care to review all warnings and informational messages so that they can be addressed or documented before the cluster is created.

Running the Validate A Configuration Wizard does the following:

- Conducts four types of tests (software and hardware inventory, network, storage, and system configuration)
- Confirms that the hardware and software settings are supportable by Microsoft support staff

You should run the Validate A Configuration Wizard before creating a cluster or after making any major hardware or software changes to the cluster. Doing this will help you identify any misconfigurations that could cause problems with the failover cluster.

## Running the Validate a Configuration Wizard

The Validate A Configuration Wizard, shown in Figure 6.6, is simple and straightforward to use, as its "wizard" name would suggest. It should be run after the Failover Clustering feature has been installed on each of the cluster nodes, and it can be run as many times as required.

**FIGURE 6.6** The Validate A Configuration Wizard

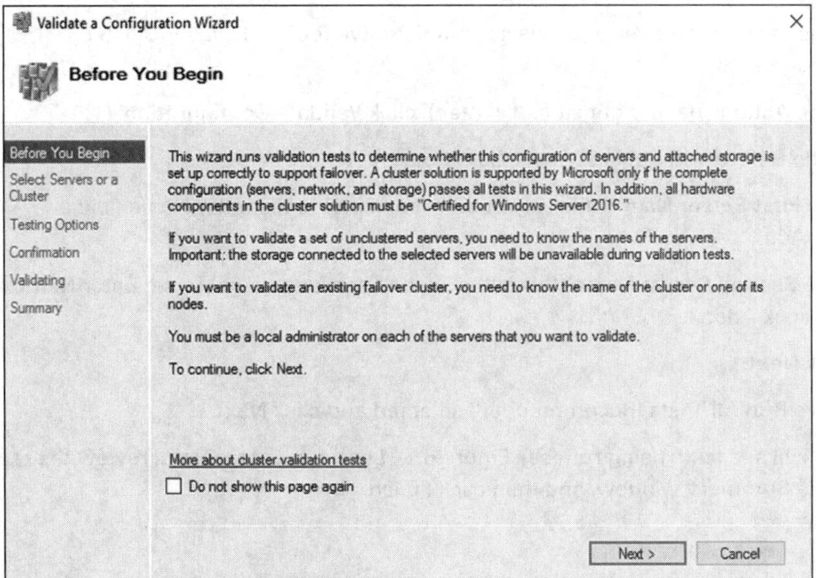

When you are troubleshooting cluster problems or have changed the configuration of the cluster hardware, it is a good idea to run the Validate A Configuration Wizard again to help pinpoint potential cluster configuration problems.

If you already have a cluster configured and want to run the Validate A Configuration Wizard, you can do so; however, you will not be able to run all of the storage tests without taking the clustered resources offline. You will be prompted either to skip the disruptive tests or to take the clustered resources offline so that the tests can complete.

Exercise 6.2 shows the exact steps to follow to run the Validate A Configuration Wizard successfully on clusters named NODEA and NODEB, which are not yet clustered.

I am using servers called NODEA and NODEB in the exercises. You need to replace these two nodes with your own two servers to complete these exercises.

**EXERCISE 6.2**

### Running the Validate A Configuration Wizard

1. Press the Windows key and select Administrative Tools > Failover Cluster Management.
2. In the Actions pane (right side of screen), click Validate Configuration.
3. At the Before You Begin screen, click Next.
4. Type **First Server Name** (this is your server's name) in the Enter Name field and click Add.
5. Type **Second Server Name** (this is the second server's name) in the Enter Name field and click Add.
6. Click Next.
7. Leave Run All Tests (Recommended) selected and click Next.
8. You will see tests being run (see Figure 6.7). Let the test complete, review the report in the Summary window, and then click Finish.

**FIGURE 6.7** Cluster Tests

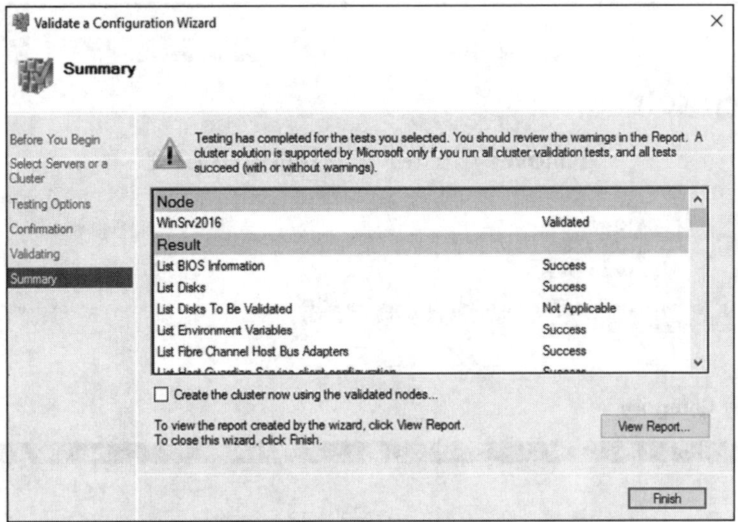


9. Close the Failover Cluster Wizard.

## Addressing Problems Reported by the Validate A Configuration Wizard

After the Validate A Configuration Wizard has been run, it will show the results, as shown in Figure 6.8. This report can also be viewed in detail later using a web browser. The report is named with the date and time the wizard was run, and it is stored in `%windir%\cluster\Reports`.

How should errors listed in the report be addressed? Often, the errors reported by the Validate A Configuration Wizard are self-explanatory; however, sometimes additional help is required. The following three guidelines should help troubleshoot the errors:

- Read all of the errors because multiple errors may be related.
- Use the checklists available in the Windows Server help files to ensure that all the steps have been completed.
- Contact the hardware vendor for updated drivers, firmware, and guidance for using the hardware in a cluster.

**FIGURE 6.8** Validate A Configuration Wizard results

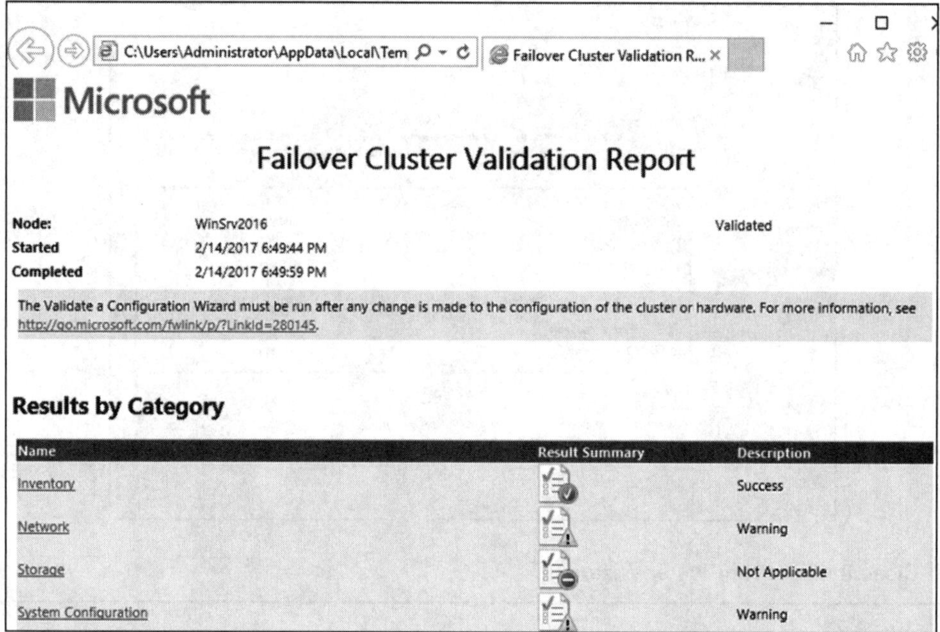


## Creating a Cluster

After you have successfully validated a configuration and the cluster hardware is in a supportable state, you can create a cluster. The process for creating a cluster is straightforward and similar to the process of running the Validate A Configuration Wizard. To create a cluster with two servers, follow the instructions in Exercise 6.3.

**EXERCISE 6.3**

### Creating a Cluster

1. Open the Failover Cluster Management MMC.
2. In the Management section of the center pane, select Create A Cluster.
3. Read the Before You Begin information and click Next.
4. In the Enter Server Name box, type **Your Server** and then click Add.
5. Again, in the Enter Server Name box, type **Your Second Server** and then click Add. Click Next.
6. At the Validation screen, choose No for this exercise and then click Next.

7. In the Access Point For Administering The Cluster section, enter **Cluster1** for the cluster name.
8. Type an IP address and then click Next. This IP address will be the IP address of the cluster.
9. In the Confirmation dialog box, verify the information and then click Next.
10. On the Summary page, click Finish.

## Working with Cluster Nodes

Once a cluster is created, a couple of actions are available. First, you can add another node to the cluster by using the Add Node Wizard from the Failover Cluster Management Actions pane.

At this point, you also have the option to pause a node, which prevents resources from being failed over or moved to the node. You typically would pause a node when the node is involved in maintenance or troubleshooting. After a node is paused, it must be resumed to allow resources to be run on it again.

Another action available to perform on a node at this time is *evict*. Eviction is an irreversible process. Once you evict the node, it must be re-added to the cluster. You would evict a node when it is damaged beyond repair or is no longer needed in the cluster. If you evict a damaged node, you can repair or rebuild it and then add it back to the cluster using the Add Node Wizard.

## Clustering Roles, Services, and Applications

Once the cluster is created, applications, services, and roles can be clustered. Windows Server 2016 includes a number of built-in roles and features that can be clustered (see Figure 6.9).

- DFS Namespace Server
- DHCP Server
- Distributed Transaction Coordinator (DTC)
- File Server
- Generic Application
- Generic Script
- Generic Service
- Hyper-V Replica Broker
- iSCSI Target Server
- iSNS Server
- Message Queuing
- Other Server
- Virtual Machine

**FIGURE 6.9** High availability roles

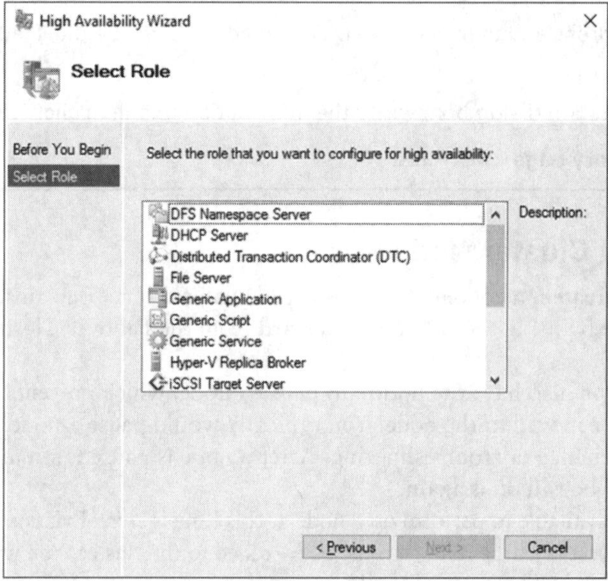


In addition, other common services and applications can be clustered on Windows Server 2016 clusters:

- Enterprise database services, such as Microsoft SQL Server
- Enterprise messaging services, such as Microsoft Exchange Server

To cluster a role or feature such as Print Services, the first step is to install the role or feature on each node of the cluster. The next step is to use the Configure A Service Or Application Wizard in the Failover Cluster Management tool. Exercise 6.4 shows you how to cluster the Print Services role once an appropriate disk has been presented to the cluster. To complete this exercise, you must have a cluster created.

**EXERCISE 6.4**

### Clustering the Print Services Role

1. Open the Failover Cluster Management MMC.
2. In the console tree, click the arrow next to the cluster name to expand the items underneath it.
3. Right-click Roles and choose Configure Role.
4. Click Next on the Before You Begin page.
5. Click Other Server on the Select Role screen and then click Next.
6. Type the name of the print server, such as **Print1**, and type in the IP address that will be used to access the print service, such as **80.0.0.34**. Then click Next.

7. At the Select Storage page, just click Next.
8. Click Next at the Confirmation page.
9. After the wizard runs and the Summary page appears, you can view a report of the tasks the wizard performed by clicking View Report.
10. Close the report and click Finish.

---

The built-in roles and features all are configured in a similar fashion. Other applications, such as Microsoft Exchange Server 2016, have specialized cluster configuration routines that are outside the scope of this exam. Applications that are not developed to be clustered can also be clustered using the Generic Application, Generic Script, or Generic Service option in the Configure A Service Or Application Wizard, as shown in Figure 6.10.

**FIGURE 6.10** Configuring a generic application

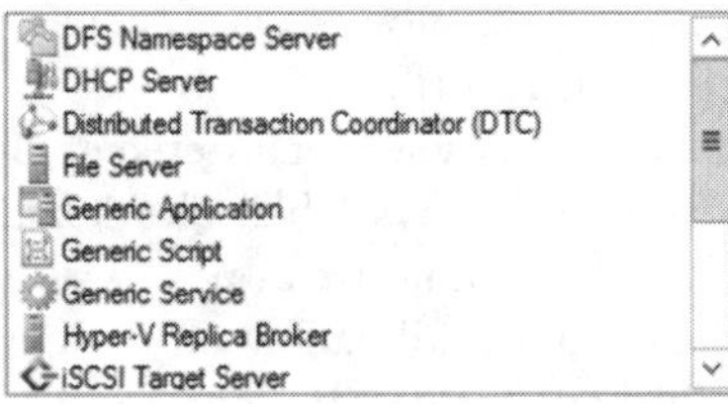


## Clustered Application Settings

Windows Server 2016 has options that allow an administrator to fine-tune the failover process to meet the needs of their business. These options will be covered in the next few sections.

*Failover* occurs when a clustered application or service moves from one node to another. The process can be triggered automatically because of a failure or server maintenance or can be done manually by an administrator. The failover process works as follows:

1. The cluster service takes all of the resources in the role offline in the order set in the dependency hierarchy.
2. The cluster service transfers the role to the node that is listed next on the application's list of preferred host nodes.
3. The cluster service attempts to bring all of the role's resources online, starting at the bottom of the dependency hierarchy.

These steps can change depending on the use of Live Migration.

In a cluster that is hosting multiple applications, it may be important to set specific nodes to be primarily responsible for each clustered application. This can be helpful from a troubleshooting perspective since a specific node is targeted for the hosting service. To set a preferred node and an order of preference for failover, use the General tab in the Properties dialog box of the clustered application.

Also, the order of failover is set in this same dialog box by moving the order in which the nodes are listed. If NODEA should be the primary node and NODEC should be the server that the application fails to first, NODEA should be listed first and selected as the preferred owner. NODEC should be listed second, and the remaining cluster nodes should be listed after NODEC.

A number of failover settings can be configured for the clustered service. The failover settings control the number of times a clustered application can fail in a period of time before the cluster stops trying to restart it. Typically, if a clustered application fails a number of times, some sort of manual intervention will be required to return the application to a stable state.

Specifying the maximum number of failures will keep the application from trying to restart until it is manually brought back online after the problem has been resolved. This is beneficial because if the application continues to be brought online and then fails, it may show as being functional to the monitoring system, even though it continues to fail. After the application is put in a failed state, the monitoring system will not be able to contact the application and should report it as being offline.

Failback settings control whether and when a clustered application would fail back to the preferred cluster node once it becomes available. The default setting is Prevent Failback. If failback is allowed, two additional options are available, either to fail back immediately after the preferred node is available or to fail back within a specified time.

The time is specified in the 24-hour format. If you want to allow failback between 10 p.m. and 11 p.m., you would set the failback time to be between 22 and 23. Setting a failback time to off-hours is an excellent way to ensure that your clustered applications are running on the designated nodes and automatically scheduling the failover process for a time when it will impact the fewest users.

One tool that is valuable in determining how resources affect other resources is the dependency viewer. The *dependency viewer* visualizes the dependency hierarchy created for an application or service. Using this tool can help when troubleshooting why specific resources are causing failures and allow an administrator to visualize the current configuration better and adjust it to meet business needs. Exercise 6.5 will show you how to run the dependency viewer.

**EXERCISE 6.5**

### Using the Dependency Viewer

1. Open the Failover Cluster Management MMC.
2. In the console tree, click the arrow to expand the cluster.
3. Click Roles.
4. Under the Roles section in the center of the screen, click one of the roles (such as Print1).
5. Right-click the role and under More Actions click Show Dependency Report.

6. Review the dependency report.
7. Close the Dependency Report and close the Failover Cluster Manager.

Exercise 6.5 generated a dependency report that shows how the print service is dependent on a network name and a clustered disk resource. The network name is then dependent on an IP address.

## Resource Properties

*Resources* are physical or logical objects, such as a file share or IP address, which the failover cluster manages. They may be a service or application available to clients, or they may be part of the cluster. Resources include physical hardware devices such as disks and logical items such as network names. They are the smallest configurable unit in a cluster and can run on only a single node in a cluster at a time.

Like clustered applications, resources have a number of properties available for meeting business requirements for high availability. This section covers resource dependencies and policies.

Dependencies can be set on individual resources and control how resources are brought online and offline. Simply put, a dependent resource is brought online after the resources that it depends on, and it is taken offline before those resources. As shown in Figure 6.11, dependencies can be set on a specific resource, such as the Generic Application.

**FIGURE 6.11** Resource dependencies

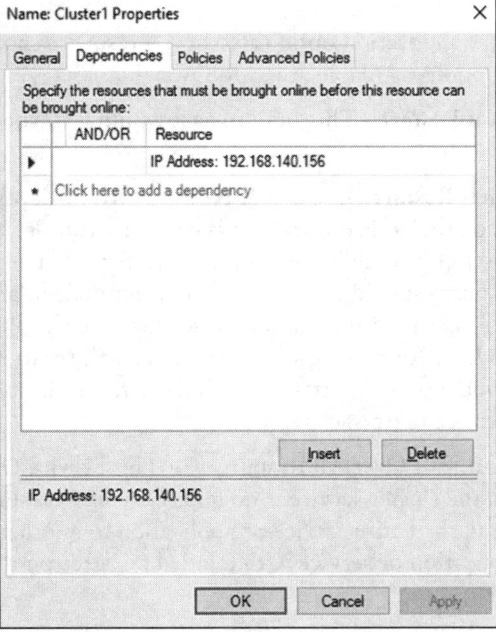

Resource policies are settings that control how resources respond when a failure occurs and how resources are monitored for failures. Figure 6.12 shows the Policies tab of a resource's Properties dialog box.

**FIGURE 6.12** Resource policies

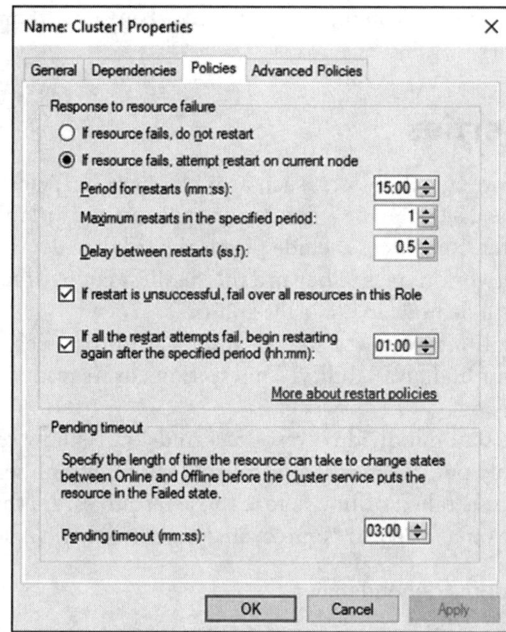


The Policies tab sets configuration options for how a resource should respond in the event of a failure. The options available are as follows:

**If Resource Fails, Do Not Restart** This option, as it would lead you to believe, leaves the failed resource offline.

**If Resource Fails, Attempt Restart On Current Node** With this option set, the resource tries to restart if it fails on the node on which it is currently running. There are two additional options if this is selected so that the number of restarts can be limited. They set the number of times the resource should restart on the current node in a specified length of time. For example, if you specify 5 for Maximum Restarts In The Specified Period and 10:00 (mm:ss) for Period For Restarts, the cluster service will try to restart the resource five times during that 10-minute period. After the fifth restart, the cluster service will no longer attempt to restart the service on the active node.

**If Restart Is Unsuccessful, Fail Over All Resources In This Service Or Application** If this option is selected, when the cluster service is no longer trying to restart the resource on the active node, it will fail the entire service or application to another cluster node. If you wanted to leave the application or service with a failed resource on the current node, you would clear this check box.

**If All The Restart Attempts Fail, Begin Restarting Again After The Specified Period (hh:mm)** If this option is selected, the cluster service will restart the resource at a specified interval if all previous attempts have failed.

**Pending Timeout** This option is used to set the amount of time in minutes and seconds that the cluster service should wait for this resource to respond to a change in states. If a resource takes longer than the cluster expects to change states, the cluster will mark it as having failed. If a resource consistently takes longer than this and the problem cannot be resolved, you may need to increase this value. Figure 6.13 shows the Advanced Policies tab.

**FIGURE 6.13** Resource Advanced Policies

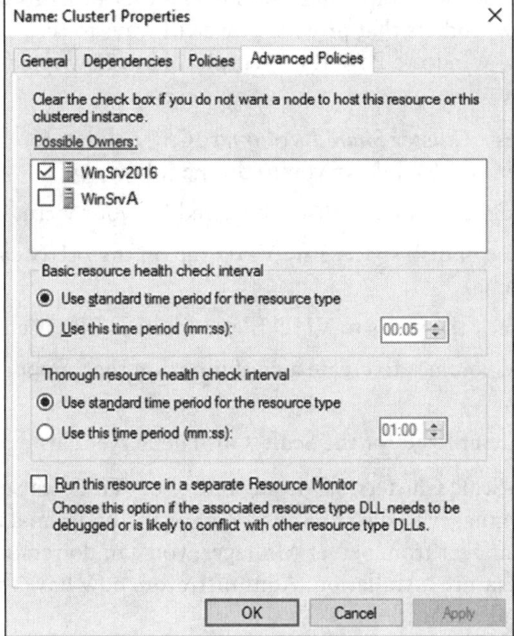


The options available on the Advanced Policies tab are as follows:

**Possible Owners** This option allows an administrator to remove specific cluster nodes from running this resource. Using this option is valuable when there are issues with a resource on a particular node and the administrator wants to keep the applications from failing over to that node until the problem can be repaired.

**Basic Resource Health Check Interval** This option allows an administrator to customize the health check interval for this resource.

**Thorough Resource Health Check Interval** This option allows an administrator to customize the thorough health check interval for this resource.

**Run This Resource In A Separate Resource Monitor** If the resource needs to be debugged by a support engineer or if the resource conflicts with other resources, this option may need to be used.

# Windows Server 2016 Clustering Features

Many new features are included in the Windows Server 2016 release for clustering. It is a rich feature set of high availability with greatly improved flexibility based on the needs of IT organizations. The new features relate to quorum behavior, virtual machine hosting, Active Directory–detached clusters, and a new dashboard.

**Windows PowerShell Cmdlets for Failover Clusters** As I have explained throughout this book, Windows PowerShell is a command-line shell and scripting tool. Windows Server 2016 clustering has new cmdlets that provide powerful ways to script cluster configuration and management tasks. Windows PowerShell cmdlets have now replaced the `Cluster.exe` command-line interface.

**Cluster Shared Volumes** *Cluster Shared Volumes (CSV)* allows for the configuration of clustered virtual machines. CSV allows you to do the following:

- Reduce the number of LUNs (disks) required for your virtual machines.
- Make better use of disk space. Any VHD file on that LUN can use the free space on a CSV volume.
- More easily track the paths to VHD files and other files used by virtual machines.
- Use a few CSV volumes to create a configuration that supports many clustered virtual machines.

CSV volumes also are utilized for the Scale-Out File Server cluster role.

**Management of Large-Scale Clusters** One advantage of Windows Server 2016 clusters is the ability for Server Manager to discover and manage the nodes in a cluster. By starting the Failover Cluster Manager from Server Manager, you can do remote multiserver management and role and feature installation. Administrators now have the ability to manage a cluster from one convenient location.

**Management and Mobility of Clustered Virtual Machines** Microsoft, as well as the industry as a whole, is moving toward the cloud and virtualization. With that in mind, administrators can now configure settings such as prioritizing the starting or placement of virtual machines in the clustered workloads. This allows administrators to allocate resources efficiently to your cluster.

**Cluster-Aware Updating** One issue that every administrator has dealt with is updating a system or application while it is running. For example, if you are running Microsoft Exchange and you want to do an Exchange update, when do you take the server offline to do the update? It always seems that someone is on the system 24 hours a day. Well, Windows Server 2016 clustering has a solution. *Cluster-Aware Updating (CAU)* is a new automated feature that allows system updates to be applied automatically while the cluster remains available during the entire update process.

**Cluster Node Fairness** Virtual Machine Load Balancing feature is new to Windows Server 2016. This new load balancing feature helps optimize the nodes in a cluster. When an organization builds a virtual machine cluster, there will be times when that cluster needs to have maintenance and certain virtual machines will be taken offline. When this happens, an unbalanced cluster (this is when some nodes are hosting VMs more often than others) may occur. This is where the VM Load Balancing feature (Node Fairness) helps the cluster. The Balancer will re-distribute VMs from an over balance node to an under balanced node. To setup Node Fairness, you would use the PowerShell command `AutoBalancerLevel` (shown below). The value input is a 1, 2, or 3. 1 is equivalent to the Low setting (move the host when showing more than 80% loaded), 2 is equivalent to Medium (move the host when more than 70% loaded) and 3 is equivalent to High (average nodes and move the host when showing more than 5% above the average).

```
(Get-Cluster).AutoBalancerLevel = <value>
```

**Cluster Operating System Rolling Upgrade** One of the problems that many IT people face is the issue with downtime while their servers get upgraded to a new operating system. Windows Server 2016 includes a new feature called Cluster Operating System Rolling Upgrade. This new feature allows an administrator to upgrade a Hyper-V or Scale-Out File Server cluster from Windows Server 2012 R2 to Windows Server 2016 without stopping the servers.

**Scale-Out File Server for Application Data** By utilizing *Microsoft Storage Spaces*, you can create a highly available clustered file share that utilizes SMB 3.0 and CSV to provide scalable access to data.

*Scale-Out File Servers* are useful for storing the following application data:

- Hyper-V virtual machine storage
- SQL Server database files

Be aware that Scale-Out File Servers are not useful at all for typical file share data because they benefit only from applications that require a persistent connection to their storage.

**Shared Virtual Hard Disks** In the previous versions of Windows, Failover Cluster nodes running as virtual machines had to use iSCSI or virtual HBAs to connect directly to SAN-based storage. With Windows Server 2016, you can set your Hyper-V virtualized cluster to use a shared VHDX virtual disk. Shared virtual hard disks can reside on the following:

- A Scale-Out File Server failover cluster
- Cluster CSV volumes

Shared virtual hard disks are extremely useful in providing highly available shared storage for the following virtualized workloads:

- SQL Server
- Virtual Machine Manager
- Exchange Server

**Virtual Machine Drain on Shutdown** When needing to perform maintenance on a Hyper-V failover cluster, you may have a lot of virtual machines on one node of a cluster. Inevitably, you will need to restart a cluster node for updates or shut it down for maintenance.

In previous versions of Windows, virtual machines running on the cluster would save their state, and then the cluster node would shut down. Windows Server 2016 helps alleviate this issue by automatically draining the virtual machines running on a node before it shuts down or restarts. Windows does this by attempting to live migrate all virtual machines on the cluster node to other nodes in the cluster when at all possible.

This feature is turned on by default, but it can be disabled through PowerShell.

**Active Directory–Detached Clusters** Previous versions of Windows Failover Clustering have depended on Active Directory to provide computer objects for the cluster name object as well as virtual computer objects. With Active Directory–detached failover clusters, communication to the cluster-form clients will use NTLM authentication rather than the normal Kerberos authentication. This is useful in maintaining high availability should a person accidently delete a virtual computer object in Active Directory that a clustered resource depends on for Kerberos authentication.

**Dynamic Witness** Earlier in this chapter, I mentioned the Dynamic Quorum model and how votes were dynamically adjusted based on the number of nodes in a cluster. In Windows Server 2016, there is a new feature called *dynamic witness* that is enabled by default when the cluster is configured to use a dynamic quorum. Since it is preferred to have an odd number of votes at any one time in a cluster, the dynamic witness will turn on or off the witness vote in order to ensure that there are an odd number of votes in the cluster.

**Tie Breaker For 50% Node Split** Like the *dynamic witness* feature just described, the Tie Breaker For 50% Node Split option in Windows Server 2016 dynamically adjusts cluster node votes in order to maintain an odd number of votes in a cluster where no witness is being used.

This is useful for a cluster in a site-aware, stretched, or geocluster configuration.

**Global Update Manager Mode** Since the first release of Microsoft Cluster Services appearing in Windows NT 4.0 Enterprise, all nodes in a cluster maintain a local database that keeps a copy of the cluster configuration. The *Global Update Manager (GUM)* is a component of the cluster that ensures that before a change is marked as being committed for the entire cluster, all nodes have received and committed that change to their local cluster database. If one or more nodes do not report back or commit a change, the cluster node is kicked out of being a member of the cluster. Another issue that can occur is that for various clustered applications, such as SQL and Exchange, their performance can be negatively impacted by the time it takes the GUM to coordinate with all the nodes of a cluster for any changes. The GUM is only as fast as the slowest node in the cluster.

With Windows Server 2016, a new feature was added to Failover Clustering called *Global Update Manager mode*. This feature allows you to configure the GUM read-write modes manually in order to greatly speed up the processing of changes by the GUM and to improve the performance of certain clustered resources.

**Turn Off IPsec Encryption For Inter-Node Cluster Communications** In network environments where IPsec is used, slow Group Policy updates and other issues can cause Active Directory Domain Services to be temporarily unavailable to cluster nodes. If the cluster intracluster communications protocol uses IPsec encryption, then these delays could cause cluster nodes to drop out of the cluster for failure to communicate in a timely manner with the rest of the nodes in the cluster. Windows Server 2016 now provides a way to turn off IPsec encryption on the cluster communication network.

**Cluster Dashboard** Starting with Windows Server 2012, Failover Clustering supports up to 64 nodes in a cluster. Keeping track of the status and resources on all of these nodes can be an administrative headache! Managing more than one failover cluster and determining what a certain cluster hosts can be painful as well. Fortunately, in Windows Server 2016, the *Failover Cluster Manager*'s main dashboard has been updated to make it easier to see the status and health of multiple clusters.

**Hyper-V Replica Broker** Starting with Windows Server 2012, Hyper-V supported continuous replication of virtual machines to another server or cluster for disaster recovery purposes. The Hyper-V Recovery Broker allows for virtual machines in a cluster to be replicated. The Hyper-V Recovery Broker keeps track of which cluster nodes virtual machines are residing on and ensures that replication is maintained.

**Hyper-V Manager Integration into Failover Cluster Manager** In Windows Server 2016, the Hyper-V Management Console is integrated with Failover Cluster Manager for managing virtual machines that are clustered. Normal Hyper-V operations such as configuring, exporting, importing, configuring replication, stopping, starting, and live migrating virtual machines are supported directly through Failover Cluster Manager.

**Virtual Machine Monitoring** Starting with Windows Server 2012, Failover Clustering supports Virtual Machine Monitoring for Windows Server virtual machines. Virtual Machine Monitoring monitors administrator-selected Windows services running within a virtual machine and will automatically restart a service if it should fail. If the service does not start for the configured number of restart attempts, the virtual machine will fail over to another node and then restart. For example, you can configure Failover Clustering to monitor the Print Spooler service on a Windows Server 2016 virtual machine. If the Print Spooler service goes offline, then the cluster will attempt to restart the Print Spooler service within the virtual machine. If the service still fails, Failover Clustering will move the virtual machine to another node.

# PowerShell Commands for Clustering

Table 6.1 is just some of the PowerShell commands that you can use to configure and manage Windows Server 2016 clustering.

**TABLE 6.1** Storage Spaces Direct PowerShell commands

| PowerShell Command | Description |
|---|---|
| Add-ClusterDisk | This command allows an admin to add a new disk to a failover cluster. The disk's logical unit number (LUN) must be visible to all cluster nodes. |
| Add-ClusterFileServerRole | This command allows an admin to create a clustered file server. |
| Add-ClusterGenericApplicationRole | This command allows you to configure high availability for an application that is normally not designed for clustering. |
| Add-ClusterGroup | This command allows an admin to add a resource group to the failover cluster. |
| Add-ClusterNode | This command allows an admin to add a node to a failover cluster. |
| Add-ClusterResource | This command allows an admin to add a resource to a failover cluster. |
| Add-ClusterResourceDependency | This command allows an admin to add a resource dependency to a failover cluster. |
| Add-ClusterServerRole | This command allows you to add the cluster server role to a server. |
| Block-ClusterAccess | This command allows an admin to block the specified users from accessing a cluster. |
| Get-Cluster | This command shows you the information about a failover clusters. |
| Get-ClusterAccess | This command shows you the permissions for a failover clusters. |
| Get-ClusterNode | This command shows you the information about the servers in a failover clusters. |
| Get-ClusterQuorum | This command shows you the information about the cluster quorum in a clusters. |
| New-Cluster | This command allows you to create a new failover cluster. |
| Remove-Cluster | This command allows you to remove a failover cluster. |

| PowerShell Command | Description |
|---|---|
| `Remove-ClusterAccess` | This command allows an admin to remove a user's access from the cluster. |
| `Remove-ClusterNode` | This command allows you to remove a node from a failover cluster. |
| `Start-Cluster` | This command allows an admin to start the Cluster service on all nodes. |
| `Stop-Cluster` | This command allows an admin to stop the Cluster service on all nodes. |
| `Stop-ClusterNode` | This command stops the Cluster service on a node. |
| `Test-Cluster` | This command allows an admin to complete validation tests for a cluster. |

# Implementing Storage Spaces Direct

Storage Spaces Direct use local-attached drives on servers to create highly available storage at a minimal cost of traditional storage devices (SAN or NAS). Storage Spaces Direct use regular hard drives that are connected to a single node of the failover cluster and these disks can be used as storage for the cluster.

To understand how Storage Spaces Direct truly works, I think it is better to first understand some other technology terms for Windows Server 2016. When an IT administrator takes a bunch of physical disks and puts them together it is called a storage pool. Storage spaces are virtual disks that are created from storage pools. Storage Spaces Direct is the evolution of Storage Spaces.

Many of the same features are used in Windows Server 2016 like Failover Clustering, Cluster Shared Volumes, and SMB.

Storage Spaces Direct utilizes disks that are connected to one node of a failover cluster and allows for the creation of pools using those disks by Storage Spaces. Storage Spaces Direct streamlines deployment by using converged or hyper-converged architecture.

Virtual Disks (Spaces) that are constructed on a pool will have their mirrors or parity (redundant data) span across the disks using different nodes of the cluster. Since replicas of the data are spread across the disks this allows for access to data in the event a node fails or is going down for maintenance.

You can implement Storage Spaces Direct in virtual machines with each VM configured with two or more virtual disks connected to the VM's SCSI Controller. Each node of the cluster running inside the virtual machine can connect to its own disks but utilizing Storage Spaces Direct allows all the disks to be part of the Storage Pool that spans the entire cluster node.

For the redundant data (mirror or parity spaces) to be spread across the nodes, Storage Spaces Direct uses SMB3 as the protocol transport.

**Networking Hardware** To communicate between servers, Storage Spaces Direct uses SMB3, including SMB Direct and SMB Multichannel over Ethernet. It is recommended to use 10+Gbe with Remote-Direct Memory Access (RDMA), or either internet Wide Area RDMA Protocol (iWARP) or RDMA over Converged Ethernet (RoCE).

**Storage Hardware** The following list shows the Storage requirements.

- 2–16 servers with locally attached SATA, SAS, or NVMe drives
- Must have at least two solid-state drives on each server and at least four additional drives.
- SATA and SAS device should be following a Host-Bus Adapter (HBA) and SAS expander.

**Failover Clustering** To connect the servers, Windows Server 2016 uses the built-in clustering feature.

**Software Storage Bus** Storage Spaces Direct has a new feature called Software Storage Bus. This allows all the servers to see all of each other's local drives by spanning the cluster and establishing a software-defined storage structure.

**Storage Bus Layer Cache** The Software Storage Bus joins the fastest drives available to the slower drives to provide server-side read/write caching that speeds up the IO and boosts data.

**Storage Pool** The storage pool is the collection of drives that form the Storage Space. It is created automatically and all qualified drives are discovered and added. It is recommended that an administrator use the default settings on one pool per cluster.

**Storage Spaces** Storage Spaces offers fault tolerance to virtual disk using mirroring, erasure coding, or both. It is thought of as distributed, software-defined RAID utilizing the drives in the pool. These virtual disks normally have resiliency when two synchronized drives or servers fail.

**Resilient File System (ReFS)** The Resilient File System (ReFS) is Microsoft's latest file system which was designed to maximize data availability, efficiently scale to large data sets across varied workloads, and provide data integrity. It includes hastening the `.vhdx` file operations such as creating, expanding, checkpoint merging, and built-in checksums to distinguish and fix bit errors. ReFS also introduced real-time tiers, based on usage, which will rotate data between "hot" and "cold" storage tiers.

**Cluster Shared Volumes** The Cluster Shared Volumes (CSV) file system unites all the ReFS volumes into a single namespace available through any server. This namespace allows every server and every volume to look and act like it's mounted locally.

**Scale-Out File Server** In converged deployments only is this necessary. It offers remote file access by using the SMB3 protocol to clients over the network. This essentially turns Storage Spaces Direct into network-attached storage (NAS).

To see step-by-step instructions on configuring and deploying Storage Spaces Direct, visit Microsoft's website at `https://technet.microsoft.com/en-us/windows-server-docs/storage/storage-spaces/hyper-converged-solution-using-storage-spaces-direct`.

## The Benefits of Storage Spaces Direct

The following are just some of the benefits of using Storage Spaces Direct with Windows Server 2016:

**Simplicity** In less than 15 minutes, an administrator can go from a standard server running Windows Server 2016 to creating a Storage Spaces Direct cluster. It's just the click of a check box if an administrator is using System Center.

**Unrivaled Performance** Storage Spaces Direct exceeds 150,000 mixed 4k random IOPS per server with reliability, low latency, built-in read/write cache, and support for NVMe drives that are mounted directly on the PCIe bus.

**Fault Tolerance** Constantly available built-in resiliency that will handle drives, servers, or component failures. Chassis and rack fault tolerance can also be configured for larger deployments. There are no complex management steps needed when hardware fails. Simply change it out for another one and the software will fix itself.

**Resource Efficiency** Greater resource efficiency with Erasure coding delivering up to 2.4x more storage. Using Local Reconstruction Codes and ReFS, real-time tiers extend to hard disk drives and mixed hot/cold workloads, all while reducing CPU usage to give the resources back to the virtual machines where they are needed.

**Manageability** Keep excessively active virtual machines in order by using Storage QoS Controls with minimum and maximum per-VM IOPS limits. Continuously monitor and alert by using the built-in Health Service. There are also new APIs that make it easier to collect cluster-wide performance statistics and capacity metrics.

**Scalability** For multiple petabytes of storage per cluster, an administrator can increase up to 16 servers and add over 400 drives. To scale out, an administrator will just need to add drives or add more servers. Storage Spaces Direct will automatically add the new drives and begin to utilize them.

## Deployment Options

When using Windows Server 2016 and installing Storage Spaces Direct, there are two deployment options that you can choose from:

### Converged

In converged, there are separate clusters for each storage and compute. The converged deployment option, also called "disaggregated," puts a Scale-Out File Server (SoFS) on top of Storage Spaces Direct to provide Network-Attached Storage (NAS) over SMB3 file shares. This allows for scaling computer/workloads separately from the storage cluster. This is essential when working with large-scale deployments such as Hyper-V Infrastructure as a Service (IaaS).

### Hyper-Converged

In hyper-converged, there is only one cluster for storage and compute. The hyper-converged deployment option runs the Hyper-V virtual machines or SQL Server databases directly on the servers delivering the storage, storing of files all on the local volumes. This removes the need to configure file server access and permissions. It also reduces the hardware costs associated for small-to-medium business or remote office/branch office deployments.

## Requirements to Set Up Storage Spaces Direct

To set up Storage Spaces Direct properly, you must make sure that all of your hardware components meet the minimum requirements. Table 6.2 was taken directly from Microsoft's website for the requirements needed and also what is actually recommended by Microsoft for proper configuration of Storage Spaces Direct.

**TABLE 6.2** Storage Space Direct requirements

| Component | Requirements |
|---|---|
| Servers | Minimum of 2 servers, maximum of 16 servers.<br>All servers should be the same make and model. |
| CPU | Minimum of Intel Nehalem or later compatible processor. |
| Memory | 4 GB of RAM per terabyte (TB) of cache drive capacity on each server, to store Storage Spaces Direct metadata.<br>Any memory used by Windows Server, VMs, and other apps or workloads. |
| Networking | Minimum of 10 Gbps network interface for intra-cluster communication.<br>Recommended: Two NICs for redundancy and performance<br>Recommended: NICS that are remote-direct memory access (RDMA) capable, iWARP or RoCE |

| Component | Requirements |
|---|---|
| Drives | Use local-attached SATA, SAS, or NVMe drives.<br>Every drive must be physically connected to only one server.<br>All servers must have the same drive types.<br>Recommended: All servers have the same drive configuration.<br>SSDs must have power-loss protection, i.e., they are "enterprise-grade."<br>Recommended: SSDs used for cache have high endurance, providing minimum of 5 drive-writes-per-day (DWPD).<br>Add capacity drives in multiples of the number of NVMe or SSD cache devices.<br>Not supported: Multi-path IO (MPIO) or physically connecting drives via multiple paths. |
| Host-bus adapter (HBA) | Simple pass-through SAS HBA for both SAS and SATA drives.<br>SCSI Enclosure Services (SES) for SAS and SATA drives.<br>Any direct-attached storage enclosures must present Unique ID.<br>Not Supported: RAID HBA controllers or SAN (Fibre Channel, iSCSI, FCoE) devices. |

## Storage Spaces Direct using Windows PowerShell

Table 6.3 includes just some of the PowerShell commands that you can use to configure and manage Storage Spaces Direct.

**TABLE 6.3** Storage Spaces Direct PowerShell commands

| PowerShell Command | Description |
|---|---|
| `Disable-NetQosFlowControl` | This command allows an administrator to turn off flow control. |
| `Enable-ClusterStorageSpacesDirect` | This command enables Storage Spaces Direct. |
| `Enable-NetAdapterQos` | This command allows an administrator to apply network QoS policies to the target adapters. |
| `Enable-NetAdapterRDMA` | This command allows an administrator to enable remote direct memory access (RDMA) on a network adapter. |
| `Enable-NetQosFlowControl` | This command allows an administrator to turn on flow control. |

**TABLE 6.3** Storage Spaces Direct PowerShell commands *(continued)*

| PowerShell Command | Description |
|---|---|
| `Enable-ClusterStorageSpacesDirect` | This command allows an administrator to enable highly available storage spaces that use directly attached storage, Storage Spaces Direct (S2D), on a cluster. |
| `Get-ClusterAvailableDisk` | This command allows an administrator to view the information about the disks that can support Failover Clustering and are visible to all nodes. But these disks are not yet part of the set of clustered disks. |
| `Get-ClusterParameter` | This command allows you to view detailed information about an object in a failover cluster. Administrators use this command to manage private properties for a cluster object. |
| `Get-NetAdapter` | This command will retrieve a list of the network adapters. |
| `Get-StoragePool` | This command allows you to see a specific storage pool, or a set of StoragePool objects. |
| `Get-StorageTier` | This command allows you to see storage tiers on Windows Storage subsystems. Use this command to see Storage Spaces Direct default tier templates called Performance and Capacity. |
| `New-Cluster` | This command creates a new cluster. |
| `New-NetQosPolicy` | This command allows an admin to create a new network QoS policy. |
| `New-NetQosTrafficClass` | This command allows you to create a traffic class (like SMB). |
| `New-Volume` | This command creates a new volume. |
| `Set-Item` | This command allows an administrator to configure the trusted hosts to all hosts. |
| `Test-Cluster` | This command allows an administrator to test a set of servers for use as a Storage Spaces Direct cluster. |
| `Update-StorageProviderCache` | This command allows you to update the cache of the service for a particular provider and associated child objects. |

# Summary

High availability is more than just clustering. It is achieved through improved hardware, software, and processes. This chapter focused on how to configure Failover Clustering in order to achieve high availability and scalability.

High availability should be approached through proper hardware configuration, training, and operational discipline. Failover Clustering provides a highly available base for many applications, such as databases and mail servers.

Finally, I showed you the benefits of using Storage Spaces Direct and I also explained how to implement Storage Spaces Direct using PowerShell commands for Windows Server 2016.

# Video Resources

There are videos available for the following exercises:

6.1

6.4

You can access the videos at `http://sybextestbanks.wiley.com` on the Other Study Tools tab.

# Exam Essentials

**Know how to modify failover and failback settings.** These settings are set on the clustered service or application, but they can be modified by settings on the resources.

**Know the hardware requirements for Failover Clustering.** Failover Clustering has very distinct hardware requirements. Know all of the components needed to set up and manage a cluster.

**Understand Storage Spaces Direct.** Storage Spaces Direct uses local-attached drives on servers to create highly available storage at a minimal cost of traditional storage devices (SAN or NAS).

**Know the PowerShell commands for clustering.** Make sure that you know how to install and manage clustering using Windows PowerShell.

**Know Storage Spaces Direct PowerShell commands.** Make sure that you know how to install and manage Storage Spaces Direct using Windows PowerShell.

# Review Questions

1. You have a Windows Server 2016 Hyper-V failover cluster that contains two nodes named NodeA and NodeB. On NodeA, you create a virtual machine named VM01 by using Hyper-V Manager. You need to configure VM01 to move to NodeB automatically if NodeA becomes unavailable. What should you do?

   **A.** In the Failover Cluster manager, configure Role actions.

   **B.** In the Hyper-V Manager, click VM01 and click Enable Replication.

   **C.** In the Hyper-V Manager, click NodeA and modify the Hyper-V settings.

   **D.** Run the PowerShell command `Enable-VMReplication`.

2. You are the administrator for a large organization that wants to implement site-aware clustering. What two PowerShell commands would you use to help you set up site-aware clustering?

   **A.** `(Get-Cluster).CrossSiteDelay = <value>`

   **B.** `(Get-Cluster).CrossSiteThreshold = <value>`

   **C.** `(Add-Cluster).CrossSiteDelay = <value>`

   **D.** `(Add-Cluster).CrossSiteThreshold = <value>`

3. What is the maximum number of nodes that can participate in a Windows Server 2016 failover cluster?

   **A.** 2

   **B.** 4

   **C.** 16

   **D.** 64

4. As an administrator, you need to create highly available storage spaces that connect to directly attached storage on the hosts. Which PowerShell command would you use?

   **A.** `Enable-ClusterStorageSpacesDirect`

   **B.** `Set-StoragePool`

   **C.** `Add-ClusterDisk`

   **D.** `Update-ClusterVirtualMachineConfiguration`

5. If you have a running cluster and need to run the Validate a Configuration Wizard again, which of the following tests may require cluster resources to be taken offline?

   **A.** Network tests

   **B.** Storage tests

   **C.** System configuration tests

   **D.** Inventory tests

6. Which of the following applications would be better suited on a failover cluster instead of a network load-balanced cluster? (Choose all that apply.)
   A. SQL Server
   B. Website
   C. Exchange Mailbox Server
   D. VPN services

7. You are the administrator for a mid-size company who wants to set up and test a cluster. What PowerShell command would you use to run a validation test on a cluster?
   A. `Test-Cluster`
   B. `Validate-Cluster`
   C. `Set-Cluster`
   D. `Add-Cluster`

8. What is the mechanism that is used in clustering to see if a node is online or if the node is not responding?
   A. Testbeat
   B. Heartbeat
   C. Testnode
   D. Pulse

9. In a four-node cluster set to a Node And File Share Majority quorum model, how many votes can be lost before a quorum is lost?
   A. One
   B. Two
   C. Three
   D. Four

10. In a three-node cluster set to a Node Majority quorum model, how many cluster nodes can be offline before the quorum is lost?
    A. Zero
    B. One
    C. Two
    D. Three

# Configuring Windows Containers

## THE FOLLOWING 70-740 EXAM OBJECTIVES ARE COVERED IN THIS CHAPTER:

✓ **Deploy Windows containers**

- This objective may include but is not limited to: Determine installation requirements and appropriate scenarios for Windows Containers; install and configure Windows Server container host in physical or virtualized environments; install and configure Windows Server container host to Windows Server Core or Nano Server in a physical or virtualized environment; install Docker on Windows Server and Nano Server; configure Docker daemon start-up options; configure Windows PowerShell for use with containers; install a base operating system; tag an image; uninstall an operating system image; create Windows Server containers; create Hyper-V containers.

✓ **Manage Windows containers**

- This objective may include but is not limited to: Manage Windows or Linux containers using the Docker daemon; manage Windows or Linux containers using Windows PowerShell; manage container networking; manage container data volumes; manage Resource Control; create new container images using Dockerfile; manage container images using DockerHub repository for public and private scenarios; manage container images using Microsoft Azure.

When reading a Windows Server book, there will always be things in that book that you will already know because previous versions of Windows had the same type of functionality. This chapter is not going to be like that.

In this chapter, I will introduce you to Windows Containers. Windows Containers are brand new to Windows Server 2016 or some versions of Windows 10.

I will teach you how to install, configure, and maintain your Windows Containers. I will also show you all of the components needed to work with containers. Unless you have already started to learn about containers, this entire chapter will be brand new material. So let's start learning about Windows Containers.

# Understanding Windows Containers

Windows Containers are independent and isolated environments that run an operating system. These isolated environments allow an administrator to place an application into its own container thus not affecting any other applications or containers.

Think of containers as virtual environments that are used to run independent applications. They load much faster than virtual machines and you can run as many containers as needed for all of the different applications that you run.

One of the nice advantages of using Windows Containers is that the containers can be managed the same way an administrator can manage an operating system. A container works the same way as a newly installed physical or virtual machine. So once you know how to configure these containers, management is much easier than configuring a physical machine.

There are two different types of containers that the Windows Container can use.

**Windows Server Containers** This container allows an administrator to isolate applications so applications can run in their own space and not affect other applications. The question that you may be asking is why not use a virtual machine? Well the advantage of Windows Server Containers is that they are already pre-built and you don't need all of the other services that a virtual machine would need to run. So Windows Containers are smaller, faster, and more efficient when isolating applications. In a Windows Server Container, the kernel is shared between all of the different Windows Containers.

**Hyper-V Containers** Hyper-V Containers and Windows Containers work the same way. The difference between the two is that Hyper-V Containers run within a virtual machine and the Windows Containers don't need to run in a Hyper-V environment. In a Hyper-V Container the container host's kernel is not shared between the other Hyper-V Containers.

## Container Terminology

As with any new technology, it is important to understand the terminology that goes along with that new technology. The first thing that you may have noticed is that a container works a lot like a virtual machine. Just like a virtual machine, the container has a running operating system within the container.

The container has a file system and the container can also be accessed through the network the same way a virtual machine does. The advantage is that a container is a more efficient operating system. But to truly understand how containers work, you need to understand all of the different components that allow containers to function properly.

**Container Host** This component can be on a physical or virtual machine and it's the component that is configured with the Windows Container feature. So the Windows Container sits on top of the Container Host.

**Container OS Image** This component provides the operating system to the container. Containers are made up from multiple images that are stacked on top of each other within the container.

**Container Image** This is the component that contains all of the layers of the container. So the Container Image contains the operating system, the application, and all of the services required to make that application function properly.

**Container Registry** This component is the heart and brain of the container. The container images are kept within the container's registry. The advantage of doing containers this way is that you can download other registries to automatically add other applications or services quickly.

**Docker Daemon** This is the component that runs the docker application. The docker daemon is automatically installed after you complete the installation of the docker application. If you need to configure the docker daemon, you would use the docker daemon file. This file is in a JSON format.

**Dockerfile** This component is used to create the container images. The advantage of using the Dockerfile is that you can automate how containers are created. Dockerfiles are batches of instructions (within a `txt` file) and commands that are called on when an image is assembled.

**Docker Hub Repositories** This component is a location where all of your images are stored. By having a central location for stored images, the images can be used among coworkers, customers, or the for the entire IT community. There are docker hub repositories on the internet and these locations allow you to grab and use images for your organization.

## Install and Configure Server Containers

So now that we have talked about what the different components are of a container, it's time that we look at installing containers on our Windows Server 2016 system. When it comes to Microsoft, it really doesn't matter if we are installing containers on a GUI based system or non-GUI based system. We are going to install the components needed by using Windows PowerShell.

But before we can look at installing and using containers, I need to show you what is required on the Windows Server 2016 system. So the first step in using containers is looking at what we need on our network and computers for containers to run properly.

## Requirements

Now that you have decided to work with containers, you need to make sure that your network meets the minimum requirements to install and work with Windows Containers. The following are the requirements for installing and working with containers:

- Computer systems (physical or virtual machines) running Windows Server 2016 (Core and with Desktop Experience), Nano Server, or Windows 10 Professional and Enterprise (Anniversary Edition).
- The boot partition must be on the `C:` drive (this does not apply if only Hyper-V Containers will be deployed).
- All critical updates must be installed on the system running the Windows Container feature.
- Docker application needs to be installed.

The following are the requirements needed if you are going to be running virtualization with containers.

- For systems running the Hyper-V containers, the Hyper-V role must be installed on the system.
- If you are going to run a Windows Container host from a Hyper-V virtual machine (also you will be hosting Hyper-V Containers), you will need to enable nested virtualization. Nested virtualization also has some requirements:
  - Operating system that allows nested virtualization (Windows Server 2016).
  - Minimum of 4 GB RAM available to the virtualized Hyper-V host.
  - The processor needs to use Intel VT-x (this is only available for Intel processors).
  - 2 virtual processors for the container host VM.

## Supported Images for Windows Containers

When I talk about setting up containers and you are getting ready to start using containers, there is one major requirement that we need to consider. The operating system on the host machine needs to be the same operating system that is used in the Windows Container. If you install a different operating system in the Windows Container, the container may load but you will most likely start to see errors and there is no guarantee that all of the container's functionality will work.

So it is very important to make sure that the version of Windows Server 2016 that you install onto the host system is the same version as you run in the Windows Container. One nice advantage to using Microsoft Windows is that you can check what version of Windows you are using.

To see what Windows version you have installed, enter into the system's Registry (`Regedit.exe`) and search the following Registry key (see Figure 7.1):

```
HKEY_LOCAL_MACHINE\Software\Microsoft\Windows NT\CurrentVersion
```

**FIGURE 7.1** Regedit version

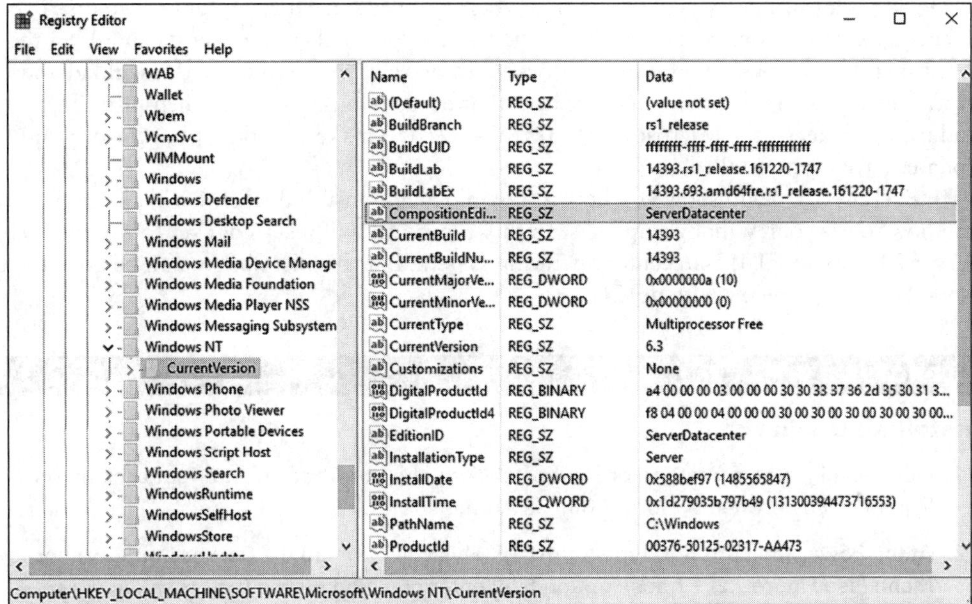


Depending on which host operating system that you are going to run will determine what operating systems you can run in the Windows Server Container or Hyper-V container. Not all operating systems are available depending on the host OS image. Table 7.1 shows you all of the supported configurations for each host operating system.

**TABLE 7.1** Supported Base Images

| Host Operating System | Windows Server Container | Hyper-V Container |
|---|---|---|
| Windows Server 2016 with Desktop | Server Core / Nano Server | Server Core / Nano Server |
| Windows Server 2016 Core | Server Core / Nano Server | Server Core / Nano Server |
| Nano Server | Nano Server | Server Core / Nano Server |
| Windows 10 Pro / Enterprise | Not Available | Server Core / Nano Server |

## Installing Docker

So the first step in setting up our Windows Containers is to install Docker. Docker is the software package that allows you to create and manipulate containers and images.

Docker is the software package that you install and the docker daemon is the application that you use to do your configuration and management. After you install docker, the docker daemon is automatically installed and configured with default settings.

Docker is a third party application that Microsoft has started using for containers. The docker application consists of a docker engine and a docker client (docker daemon). So the first thing that we need to do is install docker. To do this, you need to first download and install the docker application. Another item that needs to be completed when installing and using docker, is the Microsoft updates. You need to make sure that all of the current updates have been installed.

In Exercise 7.1, I will show you how to download and install docker. I will also show you how to get your Windows updates. In this exercise, I will install docker to a Windows Server 2016 (with GUI) Datacenter operating system. But this installation can be done on a Nano Server or a Server with no GUI.

**EXERCISE 7.1**

### Installing Docker

1. Open an elevated command prompt by clicking the Start button and right clicking on Windows PowerShell ➤ More ➤ Run as Administrator.
2. At the PowerShell prompt, type **Sconfig**. This will bring up the Server Configuration Menu (see Figure 7.2). Choose option 6 by entering 6 and hitting the Enter key. This will do an update on Windows Server 2016.

**FIGURE 7.2** Server Configuration screen

```
Administrator: Windows PowerShell
Microsoft (R) Windows Script Host Version 5.812
Copyright (C) Microsoft Corporation. All rights reserved.

Inspecting system...

===============================================================================
                         Server Configuration
===============================================================================

1) Domain/Workgroup:                    Workgroup:  WORKGROUP
2) Computer Name:                       WINSRV2016
3) Add Local Administrator
4) Configure Remote Management          Enabled

5) Windows Update Settings:             DownloadOnly
6) Download and Install Updates
7) Remote Desktop:                      Disabled

8) Network Settings
9) Date and Time
10) Telemetry settings                  Basic
11) Windows Activation

12) Log Off User
13) Restart Server
14) Shut Down Server
15) Exit to Command Line

Enter number to select an option: 6
```

3. A screen should appear asking if you want to install (A)ll updates or (R)ecommended updates only. Choose A for All updates and hit Enter. If there are any updates available, click A for installing all updates and hit Enter. The updates will be downloaded and installed.
4. If there were no updates, go to step 6. After all updates have been installed, choose option 13 to restart the server. A box will appear asking if you are sure you want to Reboot. Click Yes.
5. Login and restart the PowerShell with administrative rights.
6. At the PowerShell prompt, type the following command and hit enter to download the docker software.

```
Install-Module -Name DockerMsftProvider -Repository PSGallery -Force
```

7. If you get a message that NuGet provider needs to be installed (see Figure 7.3), choose Y and hit Enter. If this message doesn't appear, go to step 9.

**FIGURE 7.3** Install NuGet

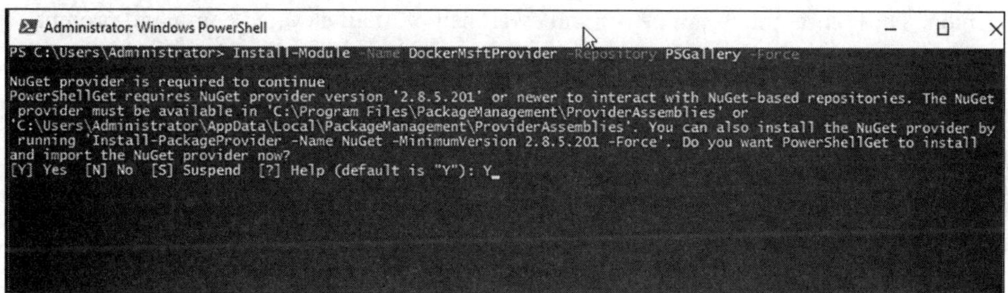


8. If you needed to install NuGet, then re-enter the following command:

```
Install-Module -Name DockerMsftProvider -Repository PSGallery -Force
```

9. Now that you have downloaded docker, it's time to install it. At the PowerShell prompt, type the following command (see Figure 7.4) and hit Enter.

```
Install-Package -Name docker -ProviderName DockerMsftProvider
```

**FIGURE 7.4** Install Docker

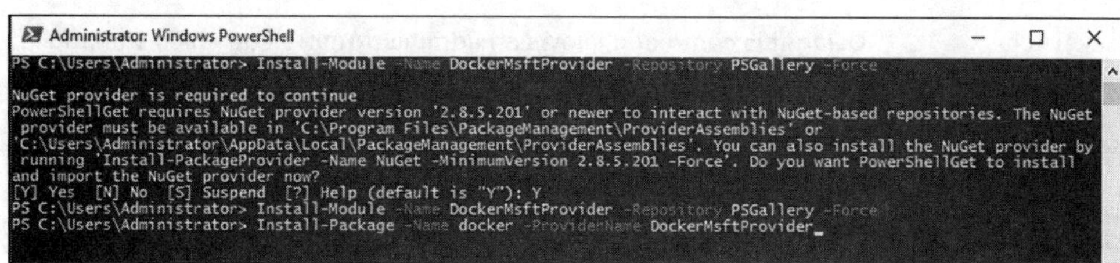

**EXERCISE 7.1** ***(continued)***

10. A message will appear that states that the package is not trusted Are you sure you want to install software from DockerDefault? Click Y and hit enter.
11. Now that docker is installed, you need to check for updates again and then reboot. So type Sconfig and choose option 6. Click A for checking for All updates. If there are any updates, click A for installing All updates.
12. After the updates complete, you will return back to the Server Configuration screen. Choose option 13. Click Yes to reboot.
13. Login to the server.

Docker is now downloaded and installed onto the Windows Server 2016 machine. The next step is to work with docker to install and configure containers.

When using Docker, there are some switches that you can use to work with Docker. Table 7.2 shows some of the Docker switches and what each switch does. These commands are what is needed if you want to manage Windows or Linux containers using the docker daemon. These commands can be run in PowerShell or at an elevated command prompt.

Table 7.2 is just a partial list of Docker commands. To see a more complete list, go to Microsoft's website at `https://docs.docker.com/engine/reference/run/`. In the left-hand window, the entire list is under Engine (Docker) CLI.

**TABLE 7.2** Docker PowerShell and command-line commands

| Command | Description |
|---|---|
| `docker attach` | This command allows an administrator to attach to a running container. |
| `docker build` | Using this command allows you to build an image from a Docker file. |
| `docker checkpoint` | Administrators can use this command to manage a Docker checkpoint. |
| `docker commit` | This command allows an administrator to debug and build a new image. |
| `docker container` | This command allows you to manage containers. |
| `docker cp` | Using this command allows an administrator to copy files and folders between the container and the local computer system. |
| `docker create` | This command gives you the ability to create a new container. |
| `docker deploy` | Administrators can use this command to create and modify a stack. |
| `docker diff` | This command allows an administrator to view changes to files or directories in the container's filesystem. |

| Command | Description |
|---|---|
| docker events | This command allows an administrator to see a server's events in real time. |
| docker exec | Administrators can use this command to run a new command in an existing container. |
| docker image | This command (along with its options) allows you to manage your images. |
| docker info | Using this command allows an administrator to view system information of the Docker installation. |
| docker kill | This command allows you to terminate running containers. |
| docker login | Administrators can use this command to log in to the docker registry of a server. |
| docker pause | This command allows an administrator to pause all processes within a container. |
| docker port | Use this command to view the port mappings for a container. |
| docker ps | This command allows you to view all of the containers. |
| docker pull | Administrators can use this command to pull an image from a registry. |
| docker push | This command allows you to push an image to a registry. |
| docker rename | This command allows you to rename a container. |
| docker restart | Using this command allows you to restart a container. |
| docker rm | Administrators can use this command to remove a container. |
| docker run | Using this command (along with the Options), an administrator can add to or override the image settings set by a developer. |
| docker save | This command allows an administrator to save images to an archive. |
| docker search | This command allows you to search the Docker Hub for images. |
| docker start | This command allows an administrator to start a stopped container. |
| docker stop | This command allows an administrator to stop a running container. |
| docker update | Administrators can use this command to update the configuration of a container. |
| docker version | This command allows an administrator to view the Docker version information. |

After docker is installed, you may want to configure the docker daemon for how docker will start and stop after a system restart or when the system needs to reboot. If you want to set a restart policy, you will want to use the `-restart` flag on the `Docker run` command.

Table 7.3 shows you all of the different startup policies that you can set on a container.

**TABLE 7.3** Docker Restart Policy

| Policy | Result |
|---|---|
| no | This setting will not automatically restart the container. This is the default setting for a container. |
| on-failure[:max-retries] | This setting will restart the container only if the container has a non-zero exit status. Also you have the ability to limit the number of restart retries that the docker daemon will attempt. |
| always | This setting will always restart the container. When the setting is set to always, docker will try to restart the container indefinitely. The container will also always start on daemon startup. |
| unless-stopped | This setting will always restart the container unless the container was stopped before the restart. |

## Install and Configure Windows Containers

So now that you have installed docker on your Windows Server 2016 system, let's take a look at how you install and configure containers.

In Exercise 7.2, I will show you how to make sure your Docker service is started. I will then show you how to install a base operating system image onto your host. I will also show you how to create Windows Server Containers.

There are dozens of pre-made Docker images. You can look at all of the different docker components at the Docker Store. Go to `https://store.docker.com` to see all of the available docker downloads (including pre-made images).

**EXERCISE 7.2**

### Installing a Base Operating System

1. Open the Services MMC by clicking Start ➢ Windows Administrative Tools ➢ Services.
2. Scroll down until you see Docker. Make sure that the Docker Service is started (see Figure 7.5). If it's not started, right click on Docker and choose Start.
3. Close Services.
4. Open Windows PowerShell with administrative privileges. To do this, click on Start and then right click on Windows PowerShell ➢ More ➢ Run as administrator.

**FIGURE 7.5** Checking the Docker service

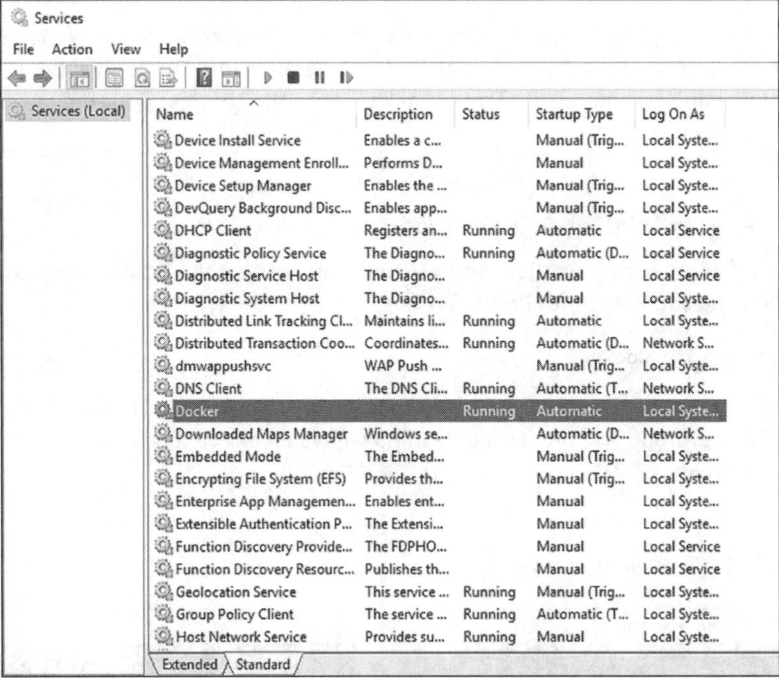

Services

File Action View Help

Services (Local)

| Name | Description | Status | Startup Type | Log On As |
|---|---|---|---|---|
| Device Install Service | Enables a c... | | Manual (Trig... | Local Syste... |
| Device Management Enroll... | Performs D... | | Manual | Local Syste... |
| Device Setup Manager | Enables the ... | | Manual (Trig... | Local Syste... |
| DevQuery Background Disc... | Enables app... | | Manual (Trig... | Local Syste... |
| DHCP Client | Registers an... | Running | Automatic | Local Service |
| Diagnostic Policy Service | The Diagno... | Running | Automatic (D... | Local Service |
| Diagnostic Service Host | The Diagno... | | Manual | Local Service |
| Diagnostic System Host | The Diagno... | | Manual | Local Syste... |
| Distributed Link Tracking Cl... | Maintains li... | Running | Automatic | Local Syste... |
| Distributed Transaction Coo... | Coordinates... | Running | Automatic (D... | Network S... |
| dmwappushsvc | WAP Push ... | | Manual (Trig... | Local Syste... |
| DNS Client | The DNS Cli... | Running | Automatic (T... | Network S... |
| Docker | | Running | Automatic | Local Syste... |
| Downloaded Maps Manager | Windows se... | | Automatic (D... | Network S... |
| Embedded Mode | The Embed... | | Manual (Trig... | Local Syste... |
| Encrypting File System (EFS) | Provides th... | | Manual (Trig... | Local Syste... |
| Enterprise App Managemen... | Enables ent... | | Manual | Local Syste... |
| Extensible Authentication P... | The Extensi... | | Manual | Local Syste... |
| Function Discovery Provide... | The FDPHO... | | Manual | Local Service |
| Function Discovery Resourc... | Publishes th... | | Manual | Local Service |
| Geolocation Service | This service ... | Running | Manual (Trig... | Local Syste... |
| Group Policy Client | The service ... | Running | Automatic (T... | Local Syste... |
| Host Network Service | Provides su... | Running | Manual | Local Syste... |

Extended / Standard

5. Now we are going to look to see if any containers are running. To do this, type `Docker info` in PowerShell and hit Enter. You will see a report (see Figure 7.6) that will show you if you have any containers running.

**FIGURE 7.6** Docker Info

Administrator: Windows PowerShell

```
Windows PowerShell
Copyright (C) 2016 Microsoft Corporation. All rights reserved.

PS C:\Users\Administrator> Docker info
Containers: 0
 Running: 0
 Paused: 0
 Stopped: 0
Images: 0
Server Version: 1.13.1-cs1
Storage Driver: windowsfilter
 Windows:
Logging Driver: json-file
Plugins:
 Volume: local
 Network: l2bridge l2tunnel nat null overlay transparent
Swarm: inactive
Default Isolation: process
Kernel Version: 10.0 14393 (14393.693.amd64fre.rs1_release.161220-1747)
Operating System: Windows Server 2016 Datacenter
OSType: windows
Architecture: x86_64
CPUs: 4
Total Memory: 8 GiB
Name: WinSrv2016
ID: PURT:42QW:TMYH:DKG4:EZBN:ALUW:CM6U:6U6V:OFEX:SRAD:IVZA:6EOI
Docker Root Dir: C:\ProgramData\docker
Debug Mode (client): false
Debug Mode (server): false
Registry: https://index.docker.io/v1/
Experimental: false
Insecure Registries:
 127.0.0.0/8
Live Restore Enabled: false
PS C:\Users\Administrator>
```

**EXERCISE 7.2 *(continued)***

6. So now you are going to install a Container image for either Microsoft Nano Server or Windows Server Core from the online Package repository. To do this, type in one of the following command into PowerShell (choose the command for the operating system that you want):

```
Docker pull microsoft/nanoserver
docker pull microsoft/windowsservercore
```

7. After your container is installed, let's go ahead and restart the Docker service. Type the following command into PowerShell:

```
Restart-Service docker
```

8. Now let's take a look at your docker information again by typing **`Docker Info`** at the PowerShell prompt. As you can see, you now have an image that you didn't have before (see Figure 7.7).

**FIGURE 7.7** Docker information

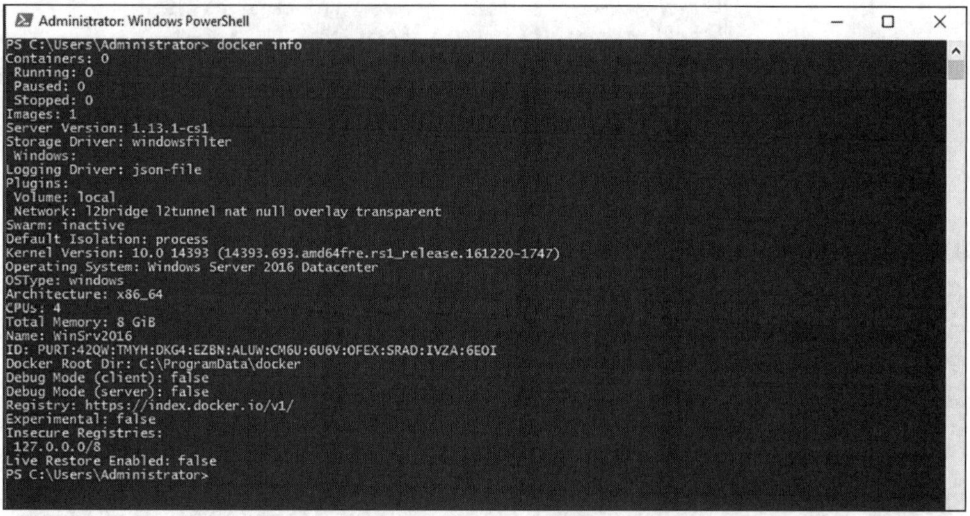

```
Administrator: Windows PowerShell
PS C:\Users\Administrator> docker info
Containers: 0
 Running: 0
 Paused: 0
 Stopped: 0
Images: 1
Server Version: 1.13.1-cs1
Storage Driver: windowsfilter
 Windows:
Logging Driver: json-file
Plugins:
 Volume: local
 Network: l2bridge l2tunnel nat null overlay transparent
Swarm: inactive
Default Isolation: process
Kernel Version: 10.0 14393 (14393.693.amd64fre.rs1_release.161220-1747)
Operating System: Windows Server 2016 Datacenter
OSType: windows
Architecture: x86_64
CPUs: 4
Total Memory: 8 GiB
Name: WinSrv2016
ID: PURT:42QW:TMYH:DKG4:EZBN:ALUW:CM6U:6U6V:OFEX:SRAD:IVZA:6EOI
Docker Root Dir: C:\ProgramData\docker
Debug Mode (client): false
Debug Mode (server): false
Registry: https://index.docker.io/v1/
Experimental: false
Insecure Registries:
 127.0.0.0/8
Live Restore Enabled: false
PS C:\Users\Administrator>
```

9. To see all of the images that you have on your system, at the PowerShell prompt type **docker images** (see Figure 7.8).

**FIGURE 7.8** Docker images

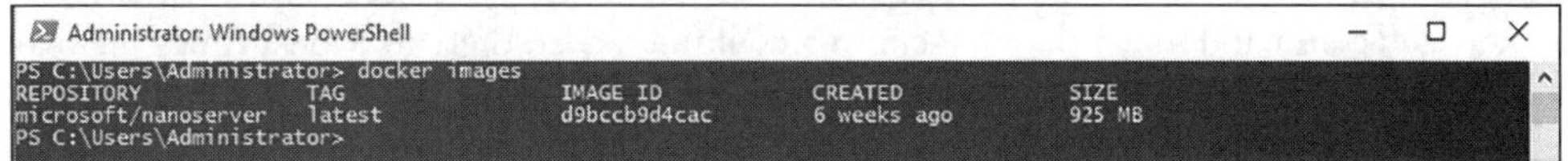


10. So now that you have seen how to grab a base image from docker, let's create a Windows Server Container with Nano Server installed. At the PowerShell prompt, type the following command:

```
docker run microsoft/dotnet-samples:dotnetapp-nanoserver
```

11. If the installation worked properly, you should see what looks like to be a small alien on your screen (see Figure 7.9). Type **`docker info`** at the PowerShell prompt and you will see that you now have a container. You will also notice that you have two images now. The one you downloaded earlier and the one you just downloaded.

**FIGURE 7.9** Container created

12. Close PowerShell.

Now that you have seen how to download an image to the systems repository, you need to see how you can turn an image into a container. To do this, you need to just use the `docker run` command to get the image into a container. Also there may be a time when you need to remove an image from a container. This is done using the `docker rm` command.

But first you need to know which image that you want to put into a container. Exercise 7.3 will show you how to see your images and then how to add an image into a container. To complete Exercise 7.3, you must have completed Exercise 7.2.

## EXERCISE 7.3

### Adding an Image to a Container

1. Open a PowerShell window with Administrative rights.
2. Type **`docker info`** into the PowerShell prompt. You should only have one container at this time.
3. Next you need to do is see what images are in our Repository. To do this, type **`docker images`** at the PowerShell window. This will show you your docker images (see Figure 7.10).

**FIGURE 7.10** Docker images

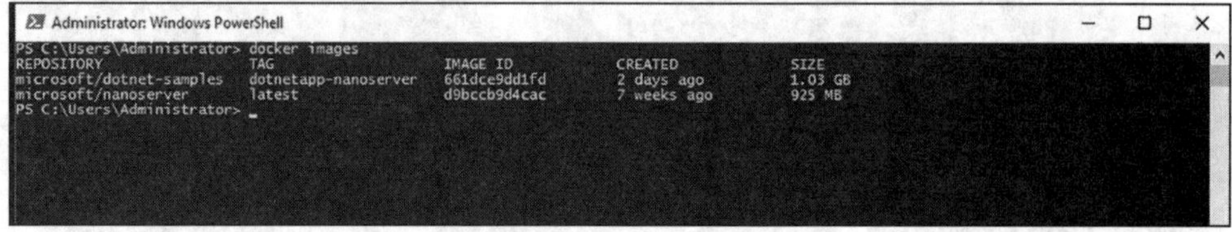


4. We need the Image ID from the Nano server or Server core that you downloaded in exercise 7.2. The Image ID for my Nano server is d9bccb9d4cac. We will use this ID to turn the image into a container. Type the following into a PowerShell prompt (your Image ID will be different) and hit enter (see Figure 7.11).

```
docker run d9bccb9d4cac
```

**FIGURE 7.11** Docker run command

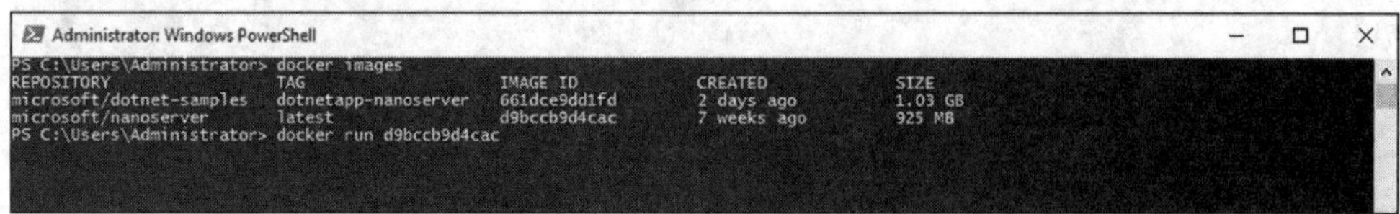

5. Type **`Docker info`** at the PowerShell prompt. You should now have two containers instead of just one (see Figure 7.12).

**FIGURE 7.12** Docker info command

```
Select Administrator: Windows PowerShell
PS C:\Users\Administrator> docker images
REPOSITORY                 TAG                     IMAGE ID       CREATED        SIZE
microsoft/dotnet-samples   dotnetapp-nanoserver    661dce9dd1fd   2 days ago     1.03 GB
microsoft/nanoserver       latest                  d9bccb9d4cac   7 weeks ago    925 MB
PS C:\Users\Administrator> docker run d9bccb9d4cac
Microsoft Windows [Version 10.0.14393]
(c) 2016 Microsoft Corporation. All rights reserved.

C:\>
PS C:\Users\Administrator> docker info
Containers: 2
 Running: 0
 Paused: 0
 Stopped: 2
Images: 2
Server Version: 1.13.1-cs1
Storage Driver: windowsfilter
 Windows:
Logging Driver: json-file
Plugins:
 Volume: local
 Network: l2bridge l2tunnel nat null overlay transparent
Swarm: inactive
Default Isolation: process
Kernel Version: 10.0 14393 (14393.693.amd64fre.rs1_release.161220-1747)
Operating System: Windows Server 2016 Datacenter
OSType: windows
Architecture: x86_64
CPUs: 4
Total Memory: 8 GiB
Name: WinSrv2016
ID: PURT:42QW:TMYH:DKG4:EZBN:ALUW:CM6U:6U6V:OFEX:SRAD:IVZA:6EOI
Docker Root Dir: C:\ProgramData\docker
Debug Mode (client): false
Debug Mode (server): false
Registry: https://index.docker.io/v1/
Experimental: false
Insecure Registries:
 127.0.0.0/8
Live Restore Enabled: false
PS C:\Users\Administrator>
```

6. Close PowerShell.

---

## Tagging an Image

Administrators have the ability to change the tags associated with the images. Many administrators use tag names as version names so that they can keep track of the different images on their machine.

By having tags that you create, it allows you to easily access the images later by its tag name. To tag an image, you use the `-t` parameter. So the following is tagging an image as `WillPanekImage`.

```
docker build -t WillPanekImage
```

## Uninstall an Operating System Image

One of the maintenance issues that many IT administrators must deal with is hard drive space. As you are downloading and using images, there may be a time when you need to remove images from our server that are no longer being used.

If you continue to download and use multiple images files, you will need to make sure that every once in a while that you look at all of your images and delete any images that are no longer valid or no longer in use.

Exercise 7.4 will show you how to remove an image file from your host system. To complete this exercise, make sure that you have completed the earlier exercises in this chapter.

**EXERCISE 7.4**

### Uninstalling an Image

1. Open a PowerShell window with Administrative rights.
2. Type **`docker images`** and get the ID number of the Nano server Image.
3. Type **`docker rm d9bccb9d4cac`** (your ID number should go where the d9bccb9d4cac number is).
4. Type docker `images`. The image is now gone.
5. Close PowerShell

## Creating New Images Using Dockerfile

One nice advantage of using docker is that you can go out to Docker's website and look at the different images that are available. There are images for operating systems, applications, and software.

But what if you can't find an image that you need? Well, then you can build your own images using Dockerfiles. When an administrator installs docker, the docker engine includes tools that the IT department can use to create these Dockerfiles. Dockerfiles are just text files that are manually created and they are compiled and turned into an image file.

If your organization decides that they want to build their own Dockerfiles, then they will get some benefits while doing just that. Some of the advantages of building your own Dockerfiles are as follows:

- Administrators can store images as code.
- Your organization can have rapid recreation of images. These images can then be used for maintenance and upgrade cycles.
- Customization for exactly what your organization wants.

So once you have installed docker, there will be some components that are included so that you can create your own Dockerfiles. These two docker components include the docker engine and the compiler (docker build command).

So if you have ever built `.ini` files or even a host file, then you understand how building a file can work. Same as many programming codes or `.ini` files, you can use the pound (#) to show comments in the file. This is very useful.

Many years ago, before I got into networking, I was a programmer. One thing that most programmers hate is when you look at someone else's coding and you have no idea what they were doing. When a coder takes the time to put in comments so that anyone can follow them and work on the code, it makes following that coder a thousand times easier. This is what the comments in the Dockerfile do. Using the pound (#) for making comments and stating exactly why each line is included, helps someone following you or if someone is trying to learn what you do.

So let's take a look at an example of a Dockerfile:

```
# Sample Dockerfile for WillPanek
# We will be using Windows Server Core as our base image.
FROM microsoft/windowsservercore
# Uses dism.exe to install the DNS role.
RUN dism.exe /online /enable-feature /all /featurename: : DNS-Server-Full-Role /NoRestart
# Sets a command or process that will run each time a container is run from the new image.
CMD [ "cmd" ]
```

So now that we can see a Dockerfile, lets break down some of the different sections that you can configure. Table 7.4 will show you some of the configuration settings that you can use.

**TABLE 7.4** Dockerfile Commands

| Command | Description |
|---|---|
| Add | This setting will copy new files, directories, or remote file URLs from a source (<src>) location to the filesystem of the image destination <dest>. |
| CMD | This setting sets the default commands that will be executed when deploying the container image. |
| Copy | This setting will copy new files or directories from a source (<src>) location to the filesystem of the image destination <dest>. |
| Escape | This setting is used to escape characters in a line and to escape a newline. Normally, the escape command is followed by the character that will represent a new line. For example: escape=\. This means that when a \ (backslash) is in the file, it will represent a new line. |
| ENV | This setting allows you to add an environmental variable. |
| Expose | This setting tells Docker that the container is listening on the specified network ports during runtime. |

**TABLE 7.4** Dockerfile Commands *(continued)*

| Command | Description |
|---|---|
| From | This setting shows the location of the container image that will be used during the image creation process. |
| Label | This setting adds metadata to an image. |
| Onbuild | This setting allows you to set a trigger that gets executed when the image is used as the base for another build. |
| Run | This setting will specify what commands are to be run in the Dockerfile process. These commands can include software installation and file, directory, and environment creation. |
| User | This setting allows you to set up a user's account that will be used during the runtime. |
| Volume | This setting allows an administrator to create a mount point and externally mounted volumes from host systems or other containers. |
| Workdir | This setting allows you to set the working directory that will be used during the runtime. |

## Understanding Hyper-V Containers

So far in this chapter we have discussed Windows Containers, but now we are going to look at Hyper-V Containers. As I stated earlier, Windows Containers share the system's kernel between all containers and the host. Hyper-V Containers are different because each Hyper-V Containers utilizes their own instance of the Windows kernel.

Since Hyper-V containers utilizing their own instance of the Windows kernel, administrators can use different versions of Windows between the host system and the image version.

Also the Windows host system needs to have the Microsoft Hyper-V role installed onto the host system. Windows Server 2016 and Windows 10 Professional and Enterprise (Anniversary Editions) both allow you to create containers and Hyper-V.

The one nice feature is that both container types, Windows Containers and Hyper-V Containers, are created, managed, and function the exact same way. The only difference is how the Hyper-V Containers have better isolation to the kernel.

When you are working with Hyper-V containers in Docker, the settings are identical to managing Windows Server containers. The one difference that you want to include in the Hyper-V Container is using the `--isolation=hyperv` parameter. The following is an example of the docker command with the Hyper-V parameters:

```
docker run -it --isolation=hyperv microsoft/nanoserver cmd
```

## Managing Container Networking

One of the features included with building containers is the ability to access the servers and data within the container the same way you would on a normal network server or Hyper-V server.

Once you have installed Docker, there will be three networks that are created automatically. You can see these networks by typing **`docker network ls`** in PowerShell (see Figure 7.13) or at an elevated command prompt.

**FIGURE 7.13** Docker Network Info

```
Administrator: Windows PowerShell
Windows PowerShell
Copyright (C) 2016 Microsoft Corporation. All rights reserved.

PS C:\Users\Administrator> docker network ls
NETWORK ID          NAME                DRIVER              SCOPE
3cb894810795        nat                 nat                 local
2fdbb2f60f2b        none                null                local
PS C:\Users\Administrator>
```

If you would like to get even more details about a specific network (see Figure 7.14), after you run the `docker network ls` command, you will need to grab the Network ID number. Then type the following PowerShell command followed by the Network ID number (my Network ID is 3cb894810795):

```
Docker network inspect 3cb894810795
```

**FIGURE 7.14** Docker Network Info

```
PS C:\Users\Administrator> docker network ls
NETWORK ID          NAME                DRIVER              SCOPE
3cb894810795        nat                 nat                 local
2fdbb2f60f2b        none                null                local
PS C:\Users\Administrator> docker network inspect 3cb894810795
[
    {
        "Name": "nat",
        "Id": "3cb89481079578852381b299f54067313fdf3472909174193ca9e742f3fa6f9d",
        "Created": "2017-02-28T16:12:41.1703268-05:00",
        "Scope": "local",
        "Driver": "nat",
        "EnableIPv6": false,
        "IPAM": {
            "Driver": "windows",
            "Options": null,
            "Config": [
                {
                    "Subnet": "172.28.144.0/20",
                    "Gateway": "172.28.144.1"
                }
            ]
        },
        "Internal": false,
        "Attachable": false,
        "Containers": {},
        "Options": {
            "com.docker.network.windowsshim.hnsid": "2444fc7a-0048-4480-b769-11b2ee5242f9",
            "com.docker.network.windowsshim.networkname": "nat"
        },
        "Labels": {}
    }
]
PS C:\Users\Administrator>
```

One nice thing about working with networks within containers is that these three networks are always available to you even when you choose only one to be part of your container. You can specify which network you want your container to run on by using the `--Network` flag setting.

When you create a container, the host network adds the container onto the host's network stack. When you are dealing with the containers network, there are very few reasons why you would even need to manage or manipulate the container's network. The only network that you may need to work with is the bridge network. The docker default bridge is created as soon as you install the Docker Engine. It creates your bridge network and its name is bridge.

## Using Docker Hub Repository

One really nice advantage of using containers is that there are hundreds of images that you can use. Docker has a public database of images that you can access.

The DockerHub repository has images for Microsoft, UNIX, Linux, and hundreds more. If you want to see what a vendor has out on the repository, just type in `docker search vendorname`. So let us take a look at what Microsoft has for you in the repository. Type **`docker search Microsoft`** (see Figure 7.15).

**FIGURE 7.15** Docker Search Microsoft

```
Administrator: Windows PowerShell
PS C:\Users\Administrator> docker search Microsoft
NAME                                     DESCRIPTION                                      STARS   OFFICIAL   AUTOMATED
microsoft/aspnet                         ASP.NET is an open source server-side Web ...    560                [OK]
microsoft/dotnet                         Official images for .NET Core for Linux an...    452                [OK]
mono                                     Mono is an open source implementation of M...    220     [OK]
microsoft/mssql-server-linux             Official images for Microsoft SQL Server o...    182
microsoft/nanoserver                     Windows Server 2016 Nano Server base OS im...    139
microsoft/windowsservercore              Windows Server 2016 Server Core base OS im...    132
microsoft/aspnetcore                     Official images for running compiled ASP.N...    101                [OK]
microsoft/iis                            Internet Information Services (IIS) instal...    94
microsoft/azure-cli                      Docker image for Microsoft Azure Command L...    77                 [OK]
microsoft/mssql-server-windows-express   Official Microsoft SQL Server Express Edit...    55
microsoft/mssql-server-windows           Official images for Microsoft SQL Server f...    31
microsoft/aspnetcore-build               Official images for building ASP.NET Core ...    25                 [OK]
microsoft/powershell                     Official PowerShell Core releases from htt...    25                 [OK]
microsoft/oms                            Monitor your containers using the Operatio...    17                 [OK]
microsoft/vsts-agent                     Official images for the Visual Studio Team...    16
microsoft/dotnet-samples                 .NET Core Docker Samples                         13                 [OK]
microsoft/powershell-nightly             Nightly builds of PowerShell Core for CI         6                  [OK]
microsoft/cntk                           CNTK images from github.com/Microsoft/CNTK...    6                  [OK]
microsoft/applicationinsights            Application Insights for Docker helps you ...    4                  [OK]
microsoft/dotnet-nightly                 Preview bits of the .NET Core CLI                3                  [OK]
berlius/microsoft-malmo                  Microsoft-malmo - artificial intelligence ...    1
microsoft/aspnetcore-build-nightly       Images to build preview versions of ASP.NE...    1                  [OK]
renerchen/microsoft                                                                       0
dreher/microsoft                         Microsoft Test Repo                              0
cvugrinec/microsoft-prep70533                                                             0
PS C:\Users\Administrator>
```

Administrators have the ability to setup a private repository so that co-workers can share and use the images that you create. After you create your images using the Docker Daemon, you can then push those images to your corporate Docker Hub repository. Administrators can add users and accounts to the Docker Hub to verify that only the organization's users are accessing the images.

If you are building images and placing those images on GitHub or Bitbucket, you can then use the Automatic build repository that is included with the Docker Hub service.

So when you are ready to start uploading corporate images to the Docker Hub, you will first need to create a Docker Hub user account (`https://cloud.docker.com/`). After you have created your account, click the Create ↓ and choose "Create Repository."

You will then be asked to put in a Docker ID namespace for your organization. The repository name needs to be unique and it can be up to 255 characters. The namespace will only allow letters, numbers, or the dash (-) and underscore (_). You are then allowed to put in a Short Description (100 characters or less) and a Full Description. Then you click the Create button and you are finished.

After your repository is created, you can push images to the repository by putting in the name of your image, your Docker Hub username, the repository name that you created earlier, and the image tag. The following is an example of the docker push command:

```
docker push <hub-user>/<repo-name>:<tag>
```

## Using Microsoft Azure for Images

If you decide to run container applications within a cluster of virtual machines, you can use the Azure Container Service. The Azure Container Service allows you to easily create, configure, and manage your virtual machine cluster of containers. The Azure Container Service uses open-source scheduling and management tools.

By using open-source tools, the Azure Container Service connects you with thousands of other users who are also designing, building, and maintaining container images.

The Azure Container Service uses the Docker format but it is also compatible with Marathon, DC/OS, Kubernetes, or Docker Swarm. Because the Azure Container Service works with all of these different formats, you have the ability to work with thousands of applications and images. But since this is Microsoft's Azure platform, you get all of the security benefits and features that Azure has to offer.

To setup the Azure Container Service, you must first setup an Azure Container Service cluster through the Microsoft portal. Once you have entered the portal, you would need to use the Azure Resource Manager template for Docker Swarm, DC/OS, and Kubernetes, or you would need to use the Azure Command Line Interface.

To setup an Azure account or to find out more information on using the Azure Container Service, visit Microsoft's website at: `https://azure.microsoft.com/en-us/services/container-service/`.

# Using PowerShell for Containers

The following table (Table 7.5) will show you just some of the available PowerShell commands that are available for using containers and Docker.

**TABLE 7.5** PowerShell Commands

| PowerShell Command | Description |
|---|---|
| `Add-ContainerNetworkAdapter` | This command allows an administrator to add a virtual network adapter to a container. |
| `Connect-ContainerNetworkAdapter` | Administrators can use this command to connect a virtual network adapter to a virtual switch. |
| `Disconnect-ContainerNetworkAdapter` | This command allows an administrator to disconnect a virtual network adapter from a virtual switch. |
| `Export-ContainerImage` | Administrators can use this command to export a container image to a file. |
| `Get-Container` | This command allows an administrator to view information about containers. |
| `Get-ContainerHost` | This command allows an administrator to view information about the host. |
| `Get-ContainerImage` | Administrators can use this command to view local container images. |
| `Get-ContainerNetworkAdapter` | Administrators can use this command to view the virtual network adapter of a container. |
| `Import-ContainerImage` | Administrators can use this command to import a container image from a file. |
| `Install-ContainerOSImage` | This command allows an administrator to install the operating system image to a base container. |
| `Install-Module` | Administrators can use this command to download a module from an online gallery. This module can then be installed on the local computer. |
| `Install-Package` | Administrators can use this command to install a software package on a computer. |
| `Install-PackageProvider` | This command allows an administrator to install a Package Management package providers. |
| `Move-ContainerImageRepository` | Administrators can use this command to move the local container image repository. |

| PowerShell Command | Description |
|---|---|
| New-Container | This command allows an administrator to create a container image from an existing container. |
| Remove-Container | Administrators can use this command to delete a container. |
| Remove-ContainerImage | This command allows an administrator to remove a container image. |
| Remove-ContainerNetworkAdapter | This command allows an administrator to remove a virtual network adapter from a container. |
| Restart-Computer | Administrators can use this command to restart a local and remote computer. |
| Set-ContainerNetworkAdapter | Administrators can use this command to configure the features of the virtual network adapter within a container. |
| Start-Container | Administrators can use this command to start a container. |
| Stop-Container | Administrators can use this command to stop a container. |
| Test-ContainerImage | This command allows an administrator to test for issues with a container image. |
| Uninstall-ContainerOSImage | Administrators can use this command to uninstall the container operating system image. |

# Summary

In this chapter, I started introducing you to Windows Containers. Windows Containers are a brand-new technology to Windows Server 2016 or some versions of Windows 10.

I also showed you how to install, configure, and maintain your Windows Containers. And I talked to you about the components that are needed to work with containers.

I then showed you some exercises for configuring Windows Server 2016 containers and also how to download and work with image files. These image files can be used to create Windows and Hyper-V containers.

In addition, I showed you how to install and work with Docker. Docker is the technology used to manage and maintain Windows Containers. I showed you how to work with Docker PowerShell and command-line switches and also how to use PowerShell to work with Windows Containers.

# Video Resources

There are videos available for the following exercises:

7.1

7.2

You can access the videos at `http://sybextestbanks.wiley.com` on the Other Study Tools tab.

# Exam Essentials

**Understand Windows Containers.** Windows Containers work a lot like virtual machines except that when you build a virtual machine, you need all of the services that make that VM run properly. Windows Containers are fast operating system builds that allow you to run applications in their own environment.

**Know the requirements for Windows Containers.** Understand that you have to have Windows Server 2016 with Docker installed. You must also make sure that all updates are current on the system. You can install containers on Windows 10 Professional and Enterprise (Anniversary Edition).

**Know the PowerShell commands used for Containers.** The Microsoft exams are going to focus on PowerShell commands. Make sure you know the PowerShell commands that are used for Docker and containers.

**Understand Docker technology.** Understand that Docker is the technology that is used to manage and maintain Windows Containers. There are preset images on Docker that you can pull down and run. Microsoft has preset Docker images that you can use and manipulate.

**Know the different Docker switches.** Understand how docker switches are used and know the main docker switches. Understand that docker switches can be run in PowerShell or at an elevated command prompt.

# Review Questions

1. You have a Windows Server 2016 server named Server. You install the Docker daemon on Server1. You need to configure the Docker daemon to accept connections only on TCP port 64500. What should you do?
   - **A.** Use the `New-NetFirewallRulecmdlet`.
   - **B.** Use the `View-ServiceWindows` PowerShell cmdlet.
   - **C.** Edit the `daemon.json` file.
   - **D.** Create a new configuration file.
2. You are the network administrator for a company that has decided to start using Windows Containers. You want to create a new container. What command allows you to create a container?
   - **A.** `docker create`
   - **B.** `docker build container`
   - **C.** `docker new`
   - **D.** `docker build`
3. You are the network administrator for a company that has decided to start using Windows Containers. You have built a bunch of containers. What PowerShell command allows you to view the containers?
   - **A.** `docker view`
   - **B.** `docker see`
   - **C.** `View-Container`
   - **D.** `Get-Container`
4. You have a Nano Server named Nano1. You deploy several containers to Nano1 that use an image named Image1. You need to deploy a new container to Nano1 that uses Image1. What should you run?
   - **A.** `Install-NanoServerPackage` cmdlet
   - **B.** `Install-WindowsFeaturecmdlet` cmdlet
   - **C.** `docker load`
   - **D.** `docker run`
5. You are the network administrator for a company that has decided to start using Windows Containers. You have created some images. What command allows you to see your images?
   - **A.** `docker images`
   - **B.** `docker info`
   - **C.** `docker view`
   - **D.** `docker see`

6. You are the administrator for your organization, which has started using containers. You need to build and use a Dockerfile. You need to compile and create an image using the Dockerfile. What command would you use?

   A. `Docker run`

   B. `Docker rm`

   C. `Docker build`

   D. `Docker compile`

7. You are the administrator for your organization, which has started using containers. You need to build and use a Dockerfile. You need to execute commands within the Dockerfile. What command would you use?

   A. `Docker run`

   B. `Docker rm`

   C. `Docker build`

   D. `Docker compile`

8. You are the network administrator for a company that has decided to start using Windows Containers. You want to delete a container. What PowerShell command allows you to delete a container?

   A. `docker delete`

   B. `docker kill container`

   C. `Remove-Container`

   D. `Delete-docker-Container`

9. You are the administrator for your organization, which has started using containers. You need to build a new image using Windows Server Core. What command would you use to get a Windows Server Core image?

   A. `Docker run microsoft/windowsservercore`

   B. `docker pull microsoft/windowsservercore`

   C. `Docker build microsoft/windowsservercore`

   D. `Docker get microsoft/windowsservercore`

10. You have been asked to start using Windows containers in your organization. Your manager wants to know what client operating systems can host containers. Which of the following client operating systems will allow for containers?

    A. Windows 10 Home

    B. Windows 7 Professional

    C. Windows 10 Enterprise (Anniversary Edition)

    D. Windows 8.1 Enterprise

# Maintaining Windows Server

## THE FOLLOWING 70-740 EXAM OBJECTIVES ARE COVERED IN THIS CHAPTER:

✓ **Install, upgrade, and migrate servers and workloads**

- This objective may include but is not limited to: Implement Windows Server Update Services (WSUS) solutions; configure WSUS groups; manage patch management in mixed environments; implement an antimalware solution with Windows Defender; integrate Windows Defender with WSUS and Windows Update; perform backup and restore operations using Windows Server Backup; determine backup strategies for different Windows Server roles and workloads, including Hyper-V Host, Hyper-V Guests, Active Directory, File Servers, and Web Servers using Windows Server 2016 native tools and solutions

In this chapter, we will start with keeping your systems updated using Windows Server Update Services (WSUS). Making sure that your users have Windows operating systems with the most current updates is one of the most important things that we can do in IT.

Microsoft is continually working to make their operating systems better and more secure. IT departments need to make sure that we keep our clients up-to-date with all of these Microsoft improvements. WSUS allows us to setup a server that deploys updates to your users.

Another important task of an IT team is to keep the network up and running quickly and efficiently. Keeping your network running is one way to make sure your end users continue to use the network and its resources without problems or interruptions. Backups are one way to make sure we can recover our network quickly and efficiently.

Remember, everyone has clients—salespeople have theirs, accountants have theirs, and so do we as system administrators. Our clients are the end users, and it's our job to make sure that our clients can always do their jobs by keeping the data secure and the network running.

When you are working with servers, it is important you make sure that your system's information is safely and efficiently backed up. Backups become useful when data gets lost due to system failures, file corruptions, or accidental deletions of information. As an IT Director, I can tell you from experience that backups are among the most important tasks that an IT person performs daily.

# Configuring Windows Server Updates

When Microsoft releases a new operating system, users may encounter issues and security deficiencies. Both of these can cause your network to have many problems. So to help fix these issues, Microsoft will release updates and security fixes on a weekly and/or monthly basis. It is important for an IT department to keep their network systems up-to-date with these fixes.

Well there are two main ways to do this. You can let your users all connect to Microsoft's website one at a time and grab updates or you can setup a Windows Server Update Services (WSUS) server to get these updates. Then that WSUS server can release the updates to your users. This helps a company because when all your users connect to Microsoft to get the same updates, it's a waste of bandwidth and time. Also, as an IT person, we may not want all of the Microsoft updates to be deployed to our clients without viewing and testing them first.

I can tell you from first hand experience that there has been times when I deployed an update from Microsoft and it caused more issues than it fixed. So having the ability to view and test updates on a test system ensures that the updates that we are deploying work the way that they are supposed to. So let's take a look at some of the tools that you need to understand when dealing with updates.

**Windows Update** This utility attaches to the Microsoft website through a user-initiated process, and it allows Windows users to update their operating systems by downloading updated files (critical and noncritical software updates).

**Windows Server Update Services (WSUS)** This utility is used to deploy a limited version of Windows Update to a corporate server, which in turn provides the Windows updates to client computers within the corporate network. This allows clients that are limited to what they can access through a firewall to be able to keep their Windows operating systems up-to-date.

## Windows Update

*Windows Update* is available for most Windows operating systems and it allows the system to receive updates from Microsoft. Examples of updates include security fixes, critical updates, updated help files, and updated drivers.

If you want to use Windows Update, an administrator would click Start ➤ Settings ➤ Update & security. You would then see the following options:

**When the Last Updates Were Done** When you enter into the Windows Update settings, the first thing you will see is when the last updates were done (if any).

**Check For Updates Button** This allows you to manually check to see if any updates are available for the operating system. When an administrator clicks this button (shown in Figure 8.1), the system will check for updates. If any updates are found, they will be downloaded and installed.

**FIGURE 8.1** Windows Update control panel

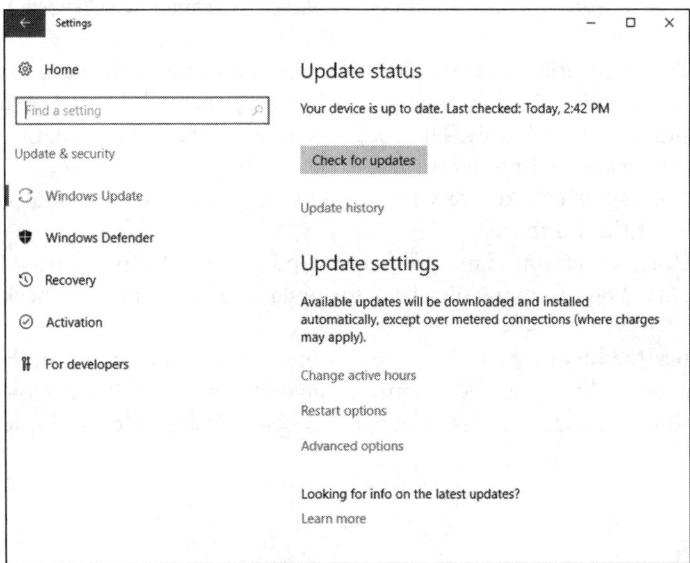

**Update History** This allows you to track all of the updates that you have applied to your server.

**Change Active Hours** This setting allows you to set your active hours on the system. So for example, you worked on this system or the server was most active from 8:00am to 6:00pm, you can set those hours so that the Windows Update knows when to download and install updates.

**Restart Options** This setting allows you to customize when the system will restart after the machine receives its updates.

**Advanced Options** This customizes what updates you receive when you use Windows Update.

The information that is collected by Windows Update includes the operating system and version number, the Internet Explorer version, the software version information for any software that can be updated through Windows Update, the Plug and Play ID numbers for installed hardware, and the region and language settings. Windows Update will also collect the product ID and product key to confirm that you are running a licensed copy of Windows, but this information is retained only during the Windows Update session and it is not stored. No personal information that can be used to identify users of the Windows Update service is collected.

Windows Server 2016 updates will recognize when you have a network connection and will automatically search for any updates for your computer from the Windows Update website (as long as an internet connection is available) or from a WSUS server (explained below).

If any updates are identified, they will be downloaded using *Background Intelligent Transfer Services (BITS)*. BITS is a bandwidth-throttling technology that allows downloads to occur using idle bandwidth only. This means that downloading automatic updates will not interfere with any other Internet traffic.

If Updates detects any updates for your computer, you will see an update icon in the notification area of the Taskbar.

As stated before, an administrator configures Updates by selecting Start ➢ Settings ➢ Update & security. You can manually check for updates by clicking the Check For Updates button.

After you click the link to see if there are any updates available, you can then choose to install the updates. After you click to install the updates, you will see a status window showing you the update status of the updates being downloaded and installed (see Figure 8.2).

**FIGURE 8.2** Seeing the Update Status

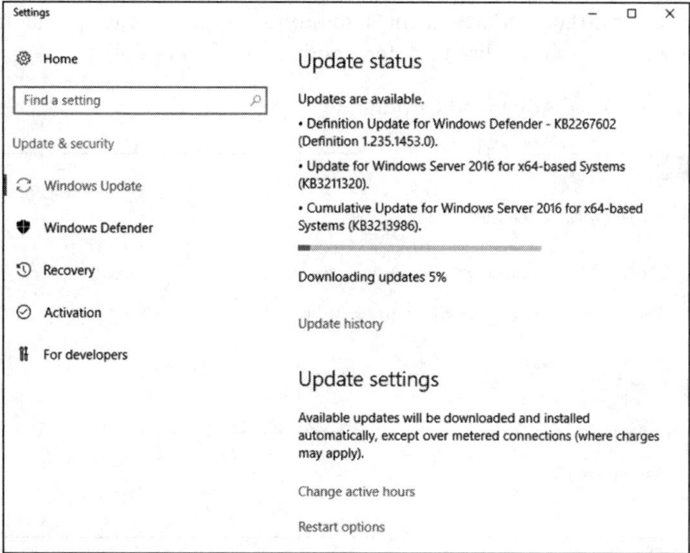


Once updates have been installed, you can click the link Update History to see all of the previous updates. When you click this link, you will be shown the updates that have been installed and also have the ability to uninstall any updates (see Figure 8.3).

**FIGURE 8.3** Viewing your Update History

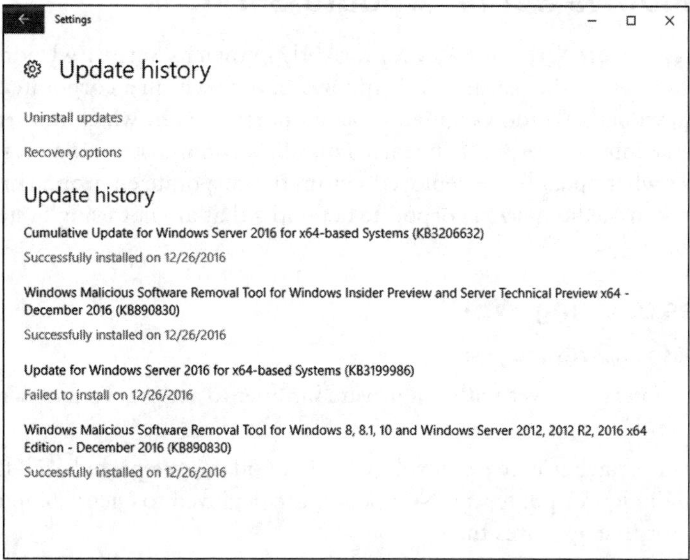

You also have the ability to set advanced options in the Updates section. One of the advanced options is to download other Microsoft updates for other Microsoft products (for example, you get Office updates at the same time you get operating system updates). Administrators also have the ability to defer updates (see Figure 8.4).

**FIGURE 8.4** Viewing Advanced Options

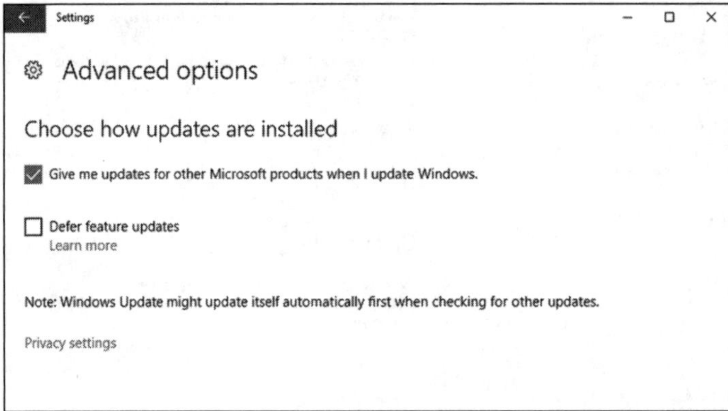


When you decide to defer updates, new Windows features will not be downloaded or installed during the upgrade process. Deferring updates will not affect the Windows Server 2016 system from getting security updates. Deferring updates will only prevent you from getting the newest Windows features as soon as they are released.

# Using Windows Server Update Services

*Windows Server Update Services (WSUS)*, formerly known as Software Update Services (SUS), is used to leverage the features of Windows Update within a corporate environment. WSUS downloads Windows updates to a corporate server, which in turn provides the updates to the internal corporate clients. This allows administrators to test and have full control over what updates are deployed within the corporate environment. WSUS is designed to work in medium-sized corporate networks that are not using System Center Essentials 2016.

## Advantages of Using WSUS

Using WSUS has many advantages:

- It allows an internal server within a private intranet to act as a virtual Windows Update server.
- Administrators have selective control over what updates are posted and deployed from the public Windows Update site. No updates are deployed to client computers unless an administrator first approves them.

- Administrators can control the synchronization of updates from the public Windows Update site to the WSUS server either manually or automatically.
- Administrators can configure Automatic Updates on client computers to access the local WSUS server as opposed to the public Windows Update site.
- WSUS checks each update to verify that Microsoft has digitally signed it. Any updates that are not digitally signed are discarded.
- Administrators can selectively specify whether clients can access updated files from the intranet or from Microsoft's public Windows Update site, which is used to support remote clients.
- Administrators can deploy updates to clients in multiple languages.
- Administrators can configure client-side targeting to help client machines get updates. Client-side targeting allows your organization's computers to automatically add themselves to the computer groups that were created in the WSUS console.
- Administrators can configure a WSUS statistics server to log update access, which allows them to track which clients have installed updates. The WSUS server and the WSUS statistics server can coexist on the same computer.
- Administrators can manage WSUS servers remotely using HTTP or HTTPS if their web browser is Internet Explorer 6.0 or newer.

## WSUS Server Requirements

To act as a WSUS server, the server must meet the following requirements:

- It must be running Windows 2008, Windows Server 2008 R2, Windows Server 2012, Windows Server 2012 R2, or Windows Server 2016.
- It must have all of the most current security patches applied.
- It must be running Internet Information Services (IIS).
- It must be connected to the network.
- It must have an NTFS partition with 100 MB free disk space to install the WSUS server software, and it must have 6 GB of free space to store all of the update files.
- It must use BITS version 2.0.
- It must use Microsoft Management Console 3.0.
- It must use Microsoft Report Viewer Redistributable 2008.
- Windows Defender should be enabled on the WSUS server.

## Installing the WSUS Server

WSUS should run on a dedicated server, meaning that the server will not run any other applications except IIS, which is required. Microsoft recommends that you install a clean or new version of Windows Server 2008, Windows Server 2008 R2, Windows Server 2012, Windows Server 2012 R2, or Windows Server 2016 and apply any service packs or security-related patches.

Exercise 8.1 walks you through the installation process for WSUS.

**EXERCISE 8.1**

### Installing a WSUS Server

1. Choose Server Manager by clicking the Server Manager icon on the Taskbar.
2. Click option number 2, Add Roles And Features. If a Before You Begin screen appears, just click Next.
3. Choose role-based or featured-based installation and click Next.
4. Choose your server and click Next.
5. Choose Windows Server Update Services (see Figure 8.5). Click the Add Features button when the dialog box appears. Then click Next.

**FIGURE 8.5** Choosing to install WSUS

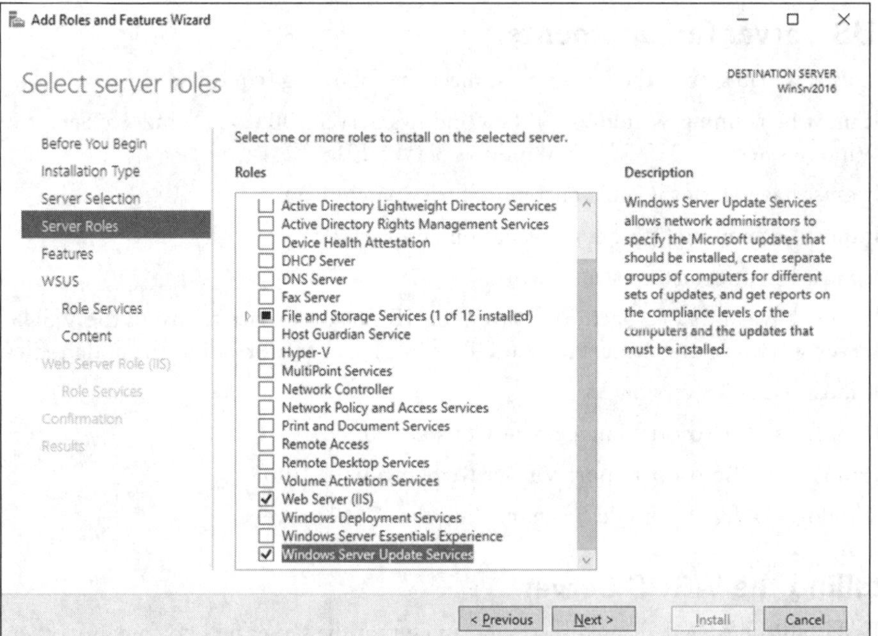

6. At the Select Features screen, just click Next.
7. At the Windows Server Update Services screen, click Next.
8. At the Select Role Services screen, make sure that WID Connectivity and WSUS Services are both checked (see Figure 8.6). Click Next.

**FIGURE 8.6** Select Role screen

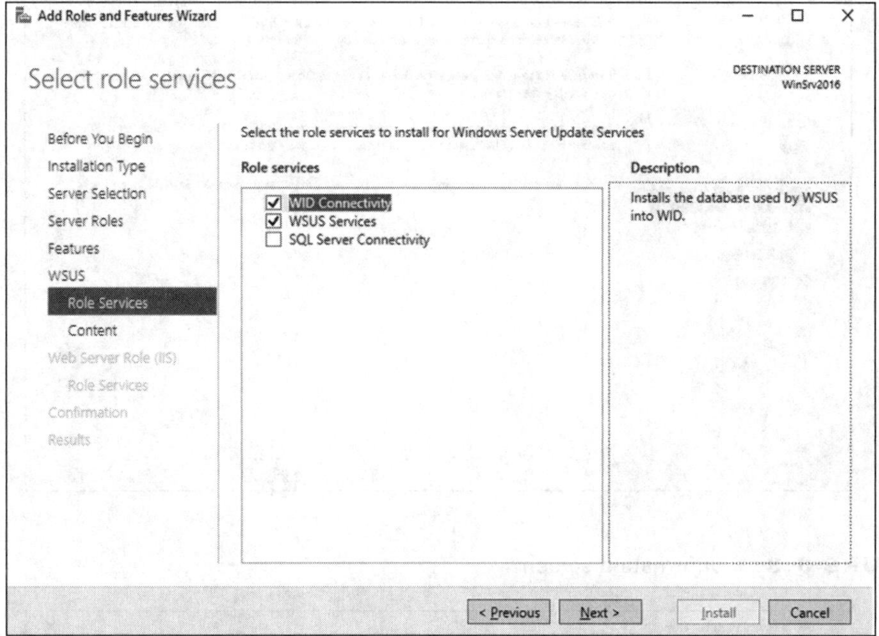


9. At the Content Location Selection screen, uncheck the box Store Updates In The Following Location and click Next (see Figure 8.7). When you uncheck this box, updates are not stored locally. They are downloaded from Microsoft only once they are approved. This will help save hard drive space.
10. At the Web Server Role screen, click Next.
11. At the Role Services screen, just accept the defaults and click Next.
12. At the confirmation screen, shown in Figure 8.8, check the box to restart the destination server automatically if required. If a dialog box appears, click Yes. Then click the Install button.

**EXERCISE 8.1 *(continued)***

**FIGURE 8.7** Content Location Selection screen

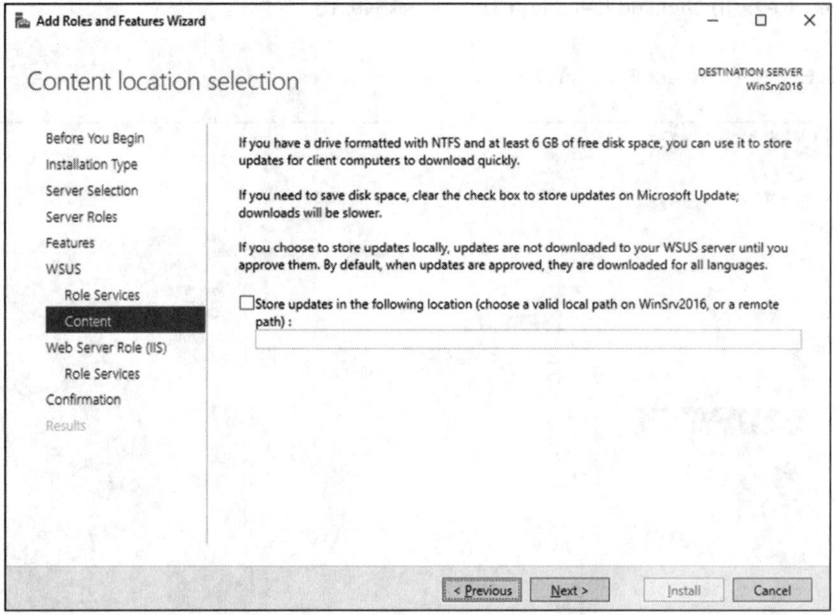


**FIGURE 8.8** Confirmation screen

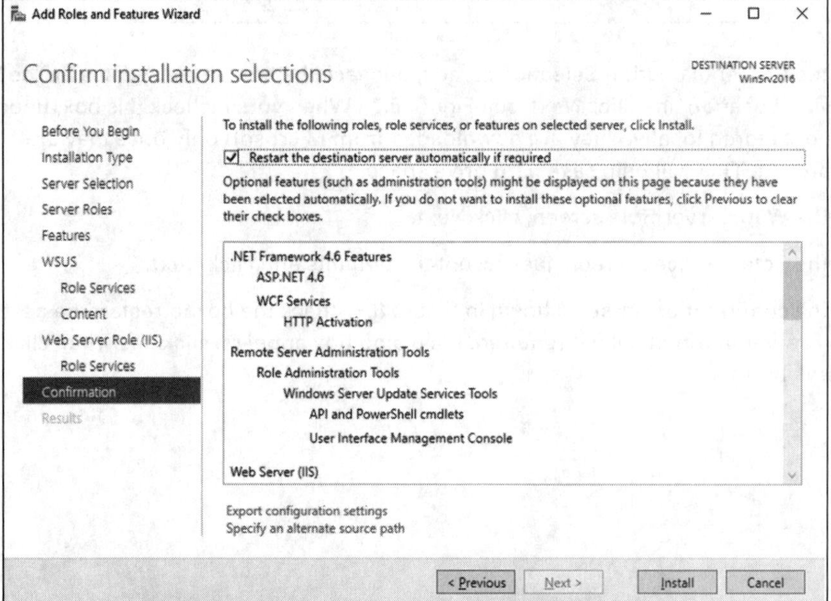

13. The installation will begin (shown in Figure 8.9), and you will see the progress. Once the installation is complete, click Close.

**FIGURE 8.9** Status screen

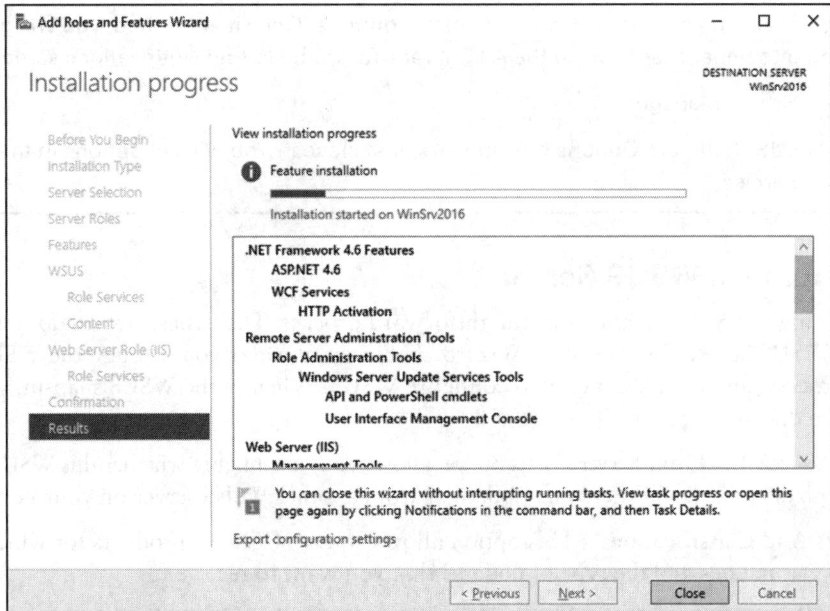


14. In Server Manager, click the WSUS link on the left side. Then click the More link (see Figure 8.10) next to Configuration Required For Windows Server Update Services.

**FIGURE 8.10** Status screen

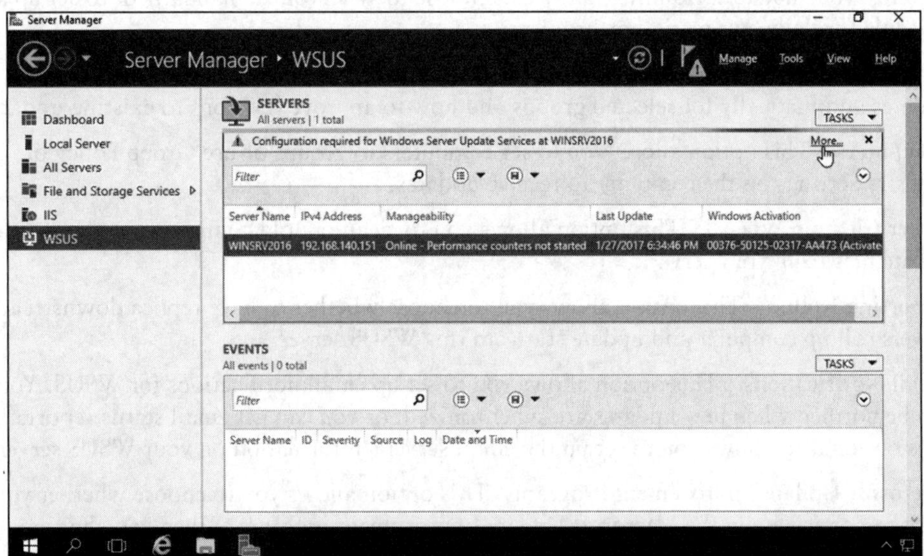

**EXERCISE 8.1 *(continued)***

15. At the All Servers Task Details And Notifications screen, click the Launch Post-Installation Tasks link.
16. The installation process will automatically continue. Once it is finished, you will see Complete under Stage. Close the All Servers Task Details And Notifications screen.
17. Close Server Manager.
18. If a WSUS Configure Options box appears, just close it. You will set options in the next exercise.

## Configuring a WSUS Server

Configuring a WSUS machine is a straightforward process. The easiest way to do it is to use the WSUS Server Configuration Wizard. This wizard walks you through the WSUS setup process, and it makes it easy to configure WSUS. When in the WSUS snap-in, you can configure different options.

**Update Source And Proxy Server** This option allows you to configure whether this WSUS server synchronizes either from Microsoft Update or from another WSUS server on your network.

**Products And Classifications** This option allows you to select the products for which you want to get updates and the type of updates that you want to receive.

**Update Files And Languages** This option allows you to choose whether to download update files and where to store these update files. This option also allows you to choose which update languages you want downloaded.

**Synchronization Schedule** This option allows you to configure how and when you synchronize your updates. Administrators can choose to synchronize manually or to set up a schedule for daily automatic synchronization.

**Automatic Approvals** This option allows you to specify how to approve installation of updates automatically for selected groups and how to approve revisions to existing updates.

**Computers** This option allows you to set computers to groups or use Group Policy or Registry settings on the computer to receive updates.

**Server Cleanup Wizard** This option allows you to clean out old computers, updates, and update files from your server.

**Reporting Rollup** This option allows you to choose whether to have replica downstream servers roll up computer and update status to this WSUS server.

**Email Notifications** This option allows you to set up email notifications for WSUS. You can be notified when new updates are synchronized, or you can get email status reports. This option also allows you to set up the email server's information on your WSUS server.

**Microsoft Update Improvement Program** This option allows you to choose whether you want to participate in the Microsoft Update Improvement program. When you choose to participate in this program, your WSUS server will automatically send information to Microsoft about the quality of your updates. This following information is included:

- How many computers are in the organization
- How many computers successfully installed each update
- How many computers failed to install each update

**Personalization** This option allows you to personalize the way that information is displayed for this server. This option also allows you to set up a to-do list for WSUS.

**WSUS Server Configuration Wizard** This option allows you to set up many of the preceding options by just using this one setup wizard.

In Exercise 8.2, you will learn how to set up some of the WSUS server options. To complete this exercise, you need to have an Internet connection that can communicate with Microsoft.

**EXERCISE 8.2**

## Setting WSUS Server Options

1. Open the Windows Server Update Services snap-in from Administrative Tools by pressing the Start key and then choosing Administrative Tools (see Figure 8.11). The Windows Server Update Services snap-in will be at the bottom of the list alphabetically.

**FIGURE 8.11** Administrative Tools

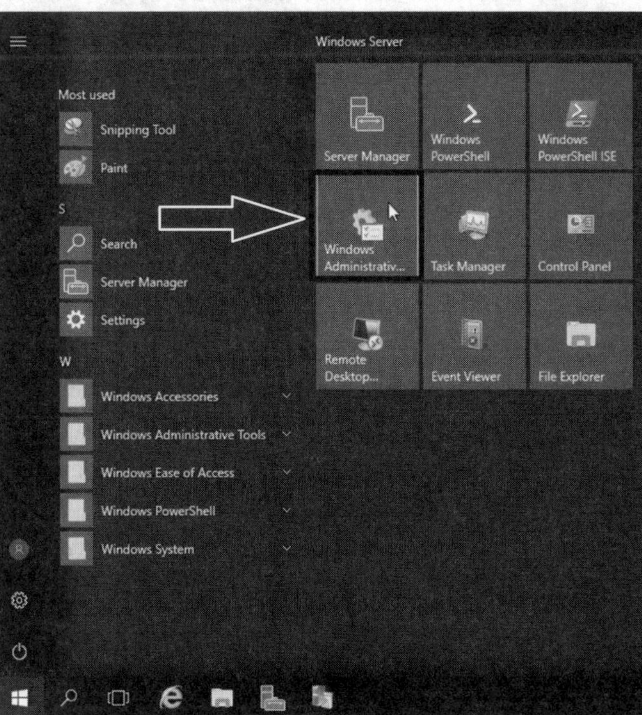

**EXERCISE 8.2 *(continued)***

2. On the left side, click the name of your server to expand the list. Then click the Options link (shown in Figure 8.12).

**FIGURE 8.12** WSUS Options

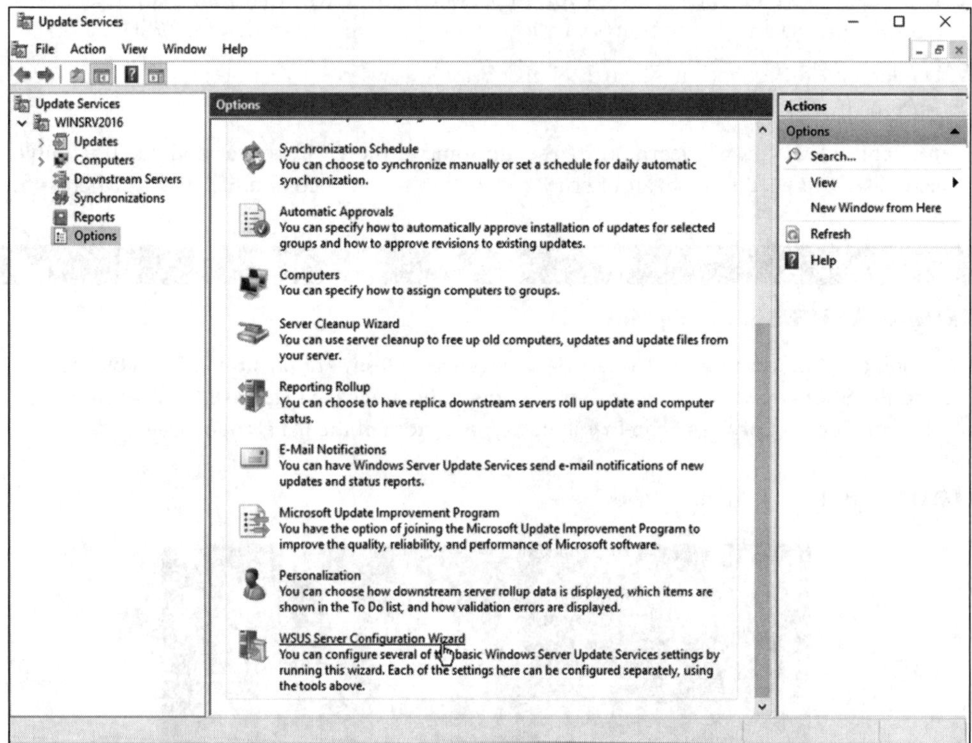


3. WSUS Server Configuration Wizard appears at the bottom of the options list. Click this link.

4. Click Next at the Before You Begin screen.

5. At the Join Microsoft Update Improvement Program screen, uncheck the Yes box and click Next.

6. At the Choose Upstream Server screen, choose Synchronize From Microsoft Update and click Next.

7. Fill in the information at the Specify Proxy Server screen if you need to use a proxy server. If you do not need a proxy server, just click Next.

8. At the Connect To Upstream Server screen, click the Start Connecting button (see Figure 8.13). This step can take a while depending on your connection speed. Once it's finished connecting, click Next.

**FIGURE 8.13** Connect to Upstream Server

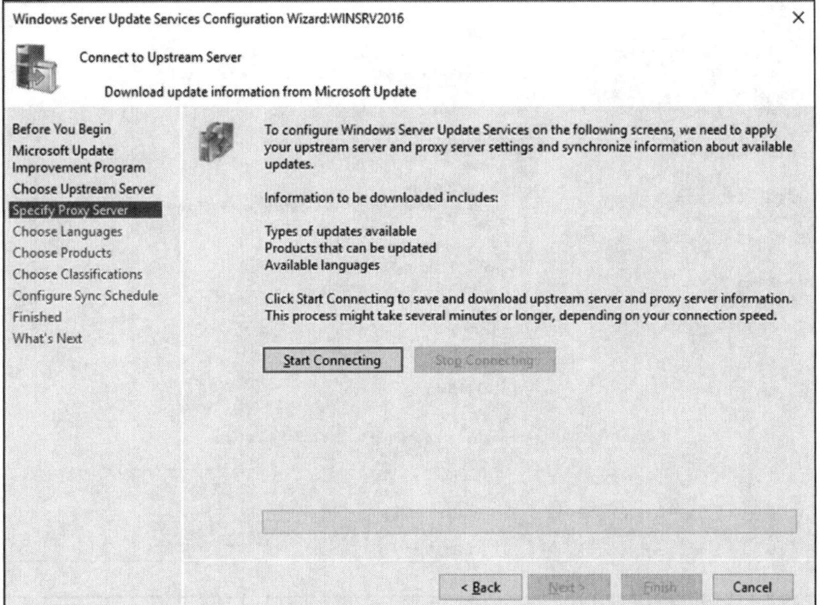


9. At the Choose Products screen (Figure 8.14), scroll down and choose the products for which you want to receive updates. Then click Next. You should only choose the products that you have in your organization. The more items you choose, the more space your network will need.

10. At the Choose Classifications screen, choose the classifications of updates you would like and click Next.

11. The Set Sync Schedule screen will appear next. At this screen, you can choose whether you want manual or automatic synchronizations. For this exercise, choose Synchronize Manually and click Next.

12. At the Finish screen, you can click Begin Initial Synchronization and click Finish. Be advised, this initial sync can take some time to finish. So if you don't have time to complete it now, you can always synchronize later.

13. Close WSUS.

**EXERCISE 8.2 *(continued)***

**FIGURE 8.14** Choose Products screen

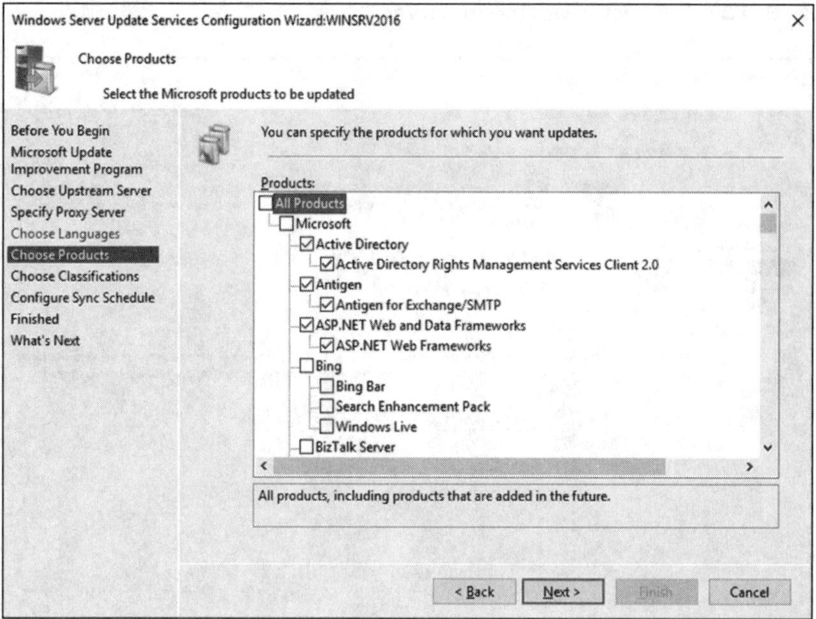


## Testing and Approving Updates

The administrator should test and approve updates before they are deployed to WSUS clients. The testing should be done on a test machine that is not used for daily tasks.

You also want to make sure that the WSUS test client has Windows Defender or a third-party antivirus-type software on it. This ensures that when the updates are loaded onto this test system, the updates will be checked against possible viruses, antimalware, spyware, or any other type of malicious software.

There are many reasons why you should pre-test the updates. There have been times in the past (and it doesn't happen a lot) when Microsoft has released an update that has caused issues on a network. Microsoft does its very best job to ensure that all updates are tested before deploying them but depending on how your network is setup; the update may not perform the same way as it was intended. So by testing updates before deploying them, you ensure that the updates will not cause your network any unseen issues.

To approve updates, from the Welcome screen, click Updates on the site's toolbar. Make your settings on the Updates page that appears.

## Viewing the Synchronization Log

To view the synchronization log, click the Reports button on the site's toolbar from the Welcome screen. The Reports page will appear. Click Synchronization Results to view the results.

### Configuring a Disconnected Network

You have the ability to use WSUS on a disconnected network. To do so, you download the updates to the Internet-connected WSUS server. After the download is complete, you can export the updates and then import the updates to the disconnected network.

## Choosing Products to Update

One of the toughest decisions that you will have to make when setting up a network and a WSUS server is which products are we (the IT department) going to allow in my network environment. The more Microsoft products that we choose, the more updates we will need.

But you have to make sure you choose the products that are needed and make sure those updates get done. Some of the products that we need to look at may not be things we think of right away. For example, we want to make sure that when we choose our products that we include Windows Defender.

As stated in the Testing and Approving Updates section, Windows Defender protects your systems against viruses, spyware, antimalware, and other malicious software. As new viruses get released, we need to make sure we protect our network systems against those viruses. By making sure we always have the up-to-date protection ensures that we can battle against these attacks.

Also, as new operating systems come out (for example, Windows Server 2016), we as IT members want to make sure that we have the latest security updates and improvements. This will not only ensure that our network runs at peak performance but it will also ensure that we fix any security loopholes that hackers may have figured out in the operating system.

## WSUS Client Requirements

WSUS clients run a special version of Automatic Updates that is designed to support WSUS. The following enhancements to Automatic Updates are included:

- Clients can receive updates from a WSUS server as opposed to the public Microsoft Windows Update site.
- The administrator can schedule when the downloading of updated files will occur.
- Clients can be configured via Group Policy or through editing the Registry.
- Updates can occur when an administrative account or nonadministrative account is logged on.

The following client platforms are the only ones that WSUS currently supports:

- Windows XP Home Edition (with Service Pack 3)
- Windows XP Professional (with Service Pack 3)
- Windows Server 2003 (SP1 or newer)
- Windows Vista
- Windows 7
- Windows 8
- Windows 8.1
- Windows 10

- Windows Server 2008 and 2008 R2
- Windows Server 2012 and 2012 R2
- Windows Server 2016

## Configuring the WSUS Clients

You can configure WSUS clients in two ways. The method you use depends on whether you use Active Directory in your network.

In a nonenterprise network (not running Active Directory), you would configure Automatic Updates through the Control Panel. Each client's registry would then be edited to reflect the location of the server providing the automatic updates.

Within an enterprise network, using Active Directory, you would typically see Automatic Updates configured through Group Policy. Group Policy is used to manage configuration and security settings via Active Directory. Group Policy is also used to specify what server a client will use for Automatic Updates. If Automatic Updates is configured through Group Policy, the user will not be able to change Automatic Updates settings by choosing Control Panel ➢ Windows Update (for Windows 8, Windows 7, Windows Server 2008, Windows Server 2008 R2, Windows Server 2012, Windows Server 2012 R2, and Windows Server 2016).

### Configuring a Client in a Non–Active Directory Network

The easiest way to configure the client to use Automatic Updates is through the Control Panel. However, you can also configure Automatic Updates through the Registry. The Registry is a database of all your server settings. You can access it by choosing Start ➢ Run and typing **`regedit`** in the Run dialog box. Automatic Updates settings are defined through `HKEY_LOCAL_MACHINE\Software\Policies\Microsoft\Windows\WindowsUpdate\AU`.

Table 8.1 lists some of the Registry options that you can configure for Automatic Updates.

**TABLE 8.1** Selected Registry keys and values for Automatic Updates

| Registry key | Options for values |
|---|---|
| `NoAutoUpdate` | 0: Automatic Updates are enabled (default). |
| | 1: Automatic Updates are disabled. |
| | 2: Notify of download and installation. |
| | 3: Autodownload and notify of installation. |
| | 4: Autodownload and schedule installation. |
| | 5: Automatic Updates are required, but end users can configure. |

| Registry key | Options for values |
|---|---|
| ScheduledInstallDay | 1: Sunday |
| | 2: Monday |
| | 3: Tuesday |
| | 4: Wednesday |
| | 5: Thursday |
| | 6: Friday |
| | 7: Saturday |
| UseWUServer | 0: Use public Microsoft Windows Update site. |
| | 1: Use server specified in WUServer entry. |

To specify what server will be used as the Windows Update server, you edit two Registry keys, which are found here:

```
HKEY_LOCAL_MACHINE\Software\Policies\Microsoft\Windows\WindowsUpdate
```

- The WUServer key sets the Windows Update server using the server's HTTP name—for example, http://intranetSUS.
- The WUStatusServer key sets the Windows Update intranet WSUS statistics server by using the server's HTTP name—for example, http://intranetSUS.

### Configuring a Client in an Active Directory Network

If the WSUS client is part of an enterprise network using Active Directory, you would configure the client via Group Policy. In Exercise 8.3, I will walk you through the steps needed to configure the Group Policy Object (GPO) for WSUS clients. The *Group Policy Management Console (GPMC)* needs to be installed to complete this exercise. If you don't have the GPMC installed, you can install it using the Server Manager utility.

**EXERCISE 8.3**

### Configuring a GPO for WSUS

1. Open the GPMC by pressing the Windows key and selecting Administrative Tools ➢ Group Policy Management.
2. Expand the forest, domains, and your domain name. Under your domain name, right-click and choose Create And Link GPO Here. Name the GPO **WSUS**, and hit Enter. Right-click the WSUS GPO and choose Edit.

**EXERCISE 8.3 *(continued)***

3. Under the Computer Configuration section, expand Policies ➢ Administrative Templates ➢ Windows Components ➢ Windows Update.
4. In the right pane, double-click the Configure Automatic Updates option. The Configure Automatic Updates Properties dialog box appears. Click the Enabled button. Then, in the drop-down list, choose Auto Download And Notify For Install. Click OK.
5. Double-click Specify Intranet Microsoft Update Service Location Properties. This setting allows you to specify the server from which the clients will get the updates. Click Enabled. In the two server name boxes, enter **//servername** (the name of the server on which you installed WSUS in Exercise 8.1). Click OK.
6. To configure the rescheduling of automatic updates, double-click Reschedule Automatic Updates Scheduled Installations. You can enable and schedule the amount of time that Automatic Updates waits after system startup before it attempts to proceed with a scheduled installation that was previously missed. Click Enabled. Enter **10** in the Startup (Minutes) box. Click OK.
7. To configure auto-restart for scheduled Automatic Updates installations, double-click No Auto-Restart For Scheduled Automatic Updates Installations. When you enable this option, the computer is not required to restart after an update. Enable this option and click OK.
8. Close the GPMC.

---

### Configuring Client-Side Targeting

Administrators can use a GPO to enable client-side targeting. Client machines can be automatically added into the proper computer group once the client computer connects to the WSUS server. Client-side targeting can be a very useful tool when an administrator has multiple client computers and the administrator needs to automate the process of assigning those computers to computer groups.

Administrators can enable client-side targeting on the WSUS server by clicking the Use Group Policy Or Registry Settings On Client Computers option on the Computers Options page.

1. On the WSUS console toolbar, click Options and then click Computer Options.
2. In Computer Options, choose one of the following options:
   - If an administrator wants to create groups and assign computers through the WSUS console (server-side targeting), click Use The Move Computers Task In Windows Server Update Services.
   - If an administrator wants to create groups and assign computers by using Group Policy settings on the client computer (client-side targeting), click Use Group Policy Or Registry Settings On Computers.
3. Under Tasks, click the Save Settings button and then click OK.

# Understanding Backups

One of the most important jobs of an IT administrator is to protect the company's data. Doesn't matter if it's setting up security and permissions or installing a new firewall, we are trying to protect our data. It truly is our number one job.

Knowing that protecting our data is our primary task means that our IT departments have to ensure that we can recover that data in the event of a major catastrophe (like a fire in the server room) or hardware failure.

If you have deployed Active Directory in your network environment, your users now depend on it to function properly in order to do their jobs. From network authentications to file access to print and web services, Active Directory has become a mission-critical component of your business. Therefore, the importance of backing up the Active Directory data store should be evident.

Backups are just good common sense, but here are several specific reasons to back up data:

**Protect Against Hardware Failures** Computer hardware devices have finite lifetimes, and all hardware eventually fails. *Mean Time Between Failures (MTBF)* is the average time a device will function before it actually fails. There is also a rating derived from benchmark testing of hard disk devices that tells you when you may be at risk for an unavoidable disaster. Some types of failures, such as corrupted hard disk drives, can result in significant data loss.

**Protect Against Accidental Deletion or Modification of Data** Although the threat of hardware failures is very real, in most environments, mistakes in modifying or deleting data are much more common. For example, suppose a system administrator accidentally deletes all of the objects within a specific OU. Clearly, it's very important to be able to retrieve this information from a backup.

**Protect Against a Major Catastrophe** As IT administrators, it's tough to think that a major catastrophe would ever happen to our company, but we have to make sure we protect our company in the event of that very possibility. Fires, earthquakes, flooding, and tornados are just some of the events that we have to consider. Because of these types of events, we have to make sure that not only do we back up our data, we also get that data offsite. When I talk about offsite, I don't mean another building on the campus. It needs to be in another city or in a very safe location (like a safety deposit box).

**Keeping Historical Information** Users and system administrators sometimes modify files and then later find out that they require access to an older version of the file. Or a file is accidentally deleted, and a user does not discover that fact until much later. By keeping multiple backups over time, you can recover information from prior backups when necessary.

**Protect Against Malicious Deletion or Modification of Data** Even in the most secure environments, it is conceivable that unauthorized users (or authorized ones with malicious intent!) could delete or modify information. In such cases, the loss of data might require valid backups from which to restore critical information.

Windows Server 2016 includes a Backup utility (called `wbadmin`) that is designed to back up operating system files and the Active Directory data store. It allows for basic backup functionality, such as scheduling backup jobs and selecting which files to back up. Figure 8.15 shows the main screen of the Windows Server 2016 Backup utility (`wbadmin`).

**FIGURE 8.15** The main screen of the Windows Server 2016 Backup utility

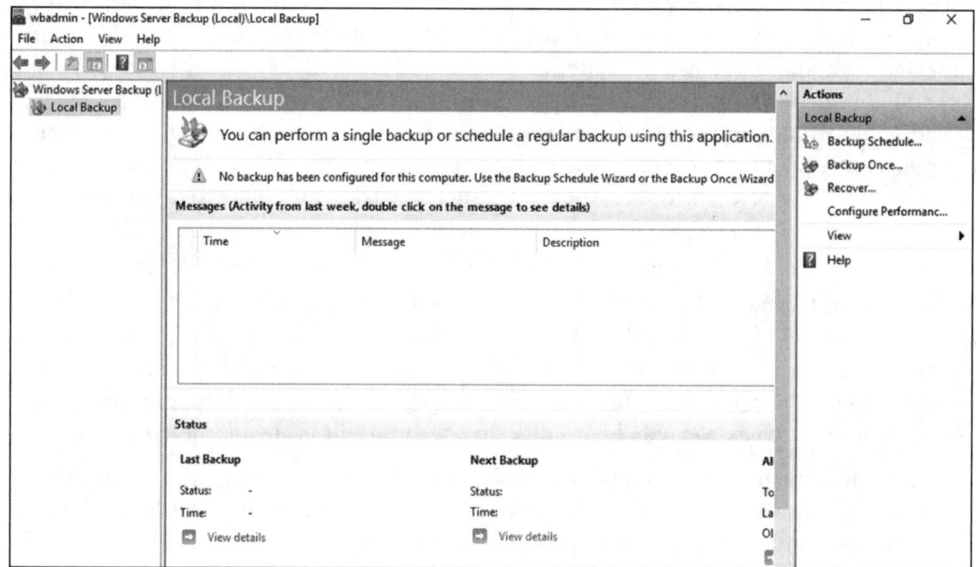


In the following sections, we'll look at the details of using the Windows Server 2016 Backup utility and how you can restore Active Directory when problems do occur.

## Overview of the Windows Server 2016 Backup Utility

Although the general purpose behind performing backup operations—protecting information—is straightforward, system administrators must consider many options when determining the optimal backup-and-recovery scenario for their environment. Factors include what to back up, how often to back up, and when the backups should be performed.

In this section, you'll see how the Windows Server 2016 Backup utility makes it easy to implement a backup plan for many network environments.

Although the Windows Server 2016 Backup utility provides the basic functionality required to back up your files, you may want to investigate third-party products that provide additional functionality. These applications can provide options for specific types of backups (such as those for Exchange Server and SQL Server) as well as disaster recovery options, networking functionality, centralized management, and support for more advanced hardware.

## Backup Types

One of the most important issues you will have to deal with when you are performing backups is keeping track of which files you have backed up and which files you need to back up. Whenever a backup of a file is made, the archive bit for the file is set. You can view the attributes of system files by right-clicking them and selecting Properties. By clicking the Advanced button in the Properties dialog box, you will access the Advanced Attributes dialog box. Here you will see the option Folder Is Ready For Archiving. Figure 8.16 shows an example of the attributes for a folder.

**FIGURE 8.16** Viewing the Archive attributes for a folder

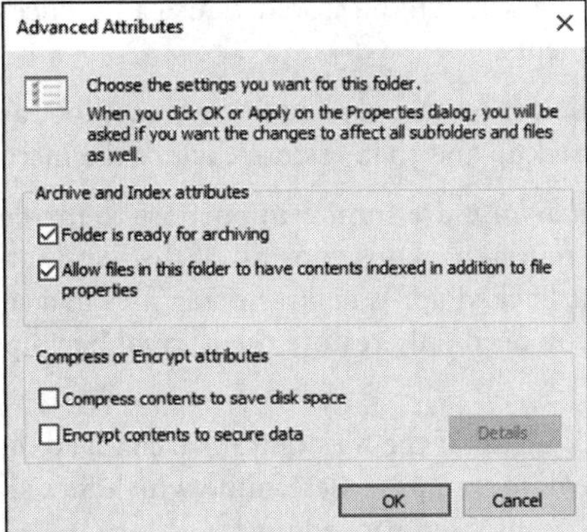


Although it is possible to back up all of the files in the file system during each backup operation, it's sometimes more convenient to back up only selected files (such as those that have changed since the last backup operation). When performing backups, you can back up to removable media (DVD) or to a network location.

It is recommended by Microsoft to do a backup to a network location or removable media. The reason for this is that if your company suffers from a disaster (fire, hurricane, and so forth), your data can all still be lost—including the backup. If you back up to a removable media source, a copy of the backup can be taken offsite. This protects against a major disaster. Several types of backups can be performed:

Although Windows Server 2016 does not support all of these backup types, it's very important that you understand the most common backup types. Most administrators use third-party software for their backups. That's why it's important to know all of the different types.

**Normal** Normal backups (also referred to as *system* or *full backups*) back up all of the selected files and then mark them as backed up. This option is usually used when a full system backup is made. Windows Server 2016 supports this backup.

**Copy** *Copy backups* back up all of the selected files but do not mark them as backed up. This is useful when you want to make additional backups of files for moving files offsite or you want to make multiple copies of the same data for archival purposes.

**Incremental** *Incremental backups* copy any selected files that are marked as ready for backup (typically because they have not been backed up or they have been changed since the last backup) and then mark the files as backed up. When the next incremental backup is run, only the files that are not marked as having been backed up are stored. Incremental backups are used in conjunction with normal (full) backups.

The most common backup process is to make a full backup and then make subsequent incremental backups. The benefit to this method is that only files that have changed since the last full or incremental backup will be stored. This can reduce backup times and disk or tape storage space requirements.

When recovering information from this type of backup method, a system administrator must first restore the full backup and then restore each of the incremental backups.

**Differential** *Differential backups* are similar in purpose to incremental backups with one important exception: Differential backups copy all of the files that are marked for backup but do not mark the files as backed up. When restoring files in a situation that uses normal and differential backups, you need only restore the normal backup and the latest differential backup.

**Daily** *Daily backups* back up all of the files that have changed during a single day. This operation uses the file time/date stamps to determine which files should be backed up and does not mark the files as having been backed up.

## Backing Up System State Data

When you are planning to back up and restore Active Directory, be aware that the most important component is known as the *System State data*. System State data includes the components upon which the Windows Server 2016 operating system relies for normal operations. The Windows Server 2016 Backup utility offers you the ability to back up the System State data to another type of media (such as a hard disk or network share). Specifically, it will back up the following components for a Windows Server 2016 domain controller:

**Active Directory** The *Active Directory data store* is at the heart of Active Directory. It contains all of the information necessary to create and manage network resources, such as users and computers. In most environments that use Active Directory, users and system administrators rely on the proper functioning of these services in order to do their jobs.

**Boot Files** *Boot files* are the files required for booting the Windows Server 2016 operating system and can be used in the case of boot file corruption.

**COM+ Class Registration Database** The *COM+ Class Registration database* is a listing of all of the COM+ Class registrations stored on the computer. Applications that run on a Windows Server 2016 computer might require the registration of various share code components. As part of the System State backup process, Windows Server 2016 stores all of the information related to Component Object Model+ (COM+) components so that it can be quickly and easily restored.

**Registry** The Windows Server 2016 *Registry* is a central repository of information related to the operating system configuration (such as desktop and network settings), user settings, and application settings. Therefore, the Registry is absolutely vital to the proper functioning of Windows Server 2016.

***Sysvol* Directory** The *Sysvol directory* includes data and files that are shared between the domain controllers within an Active Directory domain. Many operating system services rely on this information in order to function properly.

## Bare Metal Backups and Restores

One of the options you have in Windows Server 2016 is to do a *Bare Metal Restore (BMR)*. This is a restore of a machine after the machine has been completely wiped out and formatted. This type of restore is done usually after a catastrophic machine failure or crash.

Windows Server 2016 gives you the ability to back up all of the files needed for a Bare Metal Restore by choosing the Bare Metal Recovery check box (see Figure 8.17).

**FIGURE 8.17** Bare Metal Restore option

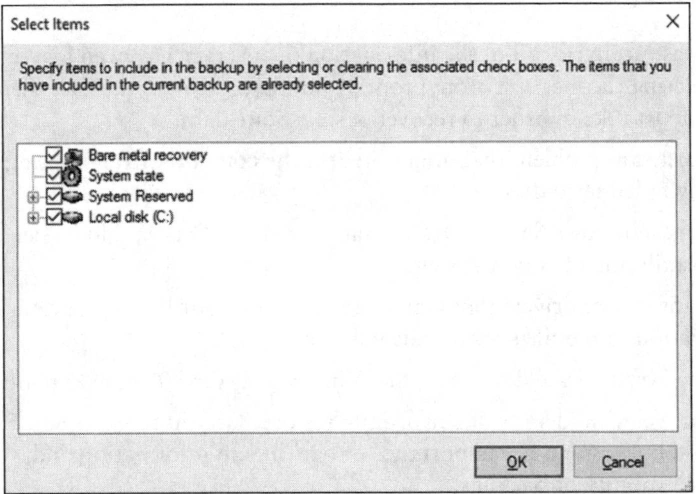


When you choose the Bare Metal Restore option in Windows Server 2016, all of the sub-options (System State, System Reserved, and Local Disk) automatically get checked.

When preparing your network for a Bare Metal Backup, you want to make sure that you have everything you need on hand to complete this type of restore. You may want to keep a copy of the server software, server drivers, and so forth on hand and ready to go, just in case you have to do a full restore.

## Scheduling Backups

In addition to specifying which files to back up, you can schedule backup jobs to occur at specific times. Planning *when* to perform backups is just as important as deciding *what* to back up. Performing backup operations can reduce overall system performance; therefore, you should plan to back up information during times of minimal activity on your servers.

To add a backup operation to the schedule, you can simply click the Add button on the Specify Backup Time window.

## Restoring System State Data

In some cases, the Active Directory data store or other System State data may become corrupt or unavailable. This could be due to many different reasons. A hard disk failure might, for example, result in the loss of data. Or the accidental deletion of an Organizational Unit (OU) and all of its objects might require a restore operation to be performed.

The actual steps involved in restoring System State data are based on the details of what has caused the data loss and what effect this data loss has had on the system. In the best-case scenario, the System State data is corrupt or inaccurate but the operating system can still boot. If this is the case, all you must do is boot into a special *Directory Services Restore Mode (DSRM)* and then restore the System State data from a backup. This process will replace the current System State data with that from the backup. Therefore, any changes that have been made since the last backup will be completely lost and must be redone.

In a worst-case scenario, all of the information on a server has been lost or a hardware failure is preventing the machine from properly booting. If this is the case, here are several steps that you must take in order to recover System State data:

1. Fix any hardware problem that might prevent the computer from booting (for example, replace any failed hard disks).
2. Reinstall the Windows Server 2016 operating system. This should be performed like a regular installation on a new system.
3. Reinstall any device drivers that may be required by your backup device. If you backed up information to the file system, this will not apply.
4. Restore the System State data using the Windows Server 2016 Backup utility.

I'll cover the technical details of performing restores later in this chapter. For now, however, you should understand the importance of backing up information and, whenever possible, testing the validity of backups.

## Backing Up and Restoring Group Policy Objects

*Group Policy Objects (GPOs)* are a major part of Active Directory. When you back up Active Directory, GPOs can also get backed up. You also have the ability to back up GPOs through the Group Policy Management Console (GPMC). This gives you the ability to back up and restore individual GPOs.

To back up all GPOs, open the GPMC and right-click the Group Policy Objects container. You will see the option Back Up All. After you choose this option, a wizard will start, asking you for the backup location. Choose a location and click Backup.

To back up an individual GPO, right-click the GPO (in the Group Policy Objects container) and choose Backup. Again, after you choose this option, a wizard will start, asking you for the backup location. Choose a location and click Backup.

To restore a GPO, it's the same process as above (backing up GPOs) except, instead of choosing Backup, you will either choose Manage Backups (to restore all GPOs) or Restore (for an individual GPO).

## Setting Up an Active Directory Backup

The Windows Server 2016 Backup utility makes it easy to back up the System data (including Active Directory) as part of a normal backup operation. We've already covered the ideas behind the different backup types and why and when they are used.

Exercise 8.4 walks you through the process of backing up the domain controller. In order to complete this exercise, the local machine must be a domain controller, and you must have a DVD burner or network location to back up the System State.

The Windows Server 2016 Backup utility is not installed by default. If you have already installed the Windows Server 2016 Backup utility, skip to step 9.

**EXERCISE 8.4**

### Backing Up Active Directory

1. To install the Windows Server 2016 Backup utility, click the Start key > Server Manager.
2. In the center console, click the link for # 2, Add Roles And Features. Click Next at the Before You Begin screen (if it appears).
3. At the Select Installation Type screen, choose role-based or feature-based installation and click Next.
4. The Select Destination Server screen appears. Choose Select A Server From The Server Pool, and choose your server under Server Pool. Click Next.
5. Click Next at the Select Server Roles screen.
6. At the Select Features screen (see Figure 8.18), scroll down and check the box next to Windows Server Backup. Click Next.

**EXERCISE 8.4 *(continued)***

**FIGURE 8.18** Selecting Windows Server Backup

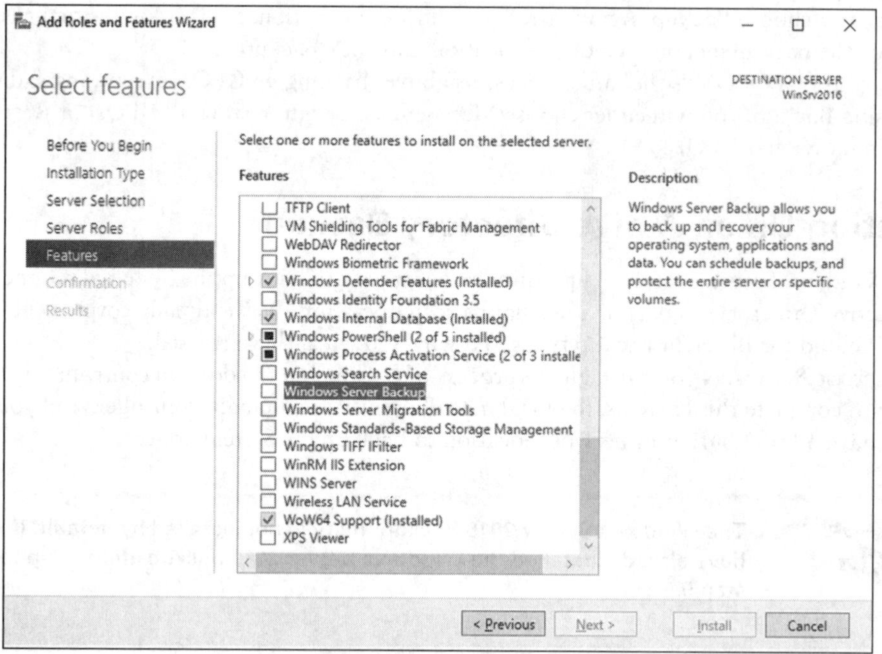


7. At the Confirmation screen, click the check box to restart the destination server automatically. This will bring up a dialog box. Click Yes, and then click the Install button.
8. Click the Close button when finished. Close Server Manager.
9. Open Windows Backup by clicking Start ➢ Administrative Tools ➢ Windows Server Backup.
10. On the left-hand side, click Local Backup. Then, under Actions, click Backup Once.
11. When the Backup Once Wizard appears, click Different Options (see Figure 8.19) and click Next.
12. At the Select Backup Configuration screen, choose Custom and click Next.
13. Click the Add Items button (see Figure 8.20). Choose System State and click OK. Click Next.

**FIGURE 8.19** Backup Options screen

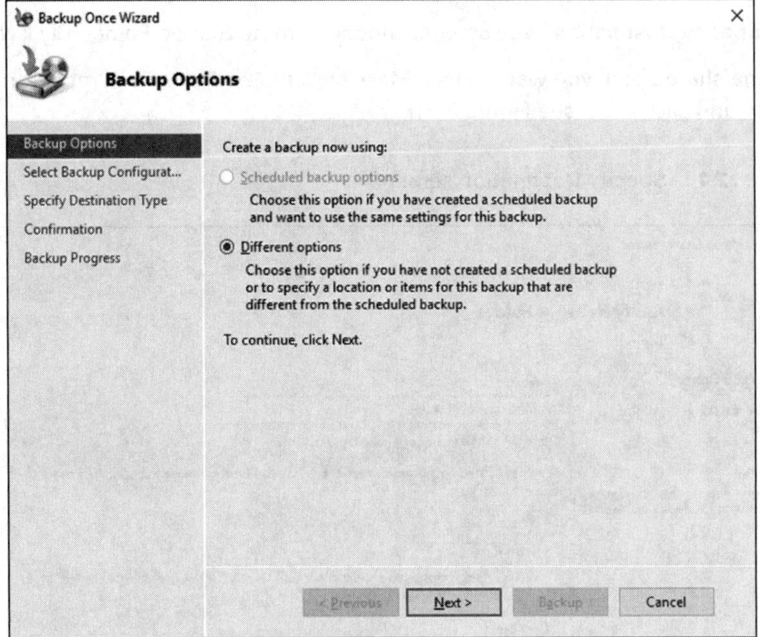


**FIGURE 8.20** Select Items for Backup screen

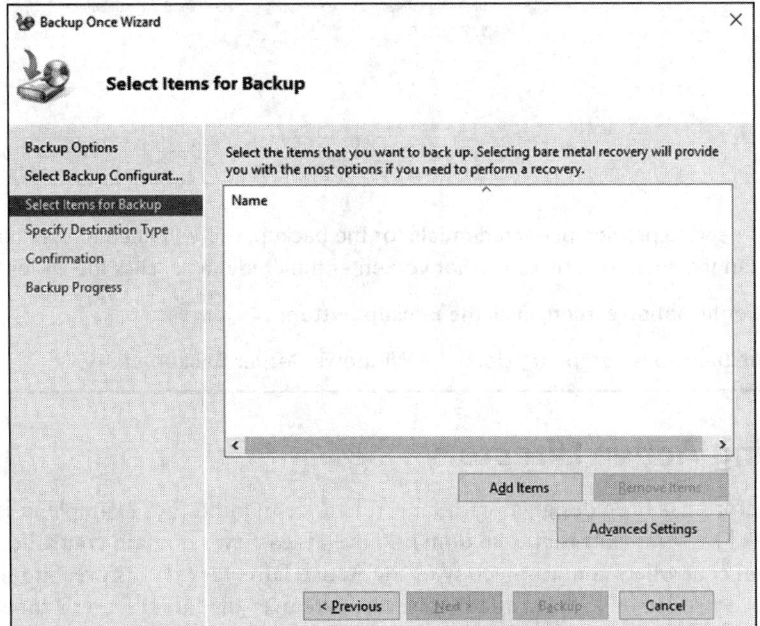

**EXERCISE 8.4 *(continued)***

14. At the Specify Destination Type screen, choose Remote Shared Folder. Click Next.
15. Put in the shared path you want to use. Make sure the Do Not Inherit radio button is selected and click Next (see Figure 8.21).

**FIGURE 8.21** Specify Destination screen

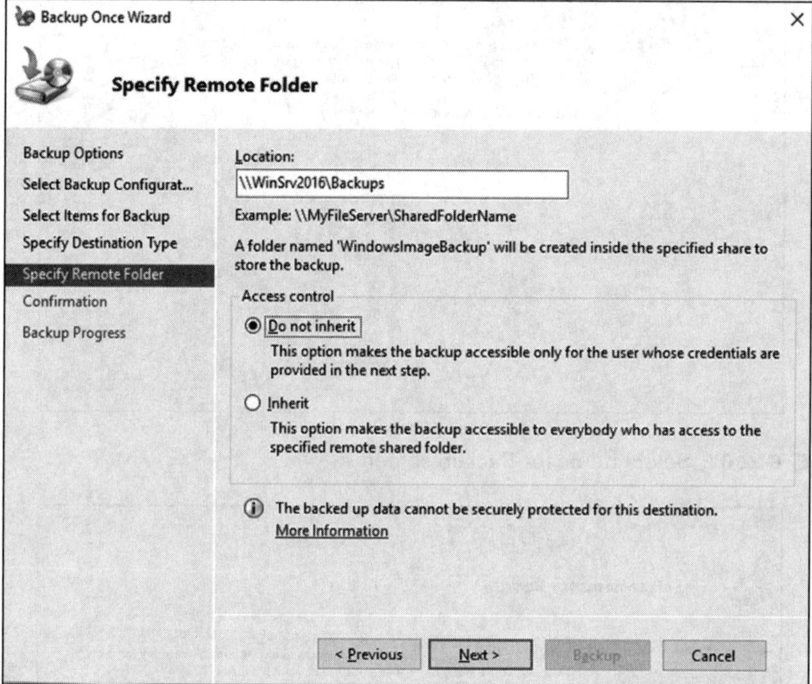


16. You will need to provide user credentials for the backup. You will need to use these credentials in the event of a restore. After you enter the credentials, click the OK button.
17. At the Confirmation screen, click the Backup button.
18. Once the backup is complete, close the Windows Server Backup utility.

## Restoring Active Directory

Active Directory has been designed with fault tolerance in mind. For example, it is highly recommended by Microsoft that each domain have at least two domain controllers. Each of these domain controllers contains a copy of the Active Directory data store. Should one of the domain controllers fail, the available one can take over the failed server's functionality.

When the failed server is repaired, it can then be promoted to a domain controller in the existing environment. This process effectively restores the failed domain controller without incurring any downtime for end users because all of the Active Directory data is replicated to the repaired server in the next scheduled replication.

In some cases, you might need to restore Active Directory from a backup. For example, suppose a system administrator accidentally deletes several hundred users from the domain and does not realize it until the change has been propagated to all of the other domain controllers. Manually re-creating the accounts is not an option because the objects' security identifiers will be different (and all permissions must be reset). Clearly, a method for restoring from backup is the best solution. You can elect to make the Active Directory restore authoritative or nonauthoritative, as described in the following sections.

## Overview of Authoritative Restore

Restoring Active Directory and other System State data is an important process should system files or the Active Directory data store become corrupt or otherwise unavailable. Fortunately, the Windows Server 2016 Backup utility allows you to restore data easily from a backup, should the need arise.

I mentioned earlier that in the case of the accidental deletion of information from Active Directory, you might need to restore Active Directory from a recent backup. But what happens if there is more than one domain controller in the environment? Even if you did perform a restore, the information on this domain controller would be seen as outdated and it would be overwritten by the data from another domain controller. This data from the older domain controller is exactly the information you want to replace. The domain controller that was reloaded using a backup would have an older time stamp, and the other domain controllers would re-delete the information from the backup.

Fortunately, Windows Server 2016 and Active Directory allow you to perform what is called an *authoritative restore*. The authoritative restore process specifies a domain controller as having the authoritative (or master) copy of the Active Directory data store. When other domain controllers communicate with this domain controller, their information will be overwritten with Active Directory data stored on the local machine.

Now that you have an idea of how an authoritative restore is supposed to work, let's move on to looking at the details of performing the process.

## Performing an Authoritative Restore

When you are restoring Active Directory information on a Windows Server 2016 domain controller, make sure that Active Directory services are not running. This is because the restore of System State data requires full access to system files and the Active Directory data store. If you attempt to restore System State data while the domain controller is active, you will see an error message.

In general, restoring data and operating system files is a straightforward process. It is important to note that restoring a System State backup will replace the existing Registry, Sysvol, and Active Directory files, so that any changes you made since the last backup will be lost.

In addition to restoring the entire Active Directory database, you can also restore only specific subtrees within Active Directory using the `restoresubtree` command in the `ntdsutil` utility. This allows you to restore specific information, and it is useful in case of accidental deletion of isolated material.

Following the authoritative restore process, Active Directory should be updated to the time of the last backup. Furthermore, all of the other domain controllers for this domain will have their Active Directory information overwritten by the results of the restore operation. The result is an Active Directory environment that has been recovered from media.

### Overview of Nonauthoritative Restore

Now that you understand why you would use an authoritative restore and how it is performed, it's an easy conceptual jump to understand a *nonauthoritative restore*. Remember that by making a restore authoritative, you are simply telling other domain controllers in the domain to recognize the restored machine as the newest copy of Active Directory for replication purposes. If you only have one domain controller, the authoritative restore process becomes moot; you can simply skip the steps required to make the restore authoritative and begin using the domain controller immediately after the normal restore is complete.

If you have more than one domain controller in the domain and you need to perform a nonauthoritative restore, simply allow the domain controller to receive Active Directory database information from other domain controllers in the domain using normal replication methods.

## Active Directory Recycle Bin

The Active Directory Recycle Bin is a great feature that allows an administrator to restore an Active Directory object that has been deleted. This feature is only available on domain controllers.

Let's say that you have a junior administrator who has been making changes to Active Directory for hours. The junior admin then deletes an OU from Active Directory. You would then have to reload the OU from a tape backup, or even worse, you may have to reload the entire Active Directory (depending on your backup software), thus losing the hours of work the junior admin has completed.

The problem here is that when you delete a security object from Active Directory, the object's security ID (SID) gets removed. All users' rights and permissions are associated with the users' SID number and not their account name. This is where the AD Recycle Bin can help.

The *Active Directory Recycle Bin* allows you to preserve and restore accidentally deleted Active Directory objects without the need of using a backup.

The Active Directory Recycle Bin works for both the Active Directory Domain Services (AD DS) and the Active Directory Lightweight Directory Services (AD LDS) environments.

By enabling (disabled by default) the Active Directory Recycle Bin, any deleted Active Directory objects are preserved and Active Directory objects can be restored, in their entirety, to the same condition that they were in immediately before deletion. This means that all group memberships and access rights that an object had before deletion will remain intact.

To enable the Active Directory Recycle Bin, you must do the following (you must be a member of the Schema Admins group):

- Run the `adprep /forestprep` command to prepare the forest on the server that holds the schema master to update the schema.
- Run the `adprep /domainprep /gpprep` command to prepare the domain on the server that holds the infrastructure operations master role.
- If a read-only domain controller (RODC) is present in your environment, you must also run the `adprep /rodcprep` command.
- Make sure that all domain controllers in your Active Directory forest are running Windows Server 2016, Windows Server 2012 R2, Windows Server 2012, or Windows Server 2008 R2.
- Make sure that the forest functional level is set to Windows Server 2016, Windows Server 2012 R2, Windows Server 2012, or Windows Server 2008 R2.

## Understanding the *ntdsutil* Utility

As you learned in the preceding section, there are times when you have to be offline to do maintenance. For example, you need to perform authoritative and nonauthoritative restores while the domain controller is offline. The main utility we use for offline maintenance is `ntdsutil`.

### *Ntdsutil.exe*

The primary method by which system administrators can do offline maintenance is through the `ntdsutil` command-line tool. You can launch this tool by simply entering **`ntdsutil`** at a command prompt. For the commands to work properly, you must start the command prompt with elevated privileges. The `ntdsutil` command is both interactive and context sensitive. That is, once you launch the utility, you'll see an `ntdsutil` command prompt. At this prompt, you can enter various commands that set your context within the application. For example, if you enter **`domain management`**, you'll be able to enter domain-related commands. Several operations also require you to connect to a domain, a domain controller, or an Active Directory object before you perform a command.

Table 8.2 provides a list of some of the domain-management commands supported by the `ntdsutil` tool. You can access this functionality by typing the command at an elevated command prompt. Once you are in the `ntdsutil` prompt, you can use the question mark to see all of the commands available.

**TABLE 8.2** `Ntdsutil` offline maintenance commands

| `Ntdsutil` **Command** | **Purpose** |
|---|---|
| `Help or ?` | Displays information about the commands that are available within the Domain Management menu of the `ntdsutil` utility. |
| `Activate instance %s` | Sets NTDS or a specific AD LDS instance as the active instance. |

**TABLE 8.2** Ntdsutil offline maintenance commands *(continued)*

| Ntdsutil **Command** | **Purpose** |
|---|---|
| Authoritative restore | Sets the domain controller for the authoritative restore of the Active Directory database. |
| Change service account | This allows an administrator to change the AD LDS service account to user name and password. You can use a "NULL" for a blank password, and you can use * to prompt the user to enter a password. |
| configurable settings | Allows an administrator to manage configurable settings. |
| DS behavior | Allows an administrator to view and modify AD DS or AD LDS behavior. |
| files | This command allows an administrator to manage the AD DS or AD LDS database files. |
| Group Membership Evaluation | Allows an administrator to evaluate the security IDs (SIDs) in a token for a given user or group. |
| LDAP policies | Administrators can manage the Lightweight Directory Access Protocol (LDAP) protocol policies. |
| metadata cleanup | Removes metadata from decommissioned domain controllers. |
| security account management | This command allows an administrator to manage SIDs. |
| Set DSRM Password | Resets the Directory Service Restore mode administrator account password. |

## *Wbadmin* Command-Line Utility

The wbadmin command allows you to back up and restore your operating system, volumes, files, folders, and applications from a command prompt.

You must be a member of the Administrators group to configure a backup schedule. You must be a member of the Backup Operators or the Administrators group (or you must have been delegated the appropriate permissions) to perform all other tasks using the wbadmin command.

To use the wbadmin command, you must run wbadmin from an elevated command prompt (to open an elevated command prompt, click Start, right-click Command Prompt, and then click Run As Administrator). Table 8.3 shows some of the wbadmin commands.

**TABLE 8.3** Wbadmin commands

| Command | Description |
|---|---|
| `Wbadmin enable backup` | Configures and enables a daily backup schedule. |
| `Wbadmin disable backup` | Disables your daily backups. |
| `Wbadmin start backup` | Runs a one-time backup. |
| `Wbadmin stop job` | Stops the currently running backup or recovery operation. |
| `Wbadmin get items` | Lists the items included in a specific backup. |
| `Wbadmin start recovery` | Runs a recovery of the volumes, applications, files, or folders specified. |
| `Wbadmin get status` | Shows the status of the currently running backup or recovery operation. |
| `Wbadmin start systemstaterecovery` | Runs a system state recovery. |
| `Wbadmin start systemstatebackup` | Runs a system state backup. |
| `Wbadmin start sysrecovery` | Runs a recovery of the full system state. |

## Backing Up Virtual Machines

One of the main questions that you have to ask yourself when it comes to backing up a Hyper-V server is, Do I back up the Hyper-V server and the virtual machines as files, or do I back up each virtual machine as its own server?

Virtual machines and the virtual hard drives that work with those virtual machines are just files that reside on a Microsoft Hyper-V server. But when they are running, they work as normal servers within the virtual environment.

Some people like to back up the Hyper-V server and its files and some like to back up the virtual machines as servers. So what is best for your company? Well, it depends on what the virtual machines do and how much storage space you have.

I have set up many companies and I have set up dozens of virtual machines and I personally like to back up the virtual machines as normal servers. I do have good reasons for this decision.

Let's say we set up a Windows Server 2016 server that works as a Hyper-V host. We then decide to load a virtual machine that will be a file server. We will do our normal daily backups once a day at night, and maybe we will even do a backup during the day at 1p.m.

At 11:30 a.m., one of your users deletes a file that was created yesterday. Before deleting the file, the user had created 25 new documents. But that one file needs to be recovered. If we back up the virtual machines as files, depending on our backup software, we will need to restore the virtual machine file from last night. Okay, problem solved, but is it? Well actually it's not. Because when we restored last night's virtual machine files, we also lost all of our changes that have happened today.

If we backed up the virtual machines as servers, we would then just need to restore the single file that was lost on that server. This would save us a lot of time and issues. But it can also cause some issues. By backing each virtual machine up as a server, your backups will require more space. So if your backup server, software, tapes, or cloud storage is large enough, then it may be best to back up each virtual machine as its own server.

# PowerShell Commands

As I have stated in other chapters, Microsoft has announced that the Windows Server 2016 exams are going to be PowerShell intensive. So in this section, I will show you some of the available PowerShell commands for updates and for backups.

So Table 8.4 will show you some of the different PowerShell commands that are available for WSUS administration.

Table 8.4 is just a partial list of PowerShell commands for WSUS. To see a complete list, visit Microsoft's website at

`https://technet.microsoft.com/en-us/library/hh826166.aspx`

**TABLE 8.4** WSUS administration commands

| PowerShell Command | Description |
|---|---|
| `Add-WsusComputer` | This command allows an administrator to add a client computer to a WSUS target group. |
| `Approve-WsusUpdate` | This allows an administrator to approve an update that can then be applied to clients. |
| `Deny-WsusUpdate` | This allows an administrator to deny an update. |
| `Get-WsusClassification` | Administrators can use this command to get the list of all WSUS classifications available on the server. |
| `Get-WsusProduct` | Administrators can use this command to get the list of all WSUS products available on the server. |

| PowerShell Command | Description |
|---|---|
| Get-WsusUpdate | This command shows you the WSUS update object and the details about that update. |
| Invoke-WsusServerCleanup | Allows an administrator to initiate the cleanup process on the WSUS server. |
| Set-WsusClassification | Sets whether the classifications of updates are enabled on the WSUS server. |

Now that you have viewed the PowerShell commands for WSUS administration, let's go ahead and take a look at the backups and recovery.

So Table 8.5 will show you some of the different PowerShell commands that are available for Backup administration.

Table 8.5 is just a partial list of PowerShell commands for backups and restores. To see a complete list, visit Microsoft's website at `https://technet.microsoft.com/en-us/library/jj902428(v=wps.630).aspx`

**TABLE 8.5** Backup and restore commands

| PowerShell Command | Description |
|---|---|
| Add-WBBackupTarget | This command allows an administrator to add a backup target to a backup. |
| Add-WBBareMetalRecovery | Allows you to select a bare metal backup to a backup so that administrators can perform bare metal recoveries. |
| Add-WBSystemState | This command includes the system state components to the backup. |
| Add-WBVirtualMachine | This command allows you to include a virtual machine file to a backup. |
| Add-WBVolume | This command adds a volume to a backup. |
| Get-WBBackupSet | Administrators can use this command to view the backups for a server. |
| Get-WBDisk | This command shows the hard drives of a computer. |

**TABLE 8.5** Backup and restore commands *(continued)*

| PowerShell Command | Description |
|---|---|
| `Get-WBJob` | Shows an administrator the current backup job. |
| `Get-WBSchedule` | Shows an administrator the current backup schedule. |
| `Get-WBVolume` | Shows the administrator the volumes on a system. |
| `New-WBPolicy` | This command creates a new backup policy. |
| `Remove-WBFileSpec` | Deletes a backup file specification from a backup. |
| `Remove-WBPolicy` | This allows you to delete a backup policy. |
| `Remove-WBSystemState` | Deletes the system state components from a backup. |
| `Remove-WBVolume` | Deletes a volume from a backup. |
| `Resume-WBBackup` | This command allows you to resume a backup. |
| `Set-WBPolicy` | With this command, you can set a new policy on a backup. |
| `Set-WBSchedule` | Administrators can set the backup schedule. |
| `Start-WBBackup` | This command starts a manual backup job. |
| `Stop-WBJob` | This command allows you to stop a backup job. |

# Summary

This chapter began with a discussion of WSUS and what Windows Update can do for your network. You learned why you would want to use a WSUS server instead of having clients manually connect to the Internet to receive their updates.

I talked about the importance of choosing which updates and which products you want to update. Also, I talked about the importance of testing updates before deploying them.

You learned about how important it is to back up and restore a Windows Server 2016 server in the event of a hardware or software failure. I also explained how some of the features, such as the Active Directory Recycle Bin and `ntdsutil`, are part of Windows Server 2016 domain controller and how these utilities make an administrator's life easier by restoring an Active Directory object or the entire Active Directory database.

# Video Resources

There are videos available for the following exercises:

8.1

8.2

You can access the videos at `http://sybextestbanks.wiley.com` on the Other Study Tools tab.

# Exam Essentials

**Understand WSUS.** Using Windows Server Update Services is one way to have your end users receive important updates from Microsoft. WSUS gives administrators the ability to download, test, and approve updates before they get released onto the network.

**Understand the various backup types available with the Windows Server 2016 Backup utility.** The Windows Server 2016 Backup utility can perform full and incremental backup operations. Some third-party backup utilities also support differential and daily backups. You can use each of these operations as part of an efficient backup strategy.

**Know how to back up Active Directory.** The data within the Active Directory database on a domain controller is part of the system state data. You can back up the system state data to a file using the Windows Server 2016 Backup utility.

**Know how to restore Active Directory.** Restoring the Active Directory database is considerably different from other restore operations. To restore some or the entire Active Directory database, you must first boot the machine into Directory Services Restore mode.

**Understand the importance of an authoritative restore process.** You use an authoritative restore when you want to restore earlier information from an Active Directory backup and you want the older information to be propagated to other domain controllers in the environment.

**Understand offline maintenance using `ntdsutil`.** The `ntdsutil` command-line tool is a primary method by which system administrators perform offline maintenance. Understand how to launch this tool by entering **`ntdsutil`** at a command prompt.

# Review Questions

1. You are the network administrator for a Fortune 500 company. You are responsible for all client computers at the central campus. You want to make sure that all of the client computers have the most current software installed for their operating systems, including software in the categories Critical Updates and Service Packs, Windows Server 2016 Family, and Driver Updates. You want to automate the process as much as possible, and you want the client computers to download the updates from a central server that you are managing. You decide to use Windows Server Update Services. The WSUS server software has been installed on a server called WSUSServer. You want to test the WSUS server before you set up group policies within the domain. You install Windows 10. Which of the following Registry entries needs to be made for the client to specify that the client should use WSUSServer for Windows Update? (Choose all that apply.)

   **A.** Use `HKEY_LOCAL_MACHINE\Software\Policies\Microsoft\Windows\WindowsUpdate\AU\UseWUServer`, and specify 0 data.

   **B.** Use `HKEY_LOCAL_MACHINE\Software\Policies\Microsoft\Windows\WindowsUpdate\AU\UseWUServer`, and specify 1 for data.

   **C.** Use `HKEY_LOCAL_MACHINE\Software\Policies\Microsoft\Windows\WindowsUpdate\AU\WUServer`, and specify `http://WSUSServer`.

   **D.** Use `HKEY_LOCAL_MACHINE\Software\Policies\Microsoft\Windows\WindowsUpdate\AU\WUServer`, and specify `WSUSServer`.

   **E.** Use `HKEY_LOCAL_MACHINE\Software\Policies\Microsoft\Windows\WindowsUpdate\WUServer`, and specify `http://WSUSServer`.

   **F.** Use `HKEY_LOCAL_MACHINE\Software\Policies\Microsoft\Windows\WindowsUpdate\WUServer`, and specify `WSUSServer`.

2. You are the administrator of a new Windows Server 2016 machine. You need to install WSUS. From where do you install WSUS?

   **A.** Add/Remove Programs

   **B.** Programs

   **C.** Server Manager

   **D.** Administrative Tools

3. You are a network administrator for your company. The network consists of a single Active Directory domain. All servers run Windows Server 2016. Windows Server Update Services (WSUS) is installed on two servers, SERVERA and SERVERB. SERVERA receives software updates from Microsoft Windows Update servers. You manually synchronized SERVERB with the Windows Update servers, and now you need to complete the WSUS configuration on SERVERB. Which of the following is *not* a step you might take to complete the configuration of WSUS on SERVERB?

   **A.** Approve the current updates.

   **B.** Set SERVERB to receive updates from SERVERA and automatically synchronize with approved updates on SERVERA.

**C.** Set SERVERB to draw updates automatically from whichever sources SERVERA is set to draw from.

**D.** Set SERVERB to receive daily updates automatically at a given time.

**4.** You are the network administrator for your company. The network consists of a single Active Directory domain. All servers run Windows Server 2016. All client computers run Windows 10. The company has 16 mobile sales representatives who are all members of the Power Users local group on their computers. From 6 p.m. until 7 a.m., the sales representatives' laptops are usually turned off and disconnected from the corporate network. The mobile sales representatives' computers must receive software updates every day with minimal user interaction. While verifying the recent updates on one of the laptops, you notice that the updates from the Windows Update servers were not applied. On the Automatic Updates tab of the System Properties dialog box of the mobile computer, what should you do to make sure that software updates are applied to the computer? (Choose three.)

**A.** Set the scheduled time to every day at 12 a.m.

**B.** Select the option Automatically Download The Updates, And Install Them On The Schedule That I Specify.

**C.** Select the option Notify Me Before Downloading Any Updates And Notify Me Again Before Installing Them On My Computer.

**D.** Select the Keep My Computer Up To Date check box.

**E.** Select the option Download The Updates Automatically And Notify Me When They Are Ready To Be Installed.

**F.** Set the scheduled time to every day at 12 p.m.

**5.** You are responsible for managing several Windows Server 2016 domain controller computers in your environment. Recently, a single hard disk on one of these machines failed, and the Active Directory database was lost. You want to perform the following tasks:

- Determine which partitions on the server are still accessible.
- Restore as much of the system configuration (including the Active Directory database) as possible.

Which of the following could be used to help meet these requirements?

**A.** Event Viewer

**B.** Performance Monitor

**C.** A hard disk from another server that is not configured as a domain controller

**D.** A valid system state backup from the server

**6.** While setting up WSUS, you need to configure the server from which you will be getting your Microsoft updates. Under which option would you set this up?

**A.** Products And Classifications

**B.** Update Files And Languages

**C.** Update Source And Proxy Server

**D.** Synchronization Schedule

7. You are the administrator of a large company and you need to ensure that you can recover your Windows Server 2016 Active Directory configuration and data if the computer's hard disk fails. What should you do?

   A. Create a complete PC Backup and Restore image.

   B. Create a backup of all file categories.

   C. Perform an Automated System Recovery (ASR) backup.

   D. Create a system restore point.

8. You need to back up the existing data on a computer before you install a new application. You also need to ensure that you are able to recover individual user files that are replaced or deleted during the installation. What should you do?

   A. Create a System Restore point.

   B. Perform an Automated System Recovery (ASR) backup and restore.

   C. In the Windows Server Backup utility, click the Backup Once link.

   D. In the Backup And Restore Center window, click the Back Up Computer button.

9. You are the administrator of a large organization. While setting up your Windows Server 2016 domain controller, you are creating a data recovery strategy that must meet the following requirements:

   - Back up all data files and folders in `C:\Data`.
   - Restore individual files and folders in `C:\Data`.
   - Ensure that data is backed up to and restored from external media.

   What should you do?

   A. Use the Previous Versions feature to restore the files and folders.

   B. Use the System Restore feature to perform backup and restore operations.

   C. Use the NTBackup utility to back up and restore individual files and folders.

   D. Use the Windows Server Backup to back up and restore files.

10. Your manager has decided that your organization needs to use an Active Directory application data partition. Which command can you use to create and manage application data partitions?

    A. `DCPromo.exe`

    B. `NTDSUtil.exe`

    C. `ADUtil.exe`

    D. `ADSI.exe`

# Understanding Monitoring

## THE FOLLOWING 70-740 EXAM OBJECTIVES ARE COVERED IN THIS CHAPTER:

✓ **Monitor server installations**

- This objective may include but is not limited to: Monitor workloads using Performance Monitor; configure Data Collector Sets; determine appropriate CPU, memory, disk, and networking counters for storage and compute workloads; configure alerts; monitor workloads using Resource Monitor

A very important task of an IT team is to keep the network up and running quickly and efficiently. Keeping your network running at its peak performance is one way to make sure your end users continue to use the network and its resources without problems or interruptions.

Sometimes, performance optimization can feel like a luxury, especially if you can't get your domain controllers to the point where they are actually performing the services for which you intended them, such as servicing printers or allowing users to share and work on files. The Windows Server 2016 operating system has been specifically designed to provide high-availability services solely intended to keep your mission-critical applications and data accessible, even in times of disaster.

The most common cause of such problems is a hardware configuration issue. Poorly written device drivers and unsupported hardware can cause problems with system stability. Failed hardware components (such as system memory) may do so as well. Memory chips can be faulty, electrostatic discharge can ruin them, and other hardware issues can occur. No matter what, a problem with your memory chip spells disaster for your server.

Third-party hardware vendors usually provide utility programs with their computers that can be used for performing hardware diagnostics on machines to help you find problems. These utilities are a good first step in resolving intermittent server crashes. When these utility programs are used in combination with the troubleshooting tips provided in this and other chapters of this book, you should be able to pinpoint most network-related problems that might occur.

In this chapter, I'll cover the tools and methods used for measuring performance and troubleshooting failures in Windows Server 2016. Before you dive into the technical details, however, you should thoroughly understand what you're trying to accomplish and how you'll meet this goal.

**Knowing How to Locate and Isolate Problems**

In a book such as this, it would be almost impossible to cover everything that could go wrong with your Windows Server 2016 system. This book covers many of the most common issues that you might come across, but almost anything is possible. Make sure you focus on the methodology used and the steps required to locate and isolate a problem—even if you are not 100 percent sure about the cause of the problem. Use online resources to help you locate and troubleshoot the problem, but don't believe everything you read (some things that are posted online can be wrong or misleading).

Test your changes in a lab environment, and try to read multiple sources. Always use Microsoft Support (`http://support.microsoft.com/`) as one of your sources because this site is most likely the right source for information. You won't be able to find and fix everything, but knowing where to find critical information that will help you in your efforts never hurts. One of the tools that many of us in the industry use is *Microsoft TechNet*. The full version of TechNet (a paid subscription) is a resource that will help you find and fix many real-world issues.

# Overview of Windows Server 2016 Performance Monitoring

The first step in any performance optimization strategy is to measure performance accurately and consistently. The insight that you'll gain from monitoring factors such as network and system utilization will be extremely useful when you measure the effects of any changes.

The overall performance monitoring process usually involves the following steps:

1. Establish a baseline of current performance.
2. Identify the bottlenecks.
3. Plan for and implement changes.
4. Measure the effects of the changes.
5. Repeat the process based on business needs.

Note that the performance optimization process is never really finished because you can always try to gain more performance from your system by modifying settings and applying other well-known tweaks.

Before you get discouraged, realize that you'll reach some level of performance that you and your network and system users consider acceptable and that it's not worth the additional effort it will take to optimize performance any further. Also note that as your network and system load increases (more users or users doing more), so too will the need to reiterate this process. By continuing to monitor, measure, and optimize, you will keep ahead of the pack and keep your end users happy.

Now that you have an idea of the overall process, let's focus on how changes should be made. It's important to keep in mind the following ideas when monitoring performance:

**Plan Changes Carefully** Here's a rule of thumb that you should always try to follow: An hour of planning can save a week of work. When you are working in an easy-to-use GUI-based operating system like Windows Server 2016, it's tempting to remove a check mark here or there and then retest the performance. You should resist the urge to do this because some changes can cause large decreases in performance or can impact functionality. Before you make haphazard changes (especially on production servers), take the time to learn about, plan for, and test your changes. Plan for outages and testing accordingly.

**Utilize a Test Environment** Test in a test lab that simulates a production environment. Do not make changes on production environments without first giving warning. Ideally, change production environments in off-hours when fewer network and system users will be affected. Making haphazard changes in a production environment can cause serious problems. These problems will likely outweigh any benefits that you may receive from making performance tweaks.

**Make Only One Change at a Time** The golden rule of scientific experiments is that you should always keep track of as many variables as possible. When the topic is server optimization, this roughly translates into making only one change at a time.

One of the problems with making multiple system changes is that although you may have improved overall performance, it's hard to determine exactly *which* change created the positive effects. It's also possible, for example, that changing one parameter increased performance greatly while changing another decreased it only slightly. Although the overall result was an increase in performance, you should identify the second, performance-reducing option so that the same mistake is not made again. To reduce the chance of obtaining misleading results, always try to make only one change at a time.

The main reason to make one change at a time, however, is that if you do make a mistake or create an unexpected issue, you can easily "back out" of the change. If you make two or three changes at the same time and are not sure which one created the problem, you will have to undo all of the changes and then make one alteration at a time to find the problem. If you make only one change at a time and follow that methodology every time, you won't find yourself in this situation.

It's important to remember that many changes (such as Registry changes) take place immediately; they do not need to be applied explicitly. Once the change is made, it's live. Be careful to plan your changes wisely.

**Ensure Consistency in Measurements** When you are monitoring performance, consistency is extremely important. You should strive to have repeatable and accurate measurements. Controlling variables, such as system load at various times during the day, can help.

Assume, for instance, that you want to measure the number of transactions that you can simulate on the accounting database server within an hour. The results would be widely different if you ran the test during the month-end accounting close than if you ran the test on a Sunday morning. By running the same tests when the server is under a relatively static load, you will be able to get more accurate measurements.

**Maintain a Performance History** In the introduction to this chapter, I mentioned that the performance optimization cycle is a continuous improvement process. Because many changes may be made over time, it is important to keep track of the changes that have been made and the results you have experienced. Documenting this knowledge will help solve similar problems if they arise. I understand that many IT professionals do not like to document, but documentation can make life much easier in the long run.

As you can see, you need to keep a lot of factors in mind when optimizing performance. Although this might seem like a lot to digest and remember, do not fear. As a system administrator, you will learn some of the rules you need to know to keep your system running optimally. Fortunately, the tools included with Windows Server 2016 can help you organize the process and take measurements. Now that you have a good overview of the process, let's move on to look at the tools that can be used to set it in motion.

# Using Windows Server 2016 Performance Tools

Because performance monitoring and optimization are vital functions in network environments of any size, Windows Server 2016 includes several performance-related tools.

## Introducing Performance Monitor

The first and most useful tool is the Windows Server 2016 *Performance Monitor*, which was designed to allow users and system administrators to monitor performance statistics for various operating system parameters. Specifically, you can collect, store, and analyze information about CPU, memory, disk, and network resources using this tool, and these are only a handful of the things that you can monitor. By collecting and analyzing performance values, system administrators can identify many potential problems.

You can use the Performance Monitor in the following ways:

**Performance Monitor ActiveX Control** The Windows Server 2016 Performance Monitor is an ActiveX control that you can place within other applications. Examples of applications that can host the Performance Monitor control include web browsers and client programs such as Microsoft Word or Microsoft Excel. This functionality can make it easy for applications developers and system administrators to incorporate the Performance Monitor into their own tools and applications.

**Performance Monitor MMC** For more common performance monitoring functions, you'll want to use the built-in Microsoft Management Console (MMC) version of the Performance Monitor.

**System Stability Index** The *System Stability Index* is a numerical value from 1 (least stable) to 10 (most stable) that represents the stability of your network. Performance Monitor calculates and creates the System Stability Index. You can view a graph of this index value. The graph can help a network administrator identify when the network started encountering problems. The System Stability Index also offers side-by-side comparisons. An administrator can view when system changes occurred (installing applications, devices, or drivers) and when system problems started to occur. This way, you can determine whether any system changes caused the problems that you are encountering.

**Data Collector Sets** Windows Server 2016 Performance Monitor includes the Data Collector Set. This tool works with performance logs, telling Performance Monitor where the logs are stored and when the log needs to run. The Data Collector Sets also define the credentials used to run the set.

To access the Performance Monitor MMC, you open Administrative Tools and then choose Performance Monitor. This launches the Performance MMC and loads and initializes Performance Monitor with a handful of default counters.

You can choose from many different methods of monitoring performance when you are using Performance Monitor. A couple of examples are listed here:

- You can look at a snapshot of current activity for a few of the most important counters. This allows you to find areas of potential bottlenecks and monitor the load on your servers at a certain point in time.
- You can save information to a log file for historical reporting and later analysis. This type of information is useful, for example, if you want to compare the load on your servers from three months ago to the current load.

You'll get to take a closer look at this method and many others as you examine Performance Monitor in more detail.

In the following sections, you'll learn about the basics of working with the Windows Server 2016 Performance Monitor and other performance tools. Then you'll apply these tools and techniques when you monitor the performance of your network.

Your Performance Monitor grows as your system grows, and whenever you add services to Windows Server 2016 (such as installing Exchange Server), you also add to what you can monitor. You should make sure that, as you install services, you take a look at what it is you can monitor.

## Deciding What to Monitor

The first step in monitoring performance is to decide *what* you want to monitor. In Windows Server 2016, the operating system and related services include hundreds of performance statistics that you can track easily. For example, you may want to monitor IPsec by monitoring connection security rules. This is just one of many items that can be monitored. All performance statistics fall into three main categories that you can choose to measure:

**Performance Objects** A *performance object* within Performance Monitor is a collection of various performance statistics that you can monitor. Performance objects are based on various areas of system resources. For example, there are performance objects for the processor and memory as well as for specific services such as web services.

**Counters** *Counters* are the actual parameters measured by Performance Monitor. They are specific items that are grouped within performance objects. For example, within the Processor performance object, there is a counter for % Processor Time. This counter displays one type of detailed information about the Processor performance object (specifically, the amount of total CPU time all of the processes on the system are using). Another set of counters you can use will allow you to monitor print servers.

**Instances** Some counters will have instances. An *instance* further identifies which performance parameter the counter is measuring. A simple example is a server with two CPUs. If you decide you want to monitor processor usage (using the Processor performance object)—specifically, utilization (the % Total Utilization counter)—you must still specify *which* CPU(s) you want to measure. In this example, you would have the choice of monitoring either of the two CPUs or a total value for both (using the Total instance).

One important thing that you want to watch when monitoring objects and counters is the average number. For example, there will be times when your CPU is at 100%. This doesn't mean that you need to buy a newer CPU or add an additional CPU. The number that you want to watch is the average CPU usage. If that is over 80% on average, then your CPU can't handle the workload of the server. If the Hard Page Faults per second average more than 5 per second, you don't have enough RAM. Make sure to watch the averages and not just whats happening at this moment.

To specify which performance objects, counters, and instances you want to monitor, you add them to Performance Monitor using the Add Counters dialog box. Figure 9.1 shows the various options that are available when you add new counters to monitor using Performance Monitor.

**FIGURE 9.1** Adding a new Performance Monitor counter

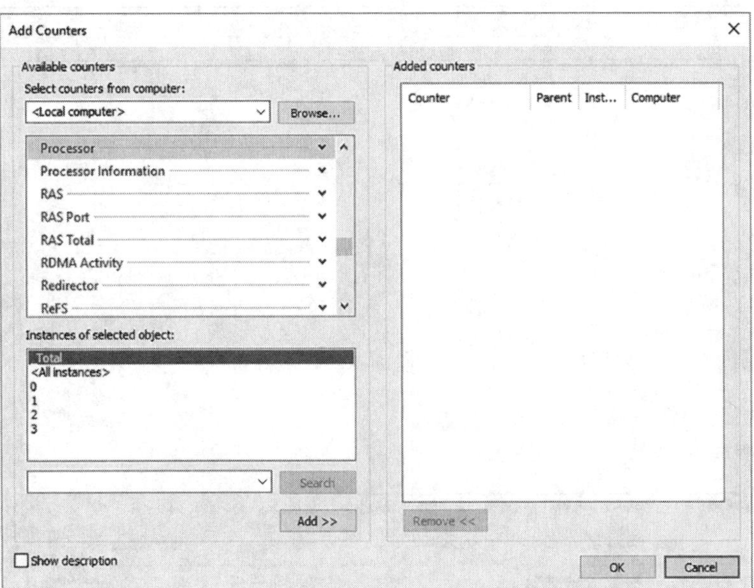

The items that you will be able to monitor will be based on your hardware and software configuration. For example, if you have not installed and configured the IIS, the options available within the Web Server performance object will not be available. Or, if you have multiple network adapters or CPUs in the server, you will have the option of viewing each instance separately or as part of the total value.

**Viewing Performance Information** The Windows Server 2016 Performance Monitor was designed to show information in a clear and easy-to-understand format. Performance objects, counters, and instances may be displayed in each of three views. This flexibility allows system administrators to define quickly and easily the information they want to see once and then choose how it will be displayed based on specific needs. Most likely, you will use only one view, but it's helpful to know what other views are available depending on what it is you are trying to assess.

You can use the following main views to review statistics and information on performance:

**Line View** The Line view (also referred to as the Graph view) is the default display that is presented when you first access the Windows Server 2016 Performance Monitor. The chart displays values using the vertical axis and displays time using the horizontal axis. This view is useful if you want to display values over a period of time or see the changes in these values over that time period. Each point that is plotted on the graph is based on an average value calculated during the sample interval for the measurement being made. For example, you may notice overall CPU utilization starting at a low value at the beginning of the chart and then becoming much higher during later measurements. This indicates that the server has become busier (specifically, with CPU-intensive processes). Figure 9.2 provides an example of the Graph view.

**FIGURE 9.2** Viewing information in Performance Monitor Line view

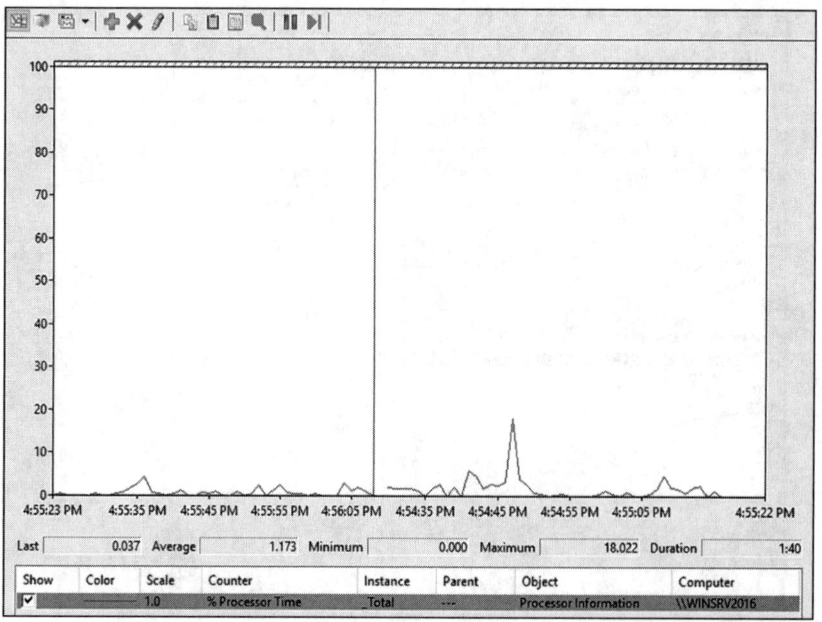

**Histogram View** The *Histogram view* shows performance statistics and information using a set of relative bar charts. This view is useful if you want to see a snapshot of the latest value for a given counter. For example, if you were interested in viewing a snapshot of current system performance statistics during each refresh interval, the length of each of the bars in the display would give you a visual representation of each value. It would also allow you to compare measurements visually relative to each other. You can set the histogram to display an average measurement as well as minimum and maximum thresholds. Figure 9.3 shows a typical Histogram view.

**FIGURE 9.3** Viewing information in Performance Monitor Histogram view

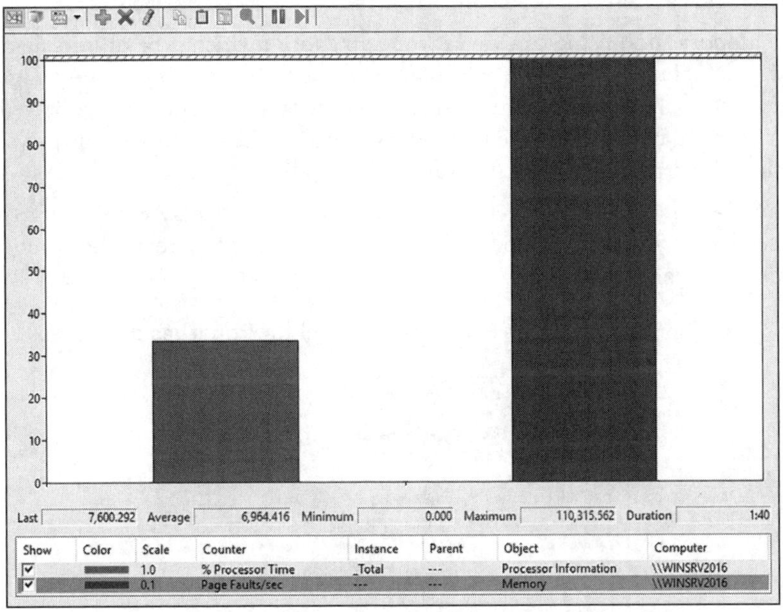

**Report View** Like the Histogram view, the *Report view* shows performance statistics based on the latest measurement. You can see an average measurement as well as minimum and maximum thresholds. This view is most useful for determining exact values because it provides information in numeric terms, whereas the Chart and Histogram views provide information graphically. Figure 9.4 provides an example of the type of information you'll see in the Report view.

**FIGURE 9.4** Viewing information in Performance Monitor Report view

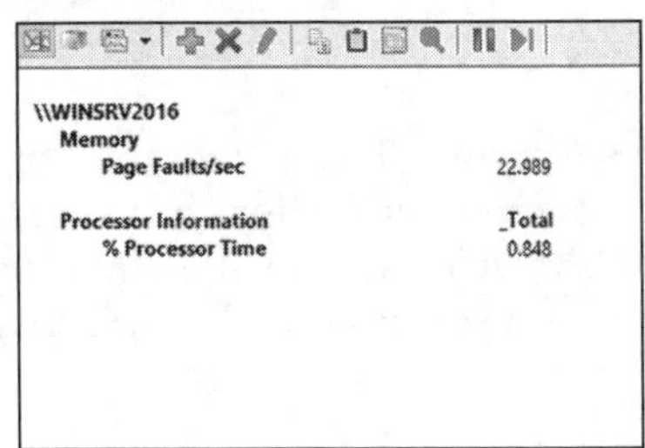

## Managing Performance Monitor Properties

You can specify additional settings for viewing performance information within the properties of Performance Monitor. You can access these options by clicking the Properties button in the Taskbar or by right-clicking the Performance Monitor display and selecting Properties. You can change these additional settings by using the following tabs:

**General Tab** On the General tab (shown in Figure 9.5), you can specify several options that relate to Performance Monitor views:

- You can enable or disable legends (which display information about the various counters), the value bar, and the toolbar.
- For the Report and Histogram views, you can choose which type of information is displayed. The options are Default, Current, Minimum, Maximum, and Average. What you see with each of these options depends on the type of data being collected. These options are not available for the Graph view because the Graph view displays an average value over a period of time (the sample interval).
- You can also choose the graph elements. By default, the display will be set to update every second. If you want to update less often, you should increase the number of seconds between updates.

**FIGURE 9.5** General tab of the Performance Monitor Properties dialog box

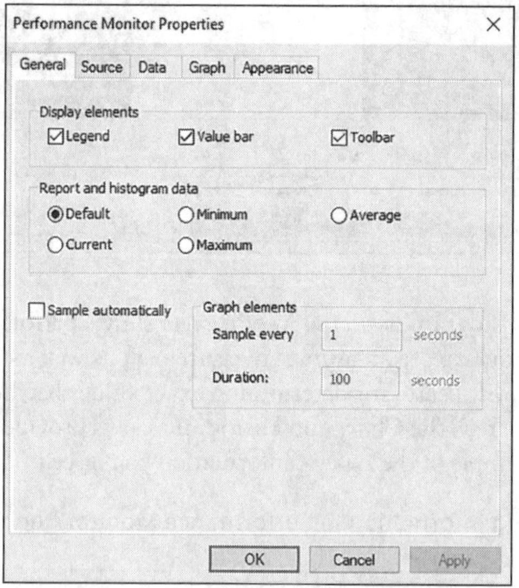


**Source Tab** On the Source tab (shown in Figure 9.6), you can specify the source for the performance information you want to view. Options include current activity (the default setting) or data from a log file. If you choose to analyze information from a log file, you can also specify the time range for which you want to view statistics. We'll cover these selections in the next section.

**FIGURE 9.6** Source tab of the Performance Monitor Properties dialog box

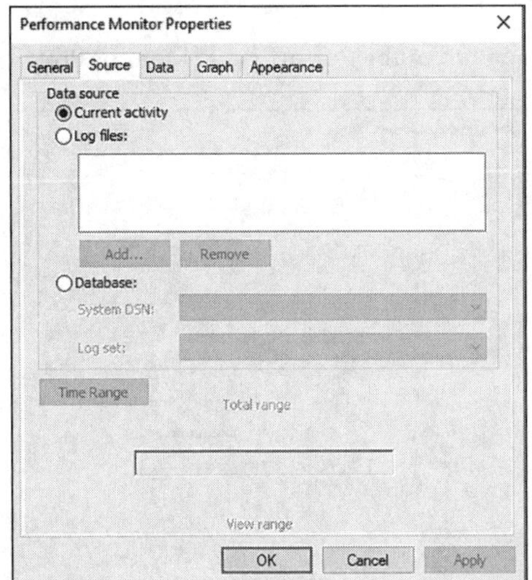


**Data Tab** The Data tab (shown in Figure 9.7) lists the counters that have been added to the Performance Monitor display. These counters apply to the Chart, Histogram, and Report views. Using this interface, you can also add or remove any of the counters and change the properties, such as the width, style, and color of the line and the scale used for display.

**FIGURE 9.7** The Data tab of the Performance Monitor Properties dialog box

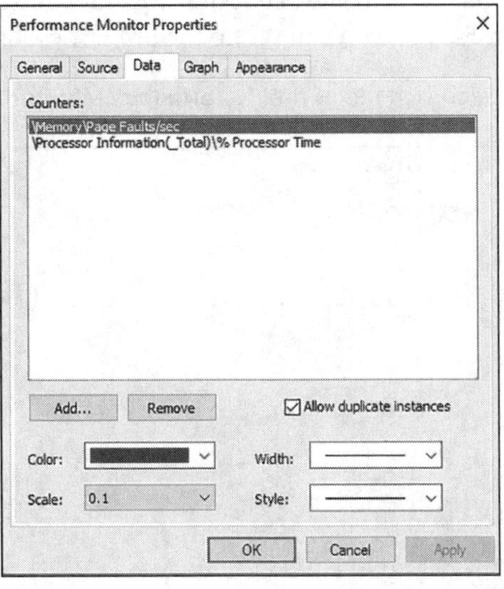


**Graph Tab** On the Graph tab (shown in Figure 9.8), you can specify certain options that will allow you to customize the display of Performance Monitor views. First you can specify what type of view you want to see (Line, Histogram, or Report). Then you can add

a title for the graph, specify a label for the vertical axis, choose to display grids, and specify the vertical scale range.

**FIGURE 9.8** The Graph tab of the Performance Monitor Properties dialog box

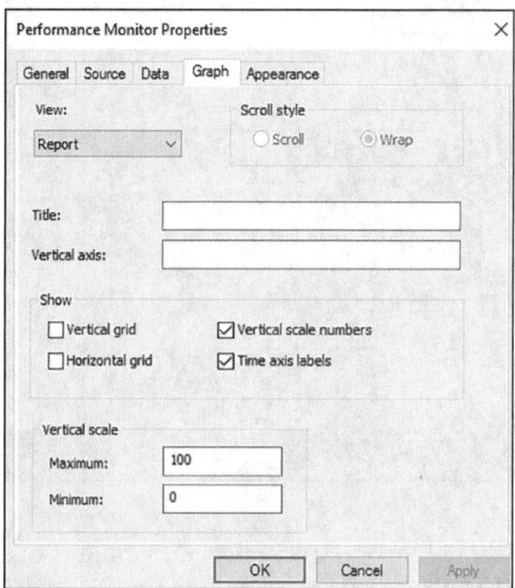


**Appearance Tab** Using the Appearance tab (see Figure 9.9), you can specify the colors for the areas of the display, such as the background and foreground. You can also specify the fonts that are used to display counter values in Performance Monitor views. You can change settings to find a suitable balance between readability and the amount of information shown on one screen. Finally, you can set up the properties for a border.

**FIGURE 9.9** The Appearance tab of the Performance Monitor Properties dialog box

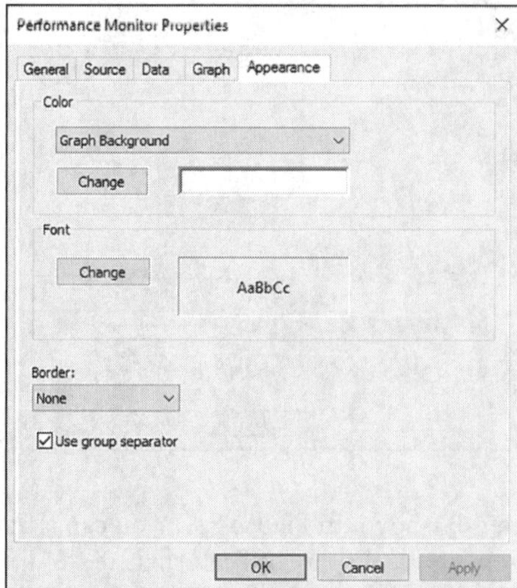

Now that you have an idea of the types of information Performance Monitor tracks and how this data is displayed, you'll take a look at another feature—saving and analyzing performance data.

## Saving and Analyzing Data with Performance Logs and Alerts

One of the most important aspects of monitoring performance is that it should be done over a given period of time (referred to as a *baseline*). So far, I have shown you how you can use Performance Monitor to view statistics in real time. I have, however, also alluded to using Performance Monitor to save data for later analysis. Now let's take a look at how you can do this.

When viewing information in Performance Monitor, you have two main options with respect to the data on display:

**View Current Activity** When you first open the Performance icon from the Administrative Tools folder, the default option is to view data obtained from current system information. This method of viewing measures and displays various real-time statistics on the system's performance.

**View Log File Data** This option allows you to view information that was previously saved to a log file. Although the performance objects, counters, and instances may appear to be the same as those viewed using the View Current Activity option, the information itself was actually captured at a previous point in time and stored into a log file.

Log files for the View Log File Data option are created in the Performance Logs And Alerts section of the Windows Server 2016 Performance tool.

Three items allow you to customize how the data is collected in the log files:

**Counter Logs** *Counter logs* record performance statistics based on the various performance objects, counters, and instances available in Performance Monitor. The values are updated based on a time interval setting and are saved to a file for later analysis.

**Circular Logging** In *circular logging*, the data that is stored within a file is overwritten as new data is entered into the log. This is a useful method of logging if you want to record information only for a certain time frame (for example, the past four hours). Circular logging also conserves disk space by ensuring that the performance log file will not continue to grow over certain limits.

**Linear Logging** In *linear logging*, data is never deleted from the log files, and new information is added to the end of the log file. The result is a log file that continually grows. The benefit is that all historical information is retained.

Now that you have an idea of the types of functions that are supported by the Windows Server 2016 Performance tools, you can learn how you can apply this information to the task at hand—monitoring and troubleshooting your Windows network.

**Real World Scenario**

### Real-World Performance Monitoring

In our daily jobs as system engineers and administrators, we come across systems that are in need of our help. . . and may even ask for it. You, of course, check your Event Viewer and Performance Monitor and perform other tasks that help you troubleshoot. But what is really the most common problem that occurs? From my experience, I'd say that you suffer performance problems many times if your Windows Server 2016 operating system is installed on a subpar system. Either the server hardware isn't enterprise class or the minimum hardware requirements weren't addressed. Most production servers suffer from slow response times, lagging, and so on because money wasn't spent where it should have been in the first place—on the server's hardware requirements.

In Exercise 9.1, I will show you how to use Performance Monitor. I will also show you how to add objects and counters and then view those items in the Line view.

**EXERCISE 9.1**

### Using Performance Monitor

1. Right-click on the Start and choose Run. Type in `Perfmon.exe` and hit the Enter key.
2. On the left-hand side under Monitoring Tools, click Performance Monitor.
3. In the center window, click the green plus sign. This will allow you to add a counter.
4. Under Available Counters, make sure Local Computer is chosen. Then expand Processor and choose % Processor Time. Click the Add button. Click OK.
5. Choose any other counters that you want to watch. If you would like to change the view, use the pull-down arrow next to the green plus sign.
6. Once you're completed, close Performance Monitor.

# Using Other Monitoring Tools

Performance Monitor allows you to monitor different parameters of the Windows Server 2016 operating system and associated services and applications. However, you can also use three other tools to monitor performance in Windows Server 2016. They are Microsoft Message Analyzer, Task Manager, and Event Viewer. All three of these tools are useful for monitoring different areas of overall system performance and for examining details related to specific system events. In the following sections, you'll take a quick look at these tools and how you can best use them.

## Microsoft Message Analyzer

Although Performance Monitor is a great tool for viewing overall network performance statistics, it isn't equipped for packet-level analysis and doesn't give you much insight into what types of network traffic are traveling on the wire. That's where the Microsoft Message Analyzer (MMA) tool comes in.

The Microsoft Message Analyzer Agent is available for use with Windows 7, Windows 8, Windows 10, Windows Server 2008 R2, Windows Server 2012, Windows Server 2012 R2, and Windows Server 2016. The agent allows you to track network packets. When you install the Microsoft Message Analyzer Agent, you will also be able to access the Network Segment System Monitor counter.

On Windows Server 2016 computers, you'll see the Microsoft Message Analyzer icon appear in the Administrative Tools program group. You can use the Microsoft Message Analyzer tool to capture data as it travels on your network.

The full version of Microsoft Message Analyzer is available at Microsoft's download server. For more information, see `www.microsoft.com/downloads/`.

Once you have captured the data of interest, you can save it to a capture file or further analyze it using Microsoft Message Analyzer. Experienced network and system administrators can use this information to determine how applications are communicating and the types of data that are being passed via the network.

For the exam, you don't need to understand the detailed information that Microsoft Message Analyzer displays, but you should be aware of the types of information that you can view and when you should use Microsoft Message Analyzer.

## Wireshark

Normally I would never talk about a third party product in a Microsoft certification book. Especially when the third party product will not be on the exam. But when we talk about Microsoft Message Analyzer, we need to mention Wireshark. Wireshark is a free downloadable software that allows you to view network packets (same as Microsoft Message Analyzer). But Wireshark has many advantages over Microsoft Message Analyzer including ease of use and ease of reading the details.

The down side to Microsoft Message Analyzer is that it is very difficult to read and understand the results. If this is something that you do daily, then you will easily understand the results. But if it's something that is done only once in a while, then Wireshark may be better for you. Wireshark is an easier networking monitor tool.

One thing that you need to make sure of when it comes to any Microsoft Message Analyzer tools is who is using them. If you go by someone's office and you see them using any Microsoft Message Analyzer tools, you need to put a stop to that instantly. Unless that person is part of IT or security, no one should be monitoring live network packets.

## Task Manager

Performance Monitor is designed to allow you to keep track of specific aspects of system performance over time. But what do you do if you want to get a quick snapshot of what the local system is doing? Creating a System Monitor chart, adding counters, and choosing a view is overkill. Fortunately, the Windows Server 2016 Task Manager has been designed to provide a quick overview of important system performance statistics without requiring any configuration. Better yet, it's always readily available.

You can easily access Task Manager in several ways:

- Right-click the Windows Taskbar and then click Task Manager.
- Press the Windows Key + R
- Press Ctrl+Alt+Del and then select Task Manager.
- Press Ctrl+Shift+Esc.

Each of these methods allows you to access a snapshot of the current system performance quickly.

Once you access Task Manager, you will see the following five tabs:

**Processes Tab** The Processes tab shows you all of the processes that are currently running on the local computer. By default, you'll be able to view how much CPU time and memory a particular process is using. By clicking any of the columns, you can quickly sort by the data values in that particular column. This is useful, for example, if you want to find out which processes are using the most memory on your server.

By accessing the performance objects in the View menu, you can add columns to the Processes tab. Figure 9.10 shows a list of the current processes running on a Windows Server 2016 computer.

**FIGURE 9.10** Viewing process statistics and information using Task Manager

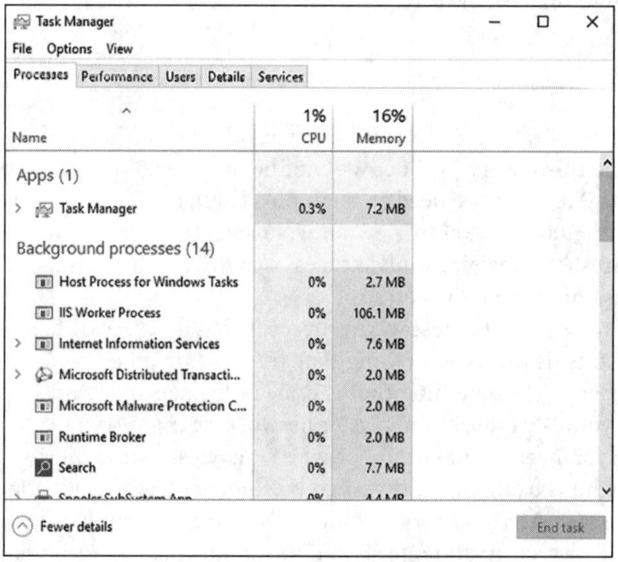

**Performance Tab** One of the problems with using Performance Monitor to get a quick snapshot of system performance is that you have to add counters to a chart. Most system administrators are too busy to take the time to do this when all they need is basic CPU and memory information. That's where the Performance tab of Task Manager comes in. Using the Performance tab, you can view details about how memory is allocated on the computer and how much of the CPU is utilized (see Figure 9.11).

**FIGURE 9.11** Viewing CPU and memory performance information using Task Manager

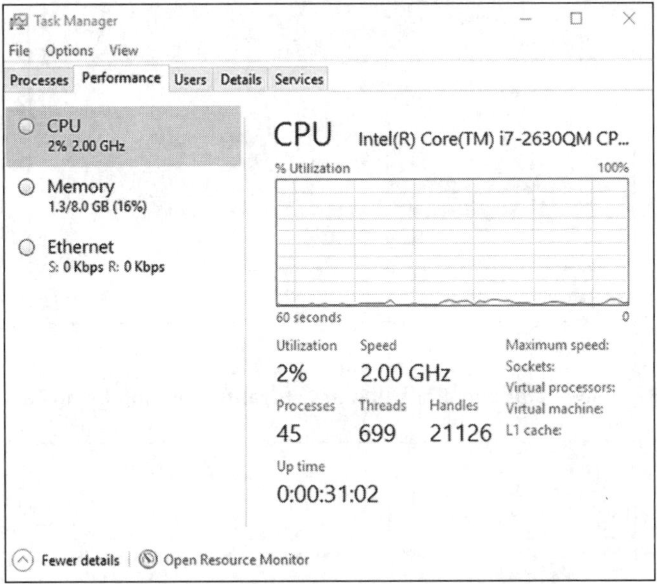


**Users Tab** The Users tab (see Figure 9.12) lists the currently active user accounts. This is particularly helpful if you want to see who is online and quickly log off or disconnect users. You can also view all of the services and applications that are being used by that user. As you can see in Figure 9.12, the Administrator account has a lot of services that are running on this system.

**Details Tab** The Details tab (see Figure 9.13) shows you what applications are currently running on the system. From this location, you can stop an application from running by right-clicking the application and choosing Stop. You also have the ability to set your affinity level here. By setting the affinity, you can choose which applications will use which processors on your system.

**Services Tab** The Services tab (see Figure 9.14) shows you what services are currently running on the system. From this location, you can stop a service from running by right-clicking the service and choosing Stop. The Open Services link launches the Services MMC.

**FIGURE 9.12** Viewing user information using Task Manager

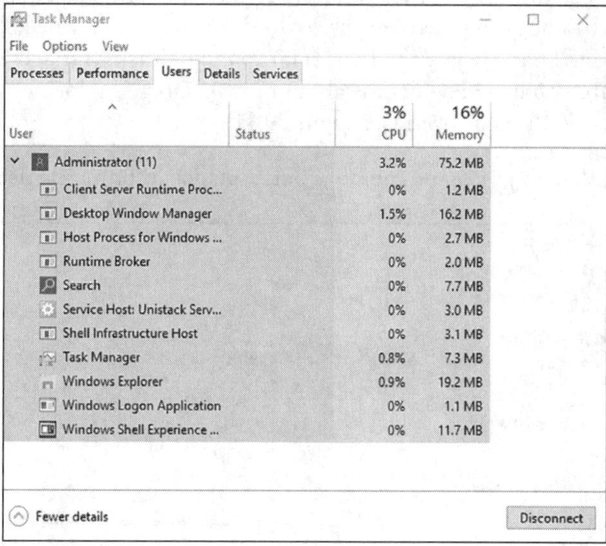


**FIGURE 9.13** Viewing applications that are currently running using Task Manager

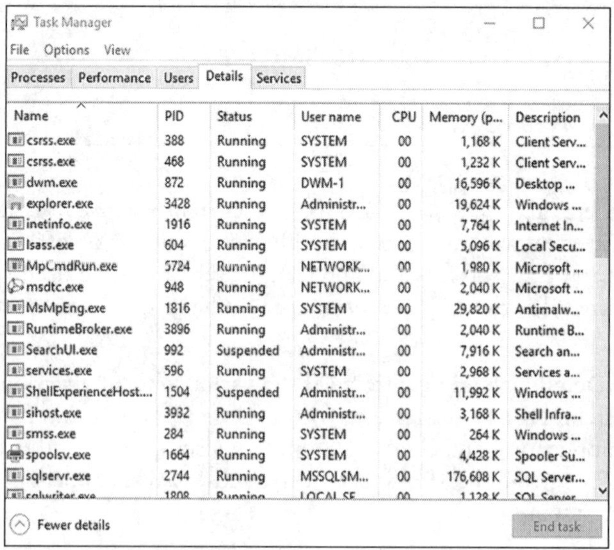

**FIGURE 9.14** Viewing services information using Task Manager

Task Manager

File Options View

Processes | Performance | Users | Details | Services

| Name | PID | Description | Status | Group |
|---|---|---|---|---|
| WsusService | 1952 | WSUS Service | Running | |
| WSusCertServer | | WSUS Certificate S... | Stopped | |
| WSearch | | Windows Search | Stopped | |
| wmiApSrv | | WMI Performance ... | Stopped | |
| WinDefend | 1816 | Windows Defende... | Running | |
| WIDWriter | 1808 | Windows Internal ... | Running | |
| WdNisSvc | | Windows Defende... | Stopped | |
| wbengine | | Block Level Backu... | Stopped | |
| VSS | | Volume Shadow C... | Stopped | |
| vds | | Virtual Disk | Stopped | |
| VaultSvc | 604 | Credential Manager | Running | |
| UI0Detect | | Interactive Service... | Stopped | |
| UevAgentService | | User Experience Vir... | Stopped | |
| TrustedInstaller | | Windows Modules... | Stopped | |
| TieringEngineService | | Storage Tiers Man... | Stopped | |
| SQLWriter | 1856 | SQL Server VSS Wri... | Running | |
| sppsvc | | Software Protection | Stopped | |
| Spooler | 1664 | Print Spooler | Running | |

Fewer details | Open Services

The Task Manager tabs can be different on Windows client machines. For example, Windows 7 has six tabs and Windows 10 has seven tabs.

As you can see, Task Manager is useful for providing important information about the system quickly. Once you get used to using Task Manager, you won't be able to get by without it!

Make sure that you use Task Manager and familiarize yourself with all that it can do; you can end processes that have become intermittent, kill applications that may hang the system, view NIC performance, and so on. In addition, you can access this tool quickly to get an idea of what could be causing you problems. Event Viewer, Microsoft Message Analyzer, and Performance Monitor are all great tools for getting granular information on potential problems.

## Event Viewer

*Event Viewer* is also useful for monitoring network information. Specifically, you can use the logs to view any information, warnings, or alerts related to the proper functioning of the network. You can access Event Viewer by selecting Administrative Tools ➤ Event Viewer. Clicking any of the items in the left pane displays the various events that have been logged for each item. Figure 9.15 shows the contents of the Directory Service log.

Each event is preceded by a blue *i* icon. That icon designates that these events are informational and do not indicate problems with the network. Rather, they record benign events such as Active Directory startup or a domain controller finding a global catalog server.

**FIGURE 9.15** Event Viewer

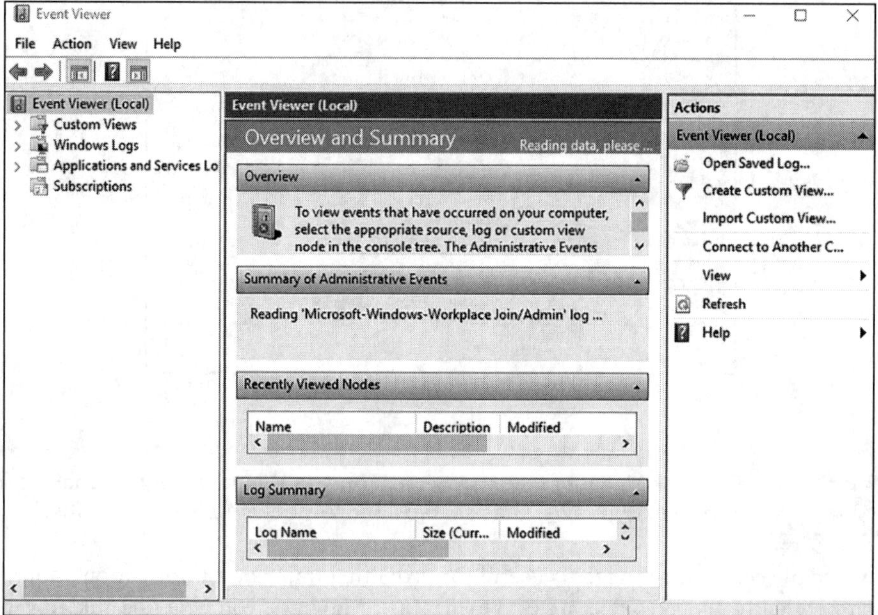


A yellow warning icon or a red error icon, both of which are shown in Figure 9.16, indicate problematic or potentially problematic events. Warnings usually indicate a problem that wouldn't prevent a service from running but might cause undesired effects with the service in question. For example, I was configuring a site with some fictional domain controllers and IP addresses. My local domain controller's IP address wasn't associated with any of the sites, and Event Viewer generated a warning. In this case, the local domain controller could still function as a domain controller, but the site configuration could produce undesirable results.

Error events almost always indicate a failed service, application, or function. For instance, if the dynamic registration of a DNS client fails, Event Viewer will generate an error. As you can see, errors are more severe than warnings because, in this case, the DNS client cannot participate in DNS at all.

Double-clicking any event opens the Event Properties dialog box, as shown in Figure 9.17, which displays a detailed description of the event.

**FIGURE 9.16** Information, errors, and warnings in Event Viewer

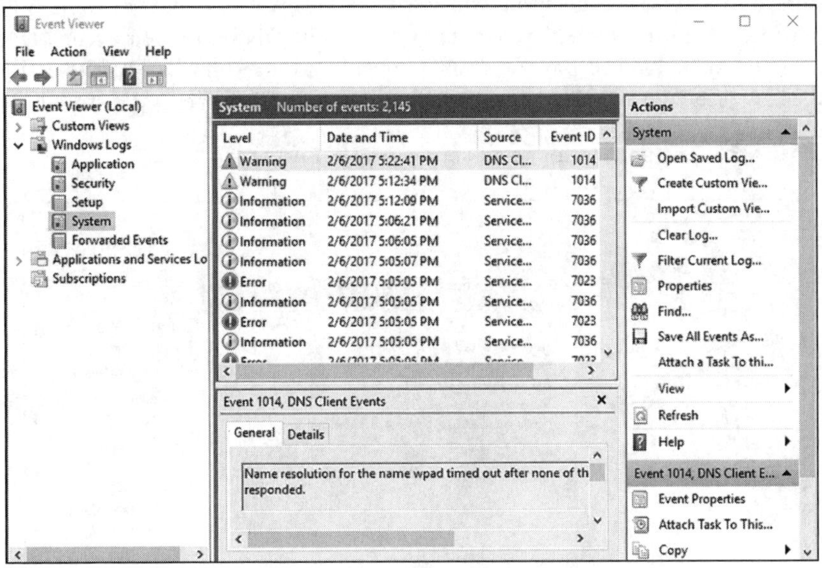

**FIGURE 9.17** An Event Properties dialog box

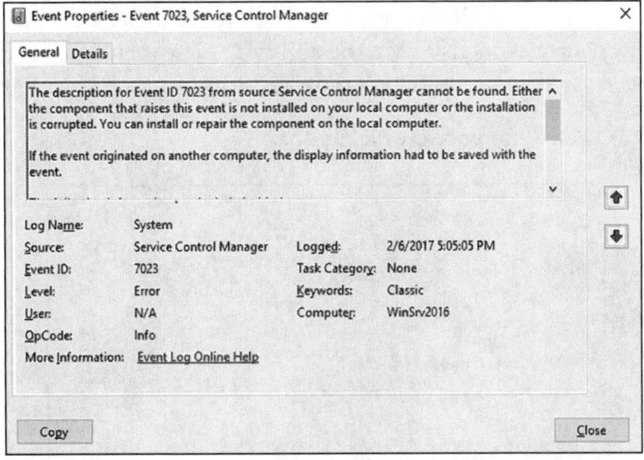


Event Viewer can display thousands of different events, so it would be impossible to list them all here. The important points of which you should be aware are the following:

- Information events are always benign.
- Warnings indicate noncritical problems.
- Errors indicate show-stopping events.

Let's discuss some of the logs and the ways you can view data:

**Applications and Services** The *applications and services logs* are part of Event Viewer where applications (for example, Exchange) and services (DNS) log their events. DNS events would be logged in this part of Event Viewer. An important log in this section is the DNS Server log (see Figure 9.18). This is where all of your DNS events get stored.

**FIGURE 9.18** The applications and services DNS Server log

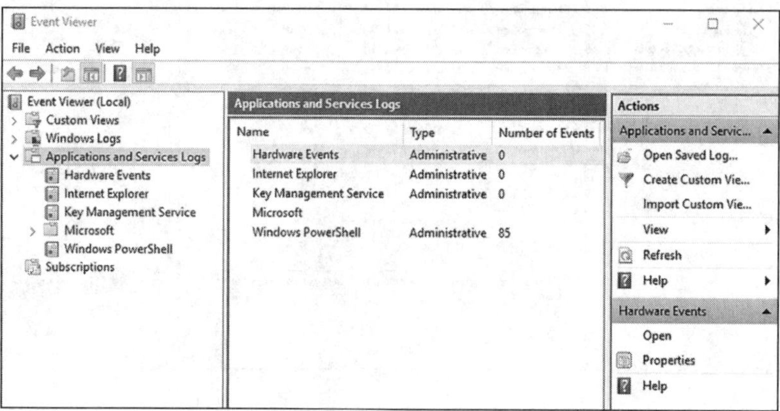


**Custom Views** *Custom views* allow you to filter events (see Figure 9.19) to create your own customized look. You can filter events by event level (critical, error, warning, and so on), by logs, and by source. You also have the ability to view events occurring within a specific timeframe. This allows you to look only at the events that are important to you.

**FIGURE 9.19** Create Custom View dialog box

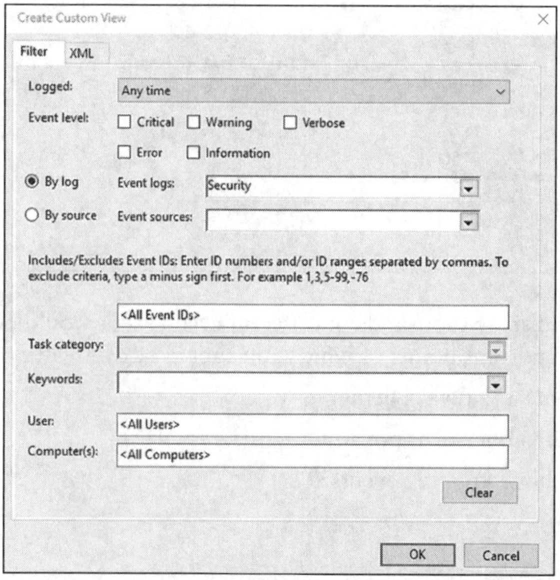

**Subscriptions** *Subscriptions* allow a user to receive alerts about events that you predefine. In the Subscription Properties dialog box (see Figure 9.20), you can define what type of events you want notifications about and the notification method. The Subscriptions section is an advanced alerting service to help you watch for events.

**FIGURE 9.20** Subscription Properties dialog box

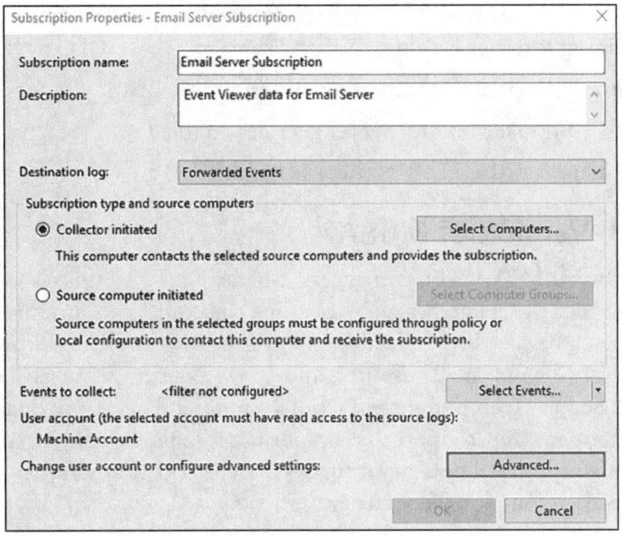

## Microsoft Baseline Security Analyzer

The *Microsoft Baseline Security Analyzer (MBSA)* is a security assessment utility that you can download from the Microsoft website at the following location:

`https://www.microsoft.com/en-us/download/details.aspx?id=755`

The filename of the download is `mbsasetup.msi`. It verifies whether your computer has the latest security updates and whether any common security violation configurations have been applied to your computer. MBSA can scan the following programs and operating systems:

- Windows 7
- Windows 8
- Windows 10
- Windows Server 2008 R2
- Windows Server 2012
- Windows Server 2012 R2
- Windows Server 2016
- IIS 5 or newer
- Internet Explorer, versions 6.0 and newer

- SQL Server 7 or newer
- Microsoft Office 2007 or newer
- Windows Media Player, versions 6.4 and newer

To use MBSA, the computer must meet the following requirements:

- It must be running Windows 7, Windows 8, Windows 10, Windows Server 2008 R2, Windows Server 2012, Windows Server 2012 R2, or Windows Server 2016.
- It must be running Internet Explorer 5.01 or newer.
- It must have an XML parser installed for full functionality.
- It must have the Workstation and Server services enabled.
- It must have Client for Microsoft Networks installed.

## Using the GUI Version of MBSA

Once you have installed MBSA, you can access it by using the Windows key and choosing Microsoft Baseline Security Analyzer or by opening the command prompt and executing `mbsa.exe`. This opens the Baseline Security Analyzer utility. You can select from Scan A Computer, Scan More Than One Computer, and View Existing Security Reports.

When you click Scan A Computer, the Pick A Computer To Scan dialog box appears. You can specify that you want to scan a computer based on a computer name or IP address. You can also specify the name of the security report that will be generated.

The following are options for the security scan:

- Check For Windows Vulnerabilities
- Check For Weak Passwords
- Check For IIS Vulnerabilities
- Check For SQL Vulnerabilities
- Check For Security Updates

If you use the Check For Security Updates option and are using WSUS, you can specify the name of the WSUS server that should be checked for the security updates.

Once you have made your selections, click Start Scan. When the scan is complete, the security report will be automatically displayed. If you have scanned multiple computers, you can sort the security reports based on issue name or score (worst first or best first).

## Using the MBSA Command-Line Utility *mbsacli.exe*

After Microsoft Baseline Security Analyzer has been installed, you can use the command-line utility `mbsacli.exe`. Enter **`mbsacli.exe/hf`** and then customize the command execution with any of the options defined in Table 9.1.

**TABLE 9.1** `mbsacli.exe /hf` command-line options

| Option | Description |
|---|---|
| -h *host name[, host name, . . .]* | Scans the specified host. You can specify that you want to scan multiple host computers by separating the hostnames with commas. |
| -fh *filename* | Scans the NetBIOS name of each computer that is to be scanned, and it saves the information as text within a file specified by `filename`. |
| -i *xxxx.xxxx.xxxx.xxxx[, xxxx.xxxx.xxxx.xxxx, . . .]* | Scans a computer based on the specified IP address. You can scan multiple computers by IP address by separating the IP addresses with commas. |
| -fip *filename* | Looks in the text file specified by *filename* for IP addresses and scans the computers with those IP addresses. The file can have up to a maximum of 256 IP addresses. |
| -d *domainname* | Scans the specified domain. |
| -n | Scans all of the computers on the local network. |

## Simple Network Management Protocol

The *Simple Network Management Protocol (SNMP)* is a TCP/IP protocol monitor. The SNMP service creates trap messages that are then sent to a trap destination. One way you might use SNMP is to trap messages that don't contain an appropriate hostname for a particular service.

When you set up SNMP, you set up communities. *Communities* are groupings of computers that help monitor each other.

Windows Server 2016 includes SNMP with the operating system. To install the service, you must use Server Manager. In Exercise 9.2, you will walk through the process of installing the SNMP service.

**EXERCISE 9.2**

### Installing SNMP

1. Open Server Manager.
2. Click option number 2, Add Roles And Features. If you see the Before You Begin screen, just click Next.
3. Choose role-based or feature-based installation and click Next.

**EXERCISE 9.2 *(continued)***

4. Choose your server and click Next.
5. Click Next at the Select Server Roles screen.
6. When the Select Features window appears, click the SNMP Services check box. If an ADD Features dialog box appears, click the Add Features button. Click Next.
7. The Confirm Installation page appears. Click Install.
8. Click Close. Exit the Server Manager application.

Now that you have installed the SNMP service, you have to set up your community so that you can start trapping messages. As stated earlier, communities are a grouping of computers to help monitor each other. After you have created the initial community, you can add other computer systems to the community.

In Exercise 9.3, you will walk through the steps to set up the SNMP service and also set up your first community name. To complete this exercise, you must have completed Exercise 9.2.

**EXERCISE 9.3**

**Configuring SNMP**

1. Open Computer Management by pressing the keyboard's Windows key and selecting Administrative Tools ➢ Computer Management.
2. Expand Services And Applications. Click Services. In the right pane, double-click SNMP Service.
3. The SNMP Service Properties window will open. Click the Traps tab. In the Community Name box, enter **Community1**. Click the Add To List button.
4. Click the General tab. Click the Start button to start the service. Click OK.
5. Close Computer Management.

## Using Resource Monitor

The Resource Monitor is another utility that allows you to view some of the resources on your server. You can access the Resource Monitor by going into the Administrative tools and choosing Resource Monitor or by typing **`Resmon.exe`** in the Run box.

Resource Monitor is a method of viewing Performance Monitoring data in a quick to view format. One advantage to using the Resource Monitor is that you can choose items that are affecting the systems performance and the view will change to show that item along with the totals.

As seen in Figure 9.21, you can use Resource Monitor to watch the system's CPU, Memory, Disk, and Network. There are 5 tabs that show you the different components. Figure 9.21 shows the Overview tab. The Overview tab allows you to watch all four hardware components in one window. Now let's take a look at each tab (which represents a component).

**FIGURE 9.21** Resource Monitor

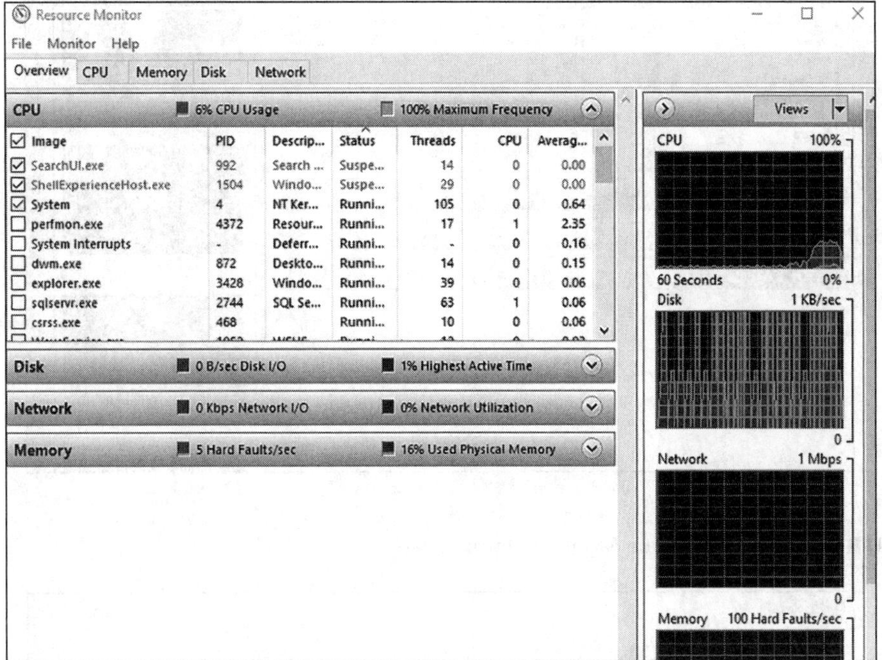


**CPU** The CPU tab (shown in Figure 9.22) will show you the total percentage of the CPU being used in a green color and it will show you the Maximum Frequency of the CPU in blue.

**Memory** This tab (shown in Figure 9.23) will show you how much memory is being used. When looking at the Resource Overview Memory window, there are two colors that you need to monitor. The current physical memory that is being used will be shown in the color green. The standby memory is shown in the color blue.

**Disk** The Disk tab (shown in Figure 9.24) will show you the total current input/output in the color green and it will show you the highest activity time. The current disk activity will be shown in green and the highest activity is shown in blue.

**FIGURE 9.22** Resource Monitor CPU tab

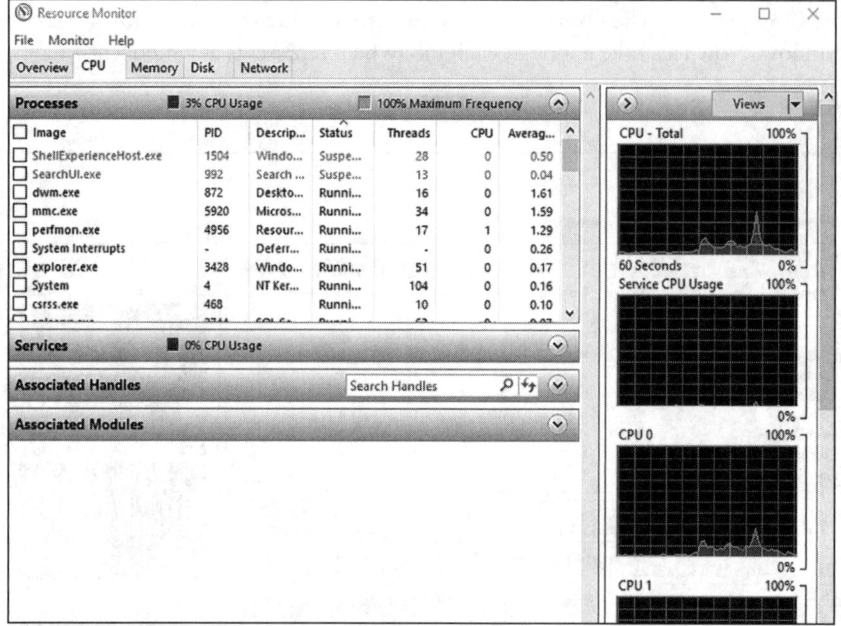

**FIGURE 9.23** Resource Monitor Memory tab

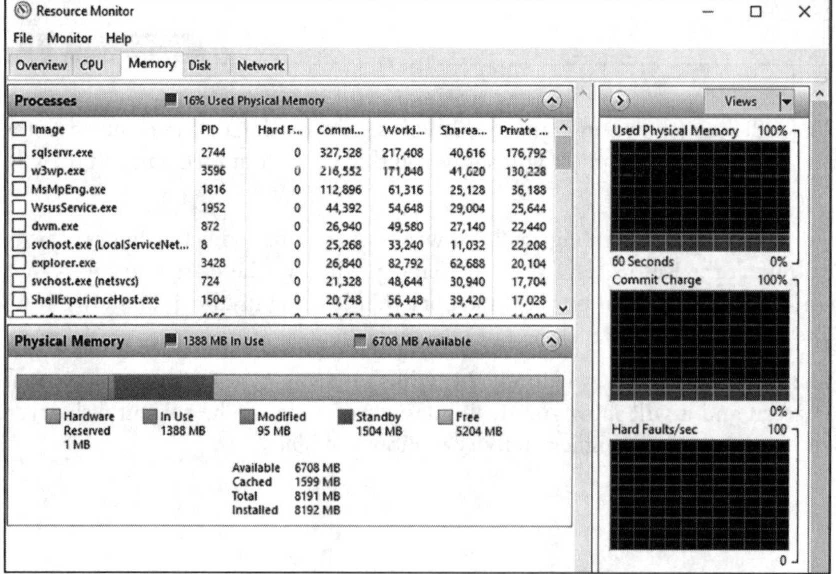

**FIGURE 9.24** Resource Monitor Disk tab

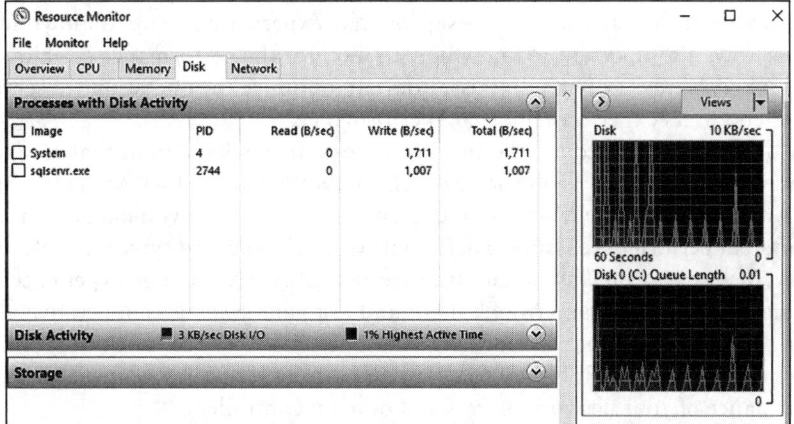


**Network** The Network tab (shown in Figure 9.25) shows you how the network traffic is operating. The window will show you the percentage of network capacity and the total current network traffic.

**FIGURE 9.25** Resource Monitor Network tab

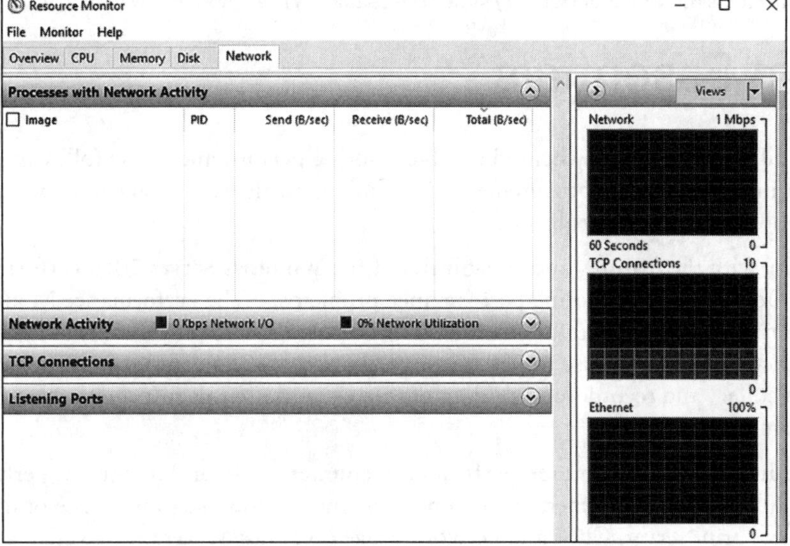


# Summary

This chapter began with a discussion of server optimization and reliability, including a look at many tools that can help you monitor and manage your systems and the basics of troubleshooting the network in times of disaster.

Monitoring performance on servers is imperative to rooting out any issues that may affect your network. If your systems are not running at their best, your end users may experience issues such as latency, or worse, you may experience corruption in your network data. Either way, it's important to know how to monitor the performance of your servers. You also looked at ways system administrators can optimize the operations of servers to ensure that end users experience adequate performance.

You also examined how to use the various performance-related tools that are included with Windows Server 2016. Tools such as Performance Monitor, Task Manager, Microsoft Message Analyzer, Resource Monitor, and Event Viewer can help you diagnose and troubleshoot system performance issues. These tools will help you find typical problems related to memory, disk space, and any other hardware-related issues you may experience.

Knowing how to use tools to troubleshoot and test your systems is imperative, not only to passing the exam but also to performing your duties at work. To have a smoothly running network environment, it is vital that you understand the issues related to the reliability and performance of your network servers and domain controllers.

# Video Resources

There are videos available for the following exercises:

9.1

You can access the videos at `http://sybextestbanks.wiley.com` on the Other Study Tools tab.

# Exam Essentials

**Understand the methodology behind troubleshooting performance.** By following a set of steps that involves making measurements and finding bottlenecks, you can systematically troubleshoot performance problems.

**Be familiar with the features and capabilities of the Windows Server 2016 Performance Monitor tool for troubleshooting performance problems.** The Performance Monitor administrative tool is a powerful method for collecting data about all areas of system performance. Through the use of performance objects, counters, and instances, you can choose to collect and record only the data of interest and use this information for pinpointing performance problems.

**Know the importance of common performance counters.** Several important performance-related counters deal with general system performance. Know the importance of monitoring memory, print server, CPU, and network usage on a busy server.

**Understand the role of other troubleshooting tools.** Windows Task Manager, Microsoft Message Analyzer, SNMP, Baseline Security Analyzer, and Event Viewer can all be used to diagnose and troubleshoot configuration- and performance-related issues.

**Understand how to troubleshoot common sources of server reliability problems.** Windows Server 2016 has been designed to be a stable, robust, and reliable operating system. Should you experience intermittent failures, you should know how to troubleshoot device drivers and buggy system-level software.

# Review Questions

1. You need to stop an application from running in Task Manager. Which tab would you use to stop an application from running?
   - **A.** Performance
   - **B.** Users
   - **C.** Options
   - **D.** Details
2. You are the network administrator for a Fortune 500 company. You are responsible for all client computers at the central campus. You want to make sure that all of the client computers are secure. You decide to use MBSA to scan your client computers for possible security violations. You want to use the command-line version of MBSA to scan your computers based on IP address. Which of the following commands should you use?
   - **A.** `mdsacli.exe /hf -i` *xxxx.xxxx.xxxx.xxxx*
   - **B.** `mdsacli.exe /ip` *xxxx.xxxx.xxxx.xxxx*
   - **C.** `mbsa.exe /hf -ip` *xxxx.xxxx.xxxx.xxxx*
   - **D.** `mbsa.exe /ip` *xxxx.xxxx.xxxx.xxxx*
3. You are the network administrator for your company. You want to look at some of the resources on the network. Specifically, you want to watch the CPU and Memory. Which tool can you use to get the most detailed information about the resources?
   - **A.** Performance Monitor
   - **B.** System Hardware Monitor
   - **C.** Event Viewer
   - **D.** Server Manager
4. What command-line command would you type to start Performance Monitor?
   - **A.** `Netmon.exe`
   - **B.** `Perfmon.exe`
   - **C.** `Performon.exe`
   - **D.** `Resmon.exe`
5. You need to view which users are running applications on a server. Which application can you use to see what users are currently connected to the server?
   - **A.** System Information
   - **B.** Resource Monitor
   - **C.** Performance Monitor
   - **D.** Task Manager

6. You are the network administrator for a large organization. You need to watch some of the main components on a server. These include the Memory, CPU, Network, and Disk. What utility can you use to get a quick overview of these four components?

   **A.** System Monitor

   **B.** Resource Monitor

   **C.** System Configuration

   **D.** Event Viewer

7. What command-line command would you type to start Resource Monitor?

   **A.** `Netmon.exe`

   **B.** `Perfmon.exe`

   **C.** `Performon.exe`

   **D.** `Resmon.exe`

8. You have been hired as a consultant to research a network-related problem at a small organization. The environment supports many custom-developed applications that are not well documented. A manager suspects that some computers on the network are generating excessive traffic and bogging down the network. You want to do the following:

   - Determine which computers are causing the problems.
   - Record and examine network packets that are coming to/from specific machines.
   - View data related only to specific types of network packets.

   What tool should you use to accomplish all of the requirements?

   **A.** Task Manager

   **B.** Performance Monitor

   **C.** Event Viewer

   **D.** Microsoft Message Analyzer

9. You need to install Microsoft Baseline Security Analyzer. How do you need to do the install?

   **A.** Download MBSA from Microsoft's website.

   **B.** Install from Server Manager.

   **C.** Use Add/Remove Programs.

   **D.** Programs

10. You need to disconnect a user running applications on a server. Which application can you use to disconnect a user currently connected to the server?

    **A.** System Information

    **B.** Resource Monitor

    **C.** Performance Monitor

    **D.** Task Manager

# Appendix Answers to the Review Questions

# Chapter 1: Installing Windows Server 2016

1. B. Windows Server 2016 Server Core is a more secure, slimmed-down version of Windows Server. Web versions of Windows Server 2016 are not available. You would use Windows Server 2016 Standard as a Web server.

2. A. The only way you can change between Server Core and the Desktop Experience is to reinstall the server. Converting from Server Core to Desktop Experience by running a PowerShell command is no longer available.

3. B. Microsoft recommends that you upgrade your Windows Server 2012 or Windows Server 2012 R2 Standard server to Windows Server 2016 Standard.

4. A. Windows Server 2012 R2 Datacenter was designed for organizations that are seeking to migrate to a highly virtualized, private cloud environment. Windows Server 2012 R2 Datacenter has full Windows Server functionality with unlimited virtual instances.

5. D. Windows Server 2016 Essentials is ideal for small businesses that have as many as 25 users and 50 devices. Windows Server 2016 Essentials has a simpler interface and preconfigured connectivity to cloud-based services but no virtualization rights.

6. C. Windows Server 2016 Essentials is ideal for small businesses that have as many as 25 users and 50 devices. It has a simple interface, preconfigured connectivity to cloud-based services, and no virtualization rights.

7. A, B, C, D. All four answers are advantages of using Windows Server 2016. Server Core is a smaller installation of Windows Server and therefore all four answers apply.

8. B. Windows Server 2016 Features On Demand allows an administrator not only to disable a role or feature but also to remove the role or feature's files completely from the hard disk.

9. D. Windows Server 2016 Nano Server uses the Current Branch for Business (CBB) servicing model. This version of servicing is a more aggressive version and it was specifically designed with the cloud in mind. As the cloud continues to quickly evolve, the CBB servicing model is meant for that lifecycle.

10. C. Windows Server 2016 has a type of domain controller called a read-only domain controller (RODC). This gives an organization the ability to install a domain controller in an area or location (onsite or offsite) where security is a concern.

# Chapter 2: Installing in the Enterprise

1. D. You would use the Sysprep utility. The `/generalize` options prevents system-specific information from being included in the image.

2. A. The DISM utility with the `/get-ImageInfo` displays information about images in a WIM or VHD file.

3. A. SIM is a graphical utility that can be used to create an answer file. Answer files can be used to automate the installation routine so that no user interaction is required.

4. C. Windows System Image Manager (SIM) is used to create unattended answer files in Windows Server 2016. It uses a GUI-based interface to set up and configure the most common options that are used within an answer file.

5. A. The `/unattend` option can be used with the `Setup.exe` command to initiate an unattended installation of Windows Server 2016. You should also specify the location of the answer file to use when using the `Setup.exe` utility.

6. D. Once you have a reference computer installed, you can use the System Preparation Tool to prepare the computer to be used with disk imaging. Image Capture Wizard is a utility that can be used to create a disk image after it is prepared using the System Preparation Tool. The image can then be transferred to the destination computer(s).

7. C. Unique information is stripped out of the installation image when you use the System Preparation Tool to create a disk image—for example, the unique SID that is applied to every computer. Unique information is then generated when the target computer is installed.

8. B. When you configure your WDS server, the remote installation folder should not reside on the system partition.

9. C. You would configure formatting and partitioning information in the Windows PE component of the answer file. The options specified in this configuration pass will occur before the image will be copied to the local computer.

10. B. The `/generalize` option prevents system-specific information from being included in the image. The `Sysprep.exe` command can be used with a variety of options. You can see a complete list by typing **`sysprep/?`** at a command-line prompt.

# Chapter 3: Configuring Storage and Replication

1. A. The iSCSI default port is TCP 3260. Port 3389 is used for RDP, port 1433 is used for Microsoft SQL, and port 21 is used for FTP.

2. A. The `Get-ShieldedVMProvisioningStatus` command allows you to view the provisioning status of a shielded virtual machine.

3. B. The `Set-VMNetworkAdapter` command allows an administrator to configure features of the virtual network adapter in a virtual machine or the management operating system.

4. C. This `Set-VMProcessor` command allows an administrator to configure the processors of a virtual machine. While the virtual machine is in the OFF state, run the `Set-VMProcessor` command on the physical Hyper-V host. This enables nested virtualization for the virtual machine.

5. C. The `Set-VMSwitch` cmdlet allows an administrator to configure a virtual switch.

6. D. The `Optimize-VHD` command allows an administrator to optimize the allocation of space in virtual hard disk files, except for fixed virtual hard disks.

7. B. The `Get-Package` command allows an administrator to view a list of all software packages that have been installed by using Package Management.

8. D. The `Get-WindowsFeature` cmdlet allows an administrator to view a list of available and installed roles and features on the local server.

9. D. The `iscsicli addisnsserver server_name` command manually registers the host server to an iSNS server. `refreshisnsserver` refreshes the list of available servers. `removeisnsserver` removes the host from the iSNS server. `listisnsservers` lists the available iSNS servers.

10. D. The `Set-VMHost` cmdlet allows an administrator to configure a Hyper-V host. These settings include network settings network adapters.

# Chapter 4: Understanding Hyper-V

1. B, D. Hyper-V can be installed on the Standard or Datacenter Editions of Windows Server 2016. Itanium, x86, and Web Editions are not supported.

2. C. The external virtual network type will allow the virtual machine to communicate with the external network as it would with the Internet, so A is wrong. The internal-only network type allows communication between the virtual machines and the host machine. Because the question says that only communication between the virtual machines should be allowed, the only valid answer is private virtual machine network. The last option, public virtual machine network, does not exist in Hyper-V.

3. A. This question focuses on the fact that you cannot change the memory if the virtual machine is running, paused, or saved. The only valid answer is to shut it down and then change the memory.

4. A. The only virtual hard disk that increases in size is the dynamically expanding disk. Thus, this is the only valid answer to this question. The fixed-size disk creates a disk of the size you specify, the differencing disk is a special disk that stores only the differences between it and a parent disk, and the physical disk uses a physical drive and makes it available to the virtual machine.

5. C. Physical hard disks cannot be configured using the Virtual Hard Disk Wizard, the Edit Virtual Hard Disk Wizard, or the New Virtual Machine Wizard. You can configure and attach a physical disk only by using the virtual machine's settings.

6. B. Hyper-V is not supported on Itanium-based systems, thus he cannot install it.

7. A, B, C. The minimum CPU requirement for running Hyper-V is a x64-based processor (Itanium is not supported), hardware Data Execution Protection must be enabled, and hardware-assisted virtualization must be enabled. There is no minimum requirement for a dual-core processor.

8. C. This question relates to the setup command used to install the Hyper-V server role on a Windows Server 2016 Server Core machine. It's important to remember that these commands are case sensitive, and that the correct command is `start /w ocsetup Microsoft-Hyper-V`, which is option C. All of the other commands will fail to install Hyper-V on a Server Core machine.

9. A, C, D. The Hyper-V Manager is available only for Windows Server 2012 R2/2012/2008 R2/2008, Windows 10, Windows 8, and Windows 7. There is no version available that runs on Windows Server 2003.

10. C. The virtual network type in which the machines communicate with each other and with the host machine is called *internal only*. In a private virtual network, the virtual machines can communicate only with each other, not with the network or the host machine. The external network type defines a network where the virtual machines can communicate with each other, with the host machine, and with an external network like the Internet.

# Chapter 5: Configuring High Availability

1. A. To create a new NLB cluster, you would use the PowerShell command `New-NlbCluster`.

2. D. Software Load Balancing allows administrators to have multiple servers hosting the same virtual networking workload in a multitenant environment. This allows an administrator to set up high availability.

3. A. The maximum number a single cluster can support is 32 computers.

4. B. If an administrator decides to use the drainstop command, the cluster stops after answering all of the current NLB connections. So the current NLB connections are finished but no new connections to that node are accepted.

5. D. If you want to stop the entire cluster from running, while in the NLB manager (type **NLBmgr** in Run command), you would right-click on the cluster, point to Control Hosts, and then choose Stop.

6. A. The PowerShell command `Stop-VMReplication` will stop virtual machine replication from happening.

7. D. The `Enable-VMReplication` command allows an administrator to enable virtual machine migration on a virtual machine host.

8. B. To use unicast communication between NLB cluster nodes, each node must have a minimum of two network adapters.

9. D. Setting the cluster affinity to Single will send all traffic from a specific IP address to a single cluster node. Using this affinity will keep a client on a specific node where the client should not have to authenticate again. Setting the filtering mode to Single would remove the authentication problem but would not distribute the load to other servers unless the initial server was down.

10. C. When setting the affinity to Class C, NLB links clients with a specific member based on the Class C part of the client's IP address. This allows an administrator to set up NLB so that clients from the same Class C address range can access the same NLB member. This affinity is best for NLB clusters using the Internet.

# Chapter 6: Understanding Clustering

1. D. The `Enable-VMReplication` PowerShell command allows an administrator to configure the automatic replication of a cluster.

2. A, B. The first PowerShell command, `(Get-Cluster).CrossSiteDelay`, is what is used to set the amount of time between each heartbeat sent to nodes. This value is in milliseconds (default is 1000).

   The second PowerShell command, `(Get-Cluster).CrossSiteThreshold`, is the value that you set for the number of missed heartbeats (default is 20) before the node is considered offline.

3. D. A Windows Server 2016 cluster consisting of servers running the x64 version can contain up to 64 nodes.

4. A. The `Enable-ClusterStorageSpacesDirect` command allows an administrator to enable highly available storage spaces that use directly attached storage, Storage Spaces Direct (S2D), on a cluster.

5. B. The storage tests require the clustered disk resource to be offline. If you need to run the storage tests, the Validate a Configuration Wizard will prompt you to make sure you want to take the resources offline.

6. A, C. SQL Server and Exchange Server are supported only on failover clusters. Websites and VPN services are network-based services, so they are better suited for NLB clusters.

7. A. Administrators would use the `Test-Cluster` command to complete validation tests for a cluster.

8. B. The cluster heartbeat is a signal sent between servers so that they know that the machines are up and running. Servers send heartbeats and after five nonresponsive heartbeats, the cluster would assume that the node was offline. Cross-Site Heartbeating is the same signal but with longer timeouts to allow for cluster nodes in remote locations.

9. B. Up to two votes can be lost before quorum can no longer be achieved. These votes can come from the file share witness or a cluster node.

10. B. In a three-node cluster, only one node can be offline before quorum is lost; a majority of the votes must be available to achieve quorum.

# Chapter 7: Configuring Windows Containers

1. C. Administrators can set any configuration option for the daemon in a JSON format.

2. A. The `docker create` command gives you the ability to create a new container.

3. D. The `Get-Container` PowerShell command allows an administrator to view information about containers.

4. D. The `docker run` command executes commands in a Dockerfile. The `Docker build` command allows you to compile and create an image and the `docker rm` command allows you to delete an image.

5. A. The `docker images` command gives you the ability to see your images. The `docker info` command allows you to see how many images you have on a host but it does not give you details about the images.

6. C. The `Docker build` command allows you to compile and create an image. The `docker run` command executes commands in a Dockerfile, and the `docker rm` command allows you to delete an image.

7. A. The `docker run` command executes commands in a Dockerfile. The `Docker build` command allows you to compile and create an image, and the `docker rm` command allows you to delete an image.

8. C. The `Remove-Container` command gives you the ability to delete a container.

9. B. The `docker pull microsoft/windowsservercore` command allows you to grab an image of Windows Server Core from the Docker website.

10. C. Windows Server 2016 and Windows 10 Professional and Enterprise (Anniversary Edition) allow you to set up containers.

# Chapter 8: Maintaining Windows Server

1. B, E. You can set the Registry key `HKEY_LOCAL_MACHINE\Software\Policies\Microsoft\Windows\WindowsUpdate\AU\UseWUServer` to 0 to use the public Windows Update server, or you can set it to 1, which means that you will specify the server for Windows Update in the `HKEY_LOCAL_MACHINE\Software\Policies\Microsoft\Windows\WindowsUpdate` key. The WSUServer key sets the Windows Update server using the server's HTTP name, such as, for example, `http://intranetSUS`.

2. C. Server Manager is the one place where you install all roles and features for a Windows Server 2016 system.

3. C. All options are valid steps to complete the configuration except option C because SERVERB cannot automatically draw updates from whichever sources are on SERVERA.

4. B, D, F. Option A schedules the updates to occur at a time when the computers are generally not connected to the corporate network. Options C and E require more user interaction than would be considered minimal. By setting updates to occur with no user interaction at noon, you satisfy the requirements.

5. D. You can recover system state data from a backup, which always includes the Active Directory database. In this case, Event Viewer and System Monitor wouldn't help you recover the database, but they might help you determine why the hard drive crashed in the first place.

6. C. The Update Source And Proxy Server option allows you to specify where you will be receiving your updates (from Microsoft or another WSUS server) and your proxy settings if a proxy server is needed.

7. A. Using images allows you to back up and restore your entire Windows Server 2016 machine instead of just certain parts of data.

8. C. The Backup Once link allows you to start a backup on the Windows Server 2016 system.

9. D. If you need to back up and restore your Windows Server 2016 machine, you need to use the Windows Server Backup MMC.

10. B. The primary method by which system administrators create and manage application data partitions is through the `ntdsutil` tool.

# Chapter 9: Understanding Monitoring

1. D. All of the applications that are running on the Windows Server 2016 machine will show up under the Details tab. Right-click the application and end the process.

2. A. If you use MBSA from the command-line utility `mdsacli.exe`, you can specify several options. You type **`mdsacli.exe/hf`** (from the folder that contains `Mdsacli.exe`) and then customize the command execution with an option such as `/ixxxx.xxxx.xxxx.xxxx`, which specifies that the computer with the specified IP address should be scanned.

3. A. Performance Monitor allows you to watch the resources on your system. You can add as many objects and counters that you want to view.

4. B. `Perfmon.exe` is the command-line command to start Performance Monitor.

5. D. All of the users that are running applications on the Windows Server 2016 machine will show up under the Users tab. Right-click the user and click the Disconnect button if you need them to be disconnected.

6. B. The Resource Monitor is another utility that allows you to view the resources on your server. You can use Resource Monitor to watch the system's CPU, Memory, Disk, and Network.

7. D. `Resmon.exe` is the command-line command to start Resource Monitor.

8. D. By using the Microsoft Message Analyzer, you can view all of the network packets that are being sent to or from the local server. Based on this information, you can determine the source of certain types of traffic, such as pings. The other types of monitoring can provide useful information, but they do not allow you to drill down into the specific details of a network packet, and they don't allow you to filter the data that has been collected based on details about the packet.

9. A. Microsoft Baseline Security Analyzer is a free download that you can get from Microsoft's website.

10. D. All of the users that are running applications on the Windows Server 2016 machine will show up under the Users tab. Right-click the user and click the Disconnect button if you need them to be disconnected.

# Index

# A

## B



## C

## D

# E



# F

# H

## I

## K



## L

## M

## N

## Q



## R

## S

## T



## U

## Z

# Comprehensive Online Learning Environment

Register on Sybex.com to gain access to the comprehensive online interactive learning environment and test bank to help you study for your MCSA Windows Server 2016 certification.

---

The online test bank includes:

- **Assessment Test** to help you focus your study to specific objectives
- **Chapter Tests** to reinforce what you've learned
- **Practice Exams** to test your knowledge of the material
- **Digital Flashcards** to reinforce your learning and provide last-minute test prep before the exam
- **Searchable Glossary** to define the key terms you'll need to know for the exam
- **Videos** created by the author to accompany chapter exercises

Go to http://www.wiley.com/go/sybextestprep to register and gain access to this comprehensive study tool package.